LINUX and UNIX
Shell Programming

LINUX and UNIX
Shell Programming

David Tansley

 Addison-Wesley

An imprint of **Pearson Education**

Harlow, England · London · New York · Reading, Massachusetts · San Francisco · Toronto · Don Mills, Ontario · Sydney
Tokyo · Singapore · Hong Kong · Seoul · Taipei · Cape Town · Madrid · Mexico City · Amsterdam · Munich · Paris · Milan

PEARSON EDUCATION LIMITED

Head Office:
Edinburgh Gate
Harlow CM20 2JE
Tel: +44 (0)1279 623623
Fax: +44 (0)1279 431059

London Office:
128 Long Acre
London WC2E 9AN
Tel: +44 (0)207 447 2000
Fax: +44 (0)207 240 5771

First published in Great Britain in 2000

© Pearson Education Limited 2000

The right of David Tansley to be identified as Author of
this Work has been asserted by him in accordance with
the Copyright, Designs and Patents Act 1988.

ISBN 0-201-67472-6

British Library Cataloguing in Publication Data
A CIP catalogue record for this book can be obtained from the British Library

Library of Congress Cataloging in Publication Data
A catalog record for this book can be obtained from the Library of Congress

The programs in this book have been included for their instructional value.
The publisher does not offer any warranties or representations in respect of their
fitness for a particular purpose, nor does the publisher accept any liability for any
loss or damage (other than for personal injury or death) arising from their use.

10 9 8 7 6 5 4 3 2 1

Typeset by CRB Associates, Reepham, Norfolk
Printed and bound in the United States of America

The Publishers' policy is to use paper manufactured from sustainable forests.

Contents

Chapter 8 **The grep family**   **82**

Chapter 9 **Introducing awk**   **96**

Chapter 10 **Using** sed   **131**

Chapter 11   Merge and divide   154

Chapter 12   Using tr   176

Chapter 19   Shell functions   291

Chapter 20   Passing parameters to scripts   320

Acknowledgements

When it comes to writing a book in the end, it's just the author and the keyboard tapping away a merry tune into the early hours of the morning. Getting there requires support and help. When I first got the 'go' to write this book from my editor Steve Temblett, we were both enthusiastic about the project. It has been a long and hard few months to get this book finished. Steve and his assistant Alison Birtwell have always met all my queries with a direct and positive response.

Thanks must also go to my employer Ace Global Markets Ltd, to Paul Taylor for his feedback on some of the scripts that are included in the book, and to Ryan Price for his comments.

I would also like to thank my children Louise and Matthew for their help. Louise for informing me of grammatical errors as I was typing away: thanks Louise! Matthew for informing me that all my typo errors looked great anyway: thanks Matthew.

This book would most certainly not have got off the ground in the first place if it were not for my wife Pauline: thanks Pauline you're great.

Introduction

This book is about shell programming or to be more precise shell and Bourne shell programming.

With LINUX now firmly taking its rightful place in the market as a viable and robust operating system, shell programming has become even more popular. No-one can say with any confidence how many LINUX users there are out there because LINUX is free, though there is a growing number of third parties selling their own LINUX variants. UNIX is still as popular as ever and growing despite a forecasted demise by IT consultants a few years ago.

If you want to learn shell programming, then this is the book for you; even if you are an intermediate shell user you will find the book a good learning and reference tool as there are some handy administrative tips and one-liners for you.

This book has been written from the outset with six main objectives in mind. These are:

- Getting the reader up to speed quickly learning about shell tools and shell programming.

- Using the book not only as a learning tool but also as a reference book.

- Using shell scripts to use your system more productively.

- Showing scripts that are clear and easily understandable.

- Making the chapters self-contained where possible for the subject covered, for ease of use.

- Showing the reader not just shell scripting but also some administrative tasks like rc.scripts and cgi scripts.

One of the annoying things about certain books on this topic was how some scripting examples were made to look complicated just to save a few lines of extra code. You won't find that sort of thing happening in this book: all the code in this book is simple but effective.

If you're reading this, then you have probably already got your own reasons for learning shell programming; great. If you want to know the main reasons for learning shell programming they are:

- The shell is a programming language all on its own; it has iteration, conditions and testing constructs and it's easy to use.

- You can create scripts quickly.

- You can automate boring manual tasks using scripts.

The Bourne shell

The Bourne shell is the standard shell shipped with all UNIX systems and is linked into the LINUX bash shell. A book about shell programming that covers all leading systems must cover the Bourne shell. There are other shells, mind you, like bash, Korn, and the C shell. If you are familiar with the bash shell, the scripts presented in this book will run on your system, because bash is backward-compatible with Bourne. If you have the Korn shell, the syntax of the shell is very close.

If you look at installation scripts you will find that over 95 per cent of them are Bourne shell scripts. This is simply because the person who wrote the script knows it will run on any UNIX or LINUX system.

Shell portability

When you write a script that you want to run on any system it has to be what is called portable. Portability of scripts has two major issues:

- script syntax of the shell you are using;

- shell commands.

The first issue is practically already solved if you are going to program with the Bourne shell: it has few or no portability problems.

Most shell scripts spend at least 20 per cent (or probably more) of their time using shell commands such as cp, mv, mkdir etc. This is where the problems of portability come in. Different system vendors have different command options on their machines; coupled with this if you have UNIX then you are either a System V or BSD user. This book uses generic scripts and command examples. I have only used options and commands that are common to both System V and BSD and in my opinion useful, throughout the book. Where there are slight differences they are pointed out with an alternative command, but these are few and far between.

Organization of the book

This book is organized as both a learning tool and a reference book, therefore do not think that you have to read each chapter in sequential order. Feel free to wander through the chapters or even start on the last chapter, if you want to knock up some cgi-based HTML pages.

The book is split into five parts, and within those parts are chapters dealing with different aspects of the shell and shell programming.

The book is full of complete working examples of scripts.

The shell

In Part 1 of this book we will cover the topics that show you how to list files using patterns, and how to change directories quickly. When you create a file, you want to make sure it has the right permissions and directories. This is also covered. Coverage is also given to file operations such as umask and group file ownerships.

To avoid endlessly searching for files you have created, a whole chapter is devoted to the find command.

When your scripts are up and running you will at some point want to run them during the night or late in the evening: you will discover how to do this in the chapter dealing with running commands unattended.

The nitty-gritty of any shell is its ability to read commands into a file or from a terminal and also display the output. This is also covered. You may want to run certain commands only if the previous command succeeded – no problem, that's covered as well.

Text file filtering

Part 2 of the book covers all the major test filtering tools. Text filtering includes all you need to know about filtering text before your scripts get hold of the information, during the script execution and the output of the text.

Topics include awk, a language by itself; grep, a text file searching utility; and sed, an in-line editor that lets you edit on the fly. We also cover sorting, merging and pasting files and records. There is also a chapter on tr, the character translation utility.

Login environment

Part 3 covers your login environment and how to customize it. Understand which files are executed when you login. Learn all about local and global variables. Uncover the mystery surrounding quoting, so you can use variables to their full power.

Basic shell programming

Part 4 of the book is all about shell scripting. The basics are explained including how to make a file executable and run it in the shell; different control constructs; and how to test for different types of conditions and take action based on that result. Once we have covered all the angles with working scripts we then look at functions. Functions are pieces of reusable code, and we will see how to use and share these functions between scripts.

Being able to pass arguments to a shell script is an important function. We look at three different methods of using commands that are passed to scripts.

By now we are putting together competent scripts, so all that we need now is some information on using colour and control characters – guess what, we cover that as well. No shell programming book should be without a file updating system, and there's a whole chapter devoted to this subject in this book. We finish off this part of the book looking at other built-in shell commands we have not yet covered.

Better scripting skills

Is there really a subject such as better scripting skills? You bet there is. That's what Part 5 of the book is all about. We look at the more advanced areas of scripting, and we cover signals and traps, so your scripts can take action if someone tries to kill them. We also look a bit more at here documents. What are here documents, you might say? They let you give input into your scripts or, to put it another way, the scripts get a touch of remote control.

Have you ever wondered how some programs get started automatically when a system boots up? It's no secret; we will look at run levels and how to put an rc.script together. If you follow the examples in this chapter you will have your own scripts up and running when your machine boots up.

There's a chapter containing a small collection of smallish but favourite scripts, which includes amongst others how to deny access to other users without touching the /etc/passwd file. If you have ever wondered how to put html pages together, send information to another page, or continuously refresh pages, we look at cgi-bin scripting using not Perl but Bourne shell scripts.

There are also two appendices, **Appendix A** which deals with the ASCII chart, and **Appendix B** which contains some useful shell commands commands.

Assumptions

I assume the person who is reading this book knows how to login into a shell, change directories, and how to use a text editor.

If you want to try out the cgi scripts that are covered in Part 4, you should really have a Web server installed and be able to run cgi scripts on your machine (though this is not a 'must have' condition).

Conventions used in this book

Throughout this book the following conventions are used:

< CTRL-key >   means hold the control key and the key specified. For instance < CTRL-O > means hold down the control key as well as the letter O.

This typeface	means a non-command example or text of special interest.
This typeface	is used for all script listings.
This typeface	is used for any command line or script input and output.

In the first two parts of the book, you will find text boxes that look like this:

If it's LINUX then...

These have been used to quickly point out differences between the BSD/ LINUX and System V command that is currently being described.

I have tested the scripts both on LINUX (Redhat) and on AIX, and some scripts have also been tested on Data Generals.

I hope you enjoy the book, not only as a learning tool but also as a reference tool. Enjoy and have fun. Stand-by to stand-to.

Any comments, or just to say hello, e-mail me at **dtansley@my-Deja.com**.

## PART 1

The shell

CHAPTER 1

File security and permissions

To stop unwanted users accessing your files, you can set permission bits on them, and on your directories. You can also specify what type of permissions the files get when they are created: this is just a small part of system security. We will not concern ourselves with the big security picture, just the files and directory part.

This chapter will cover:

- permissions on files and directories;
- the setuid;
- chown and chgrp;
- umask; and
- symbolic links.

A file is owned by the user who created it and the group the user belongs to. That user alone can then specify who can read, write and execute that file. Of course, root or the system administrator can override anything that a mere mortal user does. A file when created can be accessed in three ways:

1. By reading, so you can cat/display the file.
2. By writing, so you can edit or delete it.
3. By executing, if the file contains a script or is a program.

Permissions of a file are grouped into three different types:

1. Owner, who actually owns the file
2. Group, who is any user who belongs to that group.
3. Other, i.e. someone outside the group.

1.1 Files

When you create a file the system stores all the information you could ever want to know about it, including:

- The location of the file;

- File type;

- File size;

- Who owns it and can access it;

- The inode;

- Time last modified; and

- The permission bits of the file.

Let's look at a typical file listing, using the `ls -l` command:

```
$ ls -l
total 4232
-rwxr-xr-x   1 root    root       3756  Oct 14 04:44 dmesg
-r-xr-xr-x   1 root    root      12708 Oct  3 05:40 ps
-rwxr-xr-x   1 root    root       5388  Aug  5 1998 pwd
....
```

If we go through the output of the first two lines a step at a time, we can break down the information `ls -l` gives us.

total 4232   This field tells us how much space the files have taken up in the directory.

-rwxr-xr-x   This is the permission bits on the file. If you count all the characters excluding the first '-', you'll see that there are in fact nine of them. There is a good reason for this, as I mentioned earlier, you can specify who can access the files. These are put into the following categories (or sets):

rwx	user	these are the first three bits
r-x	group	these are the second three bits
r-x	other or the rest of the world	these are the last three bits

We'll go over these permission bits in more detail later on. A dash '-' (in place of r, w, x) within these sets means those rights have been taken away or revoked.

1   This is the number of hard links the file has.

root   This is who owns the actual file.

root   This is the default group that root belongs to (also called root!).

3578   This is the file's size in bytes, not kilobytes!

Oct 14 04:44   This is the date of the last time the file was modified.

dmesg   The actual file name.

1.2 Types of files

Remember I said to exclude the first dash when looking at the file permissions? Well, here's what the first dash means. A file can be one of seven types, designated by the first character when you do a `ls -l` command. The types are as follows:

d   This is a directory.

l   This is a symbolic link (a pointer to another file).

s   This is a domain socket.

b   This is a special block file.

c   This is a character special file.

p   This is a named pipe file.

-     This is a normal file or, more accurately, none of the above.

1.3 Permissions

Let's create a file using the touch command

```
$ touch myfile
```

Now do an `ls -l` on the directory

```
$ ls -l
-rw-r--r--   1 dave     admin        0 Feb 19 22:05 myfile
```

   We have created an empty file, and as expected the first dash tells us that we have an ordinary file. You'll find that most of your file creations will be for ordinary files and symbolic links (more on symbolic links later).

User permissions	Group permissions	Other permissions
r w -	r - -	r - -

   The next three permission bits (**rw-**) are your permissions, the owner of the file. The following (**r--**) are the group permissions that you belong to, in this case the group admin. The last three (**r--**) are the rest of the world, or anybody else. My default group admin, of which I am a member, is also displayed. Let's now look more closely at the file myfile, to see what the actual permissions mean.

Table 1.1 *Breakdown of the example listing*

(first character) **-**	Ordinary file.
(next three characters) **r w -**	These are the owner permissions.
(next three characters) **r - -**	These are the groups.
(the last three characters) **r - -**	These are for anybody else.

So each set of three characters (excluding the first) defines:

1.   Permissions for the owner of the file.

2.   Permissions of the default group you belong to (a user can belong to many groups).

3.   Permissions for anybody else on the system.

For each of these sets we have the following set permissions.

r   You can read this file.

w   You can write/amend this file.

x   You can execute this script or program.

Or to display the permissions in another form for the file myfile:

-	**r w-**	**r--**	**r- -**
Type of file	Owner can	Group	Other
is ordinary	read and write	can read	can read

You may have noticed that the file myfile wasn't created with the execute permission for the owner, the system will not let you create any file with this permission bit set. This is due to the security enforced by the system. You have to change this manually: you'll see why you don't get execute permission when we deal with the umask command later. However, you can set the execute bit on directories, but these have a slightly different meaning, which we will discuss later as well.

Understanding all these permission bits can be a bit confusing, so let's look at some examples (*see* Table 1.2).

To confuse you more, if the owner has only a read bit set, he can still write to it using file re-direction. Deleting a file is also dependent on the directory bits, as we shall see in a moment.

Table 1.2 *File permissions and what they mean*

Permission	What it means
r-- --- ---	The owner can read this, but cannot write or execute it.
r--r-- ---	The owner and the group (generally speaking the default group you belong to) can read it.
r-- r--r--	Anybody can read this, but not write or execute it.
rwx r--r--	The owner can read, write and execute it, anybody else can only read it.
rwx r-x---	The owner can read, write and execute, the group can read and execute.
rwx r-x r-x	The owner can read, write and execute; both the group and anybody else can read and execute.
rw- rw- ---	The owner and group can read and write.
rw- rw- r--	The owner and group can read and write, and anybody else can read.
rw- rw- rw-	The owner, group and anybody else can read and write. Caution should be used with this type of permission, as anybody can write to the file.

1.4 Changing permission bits

You can change the permission bits of files you own to whatever you feel comfortable with. You have to ask yourself which users need access to your files (and this also includes directories that you own). You can change the permission bits using the command chmod. This command can be used in a short way using the absolute mode or a long way using the symbolic mode. We'll look at the symbolic mode first.

1.4.1 Symbolic mode

The general format of the chmod command is

   chmod [who] operator [permissions] filename

who means:

u	The user permissions
g	The group permissions
o	The other permissions
a	Means all (user, group and other)

operator means:

+	Add a permission
-	Take away a permission
=	Set permissions

permission means:

r	Read permission
w	Write permission
x	Execute permission
s	User or group set-ID
t	Sticky bit*
l	Lock the file, other users cannot access it
u,g,o	Take away from the user, group, other

* Occasionally you may see the t when you do a listing on a file or directory. The t stands for the 'sticky bit'. If you see a 't' on a directory this means only the owner of the files contained in that directory can delete them, even if a member of a group has the same rights as the owner. But some systems are quite forgiving on this rule.

If you see a 't' on a file listing, then this means that once the script or program has been run it is to be kept in swap (virtual memory). As memory is so cheap nowadays you can pretty much ignore the use of 't' on files.

1.4.2 chmod examples

Let's now see some examples of using the chmod command. Assuming we start off with a file with the following permissions, **rwx rwx rwx**

This command	Produces this	Which means
chmod a-x myfile	rw- rw- rw-	Take away all execute permissions
chmod og-w myfile	rw- r--r--	Take away write from group and other
chmod g+w myfile	rw- rw-r--	Add write to group
chmod u+x myfile	rwx rw-r--	Add execute to owner
chmod go+x myfile	rwx rwx r-x	Add execute to group and other

When I created the file myfile it had the following permissions:

-rw-r--r--   1 dave   admin   0 Feb 19 22:05 myfile

If I now create a script within that file, and I want to make it executable to myself, and also take away read rights from the other (the rest of the world), I could type:

```
$ chmod u+x o-w myfile
```

which would give

-rwx r-- --- 1 dave   admin   0 Feb 19 22:05 myfile

I have now made the file myfile read and write executable for the owner, with read rights for my group admin.

When you want to make a script file executable to yourself, and you're not worried about the default permissions on the file, simply make it executable.

```
$ chmod u+x dt
```

1.4.3 Absolute mode

The general format for the absolute mode is:

chmod [mode] file

where mode is an octal number.

The permission part takes new meaning in the absolute mode. Each permission bit is an octal number representation. Like this:

Table 1.3 *Octal file/directory values*

Octal number	What it means
0400	Owner can read
0200	Owner can write
0100	Owner can execute
0040	Group can read
0020	Group can write
0010	Group can execute
0004	Other can read
0002	Other can write
0001	Other can execute

To specify the permissions all we have to do is look at the table to get the required permissions for the user, group and other. Now add the octal numbers up for each corresponding permission set.

Looking at the table it can be seen that the maximum mode you can give for the owner is 7, the group is 7, and the other is 7.

Taking our file example from earlier

-rw-r--r-- 1 dave   admin   0 Feb 19 22:05 myfile

the permissions would be 644 which means

0400 + 0200 (read and write for the owner) = 0600
0040   (read for the group)   = 0040
0004   (read for the other)   = 0004
                                                    0644

A better example I find on working out the octal modes is the following:

Table 1.4 *Working out symbolic modes*

User			Group			Other		
r	w	x	r	w	x	r	w	x
4 +	2 +	1	4 +	2 +	1	4 +	2 +	1

Using Table 1.4 it is more easy to work out the octal values, all you need to do is note the corresponding number under the permission bit and then add them add for the user, group and other.

    Myfile has the following permissions:

r	w	-	r	-	-	r	-	-
4 +	2		4			4		

This is the octal numbers for each permission bit set, which equals 644.

1.4.4 More chmod examples

Here are some examples using the absolute mode:

This command	Produces this	Which means
chmod 666	**rw- rw- rw-**	Set read, write to owner, group and other.
chmod 644	**rw- r--r--**	Set read, write to owner, group and other has read.
chmod 744	**rwx r--r--**	Set read, write and execute to owner, read for group and other.
chmod 664	**rw- rw- r--**	Set read, write to owner and group, read for other.
chmod 700	**rwx --- ---**	Set read, write and execute to owner only.
chmod 444	**r--r-- r--**	Set read to owner, group and other only.

    As an example suppose I wanted to change my file called yoa which had these permissions

    -rw-rw-r--   1 dave   admin   455 Feb 19 22:05 yoa and I wanted to make the file read, write and execute to the owner and read to group only, I would type:

```
$ chmod 740 yoa
-rwxr-- ---   1 dave      admin              455 Feb 19 22:05 yoa
```

If I wanted to make myfile read, write and execute for the owner and read for both group and other this command will do it.

```
$ chmod 744 myfile
-rwxr-- r--   1 dave      admin                0 Feb 19 22:05 myfile
```

To change all the permission bits for my files that were held in a directory all in one go, I would type

chmod 664 *

which would make all files read and write for user and group and read for other.
You can also drill down directories using the –R option:

chmod –R 664 /usr/local/home/dave/*

This would recursively go through all my sub-directories held under /usr/local/ home/dave, changing the permissions to read and write for the owner and group, and read for other. Be careful when using the '–R': make sure you really want to change all the files in your directory tree.

1.4.5 Absolute or symbolic, your choice

From showing examples of both the absolute and symbolic mode, it can be seen that if you choose to use the symbolic mode you cannot 'take away' or 'add' individual bits of permissions; it's a case of all or nothing. I prefer the symbolic over the absolute mode because it's so much quicker than typing the bit settings in using the absolute command.

1.5 Directories

Remember I said earlier that directories have a different meaning when you use the chmod command? Well, here's why. The 'read' bit means to be able to list the contents of the files. The 'write' bit means you can create files in this directory, so if you don't want users to leave files lying around your directory then take away this permission bit! The execute bit on permissions actually means to have the privilege to search or access that directory.

Table 1.5 *Directory permissions*

r	w	x
Yes, you can list the files in this directory	Yes, you can create/ delete files	Yes, you can search or cd into the directory

Table 1.6 *Directory permission example*

Permission/chmod	Owner	Group	Other
drwx rwx r-x (775)	Read, write, execute	Read, write, execute	Read, execute
drwx r-x r-- (754)	Read, write, execute	Read, execute	Read
drwx r-x r-x (755)	Read, write, execute	Read, execute	Read, execute

If you set your group/other permissions on a directory to --x, this means other users cannot list the contents of the directory. If that directory holds a script or program with the execute bit on, the user can still run it as long as the script/program name is known. It does not matter that the user cannot cd into it.

Permissions you have set on a directory will override whatever permissions you have on files in that directory. For example, if you have the following:

drwx r-- r-- 1 louise admin 2390 Jul 23 09:44 docs

and within the directory docs, you have the following file:

-rwx rwx rwx 1 louise admin 5567 Oct 3 05:40 pay

if a user who is a member of group admin wants to edit the file doc, they will not be able to because of the directory permissions.

It is readable by everyone, but because the execute bit for the group is not set on the directory, nobody in Louise's group can access the directory, and all they'll get is a message saying 'access denied'.

1.6 Set-uid

In Table 1.1 (*see* p. 6) there was an entry for user or group **set-ID** (suid and guid). This permission bit has been a hot potato for the last few years. Some vendors do not allow the implementation of this bit or completely ignore it even if it has been set, because of the security risk it allows. So what's all the fuss about?

The idea behind suid is that the person who is running a script where the owner has set the suid inherits the permissions of the owner of the script. So if root has a script that has a `suid` bit set and an ordinary user runs this script, he assumes root privileges for the script's run time. The same principle applies to `guid`, which assumes the privileges of the group that owns the script.

1.6.1 Why use `set-uid`?

Why use this type of script? Well here's a good case. I look after a few large database systems, and to back-up these databases requires a special system admin profile. I have created a few scripts and made them `guid`, so that certain users who I allow to run these scripts do not have to log in as the database administrator and possibly cause accidental damage to the servers. By running these scripts they get all the rights to do the database dumps and other admin stuff, but when the script ends they are back to their normal user privileges.

Quite a few UNIX commands are also `suid` and `guid`. To find out what they are, `cd` in the `/bin` or `/sbin` directory and type:

```
$ ls -l | grep '^...s'
```

The above lists `suid` files.

```
$ ls -l | grep '^...s..s'
```

The above lists `suid` and `guid` files.

Now we understand what setid is how do we set them? Here's how. For a `suid` you put 4 in front of the permission bits that you are going to set. For a `guid` you put 2 in front of the permission bits that you are going to set. To have both `suid` and `guid` add 4 and 2 together.

With the bits set, an 's' is placed over the position of the 'x'. Please note: an execute bit must be set as well; for example, if I wanted to set a `guid`, I would also make sure that group had execute permission.

If I wanted to change my file login to be `suid`, and it currently has permissions of **rwx rw- r--** (741), I need to put a 4 in front of my normal chmod permissions, so I type `chmod` 4741, which changes it to **rws rw- r--**.

```
$ chmod 4741 logit
```

1.6.2 Adding `set-uid` permission examples

Here are a couple of examples:

Table 1.7 *Adding* `set-uid` *permissions*

Doing this	Sets it to this	Which means
chmod 4755	**rws r-x r-x**	File has `suid` set, owner has read write and executes, group and others have read and execute.

Table 1.7 (*cont.*) *Adding* set-uid *permissions*

Doing this	Sets it to this	Which means
chmod 6711	**rws --s --s**	File has suid and guid set, owner has read, write and execute.
chmod 4764	**rws rw- r--**	File has suid set, owner has read, write and execute. Group has read and write, other has read.

I could also use the symbolic method to add the suid bit if I wanted. If my file had the set of permissions rwx r-x r-x, then by giving it suid:

chmod u + s < filename >

The permissions of the file would then look like: **rws r-x r-x**.

You may sometimes see an S when looking for suid files similar to rwS r-x r-x. What this means is that the execute bit has not been set under the s, so the chmod gives it an upper case S. It is a useless suid permission state; ignore it.

Note that chown does no sanity checks, and by this I mean you can give a file containing garbage any permission you like, and chown will not check it. Just because a file has an execute bit set, do not assume it is a program or script.

1.7 chown **and** chgrp

When you create a file it is owned by the creator. Once you own a file, you can then change the ownership and give it to another user, so long as this is a valid user who has an entry in /etc/passwd. This can be in the form of the actual login name of the user or the user ID, which is a number. When you change ownership of a file, the suid bit is cleared for security reasons. Only the system administrator or the actual owner of the file may give the file away to another user. If you change the owner of the file you cannot claim it back. If you want it back, go and talk to your system admin.

Here's the general format:

chown −R −h owner file

The -R means you can do a recursive change on your files throughout your sub-directories to the new owner. The -h means if you are changing a file that is a symbolic link then change the owner of the file as well.

1.7.1 chown **examples**

Here are a couple of examples:

```
$ ls -l
$ -rwxrwxrwx    1    louise    admin 345 Sep 20 14:33 project
$ chown pauline project
$ ls -l
$ -rwxrwxrwx    1    pauline   admin     Sep 20 14:33 project
```

The ownership of the file project has now changed hands from louise to pauline.

1.7.2 chgrp examples

The format of the command chgrp is the same as chown, as shown in the example below.

```
-rwxrwxrwx   1   pauline   admin    345 Sep 20 14:33 project
$ chgrp sybadmin project
$ ls -l
$ -rwxrwxrwx 1 pauline   sybadmin 345 Sep 20 14:33 project
```

User pauline has now changed the default group for the file project from admin to sybadmin (another group on the system).

1.7.3 Finding out what groups you belong to

If you want to see what groups you belong to, type:

```
$ group
$ admin sysadmin appsgen general
```

or use the **id** command

```
$ id
$ uid=0(root) gid=0(root)
groups=0(root),1(bin),2(daemon),3(sys),4(adm)
```

1.7.4 Finding out what groups other users belong to

To find out what groups another user belong you can use the command:

```
$ group matty
$ sybadmin appsgen post
```

The above command tells us that user matty belongs to the groups sybadmin appsgen and post.

1.8 umask

When you initially log in to the system a command called umask sets your default file creation mode. This command is actually the opposite of the chmod command! Your system administrator should have set this to a reasonable value so when you create files users who are not members of your group will not be able to write to them.

When you are in the shell you can use umask to alter the creation mode of files to your personal preference. This change is effective until you either log out or manually issue another umask command.

Generally, the umask is set in the /etc/profile file, which is the file everybody gets, so if you want to change the umask for everyone put an entry in that file. If you want to set it permanently for your own needs put it in your .profile or .bash_profile in your HOME directory.

1.8.1 How to work out umask values

The umask allows you to mask out file permission bits when a new file is created, and there is a umask number for each of the permission sets (owner, group, other). The maximum for a file creation is six for user, six for group and six for other. The system will not let you create a text file with executable bits, so it's up to you to add that on with the chmod command. A directory can have execute bits set, thus its number can be 7 for each of the permission sets.

The general format is

umask nnn

where nnn is the umask number 000–777.

Let's look at some examples of how this works.

Working out your umask *value*

There are a number of ways you can work out the umask value to get the required permission bits set on newly created files and directories. Table 1.8 shows the corresponding umask number to the permission bits set.

To work out what you require for the umask value, use the table using each value for the corresponding user, group and other permission sets.

To find out the umask value of 002, looking at the table, this would give a file creation mask of 664 and a directory mask of 775.

Here's another method that shows how umask values are arrived at. All we need to remember is that umask is taking away bits.

Suppose we wanted a umask of 002.

Step 1. We first write down the full file mask mode, which is 777 (read, write, execute for owner, group and everybody else).

Table 1.8 umask *permissions table*

umask	File	Directory
0	6	7
1	6	6
2	4	5
3	4	4
4	2	3
5	2	2
6	0	1
7	0	0

Step 2. In the next row note down the corresponding columns of the bits of the umask value you want. In this case it is 002.

Step 3. The next row is the result of any non-matching bits between the first and second row. This row is the directory permissions. After a bit of practice this can be done in your head.

Step 4. As files cannot be created with execute bits set, we simply strip these off.

Here's an example of the above steps, using a umask of 002.

1. Full file mask   **rwx rwx rwx (777)**
2. umask of 002   **---   ---   -w-**
3. Directory permissons **rwx rwx r-x (775)** These are the directory permissions
4. File permissions   **rw- rw- r–   (664)** These are the file permissions

Here's another example, suppose we want a umask value of 022:

1. Full file mask   **rwx rwx rwx (777)**
2. umask of 022   **---   -w- -w-**
3. Directory permissons **rwx r-x r-x (755)** These are the directory permissions
4. File permissions   **rw- r-- r-- (644)** These are the file permissions

1.8.2 Common umask values

Table 1.9 shows some common umask values and their corresponding directory and file creation bits.

Table 1.9 *Common file and directory* umask *values*

umask **number**	**Directory**	**Files**
022	755	644
027	750	640
002	775	664
006	771	660
007	770	660

To see your current settings for umask, just type umask.

```
$ umask
$ 022
$ touch file1
$ ls -l file1
$ -rw-r--r--  1 dave     admin           0 Feb 18 42:05 file1
```

To change to another setting, just put your new value after the umask command:

```
$ umask 002
```

Make sure the system has the new value.

```
$ umask
$ 002
$ touch file2
$ ls -l file2
$ -rw-rw-r--  1 dave     admin           0 Feb 18 45:07 file2
```

Always work out what you want the permissions to be before you issue the umask command. If you don't you could get some weird results; for example, if I issue a umask command with a value of 600, it will give me a creation mask of 066!

1.9 Symbolic (soft) links

There are two different types of links, soft and hard, but we'll only be looking at the soft link. A soft link is really a pointer to a file. You'll find that soft links come in very handy.

1.9.1 Using soft links saves multiple copies of files

Here's how it works. Say you have a file that contains sales information that is stored in /usr/local/admin/sales, and everybody in sales wants to look at that file. Instead of copying the file to their $HOME areas you can create a file from their $HOME area that 'points' to the actual file in /usr/local/admin/sales. Then when you need to update the sales file, you just update that one file, in /usr/local/admin/sales. The files from the sales home directory that users are pointing to can have any name they want, it does not have to be the same as the original filename.

Links also come in handy if you have lots of sub-directories and it takes time to cd down. You can create a link that points to a sub-directory buried deep down in a directory from your $HOME directory level. Another instance is if, say, you installed an application and its logs go to /usr/opt/app/log and you want it to go somewhere else, you can point it to a more convenient location.

The general format is:

ln [–s] source_path target_path

where the path can be either a directory name or filename. Let's look at an example.

1.9.2 Example of using a soft link

Suppose I have about 40 sales and admin users that log in to the system, and sales users use a sales application and admin users use an admin application. Here's what I'm going to do. First I'll delete all their profiles in their $HOME directories. I'll then create two profiles – let's call them sales.profile and admin.profile in the environment that launches them into their respective application. I'll put these profiles in /usr/local/menus/. Now I'm going to create a pointer in all the sales users' $HOME directory to the sales.profile, and do the same for the admin team. Notice I do not have to create a file at the source_path end, the ln command takes care of that. Here's how I'd do it for user matty who is part of the sales team.

```
$ cd /home/sales/matty
$ rm.profile
$ ln -s /usr/local/menus/sales.profile. profile
$ ls -al.profile
$ lrwx rwx  rwx   1  sales    admin 5567 Oct  3 05:40.profile->
/usr/local/menus/sales.profile
```

(Your listing may look slightly different.)

And that's all there is to it; now I can do the same to the admin team's profile. And if I need to alter any of the profiles, I just need to change the sales and admin instead of looking after 40 different profiles.

Here's another example. One of my network monitors puts its logs in /usr/opt/monitor/regstar, but I have all my logs point to the directory /var/adm/logs/, so that I can look at all my logs in one place, instead of cd-ing everywhere first thing in the morning. So I'll just create a link, and here's how I would do it.

```
$ ln -s /usr/opt/monitor/regstar/reg.log/var/adm/logs/monitor.log
```

When you've had enough of a link, you just delete it, but remember not to delete the actual source_path part.

You can link to a file or directory, be it on the same or a different filesystem. When you create a link, remember to have 'execute' on the directories that lead to the target_path or filename. When a link is created your source filename will have permissions of 777, or **rwx rwx rwx**, which you probably know by now, but the actual permissions of the target filename do not change.

One of the common tasks I do on a new system is to create a link from my /tmp directory to /var/tmp. I do this because some applications expect /var/tmp to be present (when it generally isn't), and some applications use this directory to stick their temp and locking files in there. To be able to keep my tmp directories together in one place I use the ln command to have a pointer from my /tmp to var/tmp.

```
$ pwd /var
$ ln -s /tmp   /var/tmp
```

Now when I do an ls -l on /var I can see the pointer from /var/tmp to /tmp

```
$ ls -l
$ lrwx rwx   rwx    1   root      root        5567 Sep  9  10:40 tmp->
/tmp
```

1.10 Conclusion

This chapter has introduced you to the basic concepts of file security. If used correctly and with a pause for thought you will have no problems. A slight slip of the fingers when typing a chmod -R command from the root directory can take ages to get the system back to its correct access permission mode, so please don't wear plasters on your fingers when you type that command!

The use of suid scripts is down to you. Use them but make sure you control and monitor their use, and please do not use 'root' enabled suid scripts.

CHAPTER 2

Using `find` and `xargs`

Occasionally you will need to find files with certain characteristics (such as permissions, ownership, size, different file types etc.) on your system. There could be many reasons for this. It could be for security reasons, general admin or maybe you've just lost a file somewhere. Find is a very powerful tool, which can drill right down through the system or just the current directory looking for the files or directories that you want to locate.

In this chapter we will cover:

- `find` options;

- examples using the different `find` options; and

- examples using `xargs` with `find`.

Because of the powerful features that come with `find` its options list is large, but it's well worth going over most of them. Even if you have a NFS system, find can drill through those too, providing the permissions are OK for it to do so.

When running a big find some people prefer to run `find` in the background, because it can take a long time to drill right through the system (I am talking about 30+ gigabytes of filesystem here).

The general format of the `find` command is:

find pathname -options [-print –exec -ok]

Let's look at parameters.

pathname	The actual path or directory where you want find to start drilling. For example use '.' for the current directory or '/' for the system's root directory.
-print	When find finds the files, this prints them to standard output.

-exec	When `find` gets the files, it executes a shell command with all the found files. The command is in the format 'command' {} \; note the space between the {} and \;
-ok	Really the same as -exec, but operating in safe mode, so you are prompted before the next command is executed.

2.1 `find` **options**

There are many options or expressions you can use with `find`, and each option is prefixed with a hyphen '-'. Let's first go over the main options before we do any examples.

-name	Find files by filename.
-perm	Find files with different access or permission bits on a file.
-prune	Use this option to stop `find` hitting the current dirrectory name specified; however, if you use the -depth option, then prune is ignored.
-user	Find files by user ownership.
-group	Find files that are a member of a certain group.
-mtime -n +n	Find files that were accessed or modified less '-' than or more '+' than x days ago. There is also an `atime` and `ctime` option with find, but they all do practically the same thing, so we'll just look at `mtime`.
-nogroup	Find files that have no valid group membership, that is no entry in /etc/groups.
-nouser	Find files that have no owner, that is no entry in /etc/passwd.
-newer file1 file2	Find files that are newer than file1 but older than file2.
-type	Find files that are a certain type, such as b – a block file d – a directory file c – a character file p – a pipe file l – a symbolic linked file f – an ordinary file.
-size c n	Find files by block 'n' size or by character length 'c', which is taken as bytes.
-depth	When finding files, look at each file first before going down the directories and its sub-directories.
-fstype	Find files on only a certain file system type, usually found in the config file /etc/fstab, which contains information about file systems on the local machine.

-mount	Use find to find files only on mounted files systems.
-follow	If find sees symbolic linked files, then chase down the source of the files.
-cpio	Find files then, using cpio, back them up to a tape device.

2.1.1 Find files by name

Using the name option is perhaps the most commonly used method with find, either by itself or in conjunction with other options. You can use some form of pattern matching for the filenames, as long as they are quoted.

No matter where you are in the system, if you want to find all *.txt files in your $HOME directory, use the '~' as the 'pathname' parameter, as the tilde sign is a shortcut for your $HOME directory.

```
$ find ~ -name "*.txt" -print
```

To find all '*.txt' files in the current directory you are in and any sub-directories:

```
$ find . -name "*.txt" -print
```

To find all filenames with at least one upper case character, in your current directory and any sub-directories:

```
$ find . -name "[A-Z]*" -print
```

To find files in /etc directory that begin with host, and any other characters after that:

```
$ find /etc -name "host*" -print
```

To find all files in your $HOME directory:

```
$ find ~ -name "*" -print or find . -print
```

To bring the system to zero per cent response time, start at the root level and drill through all directories listing 'all' files. If you want to remain on good terms with your sys admin be very careful with this option!

```
$ find / -name "*" -print
```

Find all files that begin with two lower case characters, followed by two numbers, followed by .txt. The following find command could return a file called ax37.txt.

```
$ find . -name "[a-z][a-z][0--9][0--9].txt" -print
```

2.1.2 Find files by `perm` mode

To find files on the system that have different file permissions use this option. You may want to locate files that are executable by everyone (world), or check someone's directory to see what type of permissions they have on files. When using this option it's a good idea to use the octal method for permissions.

To find files with a permission of 755 which is read, write and executable by owner and read and execute by everyone else,

```
$ find . -perm 755 -print
```

To find files that are read, write and executable for everyone (watch out for these) use this `find` command. Put a dash in front of the octal number. The perm stands for permissions and 007 is based on the notation you use for the `chmod` (absolute) mode.

```
$ find . -perm -007 -print
```

2.1.3 Ignoring directories

When you wish to search for files, but you don't want to search in a certain directory because you know the files will not be there, use `prune` to specify the directory to ignore. Be careful when using `prune` though, because if you specify '-depth' the prune option is ignored.

To display the files in the apps directory when you do not want find to search in /apps/bin:

```
$ find /apps  -name "/apps/bin" -prune  -o -print
```

2.1.4 Find files by `user` and `nouser`

To find files by owner, you supply the actual login name of that user. To find files owned by user dave in your `$HOME` directory:

```
$ find ~ -user dave -print
```

To find files owned by uucp in /etc:

```
$ find /etc -user uucp -print
```

To find files of a user that has been deleted, use the `-nouser` option. This finds files that have no valid userid in the /etc/passwd file. You do not have to supply a user name with this option; `find` will go off and do all the work. To find all files not owned by a current user in the /home directory tree:

```
$ find /home -nouser -print
```

2.1.5 Find files by `group` and `nogroup`

Like the user and nouser option, find has the same options for groups. To find all files with the group membership of 'accts' that are in the /apps directory:

```
$ find /apps -group accts -print
```

To find all files that have no valid group membership just supply the -nogroup option. Here find starts at the root of the file system.

```
$ find / -nogroup -print
```

2.1.6 Find files by modification times

To find files that were last accessed *x* days ago use this option. If your system has suddenly lost all its free space, there's probably a file out there that has grown very big in that time, and you can locate it using mtime. Use the '-' to specify files that have not been accessed in *x* number of days. Use '+' for files that have been accessed in the last *x* number of days.

To find all files that have been modified in the last five days:

```
$ find / -mtime -5 -print
```

To find files in /var/adm directory that have not been modified in the last three days:

```
$ find /var/adm -mtime +3 -print
```

2.1.7 Finding files that are newer or older in days or minutes

When you want to find files that fall between two filename modification times use newer. When using newer, be careful about the options. The general format is:

newest_file_name ! oldest_file_name.

The '!' sign is a logical operator, meaning 'not'.

Here are two files, with just over two days between their modication time.

```
-rwxr-xr-x     1 root      root          92 Apr 18 11:18  age.awk
-rwxrwxr-x     1 root      root        1054 Apr 20 19:37  belts.awk
```

This is the find command to find all files that are newer than age.awk but older than belts.awk.

```
$ find . -newer age.awk ! -newer belts.awk -exec ls -l {} \;
-rwxrwxr-x   1 root   root     62 Apr 18 11:32 ./who.awk
-rwxr-xr-x   1 root   root     49 Apr 18 12:05 ./group.awk
-rw-r--r--   1 root   root    201 Apr 20 19:30 ./grade2.txt
-rwxrwxr-x   1 root   root   1054 Apr 20 19:37 ./belts.awk
```

If you need to find files that are, say, less than two hours old you are going to be stuck using the above method, unless of course you have a file created exactly two hours ago. To get around this, you first have to create a file setting the file date/ time stamp on it. The time you set should be the time you want the search to test up to. You can do this with the touch command.

To find files that have been created within the last two hours, and the time is now 23:40 do the following:

```
$ touch -t 05042140 dstamp
$ ls -l dstamp
-rw-r--r--  1 dave      admin        0 May  4 21:40 dstamp
```

A file has been created; we'll assume the date May 4 is today for this example. The time of creation is exactly two hours before 23:40, which is 21:40.

Now we can use find with the newer option to display all files that have been modified within the last two hours.

```
$ find . -newer dstamp -print
```

2.1.8 Find files by type

UNIX or LINUX has different file types, and as we have already discussed what types they are, there is no need to go over old ground here. To find all directories in /etc:

```
$ find /etc -type d -print
```

To find all files but not directories:

```
$ find . ! -type d -print
```

To find all symbolic linked files in /etc:

```
$ find /etc -type l -print
```

2.1.9 Find files by size

You can specify the size of a file in either characters or blocks. To find files that are in character format use Nc, where N is the length in characters, but really in bytes. For block length just use the number of blocks.

Personally I always use the c option. When you are looking for file sizes, nearly everybody uses the bytes option and not blocks, except for filesystems, because it's easier to convert.

To find files that are over 1 Mb in length using the character format use:

```
$ find . -size +1000000c -print
```

To find files that are exactly 100 bytes in length in /home/apache:

```
$ find /home/apache -size 100c -print
```

To find files that are over 10 blocks in length (that's 512 bytes a block) use:

```
$ find . -size +10 -print
```

2.1.10 Find files by depth

When you use find, you probably want find to go and look at all the files first before hitting any of the directories or sub-directories. Force find to do this by using the 'depth' option. One of the reasons for using depth is when you are using find to back up a system to tape, and you want it to go through all the files first before going down all sub-directories it finds.

Find starts at the root file system searching for a file called 'CON.FILE'. It will look at each file before starting on any of the directories and sub-directories.

```
$ find / -name "CON.FILE" -depth -print
```

2.1.11 Find files by mount

To find files only on the current filesystem and not on other (mounted) filesystems use the following find option. Here we use find to search only on the current filesystem for all files that end with '.XC':

```
$ find . -name "*.XC" -mount -print
```

2.1.12 Find files using cpio

Cpio is used for file archiving to and from tape. You can use find to search all, but more probably some of, the system's directory structure, and pipe it through to cpio straight on to tape.

To use find to backup the /etc, /home and /apps directory path on to tape using cpio, make sure first that you are in the root directory:

```
$ cd /
$ find etc home apps -depth -print | cpio -ivcdC65536 -o \
  /dev/rmt0
```

(the \ at the end of the first line tells the shell that the command continues on to the next line).

In the above example note the lack of forward slashes in the path name. This is called relative path names. This is used because if the tape was needed to do a restore I can then choose where I want the restore to go on the system. For instance, work may be needed on the files first so I'd probably stick them in a separate area, do the work then copy them over to the original directory path. If I had used, say, /etc as the directory path (which is absolute addressing), then I would have no choice about where the restore went; it would go back to /etc. Carrying on with the example, I then tell find to first go into /etc/ then /home then /apps, and process each file first, before hitting the directories. All this then gets piped through to cpio to be backed up to tape.

By the way, notice on cpio I used C65536 when I could have just used the 'B' option which is 512 bytes per block. But by specifying C66536 I get a bigger block size on tape, and the block size now becomes 64k (65536/1024).

2.1.13 Using exec or OK to run shell commands

When you've found your files, you probably need to do something with them, and this is where exec comes in. Once find gets all the files, you can then use exec to run another command on them (some systems only let you run the ls or ls -l command using exec). Most users use the exec option to find old files then delete them. I strongly encourage you to first use the ls command before actually running rm, to make sure what you get is what you want deleted.

The exec option is followed by the command to run, then by two closed curly brackets ({}), a space then a backslash and finally a semicolon.

To use exec you do have to have the '-print' option on. If you're been trying out the find examples, you'll notice that find only displays the filename and the path from its current finding position.

To be able to display the found files in an ls -l format, use ls -l as the command to execute. For example:

```
$ find . -type f  -exec ls -l {} \;
-rwxr-xr-x  10 root  wheel          1222 Jan  4  1993./sbin/C80
-rwxr-xr-x  10 root  wheel          1222 Jan  4  1993./sbin/Normal
-rwxr-xr-x  10 root  wheel          1222 Jan  4  1993./sbin/Revvid
```

The above finds files that are ordinary and then uses exec to print them using ls -l.

To find files that have not been modified in the last five days in /logs, and then delete them, use:

```
$ find logs -type f -mtime +5 -exec rm {} \;
```

Using any form of file movement in the shell really needs to be checked first, just in case!

When using say `mv` or `rm`, do it in safe mode with `-ok`. It prompts you for each filename before action is carried out. In the next example `find` locates files that end in '.LOG', if they are older than five days then `find` deletes them, but prompts first.

```
$ find . -name "*.LOG" -mtime +5 -ok rm {} \;
< rm ... ./nets.LOG > ? y
```

Just hit the 'y' to delete the file, or 'n' not to delete it.

Any type of command can be run using the `-exec` option. In the next example we use grep. `Find` first searches for all 'passwd*' files, for example passwd, passswd.old, passwd.bak, then runs grep to see if there is a user 'rounder' located in the files.

```
$ find /etc -name "passwd*" -exec grep "rounder" {} \;
rounder:JL9TtUqk8EHwc:500:500::/home/apps/nets/rounder:/bin/sh
```

2.1.14 Find examples

Now that we have gone over the basic options of `find`, let's see some other `find` examples.

To find all files in your home directory, either of these will work:

```
$ find $HOME -print
$ find ~ -print
```

To find all files with file has suid set, owner has read write and executes, or group and others have read and execute:

```
$ find . -type f -perm 4755 -print
```

To find all ordinary empty files on the system, and list them with their full pathnames:

```
$ find / -type f -size 0 -exec ls -l {} \;
```

To find ordinary files older then seven days in /var/logs and delete them:

```
$ find /var/logs -type f -mtime +7 -exec rm {} \;
```

To find all files on the system who are members of the 'audit' group:

```
$ find / -name -group audit -print
```

A system audit log is created afresh every single day on one of our account systems. The log's filename is appended with a number so you can see at a glance the oldest to the newest. The admin.log is thus numbered sequentially: admin.log.001, admin.log.002 etc. This find command will delete all admin.logs that have numbers appended to them that are over seven days old. The command will check for three numbers, so it's good for up to admin.log.999.

```
$ find /logs -name 'admin.log.[0-9][0-9][0-9]' -atime +7 exec \
rm {} \;
```

Find all directories that are part of a mounted system, and then sort them:

```
$ find . -type d -print -local -mount |sort
```

To find all the rmt tape devices on the system:

```
$ find /dev/rmt -print
```

2.2 Xargs

When using the -exec option in find to process files, find passes all the located files to exec to be worked on in one go. Unfortunately on some systems there is only a limited command line length that can be passed to exec before it bombs out after running for a few minutes with an error message. The error message usually says 'Too long on Args list' or 'Args list exceeded'. This is where xargs comes in, especially when using find. Find passes on the located files to xargs and xargs grabs the files in portions and not all in one go, unlike using exec. Thus it can process the first portion of files, do its stuff, then request the next batch of the files and so on.

Let's see how xargs fits in with some find examples.

The following example goes through the system looking at each ordinary file, then uses xargs to test what type of file it is:

```
$ find / -type f -print | xargs file
/etc/protocols: English text
/etc/securetty: ASCII text
..
```

The following example goes through the entire system looking for core dumps and echos the result to /tmp/core.log file:

```
$ find. -name "core" -print | xargs echo " ">/tmp/core.log
```

The following example locates all files in /apps/audit that are read, write and executable by everyone, and takes away the write permission:

```
$ find /apps/audit -perm -7 -print| xargs chmod o-w
```

In this last example, grep is used to scan all ordinary files for the word 'device':

```
$ find / -type f -print | xargs grep "device"
```

In this last example, grep is used to scan all files in the directory for the word 'DBO':

```
$ find -name \* -type f -print | xargs grep "DBO"
```

Note the use of the '\' backslash to disable the special meaning of the asterisk to the shell.

2.3 Conclusion

Find is an excellent tool for locating different files since the user can specify the criteria on what files to locate. Using exec or xargs allows the user to run practically any command on the files once they have been located.

CHAPTER 3

Running commands unattended

When you are at the terminal or console, you do not want to run jobs that tie up your screen; you want to be getting on with other important tasks like reading your e-mail. It also makes sense to run jobs that are process or disk-intensive during off-peak hours. To enable you to run these types of tasks in the background, i.e. not on your terminal screen, there are certain commands and tools at your disposal.

In this chapter we will cover:

- setting up and submitting jobs using your own crontab file;
- submitting jobs using at;
- running jobs in the background; and
- running jobs using nohup.

Technical terms

Cron	The system scheduler. Use this for jobs that are frequently run during off-peak hours and/or during different time periods throughout the week or month(s).
At	The at command. Use this for ad hoc jobs to run at a specific time or for later during off-peak or during peak hours.
&	Use this to run a quick job now in the background.
Nohup	Use this to run commands in the background, and log off, without affecting the process.

3.1 **Cron and** crontab

Cron is the system's main scheduler for running jobs or tasks unattended. A command called crontab allows the user to submit, edit or delete entries to cron. A crontab file is a user file that holds the scheduling information. You can use crontab to run any of your scripts or one-liners every hour, or maybe just three days a week, it's up to you. Each user can have their own crontab file if they wish, but on large systems root usually disallows this and just uses one main crontab file for the whole system. Root is able to do this because of a file called 'cron.deny' and 'cron.allow' where root can specify who can and cannot have their own crontabs.

3.1.1 crontab **fields**

To be able to run tasks at certain times you need to know the format for the entries or fields in a crontab file. These are as follows:

1st column	Minutes 1–59
2nd column	Hour 1–23 (0 is midnight)
3rd column	Day_of_month 1–31
4th column	Month 1–12
5th column	Weekday 0–6 (0 is Sunday)
6th column	Command to run

The format of the crontab file is:

Minutes < > Hour < > Day_of_Month < > Month < > Weekday < > Command

The ' < > ' means a space.

A crontab entry is read left to right with Minutes being the first column. The command or task that is to be run is the last field and goes after the Weekday entry.

Within these fields you can specify ranges with a hyphen (-). For example, to run a job Monday to Friday use 1 - 5. You can also be specific using commas. For example to run a job Monday and Thursday only, use 1, 4. Continuous periods are specified with the asterisk (*). If no specific entry is required for a period then you must still use an asterisk in its place, as there must be five columns of time periods, and every column should be space-separated. All comments in a crontab file need a hash mark (#) at the beginning of the line.

3.1.2 crontab **entry examples**

Here are some examples of crontab entries:

30 21 * * * **/apps/bin/cleanup.sh**

runs a script called cleanup.sh in /apps/bin at 9:30 every night.

45 4 1,10,22 * * /apps/bin/backup.sh

runs a script called backup.sh in /apps/bin at 4:45 a.m., on the 1st, 10th and 22nd of each month.

10 1 * * 6,0 /bin/find -name "core" -exec rm {} \;

runs a find command at 1:10 a.m. only on Saturday and Sunday.

0,30 18-23 * * * /apps/bin/dbcheck.sh

runs a script called dbcheck.sh in /apps/bin at every 30 minutes past the hour, between 18:00 and 23:00.

0 23 * * 6 /apps/bin/qtrend.sh

runs a script called qtrend.sh in /apps/bin at 11:00 p.m. every Saturday.

Notice the full pathname is given for all the scripts or one-liners in the crontab file. When you run scripts from the crontab it's up to the user who supplies the script to make sure that all the scripts' full pathnames and environment variables are set correctly. Remember, though, that since the job is submitted by you, the user, cron needs to know about everything. Do not assume cron will know about any special environments that you have set up, because it won't. So make sure your scripts have all the paths and any environments defined, apart from the global environments that are set automatically.

If cron cannot run the script, the user will be mailed telling him or her why.

3.1.3 crontab **options**

The general format of the crontab is:

Crontab [-u user] -e -l -r

where:

-u   is the user login name

-e   edits the crontab file

-l   lists the crontab file

-r   deletes the crontab file

If you log in under your own userid, you do not need to specify the -u option, because cron will pick that up when you run any of the crontab commands.

3.1.4 Creating a new `crontab` entry

The first thing to do before we even think about submitting a `crontab` file into cron is to set up the `EDITOR` environment variable. This tells cron what editor to use when editing `crontabs`. If you're like 99 per cent of the UNIX and LINUX community, you'll use `vi`. So edit your `.profile` that is located in your `$HOME` directory and put the following commands in.

EDITOR = vi; export EDITOR

Now save and exit.

Create a new file called `<user>cron`, where `<user>` is your login name. For example, davecron. Now type the following.

```
# (put your own initials here) echo the date to the console every
# 15 minutes between 6pm and 6am
0,15,30,45 18-06  *  *  *  /bin/echo `date` > /dev/console
```

Now save and exit. Make sure each of the first five fields is space-separated.

The above entry will echo the date to the console every 30 minutes. If the system crashes or hangs, you get a good idea straight away by looking at the last date echoed. On some systems `tty1` is the same as console, so change the device according to your needs.

Now to place our `crontab` file in cron, type `cron` followed by the newly created filename:

```
$ crontab davecron
```

The `crontab` has now been submitted, and your entry will kick off every 30 minutes.

A copy of the file has now been placed in `/var/spool/cron`, and the filename of your `crontab` is the same as your login name (i.e. dave).

3.1.5 Listing your `crontab`

To list the `crontab` file:

```
$ crontab -1
# (crondave installed on Tue May  4 13:07:43 1999)
# DT: echo the date to the console every 30 minutes
  0,15,30,45 18-06  *  *  *  /bin/echo `date` > /dev/tty1
```

A file similar to above will be displayed. Using this listing method, it's a good idea to create a backup copy of the file in your $HOME directory:

```
$ crontab -1 >$HOME/mycron
```

When you accidentally delete your `crontab`, you can quickly reinstall it as we shall see in a moment.

3.1.6 Editing your `crontab`

When you add, edit or delete entries in your `crontab` file, you will be using `vi` as the editor, as long as the `EDITOR` variable has been set using `vi`. To edit the file:

```
$ crontab -e
```

Make any changes and exit normally as you would with any file using `vi`. When you add or edit an entry cron will do a sanity check on the fields when you save the file. It will inform you if any of the fields that have been edited or added are out of range.

Whilst we are editing the `crontab` we might as well add a new entry. Type the following:

```
#  DT: delete core files, at 3.30am on 1,7,14,21,26 days of each month
30 3  1,7,14,21,26  *  *  /bin/find -name "core" -exec rm {} \;
```

Now save and exit. It's always a good idea to put an informative comment line above each `crontab` entry, so you know what it does and when, and more importantly, who put it there.

Let's now check that `crontab` has the new information by listing the `crontab` file:

```
$ crontab -l
# (crondave installed on Tue May  4 13:07:43 1999)
# DT: echo the date to the console every 30 minutes
0,15,30,45 18-06  *  *  *  /bin/echo `date` > /dev/tty1
#  DT: delete core files, at 3.30am on 1,7,14,21,26 days of each
# month
31 3  1,7,14,21,26  *  *  /bin/find -name "core" -exec rm {} \;
```

3.1.7 Removing your `crontab`

To delete your `crontab` file type:

```
$ crontab -r
```

3.1.8 Restoring a lost `crontab`

If you accidentally deleted a `crontab` file, assuming you kept a copy of the file in your `$HOME` directory, copy it to `/var/spool/cron/<username>`, where username is your login name. Or if you cannot do that due to permission problems simply type the following:

```
$ crontab <filename>
```

where filename is the name of the copy you have in your $HOME directory.

I can recommend the above from experience, the amount of times I have accidentally deleted the crontab file. (Well, the 'r' key is right next to the 'e'...) This is probably why some system documentation recommends not editing the crontab file directly, but instead editing a copy of the file and re-submitting a new crontab entry.

Some crontab variants are a bit spooky, so be careful when issuing a directive to crontab from the command line. If you miss out any of the options, crontab will place you in an empty file or what appears to be an empty file. Hit the 'delete' (interrupt) key to exit, and do not press <CTRL-D>, or you'll lose your crontab.

3.2 The at command

The at command allows the user to submit jobs or commands to the cron demon to be executed at a later time. A later time is generally anything from ten minutes up to the next few days. If you want to run a job later than a month stick in a crontab file.

When a job has been submitted, it will keep all its current environments including directory paths, unlike crontab, which doesn't. All output from the jobs is mailed to the user, unless the output is redirected somewhere else, most probably a file.

Like cron, root can control who uses at, with the files at.allow and at.deny in /etc. But root is generally less strict on who can use at.

The basic format of at is:

at [-f script] [-m -l -r] [time] [date]

where

-f script	is the actual script name you wish to submit.
-l	lists all current jobs that are waiting to run. You can also use the command atq.
-r	removes a job. To remove a job you must also supply the ID number of the job; some variants only accept the command atrm to remove jobs.
-m	mails the user when the job has finished.
time	at is very generous with its time format; it can either be in H,HH.HHMM, HH:MM or H:M, where H and M are hours and minutes respectively. You can also use a.m. or p.m.

date   the date format is a month number and a day number, and at also recognises the words 'today' and 'tomorrow'.

OK, let's see how we can submit jobs.

3.2.1 Submitting commands and scripts using at

There are a couple of ways you can submit jobs with at, either on the command line, or using the at command prompt. Generally I prefer to use the at prompt for one-liners only, and use the command line for any scripts that I wish to submit.

For one-liner commands supply the at command with the date/time and hit return. You are then at the at prompt, so simply type in your command(s), then hit <CTRL-D> to exit. Here is an example.

```
$ at 21:10
at> find / -name "passwd" -print
at> <EOT>
warning: commands will be executed using /bin/sh
job 1 at 1999-05-05 21:10
```

The '<EOT>' is <CTRL-D>. At 21:10 a simple find command will be executed. Notice that at has assigned a unique job ID for my submitted job, 'job 1'. All the results from this command will be mailed to me when the job has been completed.

Here's a portion of my mail informing me of the output from the above at job.

```
Subject: Output from your job      1
/etc/passwd
/etc/pam.d/passwd
/etc/uucp/passwd
/tmp/passwd
/root/passwd
/usr/bin/passwd
/usr/doc/uucp-1.06.1/sample/passwd
```

The following are all valid date/time formats you can use with at:

At 6.45am May12
At 11.10pm
At now + 1 hour
At 9am tomorrow
At 15:00 May 24
At now + 10 minutes – this time specification is my own favourite.

If you wish to submit a script file to at, use the command line. Because we are submitting a script we use the -f option.

```
$ at 3.00pm tomorrow -f /apps/bin/db_table.sh
warning: commands will be executed using /bin/sh
job 8 at 1999-05-06 15:00
```

In the above example, a script called db_table.sh will be executed tomorrow at 3:00 p.m.

You can also use echo to submit jobs to at:

```
$ echo find /etc -name "passwd" -print | at now +1 minute
```

3.2.2 Listing jobs submitted

When a job has been submitted you can use the at -l to see all your jobs:

```
$ at -l
2    1999-05-05 23:00 a
3    1999-05-06 06:00 a
4    1999-05-21 11:20 a
1    1999-05-06 09:00 a
```

The first column contains the job ID, followed by the date/time the job is going to run. The last column 'a', stands for at. You can also use the atq command to get a listing of submitted jobs; atq is linked to the at command. When you submit a job, the file is copied into /var/spool/at, ready for execution at the required time.

```
$ pwd
/var/spool/at
$ ls
a0000200eb7ae4   a0000400ebd228   a0000800eb7ea4   spool
a0000300eb7c88   a0000500eb7d3c   a0000900eb7aaa
```

3.2.3 Deleting a submitted job

The format to delete a job is:

atrm [job no] or at -r [job no]

To delete a submitted job, first type at -l, to get the job ID number, then use at -r, supplying the job number to delete the actual job.

```
$ at -l
2    1999-05-05 23:00 a
3    1999-05-06 06:00 a
4    1999-05-21 11:20 a

$ atrm job 3
```

```
$ at -l
2   1999-05-05 23:00 a
4   1999-05-21 11:20 a
```

Some systems use the command at -r [job no] to delete jobs.

3.3 The & command

When you run a job in the foreground, your terminal is then tied up whilst the job is running. Running a job or command in the background, does not tie up your terminal. Use the & command.

The general format is:

command &

Why would you run a command in the background? Well, running it in the background runs it now at that instant without tying up your terminal. Tasks ideal for this are find, big print jobs, big sorts, and scripts. Please be careful with background processing: do not use commands that require user-input, or your PC will sit there doing nothing.

However, because jobs are running in the background all output would still hit your terminal. If you are running a command that puts a lot of output to the screen then it's best to redirect it to a file, using this format:

command   > out.file 2 > &1 &

The above format sends all standard output and errors to the file out.file. When you submit a job in the background its process number is displayed, which can be used to kill or monitor the process if we want.

3.3.1 Submitting a command to the background

Let's run a find that starts from the root filesystem, and we'll send any output to a file called find.dt. Find will look for a file called srm.conf.

```
$ find /etc -name "srm.conf" -print >find.dt 2>&1 &
[1] 27015
```

In the above example, after we have submitted the find command to the background, its process number, which is 27015, is displayed.

When the job has finished, a message is displayed when you next hit any key, which is generally the <return> key.

```
[1]+  Done          find /etc "srm.conf" -print
```

Here's another example. I want to run a script called ps1 that truncates and cleans up all my log files.

```
$ ps1 &
[2] 28535
```

3.3.2 Checking the process using ps

When a job is running in the background you can use the process number it displayed when you submitted it to monitor its process. Using our last example for the script ps1, we simply run the ps command with a grep for our process number:

```
$ ps x|grep 28305
28305  p1 S    0:00 sh /root/ps1
28350  p1 S    0:00 grep 28305
```

If your system does not support ps x use:

```
$ ps -ef |grep 28305
root 28305 21808   0 10:24:39  pts/2  0:00 sh ps1
root 21356 21808   1 10:24:46  pts/2  0:00 grep 28305
```

Remember that when using ps to locate running processes, ps cannot determine whether a job is running in the foreground or the background.

3.3.3 Killing a background job

To kill a running process we use the kill command. When we submitted a job to run in the background, the shell issued the process number that is associated with it. We can use this process number to kill it, using the kill command. The basic format is:

kill -signal [process_number]

Don't worry about the different kill signals at the moment; we will cover them later in the book.

To kill a job, issue the following command (your process number will be different) and hit return a couple of times. A message should be displayed informing the user that the job has been killed.

```
$ kill 28305
[1]+  Terminated            ps1
```

If no message is displayed indicating the job has been terminated, it's a good idea to wait for a minute in case the process is in the middle of terminating, then issue another `kill` command, this time with a signal option:

```
$ kill -9 28305
[1] + Killed                    ps1 &
```

When sending jobs to the background, these will be terminated the moment you log out of the system. To keep a job running after you log out use nohup, which is explained below.

3.4 The nohup **command**

If you are running a process and you don't think it will be completed by the time you log out for the day, use the nohup command. Nohup will continue processing when you exit your account. Nohup means no hang up.

The general format of the command is:

nohup command &

3.4.1 Submitting a job using nohup

Any output from your job will be redirected to a file called 'nohup.out', unless you specify otherwise with

nohup command > myout.file 2 > &1

which sends all output to the file myout.file.

Let's do an example and test that it actually does continue working after you have logged out. We'll kick off a log cleanup script called ps1.

```
$ nohup ps1 &
[1] 179
$ nohup: appending output to 'nohup.out'
```

Now exit the shell, log back in again, and run the following command:

```
$ ps x |grep ps1
  179  ?   S N  0:01 sh /root/ps1
  506  p2 S      0:00 grep ps1
```

The script is still working. Use **ps -ef |grep ps1** if your system does not support ps x.

3.4.2 Submitting several jobs at once

If you want to run several commands at once, it's best to stick them together in a script file then execute it using nohup. For example the following commands have all been piped together; stick all these commands into a file, and make it executable.

cat /home/accounts/qtr_0499 | /apps/bin/trials.awk |sort|lp

```
$ cat > quarterend
cat /home/accounts/qtr_0499 | /apps/bin/trials.awk |sort|lp
<CTRL-D>
```

Now make it executable:

```
$ chmod 744 quarterend
```

We'll also stick all the output into a file called qtr.out:

```
$ nohup ./quarterend > qtr.out 2>&1 &
[5] 182
```

3.5 Conclusion

The tools that we have discussed in this chapter are primarily for running jobs unattended. There are times when you may have to run intensive updates against large files, or carry out complex finds, which are best done out of peak work hours when the system is not so busy.

Creating scripts that clean up logs or do specific application work every night can be submitted then forgotten about; all you have to do is check the script logs. If you look after a system, then cron and the other tools can make your life a lot easier in the administration role.

CHAPTER 4

Filename substitution

When working on the command line, quite a bit of your time will be spent locating files that you want to work with. The shell offers a neat set of pattern matching or metacharacters that enables you to match filenames based on the pattern you supply. You can also use character classes to match filenames. But as it's quicker using the metacharacters on the command line, we will stick with these in this chapter.

In this chapter we will cover:

- pattern matching using any character string;

- pattern matching using single characters; and

- pattern matching using alpha or numeric characters.

Here are these special characters.

*	Matches any string including a null string.
?	Matches any one character.
[...]	Matches any characters enclosed in the square brackets.
[!...]	Matches any characters other than the characters following the explanation mark '!' inside the square brackets.

When the shell sees the above characters it knows that they are special and not the same as ordinary characters, which enables the user to match certain filenames only.

4.1 Using the *

Use the asterisk to match any part of a filename. Here we specify app*, which means list all filenames that have 'app' at the beginning of the filename and anything else after that:

```
$ ls app*
appdva          app_tapes
appdva_SLA
```

Use the asterisk to match at the beginning of the string. Here we list all documents that end with '.doc':

```
$ ls *.doc
accounts.doc    qtr_end.doc
```

You can also use the asterisk during any part of filenames you want to match. Here we say match the filenames beginning with 'cl', and any other characters after that, but they must end with .sed.

```
$ ls cl*.sed
cleanmeup.sed           cleanlogs.sed
cleanmessages.sed
```

Use the asterisk to save yourself from typing in the full directory name when you want to cd into that directory:

```
$ pwd
/etc
$ ls -l |grep ^d
. . .
. . .
drwxr-xr-x   2 root     root      1024 Jan 26 14:41 cron.daily
drwxr-xr-x   2 root     root      1024 Jun 27  1998 cron.hourly
drwxr-xr-x   2 root     root      1024 Jun 27  1998 cron.monthly
drwxr-xr-x   2 root     root      1024 Jan 26 14:37 cron.weekly
. . .
$ cd cron.w*
$ pwd
/etc/cron.weekly
```

4.2 Using the ?

Use the ? to match any single character. Here we list filenames where the first two characters can be any character, followed by an 'R', followed by any string:

```
$ ls ??R*
BAREAD
```

In the following example, we list files that start with 'conf', followed by any two characters, followed by '.log':

```
$ ls conf.??.log
conf12.log conf.23.log
conf25.log
```

To match all filenames that start with 'f', followed by any two characters, followed by any string; the end character must be an 's':

```
$ ls f??*s
ftpaccess        ftpconversions
ftpgroups        ftphosts
ftpusers
```

4.3 Using [...] and [!...]

Use [...] to match any characters inside the brackets. This method also supports ranges by separating the range with a dash. To list all filenames that start with an 'i' or 'o':

```
$ ls [io]*
inetd.conf  initrunlvl
inputrc     issue
info-dir    inittab
ioctl.save  issue.net
```

To match filenames that begin with 'log.', followed by a single number, followed by any other character. The [0–9] means any single number. The asterisk takes care of multiple numbers:

```
$ ls log.[0-9]*
log.0323  log.0324
log.0325  log.0326
```

To list all filenames that have the same criteria as above but with no numbers, use the negation symbol (!) inside the bracket. [!0–9]* means it must not start with a digit.

```
$ ls log.[!0-9]*
log.sybase
```

To match filenames that start with 'LPS', where the next two characters can be anything, but the next character must be a '1':

```
$ ls LPS??[1]
LPSI91  LPSO91
```

To match filenames that start with 'LPS', followed by any two characters, followed by an nn-digit, followed by anything:

```
$ ls LPS??[!0-9]*
LPSOSI        LPSILP
LPSOPS        LPSPOPQTR
```

To match filenames starting with an upper case letter only:

```
$ ls [A-Z]*
```

To match filenames starting with a lower case letter only:

```
$ ls [a-z]*
```

To match only numbered filenames use:

```
$ ls [0-9]*
```

To match all your .files (hidden files, like .profile, .rhosts, .history, etc.):

```
$ ls .*
```

4.4 Conclusion

Using metacharacters to match filenames greatly reduces the time you spend searching for filenames. The use of metacharacters is a very powerful tool in pattern matching, as we shall see when we deal with metacharacters in more detail when we discuss regular expressions.

CHAPTER 5

Shell input and output

To be able to read data into your scripts you have a few different methods available to you: use the standard input which is your keyboard, or assign a file as the input. The same goes for the output: unless you specify a file as the output, the standard output will always go to your terminal screen. If you have errors that are generated from the commands that you use, you probably do not want these messing up your screen, so you can redirect these messages to another output, generally a file.

Most of the commands that use standard input usually specify files as their standard input – why key in a load of data, when it can be read in via a file?

In this chapter we will cover:

- using standard input, output and errors; and
- redirection of input and output.

This chapter is all about using the shell for input and output for all your data and information, with a bit of redirection.

5.1 echo

Use echo to display lines of text or variables or to direct strings into files. The general format is:

echo string

The echo command comes with many features, but the most useful ones are as follows:

\c   do not go to the next line

\f   formfeed

\t   tab

\n   newline

To keep the prompt at the end of your string use:

```
$ echo  "What is your name :\c"
$ read name
```

The output from the above would display:

```
What is your name :□
```

where '□' is the cursor.

To echo a string and let the cursor go to the next line use:

```
$ echo "The red pen ran out of ink"
```

You can put variables within echo statements as well as escape codes. In this example, the terminal bell is rung, your $HOME directory is displayed, and the command tty is evaluated by the shell.

```
$ echo "\007your home directory is $HOME, you are connected on `tty`"

your home directory is /home/dave, you are connected on /dev/ttyp1
```

If it's LINUX then...

You have to put a '-n' after the echo to suppress the new line:

```
$ echo -n "What is your name :"
```

You have to put a '-e' after echo for the escape code to work:

```
$ echo -e "\007your home directory is $HOME, you are connected on `tty`"

your home directory is /home/dave, you are connected on /dev/ttyp1
```

To have blank lines after your string is echoed, use the \n newline option.

```
$ pg echod
#!/bin/sh
echo  "this echo's 3 new lines\n\n\n"
echo "OK"
```

When run, this gives as output:

```
$ echod
this echo's 3 blank lines



OK
```

You can put tabs in your echo statements, simply remember to use the backslash first:

```
$ echo "here is a tab\there are two tabs\t\tok"
here is a tab   here are two tabs                ok
```

If it's LINUX then...

Remember to put a '-e' after the echo statement for the escape code to work:

```
$ echo -e "here is a tab\there are two tabs\t\tok"
here is a tab   here are two tabs                ok
```

To echo strings into a file use the > sign. This example echoes a string to a file called myfile:

```
$ echo "The log files have all been done" > myfile
```

or to append to myfile, which means do not overwrite the contents already present:

```
$ echo "$LOGNAME carried them out at `date` " >>myfile
```

Let's now see the contents of the file myfile:

```
$ pg myfile
The log files have all been done
root carried them out at Sat May 22 18:25:06 GMT 1999
```

One of the many problems that usually crop up for users new to the shell concerning the echo command is how to include a double quote within an echo statement. A quote is a special character, so it has to be escaped with a backslash. Suppose we want to echo this string to the screen, "/dev/rmt/0", as long as we put the backslashes in front of the quotes we are OK.

```
$ echo "\"/dev/rmt0"\"
"/dev/rmt0"
```

5.2 `read`

Use `read` to take information from the keyboard or from a line of text from a file and assign it to a variable. If you specify only one variable then the read will assign all input to that variable until it sees an end-of-file marker or the shell sees a carriage return.

The general format is:

read variable1 variable2 . . .

One variable has been specified, which holds all text until the return key has been hit:

```
$ read name
Hello I am superman
$ echo $name
Hello I am superman
```

Here, we assign two variables to hold a first and a second name. The shell will use the space bar as the separator for each variable.

```
$ read name surname
John Doe
$ echo $name $surname
John Doe
```

If you type in too many fields of text, the shell will assign all the leftover text to the end variable. Here is an example; suppose we have the variable's name and surname again, but this time type in three names to see what happens:

```
$ read name surname
John Lemon Doe
$ echo $name
John
$ echo $surname
Lemon Doe
```

We typed in the string 'John Lemon Doe', and the first variable was assigned, but as the shell ran out of variables for assignment, it stuck all the text we entered into the last variable.

One way to avoid possible confusion from the user is to use each `read` for each variable only, like this:

```
$ pg var_test
#!/bin/sh
# var_test
echo "First Name :\c"
```

```
read name
echo "Middle Name :\c"
read middle
echo "Last name :\c"
read surname
```

When you run the above you can then tell the user what type of information goes in what field.

```
$ var_test
First Name : John
Middle Name : Lemon
Surname : Doe
```

If it's LINUX then...

Remember to use the '-n' echo option.

```
$ pg var_test
#!/bin/sh
# var_test
echo "First Name :\c"
read name
echo "Middle Name :\c"
read middle
echo "Last name :\c"
read surname
```

5.3 cat

cat is a very simple but versatile file display and file creator which is also handy for displaying control characters. When using cat be warned that it will not pause between page breaks; it literally displays the whole file in one go. If you need to see a file a page at a time then use 'more' or pipe the output from cat through to another pager, like this:

```
$ cat myfile | more
```

or

```
$ cat myfile | pg
```

The general format is:

cat [options] filename1 ... filename2 ...

cat's most useful option is:

-v   Display control characters.

To display a file called myfile:

```
$ cat myfile
```

To display three files called myfile1, myfile2 and myfile3:

```
$ cat myfile1 myfile2 myfile3
```

To create a file called bigfile that contains the contents of the files myfile1, myfile2 and myfile3, redirect (more on this is a moment) the output to the new file:

```
$ cat myfile1 myfile2 myfile3 >bigfile
```

To create a new file and also enter some text, you need only to redirect the output from cat to a filename, type some text in, and when you have finished hit <CTRL-D> to terminate. A very simple editor!

```
$ cat > myfile
This is great
<CTRL-D>
$ pg myfile
This is great
```

To see all control characters in a file, this is a good post mortem test on all DOS files that have been ftp-ed across to UNIX. Here all control characters <CTRL-M> are displayed at the end of each line.

```
$ cat -v life.tct
ERROR ON REC AS12^M
ERROR ON REC AS31^M
```

One of note caution here; if you just type cat and hit return, it will wait there for you to type in some characters. If you do decide to type text in then it will echo what you type in (of course) but it will also echo the text back to you as well; simply hit <CTRL-D> to terminate cat.

5.4 Pipes

The pipe command lets you take the output from one command and use it as input to another command. The pipe is represented by the bar (|) sign. The general format is:

command1 | command2

where the '|' is the pipe.

In the following example, a file listing is carried out on the current directory, and all files are displayed or would be if the pipe was not there. The shell sees the pipe, takes all the files and gives them to the command on the right of the pipe, so that in essence the pipe is doing exactly what its name implies: piping the information from one side to the other. In this case grep then searches through this output looking for the pattern quarter1.doc:

```
$ ls | grep quarter1.doc
quarter1.doc
```

Let's see that example again but this time using a diagram to explain what's happening.

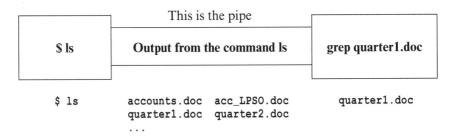

```
$ ls               accounts.doc  acc_LPS0.doc        quarter1.doc
                   quarter1.doc  quarter2.doc
                   ...
```

Sed, awk and grep go together well in using pipes especially for one-liners. Using the output from the who command gets pipe through to awk to display the usernames and their terminal connections.

```
$ who | awk '{print $1"\t"$2}'
matthew    pts/0
louise     pts/1
```

To see all your registered mounted file systems, use pipe to pass the output from df to awk, where awk then prints the first column. Use pipe again to take this output and pass it through grep to get rid of the 'filesystem' header information.

```
$ df -k | awk '{print $1}'| grep -v "Filesystem"
/dev/hda5
/dev/hda8
```

```
/dev/hda6
/dev/hdb5
/dev/hdb1
/dev/hda7
/dev/hda1
```

Of course you may prefer to have the partition names only from the above output, and not the '/dev/' part, which is no problem; we simply use another pipe and use a sed command after it.

```
$ df -k | awk '{print $1}'| grep -v "Filesystem"|sed s'/\/dev\///g'
hda5
hda8
hda6
hdb5
hdb1
hda7
hda1
```

In this example, a file is sorted and the output via pipe is sent to the printer:

```
$ sort myfile | lp
```

5.5 tee

The tee command acts the way it is pronounced. It takes the input and sends one copy to the standard output and another copy to a file. If you want to see your output and save it to a file at the same time, then this is the command for you.

The general format is:

tee -a files

where, '-a' means append all output to a file.

Tee comes in handy when you are running commands or scripts and you want to keep a log of the output.

Let's look at an example. Using the who command, the output is sent to the screen and a copy is sent to a file called who.out.

```
$ who | tee who.out
louise     pts/1     May 20 12:58 (193.132.90.9)
matthew    pts/0     May 20 10:18 (193.132.90.1)


cat who.out
louise     pts/1     May 20 12:58 (193.132.90.9)
matthew    pts/0     May 20 10:18 (193.132.90.1)
```

The figure below shows that example again.

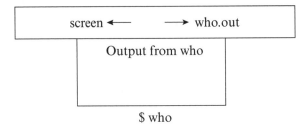

In the next example a cpio command is run to back up files to a tape and at the same time to log the output to a file called tape.log. As the file will be continuously appended to by cpio, use the -a option.

```
$ find  etc usr/local home -depth -print | cpio -ovC65536 -O \
/dev/rmt/0n | tee -a tape.log
```

In the above command, the backslash after the -O option means let the shell know that the command continues on the next line.

You can create simple echo statements before calling your scripts to tell the user who is running the script where the output of this script will be kept.

```
$ echo " myscript is now running, check out any errors...in
myscript.log" | tee -a myscript.log
```

```
$ myscript | tee -a myscript.log
```

You do not have to send the output to a file if you do not want to; instead you can send it to a terminal. This sends a warning to the system's console that a disk cleanup is now being carried out.

```
$ echo "stand-by disk cleanup starting in 1 minute" | tee/dev/console
```

You can specify different commands to all go to the same log file, but just remember to use the -a option.

```
$ sort myfile | tee -a accounts.log
```

```
$ myscript | tee -a accounts.log
```

5.6 Standard input, output and errors

When using commands in the shell, the shell associates each process with an open file, and references these open files by using numbers called file descriptors. As numbers are not very easy to remember, the shell gives them (file) names as well.

Here are the file descriptors and their more common names.

Files	File descriptor
Input file – standard input	0
Output file – standard output	1
Error output file – standard error	2

There are actually 12 file descriptors, but as can be seen from the above table, 0,1, and 2 are reserved for the 'standard' input, output and errors. You are free to use descriptors 3 to 9.

5.6.1 Standard input

Standard input is file descriptor '0'. This is where input goes into commands, either via the keyboard which is the default, or from the output of other commands.

5.6.2 Standard output

Standard output is file descriptor '1'. This is where all the output from your commands goes; the default is the screen, but you can send it to a file.

5.6.3 Standard error

Standard error is file descriptor '2'. This is where all errors from your commands go; the default is the screen, but again you can send it to a file. You may be wondering why there is a special file for errors; well, some people like to keep their errors in a separate file, especially when processing large data files, where a lot of errors might be raised.

If you do not specify a file descriptor, then the default (your screen, or to be more accurate, your terminal) is assumed.

5.7 File redirection

When issuing commands, you can specify where you want the standard input, output and errors to go, and to be able to do this you need to do a bit of redirection. A combination of the most useful redirections with corresponding file descriptors is shown in Table 5.1.

When using standard error in redirection, you must use a file descriptor, but for standard input and output this is optional. Table 5.1 shows both methods for completeness.

Table 5.1 *Common file redirection commands*

Command > filename	Send standard output to a new filename
Command > > filename	Send standard output to filename (appended)
Command 1 > filename	Send standard output to filename
Command > filename 2 > &1	Send all output (including errors) to filename
Command 2 > filename	Send standard error to filename
Command 2 > > filename	Send standard error to filename (appended)
Command > > filename 2 > &1	Send all output (including errors) to filename (appended)
Command < filename > filename2	Command gets its input from filename and sends command output to filename2
Command < filename	Command gets its input from filename
Command < < delimiter	Read standard input until delimiter encountered
Command <&m	Read standard input from file descriptor m
Command >&m	Write standard output to file descriptor m
Command <&-	Close standard input

5.7.1 Redirecting standard output

Let's look at the standard output. In the next command, the login ID fields from /etc/passwd are sorted by name. The output from this command is directed to a file called sort.out. One word of caution here when using sort output (or indeed any command that expects a file as input): make sure that the redirection operator is two spaces from the sort command, otherwise sort will think that it is an input file.

```
$ cat passwd | awk -F: '{print $1}'| sort  1>sort.out
```

Looking at our table we could have used the following, which would have produced the same output:

```
$ cat passwd | awk -F: '{print $1}'| sort >sort.out
```

You can redirect output to an appended file from many commands.

```
$ ls -l | grep ^d >>files.out
$ ls account* >> files.out
```

In the above, all `grep`'s output, which lists directories only and output from an `ls` command matching filenames that start with 'account', have been appended to the file `files.out`.

To redirect standard output to a new file, use '> `filename`'. Here, all the output from an ls command is directed to a file called `ls.out`:

```
$ ls >ls.out
```

To append to an already created file or to create a new file if the file is not present, use '>>`filename`':

```
$ pwd >>path.out
$ find . -name "LPSO.doc" -print >>path.out
```

To create an empty zero length file use '>`filename`':

```
$ >myfile
```

5.7.2 Redirecting standard input

You can use the standard input to take or give input to commands. You will meet this in the `awk` chapter. Below is an example on giving the input to a command.

```
$ sort < names.txt
```

The `sort` command is given its input using redirection, but I could also have used:

```
$ sort names.txt
```

Taking the above example a step further, if I wanted to produce an output file from the `sort` command, I simply stick an output redirection in telling the `sort` to send all output to a file called names.out. No output will go to the screen (apart from any errors):

```
$ sort <names.txt > names.out
```

To mail a user from the command line, if message is in a file, just redirect the file into mail. Here, user louise gets sent mail, with the message enclosed in a file called `contents.txt`:

```
$ mail louise < contents.txt
```

The redirection '`command << delimiter`' is a useful command more commonly called a 'here' document. We will see this in action when we deal with here documents later on in the book. But for now, this is how it works. The shell takes all lines after the 'delimiter' as input until it encounters the 'delimiter' again, and the shell then knows to terminate the redirection. This command is very useful for doing automatic or remote routines. You can specify any 'delimiter'; the word 'EOF', is quite popular, but it's up to you. I like to use MAYDAY, but that's just me. You can pass variables into the here document as well. Here's an example. A file is created called 'myfile' with a little text, using the variables TERM and LOGNAME.

```
$ cat >> myfile <<MAYDAY
> Hello there I am using a $TERM terminal
> and my user name is $LOGNAME
> bye...
> MAYDAY

$ pg myfile
Hello there I am using a vt100 terminal
and my user name is dave
bye...
```

5.7.3 Redirecting standard error

To redirect standard errors you specify the file descriptor '2'. Let's first look at an example, since they always explain better. Here grep searches for a pattern called 'trident' on a file called missiles.

```
$ grep "trident" missiles
grep: missiles: No such file or directory
```

grep reports no such file, and sends its errors to the terminal which is the default. Let's now send all errors to a file, in fact to the system dustbin, '/dev/null'.

```
$ grep "trident" missiles 2>/dev/null
```

All error output (remember this example returned errors, with 'no file') is sent to /dev/null, not to the screen.

If you were working on more important files, then you would probably want to save your errors. Here's the same command again, but this time going to a file called grep.err:

```
$  grep "trident" missiles 2>grep.err
$ pg grep.err
grep: missiles: No such file or directory
```

You can also send errors to an appended file. This method is useful if you are running a batch or group of commands to do a common task. Two grep commands are used with the errors both going to the same file; as we are appending with the '> >', the errors (if any) from the second grep will not overwrite the first lot of errors.

```
$ grep "LPSO" * 2>>account.err
$ grep "SILO" * 2>>account.err
```

5.8 Combining standard output and error

A neat way of quickly identifying errors is first to direct the output to a file, then direct the errors to another file. Here's an example.

I have two account files, one that contains information, another that does not (but I do not know this). I want to redirect both files to an output file called `accounts.out`.

```
$ cat account_qtr.doc account_end.doc 1> accounts.out 2> accounts.err
```

Now if I have errors, it will be contained in the file `accounts.err`.

```
$ pg accounts.out
AVBD 34HJ    OUT
AVFJ    31KO  OUT
. . .
```

```
$ pg accounts.err
cat: account_end.doc: No such file or directory
```

Without previously knowing if the second file 'account_end.doc' contained information, using the above redirection for output and errors has quickly helped me identify that the file 'account_end.doc', is the source of my problem.

5.9 Merging standard output and standard error

When merging output and errors, the shell evaluates the command from left to right, which is really all you need to know when putting mergers together. Here's an example.

```
$ cleanup >cleanup.out 2>&1
```

In the above example the script cleanup directs all output (>) to a file called cleanup.out, and all errors (2), are directed to (>) the same place as the output (&1), which is cleanup.out.

```
$ grep "standard" * > grep.out 2>&1
```

In the above example all output from the grep command is put into the output file grep.out. When you use here documents, you will probably need to capture all the output to a file in case errors are encountered. To do this you need to use 2>&1 as part of the command. Here's how to do it:

```
$ cat>> filetest 2>&1 <<MAYDAY
> This is my home $HOME directory
> MAYDAY
```

```
$ pg filetest
This is my home /home/dave directory
```

The above example illustrates how to capture all the output to a file. This is probably not much good when you are doing a cat command, but if you are connecting to DBMS products (like sybase with isql) or ftp, it is vital that you capture all errors and not let them run off the screen somewhere, especially if you are not around.

5.10 exec

The exec command is used to replace the current shell; in other words a subshell is not started. When using this command all existing environments are cleared to start afresh. The general format is:

exec command

where command is generally a script.

The best description I can think of in explaining exec is to think of it as trampling over your current shell.

When the script has finished the session can be terminated. One of the many uses of exec is to run added security scripts, usually put at the end of the user's .profile file. If the user inputs an invalid response, the shell is closed and they are back at the login prompt. Exec is also popular when opening files with file descriptors.

Be aware when using exec with file descriptors that it will not overwrite your current shell; this is the only occasion it will not.

5.11 Using file descriptors

To open and close files using file descriptors use exec. In the following example, I have chosen file descriptor 4, but I could have chosen any number from 4 to 9. This little script does nothing but reads two lines of a stock file and echoes the lines back.

The first line saves the standard input using file descriptor 4 and then opens the file for reading. The next two lines read in two lines of text. The last line closes the standard input using file descriptor 4. The rest of the script echoes out the contents that were read in using the variables line1 and line2.

```
$ pg f_desc
#!/bin/sh
# f_desc
exec 4<&0 0<stock.txt
read line1
read line2
exec  0<&4
```

```
echo $line1
echo $line2
```

Here is that little stock file stock.txt:

```
$ pg stock.txt
Crayons Assorted 34
Pencils Light    12
```

Here is the output when the script is executed:

```
$ f_desc
Crayons Assorted 34
Pencils Light    12
```

The above example is a fairly basic use of file descriptors. It does no processing of any importance. When we cover iteration, we will see how to use file descriptors to copy text files as an alternative method to using the `cp` command.

5.12 Conclusion

Throughout this book you will encounter redirections, because it is an important part of the shell that allows you to get input into commands. Separating the errors, if any, to a separate destination enables you to track down problems fast.

One area we have not covered is the use of the shell's file descriptors (3–9). To be able to use these file descriptors you really need to use iteration methods, and we'll look again at file descriptors when we deal with iteration.

CHAPTER 6

Command execution order

When executing commands, you occasionally need to know that one command has completed successfully or failed before carrying on with another command. For example, suppose you wanted to copy all the files from one directory to another directory, then delete the source directory. You'll want to know for sure that the copy went OK first before you blitz the original directory, otherwise you could lose all your source directory contents.

In this chapter we will cover:

•   command execution control; and

•   command grouping.

The shell has a couple of commands that will not execute the second commands unless the first went OK or execute the second command if the first one failed. The operators that can take care of these types of situations are the command operators && and ||. The commands can be scripts or system commands.

The shell also offers commands where you can execute a group of commands either in the current shell or subshell, which are () and {}.

6.1 Using &&

Here's the general format of &&:

command1 && command2

The operation of these commands is fairly straightforward. The command on the left of the && (command1) must be returned true (successfully executed) if the command on the right (command2) is to be executed; or to put it another way, 'If this command works' && 'then execute this command'.

Here's a simple example that illustrates the use of the &&:

```
$ cp justice.doc justice.bak && echo "if you are seeing this then cp was
OK"

if you are seeing this then cp was OK
```

The copy was successful, so the command on the right of the && (the echo command) was executed.

For a more practical example:

```
$ mv /apps/bin /apps/dev/bin && rm -r  /apps/bin
```

In the above example, the directory /apps/bin is to be moved to /apps/dev/bin; if this fails then the deletion of the directory /apps/bin will not happen.

In the following example, a file is to be sorted with the output going to a file called quarter.sort; if this is successful, the file will be printed.

```
$ sort quarter_end.txt > quarter.sorted && lp quarter.sorted
```

6.2 Using ||

The general format of the || is:

command1 || command2

The operation of the || is slightly different. If the command on the left of the || (command1) fails then execute the command on the right of the || (command2); or to put it another way, 'If this command fails' || 'then execute this command'.

Here's another simple example that illustrates the use of the ||:

```
$ cp wopper.txt oops.txt || echo "if you are seeing this cp failed"

cp: wopper.txt: No such file or directory
if you are seeing this cp failed
```

The copy has failed so now the command on the right-hand side of the || is executed.

A more practical example is this. I want to extract the first and fifth fields from an accounts file and stick the output into a temp file. If the extraction does not work, I want to be mailed.

```
$ awk '{print$1,$5}' acc.qtr >qtr.tmp || echo "Sorry the payroll
extraction didn't work" | mail dave
```

You don't always have to use system commands; here I run the script comet on a file called `month_end.txt`. If the script bombs out, the shell should terminate (exit).

```
$ comet month_end.txt || exit.
```

6.3 Grouping commands using () and { }

To run several commands as a group effort all at once, the shell provides two methods. You can either run the group in the current shell or in a subshell.

To run a list of commands in the current shell, separate each command with a command separator, and enclose the list with round brackets.

The general format is:

(command1; command2; . .)

To run a command in the subshell do exactly the same but use { } instead of (). The general format is:

{command1; command2; . .)

I do not use these methods by themselves very often. The only time I use these grouping operators is in conjunction with the && or ||.

Going back to our comet script example, if the script comet failed I would probably want to execute two or more commands, not just one. Using the grouping method I can do this. Here's the original example:

```
$ comet month_end.txt || exit
```

Now if the comet script failed, and I wanted to mail myself, and then exit, all I need to do is:

```
$ comet month_end || (echo "Hello, guess what! Comet did not work"|mail
dave; exit)
```

If I had just used command separators without the grouping the shell would automatically go to the last statement, which is exit.

Going back to the sort example using the && operator, here it is below:

```
$ sort quarter_end.txt > quarter.sorted && lp quarter.sorted
```

Using the grouping method, if the `sort` command worked, copy the output file to a log area and then print the file.

```
$ sort quarter_end.txt > quarter.sorted && ( cp quarter.sorted /logs/
quarter.sorted; lp quarter.sorted )
```

6.4 Conclusion

Using the `&&` and `||` operators is very helpful when creating decision-making statements. It can also save your skin if you do not want the second command executed because the first failed. These methods give you control over what actions are to be taken based on the exit status of the commands on the left-hand side of the `&&` or `||`.

## PART 2

Text filtering

CHAPTER 7

Introducing regular expressions

As you become more familiar with UNIX or LINUX, there is one subject you will bump into repeatedly, and that is regular expressions. As you use the shell, the need to extract more than just a basic string from a file soon outgrows it. For example, you may want to extract a word where the first two characters are, say, upper case followed by four numbers. You cannot do this in the shell unless you use some form of regular expression.

In this chapter we will cover:

- matching at the beginning and end of line;

- matching sets of data;

- matching only alpha or numeric or both; and

- matching character ranges.

When we want to extract or filter text from a file or an output of a command we can use what is called regular expressions (RE). Regular expressions are a collection of special, and sometimes not so special, character patterns.

To extract or catch certain information, we give it a pattern of rules to which the extraction should adhere. These rules come in the form of special characters or metacharacters, which are characters we use for pattern matching. We can also use normal characters to search as part of our pattern; for example, A will search for A, and x will search for the letter x.

All of the big filtering text tools that come with the system allow the use of regular expressions in some form, but there is also an extended set of meta-characters. We will cover only one of these and that is the occurrence expression. The reason that for this is that some systems group the occurrence pattern into the basic set of metacharacters. I believe this is a sound idea and so I will also include this as a member of the basic set.

The basic metacharacters covered in this chapter will work on grep and sed. They will also work for awk apart from the {\\} occurrence metacharacter.

Table 7.1 shows the basic set of metacharacters.

Table 7.1 *The basic set of metacharacters and their meanings*

^	Will match the beginning of the line only.
$	Will match the end of the line only.
*	A single character followed by an *, will match zero or more occurrences.
[]	Character enclosed inside the [] will be matched. This can be a single or range of characters. You can use the - to include a range inclusively. Instead of saying [12345] use [1-5].
\	Use this to escape the special meaning of a metacharacter. Some metacharacters have special meanings to the shell. The \ disables the meaning.
.	Matching any single character.
pattern \{n \}	Use this to match a specific number of occurrences specified by n that contains the preceding pattern
pattern \{n,\}m	As above but match at 'least' n occurrence of the preceding pattern.
pattern \{n,m\}	Matches any number of occurrences between n and m of the preceding pattern.

Let us go over the special characters in more detail.

7.1 Matching a single character with a period

You can match any single character with a '.' For example if we wanted to match a string that started with beg followed by any character and ended with an n, we could use beg.n. This would match begin and began amongst others.

We could also use it to match certain permissions from a ls -l command.

   ...x..x..x

This would match all the execute permissions for owner, group and other:

drwxrwxrw-	**– no match**
-rw-rw-rw-	**– no match**
-rwx-rwxr-x	**– match**
-rwx-r-x-r-x	**– match**

Suppose you are filtering a text file, and you need to match all codes with an XC after the first four characters within a 10-character field. This would do it:

....XC....

What we have said in the above example is that the first four characters can be anything, the next two must be *XC* and the last four characters can also be anything. Running this against the following:

1234XC9088   – match
4523XX9001   – no match
0011XA9912   – no match
9931XC3445   – match

Please note that the period allows the match of 'any' character in the ASCII set, be it an alpha or numeric character.

7.2 Matching a string or character at the beginning of a line with a ^

Using the ^ allows you to match words or characters at the beginning of the line only. We could for example do a `ls -l` and match only directories, which we can do because if the first character of a `ls -l` is a 'd' then it's a directory.

^d
drwxrwxrw-   – match
-rw-rw-rw-   – no match
drwx-rwxr-x   – match
-rwx-r-x-r-x   – no match

Returning to our code example, using **^001**, this would match 001 at the beginning of the line:

1234XC9088   – no match
4523XX9001   – no match
0011XA9912   – match
9931XC3445   – no match

We can also combine various pattern matching, for example,

^...4XC....

would return:

1234XC9088	– match
4523XX9001	– no match
0011XA9912	– no match
9931XC3445	– no match
3224XC193	– no match

Here we have said to start at the beginning of the line, and match any three characters, followed by a 4XC, and any four characters after that. You will find using the ˆ character is very common in using the regular expressions because a lot of extraction you will need will generally be at the start of the line.

To match only fields that have a character of the number '1', that is four characters in from the beginning of the line, we could do:

ˆ...1

which would return:

1234XC9088	– no match
4523XX9001	– no match
0011XA9912	– match
9931XC3445	– match

Suppose you wanted to match all words that started with *comp* at the beginning of the line, this would do it:

ˆcomp

Now suppose you wanted to further refine the pattern so that it should return all words that start with *comp*, which have any two letters after that, but must end with *ing*. Here's one way:

ˆcomp..ing

The above example is a bit obvious and maybe not very useful, but the idea is to show you how you can mix a regular pattern.

7.3 Matching a string or character at the end of a line with $

You could say that the opposite of the ˆ is the $, which lets us match a string or character at the end of the line. The dollar sign goes at the end of the word you want to match. Suppose we wanted to match all lines that end with the word *trouble*, this would do it:

trouble$

Similarly, using **ld$** would return all words ending with *ld* at the end of each line.

If we wanted to match all empty lines, we could do this as follows:

^$

This says start at the beginning of the line, and end at the end of the line. As there is no pattern involved it will return only blank lines.

If we wanted to return lines that contained only one character, we could do this:

^.$

Unlike the blank lines example, there is a pattern between the start and the end of line, which is any single character.

If we wanted to match the word `jet01` at the end of a line, this would do it:

jet01$

7.4 Matching a single or string of characters with *

Using this special character allows us to match repeatedly any number of occurrences of any character or string. One example is:

compu*t

will match the character *u* once or repeatedly:

computer
computing
compuuuuute

Here's another example:

10133*

will match

101333
10133
101344444

7.5 Escaping the meaning of a special character using \

We may want to search for strings or characters they may sometimes contain a character that is considered a special character. What is a special character? For general purposes you may consider any of the following characters to be special characters

$. ' " * [ ] ^ | ( ) \ + ?

Suppose we wanted to match any lines that had a period '.' in them. We know a '.' is a special character that lets you match any single character, so we need to disable this meaning. Here's how we would do it:

\.

The above says do not treat the character after the backslash as a special character, but treat it literally; in this case, treat it as a period.

Suppose we want to match any lines containing a caret in them. We put the backslash in to turn off the special meaning of the character ^, as follows:

\^

If you wanted to match all files that ended with *.pas* within a regular expression we could do this as follows:

*\.pas

which means disable the special meaning of the character *.

7.6 Matching ranges or sets using [ ]

To match certain specific characters or ranges of characters use [ ]. You can separate the different characters that you want to match inside the brackets with commas; this is not mandatory (some systems do moan if you don't use commas on complex expressions) but it does make the pattern more readable.

To specify a range of characters use the dash (-). This specifies a set or range where the range starts on the left-hand side of the dash and finishes on the right-hand side of the dash.

You should always use the [ ] when you want to home in on a string match.

Suppose we wanted to match any single number, we could use:

[0123456789]

However, there is an easier method by using the dash (-):

[0-9]

or any lower case letter

[a-z]

To match any case of letter we would use:

[A-Za-z]

This specifies a range of letters from A-Z and a-z, catching both combinations.
If we wanted to catch any letter or number, try this:

[A-Za-z0-9]

We can also specify what the characters are to be using any case combination.
Suppose we wanted to match a word beginning with the letter *s*, having any letter in
the middle but ending with *t*. This would do it:

s[a-zA-Z]t

This would of course bring back upper and lower case mixed words. If we wanted to
match all lower case we would use:

s[a-z]t

If we wanted to match all words that were either *Computer* or *computer*, we would
do it like this:

[Cc]omputer

To catch a combination of the following words such as scout, shout, bought
we could use the expression

[ou].*t

which matches any letter that starts with an o or u, followed by any character, any
number of times and ending in a 't'.
Maybe you want to match all words that have system followed by a period.
Where the 'S' could be in upper or lower case, use:

[S,s]ystem\.

The use of the [] is very good at limiting the range or scope of your pattern match. You'll find it useful to use the * with the [], to match repeatedly:

[A-Za-z]*

will match all words.

Remember the use of the ^ symbol, when used directly inside the first bracket, means to negate or not to match what is inside the bracket.

[^a-zA-Z]

will match any non-alpha character, while

[^0-9]

will match any non-numeric character.

Looking at the last example, you have probably already guessed that you can use any special character to search on apart from the ^.

7.7 Matching a specific number of occurrences with \{ \}

Using the * allows us to match any number of matches, but if we want to match only a certain number of occurrences, that's where \{ \} comes in. There are actually three options in using this pattern match, which are:

pattern \{n\}	Match n occurrences of the pattern
pattern \{n,\}	Match at least n occurrences of the pattern
pattern \{n,m\}	Match occurrences of the pattern between n and m, where n and m are integer numbers between 0 and 255

Looking at the first examples, suppose we wanted to match only three occurrences of the letter AA, but ending in the letter B, this would do it:

A\{2\}B

This would give me **AAB** in a match.

If we wanted to match at least four occurrences of the letter A I could do:

A\{4,\}B

which would give **AAAAB** or **AAAAAAAB**, but not **AAAB**.

I could now give it a range of say, match between two and four occurrences only of the letter A:

A\{2,4\}B

This would result in returning **AAB**, **AAAB**, **AAAAB** but not **AB** or **AAAAAB** and so on.

Suppose we wanted to extract codes from the following list:

1234XC9088
4523XX9001
0011XA9912
9931XC3445

The codes must have the following format. The first four characters have to be numeric, followed by the next two that must be **XX**, followed by any four numbers. Here's how to do it:

[0-9]\{4\}XX[0-9]\{4\}

Let's see what this expression is saying:

1. Match only four occurrences of numbers.

2. Followed by the codes **XX**.

3. Followed by four occurrences of numbers.

Using the above would yield the following:

1234XC9088 – **no match**
4523XX9001 – **match**
0011XA9912 – **no match**
9931XC3445 – **no match**

When writing regular expressions, it can be a bit of a hit and miss affair to start off with, and a good rule is writing down the output you expect before writing the actual regular expression. This way, when you get it wrong, you can then make gradual changes on the expression eliminating the unwanted text until the exact text that you require comes back. To save you time in working out basic patterns, Table 7.2 gives some examples, in no particular order.

Table 7.2 *Useful regular expression examples*

^	beginning of line
$	end of line
^[the]	lines beginning with the

Table 7.2 *Useful regular expression examples* (cont.)

[Ss]igna[lL]	matches the words signal, signaL, Signal, SignaL
[Ss]igna[lL]\.	as above, but with a period
[mayMAY]	lines containing upper or lower case letters/word may
^USER$	the word USER as the only word on a line
[tty]$	lines ending with tty
\.	lines with a period
^d..x..x..x	directory listings with execute set for user, group and other
^[^l]	exclude directory listings of linked directories
[.*0]	anything before or after the 0
[000*]	three or more zeros
[iI]	lower or upper case I
[iL][nN]	lower or upper case I or n
[^$]	blank line
[^.*$]	will match anything in line
^......$	line containing six characters
[a-zA-Z]	any single letter
[a-z][a-z]*	at least one lower case letter
[^0-9\$]	not a number or dollar sign
[^0-0A-Za-z]	not a letter or number, a symbol
[123]	number between 1 and 3
[Dd]evice	the word Device or device
De..ce	first two characters De followed by any two, ending with ce
\^q	lines starting with ^q
^.$	lines with only one character
^\.[0-9][0-9]	lines starting with a period and two numbers
'"Device"'	the word 'device'
De[Vv]ice\.	the word DeVice or Device.
[0-9]\{2\}-[0-9]\{2\}-[0-9]\{4\}	date format dd-mm-yyyy
[0-9]\{3\}\.[0-9]\{3\}\.[0-9]\{3\}\.[0-9]\{3\}	ip address format nnn.nnn.nnn.nnn
[^.*$]	will match anything in a populated line

7.8 Conclusion

Knowing regular expressions and how to use them is an important part of shell programming, making the difference between an OK script and a good script. It saves you time in coding if you know what text to extract in one command, instead of using three or four different commands to get the same result.

Now that we have gone over the basic special characters used for regular expressions, wouldn't it be great if there were some examples of these? It's OK to see regular expressions explained, but we really want to see some working examples.

Well, we'll see plenty of examples when we cover `grep`, `sed` and `awk`.

CHAPTER 8

The `grep` family

Grep, I believe, is one of the most widely used tools in UNIX or LINUX. Grep (**g**lobal **r**egular **e**xpression **p**rint) allows you to search through a text file or text files for a pattern. If the pattern is found, `grep` will print out all the lines that contain that pattern. Grep supports the regular expressions (basic) as well as the extended set. Grep comes in three variations, which are:

Grep: This is the standard `grep`. It has been around the longest and is the one we'll focus on.

Egrep: Extended `grep`. This supports the basic and extended regular expression range except for the use of the \{ pattern range. There are a couple of other patterns egrep gets picky on, but we won't discuss them here.

Fgrep: Fast `grep`. Allows you to search for a string instead of a pattern. Don't get confused by the word 'fast', it isn't really, it's just the same speed as `grep`.

In this chapter we will cover:

- `grep` options;

- general pattern matching with `grep`;

- matching only alpha or numeric or both; and

- matching character ranges.

There should really be only one `grep` command, but unfortunately there is not a single pattern procedure that can cope with all three `grep` parameters rolled into one, and still retain the speed of the separate variations of `grep`. The GNU `grep` though has come a long way towards harnessing the three `greps`, and it does not distinguish between the basic and extended set of metacharacters.

I said in the last chapter that we would be dealing only with the basic regular expression set, but we will also look at some extended pattern matching when we look at egrep. Primarily, however, we'll be looking at grep. Patterns that work in grep also work in fgrep and egrep.

Before we start you may want to insert this text into a file, and hit the <tab> key after every column: that's our field separator. Most of our grep examples will be using this file, and we'll call this order parts file 'data.f'. Don't you just hate it when you type a file containing information you know nothing about? Well I do, so here is a quick record structure.

1st column: **City location number**
2nd column: **Month**
3rd column: **Store code and year of opening**
4th column: **Product codes**
5th column: **Unit price of product**
6th column: **Identity code**
7th column: **Qty amount**

```
$ pg data.f
48    Dec    3BC1997    LPSX  68.00 LVX2A 138
483   Sept   5AP1996    USP   65.00 LVX2C 189
47    Oct    3ZL1998    LPSX  43.00 KVM9D 512
219   dec    2CC1999    CAD   23.00 PLV2C 68
484   nov    7PL1996    CAD   49.00 PLV2C 234
483   may    5PA1998    USP   37.00 KVM9D 644
216   sept   3ZL1998    USP   86.00 KVM9E 234
```

8.1 grep

The general format is:

   grep [options] basic regular expression [file]

where basic regular expression can be a string.

8.1.1 Please quote me

When you supply a string in a grep command it is good form to enclose it with double quotes. Like this: "mystring". There are two reasons for this. It stops the shell from misintepreting them as something else. Secondly, you may want to search for a string that contains a couple of words, like this: "jet plane". If you don't surround the string with quotes it will think the word 'plane' is a file, and you'll get error messages about non-existent files.

You should also use double quotes when using variables, like this: grep "$MYVAR" filename, if you do not you will get no data returned.

Use single quotes when you want to use pattern matching.

8.1.2 `grep` options

The most useful options are:

-c   print only the count of matching lines.

-i   ignore upper/lower case, treat upper and lower case as the same (this only works for single characters).

-h   do not display the names of the files when searching through multiple files.

-l   print only the names of the files containing matches when searching through multiple files.

-n   display all matching lines with their line number.

-s   please do not display error messages on non-existent or non-text files.

-v   print all lines except those that contain a match.

8.1.3 Searching more than one file

If I wanted to search for the string `"sort"` in all my .doc files in my directory I would do this:

```
$ grep "sort" * .doc
```

Or I could search through all the files that have the word "sort it".

```
$ grep "sort it" *
```

Let's now see how some of these `grep` options work against our text file.

8.1.4 Line matches

```
$ grep -c "48" data.f
$ 4
```

Grep has returned the number 4; it's saying it has found four lines that contain the string 48.

Let's see what those lines are, using the 48 as the string:

```
$ grep "48" data.f
48      Dec     3BC1997 LPSX    68.00   LVX2A   138
483     Sept    5AP1996 USP     65.00   LVX2C   189
484     nov     7PL1996 CAD     49.00   PLV2C   234
483     may     5PA1998 USP     37.00   KVM9D   644
```

8.1.5 Line numbers

We can see what line numbers match our pattern with:

```
$ grep -n "48" data.f
1:48     Dec     3BC1997  LPSX     68.00   LVX2A   138
2:483    Sept    5AP1996  USP      65.00   LVX2C   189
5:484    Nov     7PL1996  CAD      49.00   PLV2C   234
6:483    May     5PA1998  USP      37.00   KVM9D   644
```

The numbers are output on the first column, followed by each matching line that contains 48.

8.1.6 Do not match

Let's now see all the lines that don't match the text string 48:

```
$ grep -v "48" data.f
47       Oct     3ZL1998  LPSX     43.00   KVM9D   512
219      Dec     2CC1999  CAD      23.00   PLV2C    68
216      Sept    3ZL1998  USP      86.00   KVM9E   234
```

8.1.7 Getting an exact match

You probably noticed that when we tried to extract the string "48" in earlier examples, it returned other strings that contained "48" in them like 483 and 484. We can be more specific if we want just 48 from our file; notice that there is a <tab> after each field, which we can put in our search pattern, like this:

```
$ grep "48<tab>" data.f
48       Dec     3BC1997  LPSX     68.00   LVX2A   138
```

The <tab> sign means hit the tab key.

A more efficient way of getting an exact match using grep is to append the string you want extracted with '\>'. Suppose I now only want to extract 48, here's how to do it:

```
$ grep '48\>' data.f
48       Dec     3BC1997  LPSX     68.00   LVX2A   138
```

8.1.8 Being case-sensitive

By default grep is case-sensitive. If you want to search for non-case-sensitive strings you'll have to use the -i switch. We have the month Sept both in upper and lower case in our data.f file, so to get both versions of the month we would use:

```
$ grep -i "sept" data.f
483      Sept    5AP1996  USP      65.00   LVX2C   189
216      sept    3ZL1998  USP      86.00   KVM9E   234
```

8.2 grep **and regular expressions**

Using regular expressions we can now apply some rules to our pattern matching and be more selective about the information we want extracted. When we are using regular expressions it's always a good idea to use single quotes, as this stops any special pattern you use in grep from being interpreted in strange ways by the command shell.

8.2.1 Pattern ranges

Suppose we wanted to get all the city locations that were either a 483 or 484 code. From the last chapter we know by using the [] brackets that we can specify a range of characters; here we specify that this will start with 48 and end with 3 or 4, thus extracting 483 or 484.

```
$ grep '48[34]' data.f
483     Sept    5AP1996  USP    65.00   LVX2C   189
484     nov     7PL1996  CAD    49.00   PLV2C   234
483     may     5PA1998  USP    37.00   KVM9D   644
```

8.2.2 Don't match at the beginning of a line

If we wanted to extract all records that do not have a '48' at the beginning of the line, we can use the ^ sign inside the square brackets. Using the ^ at the beginning of the pattern states that the search should begin at the beginning of each line.

```
$ grep '^[^48]' data.f
219     dec     2CC1999 CAD    23.00   PLV2C   68
216     sept    3ZL1998 USP    86.00   KVM9E   234
```

8.2.3 Trapping upper and lower cases

When we used the -i switch we disabled case sensitivity for the month Sept; here is another way of doing the same filter. Using the [] range pattern let's extract all information that has sept or Sept in the line:

```
$ grep '[Ss]ept' data.f
483     Sept    5AP1996 USP    65.00   LVX2C   189
216     sept    3ZL1998 USP    86.00   KVM9E   234
```

If we wanted to extract all months that had Sept, no matter if it was upper or lower case, and all locations that were 483, we could use a command called a pipe that takes the output from the command on the left of the bar (|) and uses it as input for the command on the right of the bar. Here's an example:

```
$ grep '[Ss]ept' data.f | grep 483
483     Sept    5AP1996  USP     65.00   LVX2C   189
```

We don't have to put the filename on the second grep command, because the input for that comes from the output of the first grep result.

8.2.4 Matching any characters

If we wanted to extract all identity codes that started with an L and ended with a D, we could use the following, because we know the codes are five characters in length:

```
$ grep 'K...D' data.f
47      Oct     3ZL1998  LPSX    43.00   KVM9D   512
483     may     5PA1998  USP     37.00   KVM9D   644
```

We could do a slight variation on the above by extracting all codes where the first two characters were upper case letters, followed by any two characters and ending with a C:

```
$ grep '[A-Z][A-Z]..C' data.f
483     Sept    5AP1996  USP     65.00   LVX2C   189
219     dec     2CC1999  CAD     23.00   PLV2C    68
484     nov     7PL1996  CAD     49.00   PLV2C   234
```

8.2.5 Date searching

A common search pattern is finding dates. Here we'll find all the records where the store codes start with a 5 and end in 1996 or 1998. We'll use this pattern '5..199[68]', which means that the first character should be a five, followed by any two digits, then 199, and the remaining two numbers can be either a 6 or 8.

```
$ grep '5..199[6,8]' data.f
483     Sept    5AP1996  USP     65.00   LVX2C   189
483     may     5PA1998  USP     37.00   KVM9D   644
```

Another method we could use to get all records that have '1998' in them is by using the expression [0-9]\ {3\} [8], which means any single number repeated three times followed by an 8, although this method is not as effective as the last example:

```
$ grep '[0-9]\ {3\}[8]' data.f
47      Oct     3ZL1998  LPSX    43.00   KVM9D   512
483     may     5PA1998  USP     37.00   KVM9D   644
216     sept    3ZL1998  USP     86.00   KVM9E   234
```

8.2.6 Combining ranges

Staying with the use of the [] brackets to extract information, suppose we want to get city codes where the first character could be any number, the second character between 0 and 5 and the third between 0 and 6. If we use this pattern we'll get the following output:

```
$ grep '[0-9][0-5][0-6]' data.f
48      Dec     3BC1997 LPSX    68.00   LVX2A   138
483     Sept    5AP1996 USP     65.00   LVX2C   189
47      Oct     3ZL1998 LPSX    43.00   KVM9D   512
219     dec     2CC1999 CAD     23.00   PLV2C    68
484     nov     7PL1996 CAD     49.00   PLV2C   234
483     may     5PA1998 USP     37.00   KVM9D   644
216     sept    3ZL1998 USP     86.00   KVM9E   234
```

Well, we certainly got a lot of information back. What we want is included but we also got other records we didn't want. However, looking at our pattern, all records that have been returned are the correct ones according to our rules. We need to specify that the pattern must start at the beginning of each line. We can use the ˆ for that.

```
$ grep '^[0-9][0-5][0-6]' data.f
216     sept    3ZL1998 USP     86.00   KVM9E   234
```

Now that's what I call a good return!

8.2.7 Occurrences in a pattern

If we want to extract any row that has a number 4 repeated at least twice, we could use this:

```
$ grep '4\{2,\}' data.f
483     may     5PA1998 USP     37.00   KVM9D   644
```

Using the comma states that the occurrence should be at least twice.

Along the same lines, if we wanted to get all records that contained at least 999 (three 9s) we could use this:

```
$ grep '9\{3,\}' data.f
219     dec     2CC1999 CAD     23.00   PLV2C    68
```

If you want to search for only so many occurrences then take the comma out. This will search for only two occurrences of the number 9.

```
$ grep '9\{2\}' data.f
```

There may be a need to match between, say, two and six occurrences of a number or maybe a letter. This will match between two and six occurrences of the number 8 that ends with 3:

```
$ grep '6\{2,6}3'  myfile
```

83	– no match
888883	– match
8884	– no match
88883	– match

8.2.8 Using grep to match either or all patterns

A nice little extension to the grep command is the -E parameter, which allows you to use extended pattern matching. For example, let's say we want to extract all city codes with either a 219 or 216 prefix. We can use this:

```
$ grep -E '219|216' data.f
219     dec     2CC1999  CAD     23.00   PLV2C   68
216     sept    3ZL1998  USP     86.00   KVM9E   234
```

8.2.9 Blank lines

If you wanted to search for blank lines in a file you can combine the ˆ and $, and perhaps use the -n to display the actual line numbers.

```
$ grep '^$' myfile
```

8.2.10 Matching special characters

If you wish to search for characters that have special meanings, like one of the following, $. ' " * [ ] ˆ ( ) | \ + ?, then you must place a \ in front of them. Suppose you want to search for all lines that contain a period (.), you would do this:

```
$ grep '\.' myfile
```

Or maybe for a double quote

```
$ grep '\"' myfile
```

In the same instance if you are searching for, say, a filename called conftroll.conf that is in a file, you should use:

```
$ grep 'conftroll\.conf' myfile
```

8.2.11 Searching for formatted filenames

Using regular expressions we can match any filename we want. On our systems we have a standard file naming format for document files. Up to the first six characters are lower case, followed by a dot, followed by two characters which are upper case. If I wanted to locate these type of filenames from a file called `filename.deposit` which contains all our document filenames I would do this:

```
$ grep '[^a-z]\{1,6/}\.[^A-Z]\{1,2/}' filename.deposit
yrend.AS        – match
mothdf          – nomatch
soa.PP          – match
qp.RR           – match
```

8.2.12 Searching for ip addresses

Part of my job is looking after our DNS servers, which means maintaining a lot of ip addresses that cover different networks. Our address ip file can contain over 200 addresses. Sometimes I want to look at just, say, the 'nnn.nnn' network addresses, and forget about the rest that have only two digits in the second part, i.e. nnn.nn.. To extract all these nnn.nnn. addresses, use [0-9]\{3\}\.[0-0\[3\}\. This expression is saying any number repeated three times followed by a period, any number repeated three times followed by a period.

```
$ grep '[0-9]\{3\}\.[0-0\[3\}\.' ipfile
```

8.3 Class names

Grep also allows the use of international character pattern matching or class name form of pattern matching.

Table 8.1 *Class names and their regular expression equivalent*

Class	Regular expression equivalent
[[:upper:]]	[A-Z]
[[:lower:]]	[a-z]
[[:digit:]]	[0-9]
[[:alnum:]]	[0-9a-zA-Z]
[[:space:]]	same as a space or a tab
[[:alpha:]]	[a-zA-Z]

Let's use a couple of examples on our file to see how these work. We want to extract all the product codes that start with a '5' and have at least two upper case letters following them. This will do it:

```
$ grep '5[[:upper:]][[:upper:]]' data.f
483      Sept    5AP1996  USP     65.00      LVX2C  189
483      may     5PA1998  USP     37.00      KVM9D  644
```

If we wanted to get all product codes that ended a 'P' or 'D' we could do this:

```
$ grep '[[:upper:]][[:upper:]] [P,D]' data.f
483      Sept    5AP1996  USP     65.00      LVX2C  189
219      dec     2CC1999  CAD     23.00      PLV2C  68
484      nov     7PL1996  CAD     49.00      PLV2C  234
483      may     5PA1998  USP     37.00      KVM9D  644
216      sept    3ZL1998  USP     86.00      KVM9E  234
```

8.3.1 Pattern matching with wildcards

Let's take a look at the use of wildcards in using grep. Suppose we have a file like this:

```
$ pg testfile
looks
likes
looker
long
```

Here is what is displayed when using the following grep pattern:

```
$ grep 'l.*s' testfile
looks
likes

$ grep 'l.*k.' testfile
looks
likes

$ grep 'ooo*' testfile
looks
```

If you want to find a word only at the end of a line, try this:

```
$ grep 'device$' *
```

That will search all files for lines that have the word 'device' at the end of each line.

8.4 `grep` **on the system**

If we want to use `grep` to get information from our system, this is easily accomplished from what we have just learnt. In these examples, we'll be using the `pipe` command, i.e. that the bar sign (|) takes the output from the left of the bar and uses it for input for the command on the right.

8.4.1 Directories

If you want to search a directory for directory listings only we can do this:

```
$ ls -l | grep '^d'
```

or search a directory and don't include any directories:

```
$ ls -l | grep '^[^d]'
```

If we want to search for directories that have executable files set by group and other:

```
$ ls -l | grep '^d.....x..x'
```

8.4.2 `passwd` **file**

```
$ grep "louise" /etc/passwd
louise:1xAL6GW9G.ZyY:501:501:Accounts Sect 1C:/home/accts/louise:
/bin/sh
```

The above searches the /etc/passwd file to see if there is an entry for louise. What if you typed the following by mistake:

```
$ grep "louise" /etc/password
```

You will get an error stating grep 'No such file or directory'.

All this is saying is that you have typed a filename that does not exist. If we use the -s switch in grep we can silence these error messages.

```
$ grep -s "louise" /etc/password
$
```

You are returned to the command prompt, with no errors about non-existent files.
If your version of grep doesn't support the -s switch you can use this instead:

```
$ grep "louise" /etc/password >/dev/null 2>&1
```

which means send the output of the command matches or errors (2 > &1) to the system's bucket. Most system administrators call /dev/null the bit bucket, it doesn't really matter; you can think of it as a bottomless pit. What goes in never comes out, and it never gets full!

The two above examples are not much good. I mean, we would like to know if the search was successful wouldn't we? Later on in the book, we'll discover how to use the exit codes of grep to take action even if a search hasn't been successful.

When using grep you may want to save the output of your search. You can redirect it to a file.

```
$ grep "louise" /etc/passwd >/tmp/passwd.out
```

This puts it into the directory /tmp with a filename called passwd.out.

8.4.3 Using the ps command

If you want to see if a certain process is running on your system, use grep with the ps x command. ps x means show a full listing of all processes running on the system. To see if my DNS server is running (usually called named) we can do this:

```
$ ps ax | grep "named"
PID  TTY  STAT TIME  CMD
211  ?    S    4.56  named
303  3    S    0.00  grep named
```

The output also includes our grep command, because grep has created a process to find the match, and ps will pick it up. To disregard the grep in the ps command use the -v option in grep.

```
$ ps ax | grep named |grep -v "grep"
211  ?    S    4.56  named
```

If the ps x command doesn't work on your system, use ps -ef instead.

8.4.4 Using grep on a string

grep is not only reserved for files; you can also use grep on strings. All you need to do is echo the string then pipe it through to grep.

```
$ STR="Mary Joe Peter Pauline"
$ echo $STR | grep "Mary"
Mary Joe Peter Pauline
```

Match has been found.

```
$ echo $STR | grep "Simon"
```

No match has been found so there is no output.

8.5 egrep

egrep stands for expression or extended grep depending on who you listen to. Egrep accepts the full range of regular expressions. One of the nice features of egrep is that you can store your strings in a file and pass them into egrep. We do this with the -f switch. If we create a file called grepstrings and then type 484 and 47 into it:

```
$ pg grepstrings
484
47
$ egrep -f grepstrings data.f
```

this would match all records with 484 or 47 in them. The -f switch really becomes useful if you want to match a lot of patterns, and typing them in on the command line becomes awkward.

If we want to search for store codes 32L or 2CC we can use the bar sign (|), which means one or the other or both (all), separated by the bar sign.

```
$ egrep '(3ZL|2CC)' data.f
47      Oct    3ZL1998  LPSX    43.00   KVM9D   512
219     dec    2CC1999  CAD     23.00   PLV2C   68
216     sept   3ZL1998  USP     86.00   KVM9E   234
```

You can use as many bars as you want. If we wanted to see if users louise, matty or pauline were logged into the system we could use the who command and pipe the output through to egrep.

```
$ who | egrep (louise|matty|pauline)
 louise pty8
 matty tty02
pauline pty2
```

You can also exclude certain strings using the caret sign (^). If I wanted to see who was on the system, but I did not want to know if users matty and pauline were on I could do this:

```
$ who | egrep -v '^(matty|pauline)'
```

If you want to search a directory listing for files that were called shutdown, shutdowns, reboot or reboots, this is easily accomplished with egrep.

```
$ egrep '(shutdown | reboot) (s)?'  *
```

8.6 Conclusion

I hope I have demonstrated the flexibility of grep, which is a very powerful and popular tool. Like many of the UNIX tools, it has been ported to DOS. If you want to search for a string or pattern quickly through files then grep's your buddy, it's as simple as that. Grep is an important tool in shell programming, as we'll discover later on in the book, when used with other UNIX tools and in variable substitutions.

CHAPTER 9

Introducing awk

If you want to format reports or extract chunks of data from large text files then awk will do the job. It is perfect for text scanning and manipulating data.

From my experience of all the shell filtering tools awk is the most difficult to master in its entirety. I do not know why, maybe it's to do with its syntax, or its not very meaningful error messages. You'll get to know the 'Bailing out' and 'awk: cmd.line:' error messages quite well as you progress through the awk language. That's right, awk *language*: awk is a programming language all on its own. You may be wondering why I have included awk in a shell book. Good question, so here's the good answer. Awk by itself may be a demon to learn, but using awk in conjunction with other tools such as grep and sed makes your job as a shell programmer a lot easier.

This chapter will not cover all of awk's many features, nor will it teach you how to write advanced awk scripts, that would take practically a book by itself. This chapter aims to show you the power of awk one-liners, and how to extract information from text files and strings.

In this chapter we will cover:

- extracting fields;

- matching with regular expressions;

- comparing fields;

- passing values to awk; and

- basic awk one-liners and scripts.

Nearly all my scripts have awk commands in them, usually combined with sed or grep, to get information out of a text file or a string. To get the information you want, the text must have a structured format, and by this I mean the fields must be separated by a field delimiter. This can be anything, and can be specified when you invoke awk, as we'll see later.

Awk is named after the people who developed the language, Aho, Weninberger and Kernigham. There are also nawk and gawk, which have extended text processing features, but we will not cover them in this chapter.

At its most basic function, awk's task is to scan and extract information from a text file or string, based on the criteria given to it. When awk has got this information, you can then do other text manipulating functions. Full blown awk scripts are generally used to format reports from text files.

9.1 **Calling** awk

There are three ways awk can be invoked. You can either specify awk on the command line like this:

> **awk [-F field-separator] 'commands' input-file**(s)

where 'commands' are the actual awk commands. This method is the one that we will use most in this chapter.

In the above example the use of the -F field separator is optional, as awk uses the <space> as a default field separator. So if you are scanning text which has spaces between fields you don't have to specify this option; however if you're scanning the passwd file, for example, then those fields are separated by a colon, so you'll have to state this with the -F option, like this:

> **awk -F: 'commands' input-file**

The second method is to insert all the awk commands in a file then make the awk program executable and have the awk command interpreter as the first line of the script, so it can be called by just typing the script name.

In the above two examples of calling awk, please note the use of single quotes that enclose the awk commands.

The third method is to insert all the awk commands in a separate file and then call it:

> **awk -f awk-script-file input-files(s)**

The -f option states that the awk script is held in the file awk-script-file. The input-file(s) are the files you want awk to scan.

9.2 awk **script**

When specifying awk on the command line, an awk script consists of various actions and patterns.

When awk reads in the records or lines one at a time if looks to see if the -F or the FS option (more on FS later) has been set. If it has it will use this to separate the fields, but if the -F option has not been set then awk will assume that a <space> is the field separator, and it will continue to do this until it hits a new line. When a new line has been reached it then knows it has read in a whole record, and will then start on the next line reading in the next record. This reading process for each record continues until the end-of-file has been reached, or no more text exists.

Using Table 9.1 as a guide, awk reads in the file one line at a time, finds a field separator (in this case a hash symbol '#') and assigns it as field-n, until it reaches a new line (which is the default record separator). Then it classes this line as a record. Awk then starts all over again reading in the next line.

Table 9.1 *How* awk *reads records from a file*

< Field-1 >	< sep >	< Field-2 >	< sep >	< Field-3 >	< sep >	< Field-4 and new line >
P.Bunny (Record 1)	#	02/99	#	48	#	Yellow \n
J.Troll (Record 2)	#	07/99	#	4842	#	Brown-3 \n

9.2.1 Patterns and actions

Any awk statement can consist of a pattern or action, and there can be many statements in an awk script. The pattern part decides when an action statement should be triggered or what should trigger it. The action is what we want to do with the data. If you omit the pattern part, the action will always be carried out.

Patterns can be any conditional, compound statement or regular expression. The pattern also contains two special parts that are called BEGIN and END. You can use the BEGIN statement to set counters and print headings. The BEGIN statement is used before any text scanning is actually carried out on the input file. The END statement is used to print totals and end-of-report statements after awk has finished scanning all the text. If you do not specify a pattern, awk will always match or print the line(s).

An action is specified by enclosing the statements within curly brackets {}. Actions are mostly used for printing, but for longer scripts will generally include if and iteration (looping) statements as well as iteration exit constructs. If you do not specify what action to take, awk will print out the whole record it is currently scanning.

We'll meet some of these patterns and actions in examples further on.

9.2.2 Fields and records

When awk is executed the fields that it scans are referenced by $1, $2 ... $n. This method is called field identity. Using these field identities it is easy to work on each field for further processing.

To reference the first and third fields only we would use $1, $3 – note the use of the comma separating the fields. If we wish to print all the fields in a record that had five fields we do not have to specify $1, $2, $3, $4, $5; instead we can use $0, which means all fields. When awk scans and it reaches a new line it assumes that it has reached the end of the record for these fields, and will then carry on starting at the next line reading in the new record and assigning the fields. Before we carry on, do not confuse this $ sign with the shell's $ sign: they are different!

To print individual fields or all fields we use the 'print' command, which is an action (action statements are enclosed with curly brackets).

Extracting fields

Let's look at a couple of examples before we carry on. We'll use this text file called grade.txt which contains some entries from a local karate database.

```
$ pg grade.txt
M.Tansley    05/99    48311   Green     8    40   44
J.Lulu       06/99    48317   green     9    24   26
P.Bunny      02/99    48      Yellow    12   35   28
J.Troll      07/99    4842    Brown-3   12   26   26
L.Tansley    05/99    4712    Brown-2   12   30   28
```

We have seven fields in this text file, containing (1) name, (2) date of grade, (3) student serial number, (4) belt awarded, (5) age of person, (6) points gained so far in competition, and (7) maximum points available from competitions.

Because each field is separated by spaces we do not have to use the -F option to specify a different field separator or delimiter. Let's now scan the file and get some data out.

For clarity of display in the examples I have expanded the spaces so the individual fields can be viewed more easily.

A quick brief about saving awk output

There are a couple of ways you can save the output from your awk scripts from the shell prompt. The easiest way is to use the redirection sign '> filename'. The following example will redirect all output to a file called wow.

```
$ awk '{print $0}' grade.txt >wow
```

If you use this method please be aware that no output will appear on the screen as it will go straight to the file. Only use this method when you're happy that you're getting the right results. Also it will overwrite what was in the file previously.

The second way is to use the tee command, which will show the output on the screen as well as going to a file. Some people prefer this when testing their output. For example to redirect output to the screen and to a file called 'delete_me_and_die', I would use this command, at the end of my awk command '| tee delete_me_and_die'. For example:

```
$ awk '{print $0}' grade.txt | tee delete_me_and_die
```

Using standard input

Before we get too far into this chapter a quick note on using input for the awk scripts; actually this applies to any script that takes its input from standard input. To run the scripts in this chapter we will use this format awk_script input_file. For example:

```
$ belts.awk grade_student.txt
```

But we can use any of the following instead.
Using a bit of redirection:

```
$ belts.awk < grade2.txt
```

Or a pipe:

```
$ grade2.txt|belts.awk
```

Printing all records

```
$ awk '{print $0}' grade.txt
```

Awk reads in each record, and as we have no pattern and only an action part that says {print $0} (print out all the records). As this is an action we enclosed the statement with curly brackets. The above command prints the whole file.

```
M.Tansley   05/99   48311   Green     8    40   44
J.Lulu      06/99   48317   green     9    24   26
P.Bunny     02/99   48      Yellow    12   35   28
J.Troll     07/99   4842    Brown-3   12   26   26
L.Tansley   05/99   4712    Brown-2   12   30   28
```

Printing individual records

Now suppose we wanted to just print out the names of the pupils and the belts they have been awarded. By looking at the columns of the fields we know we need 'field-1' and 'field-4', so by using $1 and $4 and not forgetting to separate them with a comma we have:

```
$ awk  '{print $1,$4}' grade.txt
M.Tansley    Green
J.Lulu       green
P.Bunny      Yellow
J.Troll      Brown-3
L.Tansley    Brown-2
```

Printing report headers

The output from the last command could do with some spacing between the names and belts column to make it more presentable. We can fix this by putting tabs between the output of the fields. To put a tab in we use \t – shorthand notation for a tab; we'll cover shorthand notation in more detail later on. We could also put an informative header for the output of the text, titled 'Name and Belt' which will also contain an underline. To underline text we can use \n which forces a new line and starts printing the text that follows the \n on the next line. We put the text header in the BEGIN pattern part. Because we are printing the header, it will be classed as an action, so we'll enclose it with curly brackets. This heading will be printed before awk looks at the first record.

```
$ awk  'BEGIN {print "Name     Belt\n--------------------------------"}
{print $1"\t"$4}' grade.txt

Name           Belt
--------------------------------------
M.Tansley      Green
J.Lulu         green
P.Bunny        Yellow
J.Troll        Brown-3
L.Tansley      Brown-3
```

Printing report trailers

If we want an 'end of report' line we can use the END statement, but remember this END action will be executed after all text processing on the file is done. The END statement fits in just after the main action part. We can stick in a simple header line as well for completeness:

```
$ awk 'BEGIN {print "Name\n-------"} {print $1} END {"end-of-report"}'
grade.txt
```

```
Name
-------
M.Tansley
J.Lulu
P.Bunny
J.Troll
L.Tansley
end-of-report
```

Bailing out with awk error messages

It is almost guaranteed using awk that you will come across errors in your commands. Awk will try to print out the offending line, but as most awk commands are one-liners, that isn't much help.

The messages are not always (actually I'd say never) very descriptive. Using the above example, I have missed out a double quote; here's what awk sends back to me:

```
$ awk 'BEGIN {print "Name\n-------} {print $1} END {"end-of-report"}''
grade.txt

awk: cmd. line:1: BEGIN {print "Name\n-------} {print $1} END
{"end-of -report"}
awk: cmd. line:1: ^ unterminated string
```

When I first got into awk, I was really frustrated with the lack of descriptions on the error messages, but through experience, and a long learning curve, I now go by the following rules. Here's what to look for when you get awk errors:

- Make sure the entire awk command(s) are enclosed in single quotes.

- Make sure all quotes inside the commands are paired off.

- Make sure you have enclosed curly brackets with action statements and round brackets with conditional statements.

- You may have forgotten to include curly brackets completely; you may think you do not need then, but awk thinks it does and will complain.

If you supply a file that is not present, you will get this type of message:

```
$ awk 'END {print NR}' grades.txt

awk: cmd. line:2: fatal: cannot open file 'grades.txt' for
reading (No such file or directory)
```

Supplying awk input from the keyboard

Let's see what happens if we do not supply the input-file 'grade.txt' on the command line.

```
$ awk 'BEGIN {print "Name  Belt\n-------------------------------"}
        {print $1"\t"$4}'
```

```
Name                Belt
-------------------------------
>
```

The BEGIN part has printed the header, but awk just sits there and waits; we have not been returned to the shell prompt. This is because awk is expecting input from the keyboard. As no input-file was given, it assumes you are going to supply the data. If you wish, you could manually type in some related text and hit <CTRL-D> when you have finished typing. If you have typed in the correct field separator awk will then process normally as in the first example. This process though should not be practised too often, as it is open to far too many typos.

9.2.3 Regular expressions and operators in awk

When we covered the grep chapter, we saw quite a lot of examples using regular expressions. We won't use the same examples here, but we'll see how you can use regular expressions in awk with condition operators.

You specify a regular expression by enclosing it with forward slashes: '/regular_expression/'. For example, if I wanted to search for the string 'Green' in our text file we would use /Green/, which would search for all occurrences of the word 'Green'.

9.2.4 Metacharacters

Here are the characters we use for regular expression matching in awk. For a detailed explanation of these look back at Chapter 7 *Introducing regular expressions*.

\ ^ $. [] | () * + ?

There are two characters we didn't cover in Chapter 7 because these work in awk but not in grep or sed; they are:

+ Use the + to match one or more characters.
   For example, to match one or more of the letter t /t+/ or to match any lower case string use /[a-z]+/
? This will match up to one occurrence of the pattern.
   For example, to match XYZ or YZ use /XY?Z/

9.2.5 Conditional operators

Table 9.2 shows awk's conditional operators. We'll see some examples of these operators next.

Table 9.2 Awk's *conditional operators*

Operator	Description
<	Less than
< =	Less than or equal to
= =	Equal to
! =	Not equal to
> =	Greater than or equal to
˜	Matched by regular expression
!˜	Not matched by regular expression

Matching

To be able to match a pattern against a field number we can use the tilde sign (˜) which tells awk that a regular expression match will follow. We can also use an 'if' clause. When we use the word 'if' in awk we enclose the condition part in brackets ().

Looking at our file grade.txt, if you wanted to see only brown belts, and we know that the belt grades are 'field-4', we can now write an expression which means if 'field-4' contains 'Brown' then print it. This is the expression, '{if ($4 ˜ /Brown/) print }'. If the condition is met, we want to print the matching records, and because this is an action, we need to enclose the whole statement with curly brackets.

```
$ awk  {if($4~/Brown/) print $0}' grade.txt
J.Troll     07/99   4842    Brown-3  12    26       26
L.Tansley   05/99   4712    Brown-2  12    30       28
```

When a match is found awk will by default print the whole record unless you tell it otherwise. Using the if statement can be a bit difficult at first, but don't worry as there are many ways to skin a cat. This statement will work as well. The following example means if any of the records contain the pattern 'Brown', print it.

```
$ awk  '$0 ~ /Brown/' grade.txt
J.Troll     07/99   4842    Brown-3  12    26       26
L.Tansley   05/99   4712    Brown-2  12    30       28
```

Exact match

Suppose we wanted to to do an exact match on a string if, say, you were searching for a student serial number of '48'. By looking at the file, there are other serial numbers that also have 48 within them. If we were to search on the serial number 48 awk would return all other serial numbers that had 48 in their numbers, from 'field-3':

```
$ awk  '{if($3~/48/) print $0}' grade.txt
M.Tansley   05/99     48311  Green    8     40    44
J.Lulu      06/99     48317  green    9     24    26
P.Bunny     02/99     48     Yellow   12    35    28
J.Troll     07/99     4842   Brown-3  12    26    26
```

To be able to do an exact match use the equals sign '= =' by putting the string in quotes, like this, '$3=="48"', which ensures only '48' will be matched and nothing else.

```
$ awk '$3=="48" {print $0}' grade.txt
P.Bunny     02/99     48         Yellow   12    35    28
```

Not matched

Sometimes you want to be able to scan information and extract items that do NOT match. Well the opposite to the compare sign is the !~, which means not matched. When we used the matched example earlier we searched for brown belts, so let's now see all the non-brown belts. This is the expression '$0 !~ /Brown/', which means if any record does not contain the pattern 'Brown', print it.

Remember, by default awk will print all matching records so we do not need an action part in this case.

```
$ awk  '$0 !~ /Brown/' grade.txt
M.Tansley   05/99     48311  Green    8     40    44
J.Lulu      06/99     48317  green    9     24    26
P.Bunny     02/99     48     Yellow   12    35    28
```

We could have targeted just the belt grade field 'field-4' and done the test this way:

```
$ awk '{if($4!~/Brown/) print $0}' grade.txt
M.Tansley   05/99     48311  Green    8     40    44
J.Lulu      06/99     48317  green    9     24    26
P.Bunny     02/99     48     Yellow   12    35    28
```

If we had used the command, awk '$4 != "Brown" {print $0}' grade.txt, it would have returned wrong results, because we have enclosed brown in quotes, and so it will search for 'Brown' only and not 'Brown-2' or 'Brown-3' grades. Of course if we wanted to search for belts that are NOT Brown-2, we could have done this:

```
$ awk '$4 != "Brown-2" {print $0}' grade.txt
```

Less than

Let's see which students have obtained their target points (total points possible). For this test all we have to do is test if points gained 'field-6' is less than total possible points 'field-7'. We'll also put a little motivation message on the report as well.

```
$ awk '{if ($6 < $7) print $0 "$1 Try better at the next comp"}'
grade.txt
M.Tansley Try better at the next comp
J.Lulu Try better at the next comp
```

Less than or equal to

To include the 'or equal to' only requires a small amendment to our operator, and the records that satisfy this condition will also include those from the above example.

```
$ awk '{if ($6 <= $7) print $1}' grade.txt
M.Tansley
J.Lulu
J.Troll
```

Greater than

No surprises here on the greater than sign. Here it is:

```
$ awk '{if ($6 > $7) print $1}' grade.txt
L.Tansley
P.Bunny
```

I hope that you've got the idea now on the basic use of operators.

Trapping upper and lower case

If we want to be able to search for information, be it upper or lower case, we can use the [] sign. Remember when we covered regular expressions, we found that we can specify any characters/words in the brackets to be matched. So if we want to extract all green belts whether the first letter is either in upper or lower case from our file this expression would do it. '/[Gg]reen/':

```
$ awk '/[Gg]reen/' grade.txt
M.Tansley   05/99      48311   Green    8    40    44
J.Lulu      06/99      48317   green    9    24    26
```

Any characters

If we want to extract all names where the fourth character is an 'a' from the first field we use the period '.' notation. The expression '/^...a/' means the first three characters from the beginning of the line (or field in this case) can be any character followed by an 'a'. The caret sign '^' means to start from the beginning of the line.

```
$ awk '$1 ~/^ ... a/' grade.txt
M.Tansley   05/99      48311   Green    8    40    44
L.Tansley   05/99      4712    Brown-2  12   30    28
```

Match either

If we wish to extract belts that are either yellow or brown, we can use the bar sign (|) which means return patterns that are on either side of the '|'. Be aware when using the bar sign that the statement must be enclosed with round brackets.

```
$ awk '$0~/(Yellow|Brown)/' grade.txt
P.Bunny      02/99    48      Yellow   12   35   28
J.Troll      07/99    4842    Brown-3  12   26   26
L.Tansley    05/99    4712    Brown-2  12   30   28
```

In the example above all belts that are either Yellow OR Brown are output.
    We can also use this method to get the same results as we did using the [] expression to find a Green or green belt.

```
$ awk '$0~/(Green|green)/' grade.txt
M.Tansley    05/99    48311   Green     8   40   44
J.Lulu       06/99    48317   green     9   24   26
```

Beginning of line

You do not always have to specify the field number you require. If you want to find all codes that have '48' at the beginning of a line from a text file you can simply use the caret ^ sign, like this:

```
$ awk '/^48/' input-file
```

    Using the expressions that we covered in Chapter 7 I have shown how some of these can be used in awk. As I mentioned at the beginning of Chapter 7 all those expressions (apart from occurrences) are quite legal in awk.
    Compound patterns or compound operators are used to form complex logic operators; the level of complexity is really up to you. All you really need to know about compounds is that this is an expression that combines other patterns, and the expression is carried out by using the following logical operators.

&& AND: both sides of the statement must be true for the match

|| OR: either or both sides of the statement must be true for the match

!   NOT: both sides of the equation will be inverted

AND

If you wanted to print a record if only 'P.Bunny' was present and only if the belt was 'Yellow' we could do this. '($1=="P.Bunny" && $4=="Yellow")' means a match has been found if the statement on the left-hand side of the && is true and the statement on the right-hand side of the && is true. Here's the full command:

```
$ awk '{if ($1=="P.Bunny" && $4=="Yellow")print $0}' grade.txt
P.Bunny      02/99     48     Yellow   12   35   28
```

OR

If we wanted to see all 'Yellow' or 'Brown' belts you could use the OR command, which says either or both of the statements on either side of the || sign can be true.

```
$ awk '{if ($4=="Yellow" || $4~/Brown/) print $0}' grade.txt
P.Bunny     02/99    48       Yellow  12    35    28
J.Troll     07/99    4842     Brown-3 12    26    26
L.Tansley   05/99    4712     Brown-2 12    30    28
```

9.2.6 awk built-in variables

Awk has a number of built-in variables that allow you to get more information about your environment. You can also change some of the variable values. Table 9.3 shows the most useful ones, and a brief explanation of each variable follows.

Table 9.3 *Awk's built-in variables*

ARGC	The number of command-line arguments
ARGV	The array of command-line arguments
ENVIRON	Holds the current system environment variables in the array
FILENAME	The name of the current file awk is scanning
FNR	The record number in the current file
FS	Sets the input field separator; same as the command-line -F option
NF	Number of fields in the current record
NR	The number of records read so far
OFS	Output field separator
ORS	Output record separator
RS	Controls the record separator

The **ARGC** holds the number of command-line arguments that are passed to the awk script. **ARGV** are the elements of the array **ARGC**. They are accessed by referencing **ARGV[n]**, where n is the command-line argument you wish to access.

ENVIRON holds all the environment variables that are set. To access the individual variables you use the actual variable name, for example ENVIRON["EDITOR"]= ="vi".

FILENAME holds the current input-file the script is actually working on. Because awk can process many files this variable, if accessed, will tell which file is being scanned at that time.

FNR holds the current record awk is working on; its value when accessed is less than or equal to **NR**. If you are accessing many files in a script this variable will be reset for each new input-file.

FS is used to set the field separator within awk, which is the same as setting it with the -F option on the command line. By default it is a space; if you wish to access files that are comma-delimited then you assign the comma like this: FS=",".

NF holds the number of fields for each record and is set after each record has been read.

OFS allows you to specify the output field separator, which by default is a space. If you want to set it as a # then do this: OFS="#".

ORS is the output record separator, which by default is a new line (\n).

RS is the record separator, which by default is a newline (\n).

9.2.7 NF, NR and FILENAME

Let's look at a couple of examples using the built-in variables.

A quick way to tell how many records you have is to use NR. When I've exported a database file, I want to be able to tell quickly how many records it has, so I can compare the exported to the original for possible errors during the export process. This does the job; it prints only the number of records in the input-file; 'print NR' is part of the END statement.

```
$ awk 'END {print NR}' grade.txt
```

In the following example all the student records are printed with the record numbers. We can use NF awk variable to display how many fields there are in each record read. The END part prints the current input filename.

```
$ awk '{print NF,NR,$0}END{print FILENAME}' grade.txt
7  1 M.Tansley  05/99  48311  Green    8    40    44
7  2 J.Lulu     06/99  48317  green    9    24    26
7  3 P.Bunny    02/99  48     Yellow  12    35    28
7  4 J.Troll    07/99  4842   Brown-3 12    26    26
7  5 L.Tansley  05/99  4712   Brown-2 12    30    28
grade.txt
```

When you want to extract information from a file, it's always good practice to check first that there are actually records in the file. In the following example I do not want to search for any Brown belts unless there is at least one record in the file. This is accomplished using the AND compound statement. The example means if there are more than zero records present and the string 'Brown' is present (which we know it is), print it.

```
$ awk '{if (NR >0 && $4~/Brown/)print $0}' grade.txt
J.Troll     07/99  4842   Brown-3 12   26     26
L.Tansley   05/99  4712   Brown-2 12   30     28
```

A good use of using the NF function is that you can pull off the directory you are in by echoing the $PWD variable to awk; all we need to do is specify that the field separator is '/'.

```
$ pwd
/usr/local/etc
$ echo $PWD | awk -F/ '{print $NF}'
etc
```

Here's another use, pulling off the filename only.

```
$ echo "/usr/local/etc/rc.sybase" | awk -F/ '{print $NF}'
rc.sybase
```

9.2.8 awk operators

When using the operators in awk the primary expressions can be classed as numeric, string, variables, fields and array elements. We've met some of these already, but for completeness here is the list of operators.

You can use any of the following operators to make expressions.

= += *= /= %= ^=	Assignment operators
?	Conditional expression operator
|| && !	OR, AND, NOT (we covered these in the last section)
~ !~	Matching operators, match and non-match
< <= == != => >	Relational operators
+ - * / % ^	Arithmetic operators
+ + --	Prefix and postfix

Some of the examples we have covered have included a few of the awk operators, so we'll just have a look at some we haven't covered yet.

Assigning input fields to field variable names

When using awk it's occasionally a good idea to assign meaningful names to the fields, which can make the commands easier to understand if you're doing pattern matching or other relational operations. The general construct on variable name assigning is 'name=$n, where name is the variable you want to call this field and $n is the actual field number. If you want to assign the variable 'name' to the students' names and 'belts' to the students' grades, this will do it: 'name=$1; belts=$4', notice the use of the semi-colon, which separates the awk commands. In this example we have reassigned the student names field to name and the grade field to belts. We then test for any Yellow belts in the belts field and then finally print out the name and belt.

```
$ awk '{name=$1;belts=$4; if(belts ~/Yellow/)print name" is belt
"belts}' grade.txt
P.Bunny is belt Yellow
```

Comparing fields with values

There are two ways to test if a numeric field is less than another numerical field.

1   Have the number assigned within the BEGIN part to a variable name.

2   Use the actual number when you do the relational test.

Generally it's a good idea to set any values in the BEGIN part, which saves messing around with the actual awk expression commands, when you have to amend them.

When using relational type operators always enclose the statements with round brackets.

Let's see all students who have obtained fewer than 27 points in their competitions.

The use of quotes around the number you want to test against is optional. "27", 27 will both yield the same results.

```
$ awk '{if($6 < 27)print$0}' grade.txt
J.Lulu      06/99   48317   green    9    24      26
J.Troll     07/99   4842    Brown-3 12   26      26
```

For the second example we first assign the number to a name, let's call it BASELINE. As we are giving it a value we can set it in the BEGIN part.

```
$ awk 'BEGIN {BASELINE="27  "}{if($6 < BASELINE)print$0}'  grade.txt
J.Lulu      06/99   48317   green    9    24      26
J.Troll     07/99   4842    Brown-3 12   26      26
```

Changing numeric field values

When you make changes to any of the fields using awk, it's important to remember that the actual input file is NOT changed, only awk's copy which is kept in the buffer. Awk will recognize the change and it is reflected in the NR or NF variable values.

To change numeric fields we simply reassign the field identity with a new value, like this: '$1=$1+5'. This would add '5' to the value of field-1. Make sure that the field you are adding or subtracting is a numeric.

To change M.Tansley's 'points scored so far' field from its current value of '40' to '39', I would use this assignment: '$6=$6-1' – of course I would have to make sure first that I had matched the name first with a = =, before I carried out this alteration.

```
$ awk '{if($1=="M.Tansley") $6=$6-1; print $1, $6, $7}' grade.txt
M.Tansley   39  44
J.Lulu      24  26
P.Bunny     35  28
J.Troll     26  26
L.Tansley   30  28
```

Changing text fields

Changing text fields is again a reassignment of the field. All that needs to be done is to give the field a new string value. To add J.Troll's middle initial, so that the name becomes J.L.Troll, I use the expression '$1="J.L.Troll"', remembering to enclose the string in double quotes ("") and closing each statement up with round brackets.

```
$ awk '{if($1=="J.Troll") ($1="J.L.Troll"); print $1}' grade.txt
M.Tansley
J.Lulu
P.Bunny
J.L.Troll
L.Tansley
```

Displaying only the changed record

The field changes we have been making are on a small file, so printing out all the records to see the changes is not much of a problem. But if you have a large file – say over 100 records – you don't want to see all the records for just one change. To just print out the changed record we use the curly brackets after the pattern, so that we get 'pattern then action based on the result of the pattern'. It may seem confusing, so here's the last example with just the changed record printed out. Notice the position of the curly brackets.

```
$ awk '{if($1=="J.Troll") {$1="J.L.Troll";print $1}}' grade.txt
J.L.Troll
```

Creating a new output field

When processing data in awk, it's a good idea to occasionally create a new field when doing calculations based on other fields. A new field in awk is created by assigning the new field identity from an assignment of other fields. To create a new field that is based on the addition of other fields you can type '{$4=$2 + $3}'. Assuming the records hold three fields, we have created a new field, field-4, that holds the addition result of 'field-2' and 'field-3'.

We will now create a new field 'field-8' that holds the difference between 'points scored so far' and 'max points available' from our grade.txt file. The expression should be '{$8=$7-$6}'. We first test that the 'points so far' field is less than 'max points available' for each student, so the new field will print only those names where there is actually a difference in value. We will also put in a tab in the BEGIN part to align the report headings.

```
$ awk 'BEGIN{ print "Name\t Difference"}{if($6 <$7) {$8=$7--$6; print
$1,$8}}' grade.txt
Name        Difference
M.Tansley   4
J.Lulu      2
```

We could of course make the new fields more meaningful and assign a variable name to them, like this:

```
$ awk 'BEGIN{ print "Name\t Difference"}{if($6 <$7) {diff=$7-$6; print
$1,diff}}' grade.txt
M.Tansley    4
J.Lulu       2
```

Adding columns

To add column numbers or running totals, we use the $+=$ sign. The variable to hold the result of the adding goes on the left-hand side of the sign. The field you are adding ($1... etc.) to the variable goes on the right of the sign. So to add $1 to a variable called 'total' we would use 'total+=$1'. Column adding is quite popular: how many times have you had files where you want to add the totals together but couldn't be bothered to get the calculator out? In awk it's simple, as we'll see with the next example.

To add all the students' 'points gained' together all we do is use this expression 'tot+=$6', where tot will hold the results of the addition as awk reads through the file. We'll put a little end of report trailer statement in the END part which will also print the total when all records have been read. We do not have to tell awk to print all the records, as it will do this by default, when each pattern is matched.

```
$ awk '(tot+=$6); END{print "Club student total points :" tot}'
grade.txt
M.Tansley    05/99    48311  Green    8    40    44
J.Lulu       06/99    48317  green    9    24    26
P.Bunny      02/99    48     Yellow   12   35    28
J.Troll      07/99    4842   Brown-3  12   26    26
L.Tansley    05/99    4712   Brown-2  12   30    28
Club student total points :155
```

If a file is large then you might just want to print the result part, and not see all the records. To do this just enclose the () with the curly brackets on the outside of the statement like this:

```
$ awk '{(tot+=$6)}; END{print "Club student total points :" tot}'
grade.txt
Club student total points :155
```

Adding file sizes

When looking at files in directories I want to be able to see the total sizes of all my file types quickly, but I want to exclude sub-directories. I can do this by piping ls -l through to awk, then using awk to exclude the first character if it is a 'd' (by using a regular expression). I can then add the file size column, and then print each file with its size and the total of file sizes at the end.

In this example here's what my ls -1 brings up. Notice the first character is a 'd' on the second file, which tells me it's a directory, the column on this listing for the file size is column 9 and the filenames are column 5. You may have to change this number if your system brings the sizes/filenames up in a different column,

-rw-r--r--	1 root	root	80	Apr	11	18:56	acc.txt
drwx------	2 root	root	1024	Mar	26	20:53	nsmail

Columns   1   2 3   4   5   6   7   8   9

The regular expression below says it must start at the beginning of the line ^, and to exclude any character that is a 'd'. So we end with ^[^d].

Using this pattern we can print the filenames and their sizes, then add up each of these sizes putting the result into 'tot' variable.

```
$ ls -1 | awk ' /^[^d]/ {print $9"\t"$5} {tot+=$5} END
{print "total KB:"tot}'
dev_pkg.fail    345
failedlogin     12416
messages        4260
sulog           12810
utmp            1856
wtmp            7104
total KB:41351
```

9.2.9 Built-in string functions

Awk has some powerful string functions. Table 9.4 lists of some of them.

The gsub function is a bit like sed's search and replace. It allows you to substitute globally a string or characters (r) for another string or characters (s). This

Table 9.4 Awk's *built-in string functions*

gsub(r,s)	Substitute s for r globally in $0
gsub(r,s,t)	Substitute s for r globally in t
index(s,t)	Return the first position of string t in s
length(s)	Return length of s
match(s,r)	Test if s contains a substring match by r
split(s,a,fs)	Split s into array a on fs
sprint(fmt,exp)	Return the exp formatted according to fmt
sub(r,s)	Substitute s for the leftmost longest substring of $0
substr(s,p)	Return suffix of s starting at p
substr(s,p,n)	Return substring of s of length n starting at p

is carried out in the form of a regular expression. The first function is carried out on the current record $0. The second gsub function allows you to specify the target; however, if you do not specify the target, the replacement is done on $0.

The index (s,t) function will return the first position of the search string (t) that is in the target string (s). The length function will return the total number of characters within the string (s). The match function tests if the string (s) contains a match defined by the regular expression (r). The split function will split the string (s) into the specified array (a), using the field separator fs. The sprint function is like the printf function (we'll meet this later on). It will return the result string (exp) based on formatted output (fmt). The sub (r,s) function willl substitute (s) for the leftmost longest substring of $0, matched by (r). The substr (s,p) returns the suffix of string (s) starting at position (p) in the string. Substr (s,p,n) is the same as above, but you can specify the length (n) of the substring.

Let's see how some of these string functions work in awk.

gsub

To substitute globally a string for another in the current record, we have to use the regular expression format, '/target pattern/,replace pattern/'. If we wanted to change the student number of 4842 to 4899 we could do this:

```
$ awk 'gsub(/4842/,4899) {print $0}' grade.txt
J.Troll      07/99      4899    Brown-3  12    26   26
```

index

To search the target string (s) for the first occurrence of (t), we enclose the string in quotes. To find where the string 'ny' first occurs in the target string 'Bunny', returning how many characters along, we can do this:

```
$ awk 'BEGIN {print index("Bunny","ny")}' grade.txt
4
```

length

To return the length of a string all we need to to do is supply the string. The following example checks we have a 'J.Troll' then prints the name and the length of the string, returning how many characters make up the person's name.

```
$ awk '$1=="J.Troll" {print length($1)" "$1}' grade.txt
7 J.Troll
```

Here's another way of finding out the length of a string, when the string is quoted.

```
$ awk 'BEGIN {print length("A FEW GOOD MEN")}'
14
```

`match`

Match allows you to test if the target string contains part of the search string. You can use regular expressions if you wish for the search part. It will return a number where it has found the occurrence if successful. If no occurrence has been found, it will return a zero. The first example tests whether 'd' is in the string ANCD; it isn't, so a zero is returned. The second example tests whether 'D' is in the string ANCD; it is, and it returns how many characters along to the first occurrence. The third example tests for the occurrence of 'u' in the student 'J.Lulu'.

```
$ awk 'BEGIN {print match("ANCD",/d/)}'
0
$ awk 'BEGIN {print match("ANCD",/C/)}'
3
$ awk '$1=="J.Lulu" {print match($1,"u")}' grade.txt
4
```

`split`

You can use `split` to return the number of elements in an array from a string. Here's how it works. If you had a string containing, say, part numbers separated by a dash '-', like this, AD2-KP9-JU2-LP-1, and you wanted to put them into an array, using `split` you would specify the separator, and what the array is to be called. For our part number example the command would be split ("AD2-KP9-JU2-LP-1", `parts_array,"-"`), and `split` would then return the number of indexes, in this case it would be 4.

Here's another example using a different separator.

```
$ awk 'BEGIN {print split("123#456#678", myarray, "#")}'
3
```

In the previous example, split returns the number of indexes for the array called myarray. The array myarray would then look like this internally:

Myarray[1]="123"
Myarray[2]="456"
Myarray[3]="678"

We'll take a look at arrays at the end of the chapter.

`sub`

Use `sub` to find and replace the first occurrence of the pattern. If I had a string called STR containing 'poped pope pill' and I ran the following `sub` command on it: 'sub(/op/,"OP",STR)', it would hit the first occurrence only of the pattern 'op', change it and return the following, 'pOPed pope pill'.

In our text file the student J.Troll's record has two values the same, 'points gained' and 'max points available' which are both set at 24. To change only the first occurrence of 24 to 29 and leave the second untouched, you can do this command 'sub (/26/, "29",$0)', which will only hit the first occurrence of 24. First make sure that we have J.Troll's record.

```
$ awk '$1=="J.Troll" sub(/26/,"29",$0)' grade.txt
M.Tansley   05/99    48311   Green     8     40    44
J.Lulu      06/99    48317   green     9     24    29
P.Bunny     02/99    48      Yellow    12    35    28
J.Troll     07/99    4842    Brown-3   12    29    26
L.Tansley   05/99    4712    Brown-2   12    30    28
```

substr

Substr is a useful function. It returns the part of the string that you tell it to, using the starting position and how much you want returned. Here are a couple of examples.

```
$ awk '$1=="L.Tansley" {print substr($1,1,5)}' grade.txt
L.Tan
```

In the above example, we have stated that we want to return the first five characters starting at the first character from 'field-1'.

If you put a value in the 'how much you want returned' part and that number is far greater than the actual length of the string, awk will return all the characters of the string, starting from the position number you gave it. To extract the surname part only of L.Tansley, we know we need to start three characters in and the length I want is seven characters. But by putting in 99 as the length, awk will still return what we want.

```
$ awk '$1=="L.Tansley" {print substr($1,3,99)}' grade.txt
Tansley
```

The other substr variation is where the part of the string returned is the suffix, or the characters after the starting position. You supply the string and then just the starting position from which you want the substring returned. To get only the surnames from the text file, I need to start at the first character and go three characters in.

```
$ awk '{print substr($1,3)}' grade.txt
Tansley
Lulu
Bunny
Troll
Tansley
```

Here's another example, using a string defined within the BEGIN part. It returns what's left after seven characters have been chopped from the string.

```
$ awk 'BEGIN {STR="A FEW GOOD MEN"}END{print substr(STR,7)}' grade.txt
GOOD MEN
```

Passing strings from the shell to awk

I said at the beginning of this chapter that a lot of awk will be just one-liners, and a few of them will be string manipulation. You'll do these one-liners *in situ* within your scripts as we progress through the book. To show you how easy it is to do one-liners that pass variables to an awk command line, here are some examples with a brief explanation on each one.

Echo the string 'Stand-by' using pipe through to awk and return the length of it:

```
$ echo "Stand-by" |awk '{print length($0)}'
8
```

Assign the variable STR a filename, pipe to awk and return the filename without the extension:

```
$ STR="mydoc.txt"
$ echo $STR| awk '{print substr($STR,1,5)}'
mydoc
```

Assign the variable STR a filename, pipe to awk and return the filename's extension only:

```
$ STR="mydoc.txt"
$ echo $STR| awk '{print substr($STR,7)}'
txt
```

9.2.10 String escape sequences

When using strings or regular expressions, you may want to include a new line in the output or search for a metacharacter.

When printing a new line (a new line is the character \n) we give it an escape sequence, so awk does not misinterpret the meaning. We can escape it by giving it a special meaning by putting a backslash before the character. For instance to force awk to print a new line we use \n.

If you are using regular expressions and want to search for the curly bracket ({), just put a backslash in before the character, like '/\{/'. This will disable the special meaning that the bracket has in awk.

There are other escape sequences awk recognizes, and these are shown in Table 9.5.

Table 9.5 *Escape sequences you can use with* awk

\b	Backspace
\f	Form feed
\n	New line
\r	Carriage return
\t	Tab
\ddd	Octal value
\c	Any other special character. For example \\ means a backslash sign.

Using some of the above sequences, we'll print May Day, with a tab between the May and Day, followed by two new lines, then print May again, then print Day again, but this time using the octal numbers 104, 141, 171 for D, a, y respectively.

```
$ awk 'BEGIN {print"\n\May\tDay\n\nMay \104\141\171"}'
May     Day

May     Day
```

Note: \104 is the octal number for ASCII D, \141 is the octal number for ASCII a, etc.

9.2.11 awk output functions (printf)

All our examples concerning output so far have just been printed to the screen, without any format, apart from the tab. Awk provides several options in a function called printf, that allow you to format the output in several different ways. For example you can have fixed column output, and right and left justification.

Each printf function (format control character) begins with a % sign and ends with a character that determines the conversion. The conversion may contain three modifiers.

The basic syntax for using the printf function is printf ([format control specifier], arguments). The format control specifiers are generally supplied in quotes.

9.2.12 printf modifiers

Table 9.6 Awk printf *modifiers*

-	Left justify
Width	Pad the field as needed, leading 0 pads with zeros
.prec	Maximum string width, or digits to the right of decimal point

printf *format control character specifiers*

Table 9.7 Awk *printing formats*

%c	ASCII character
%d	Decimal integer
%e	Floating point number – scientific
%f	Floating point number i.e. (123.44)
%g	Let awk decide which floating point conversion to use, e or f
%o	Unsigned octal number
%s	String containing characters
%x	Unsigned hexadecimal number

Character conversion

To see the equivalent of 65 in ASCII, you can pipe the number 65 through to awk. printf then does the conversion to the ASCII character. I've also stuck a new line in. This is because printf does not put a new line in for you by default.

```
$ echo "65" | awk '{printf "%c\n",$0}'
A
```

Of course I could have used awk in this way, which produces the same result:

```
$ awk 'BEGIN {printf "%c\n",65}'
A
```

The format for all the character conversions is the same. Here we see what '999' turns out like when we use the floating point conversion. It goes to six decimal places when an integer is passed to it.

```
$ awk 'BEGIN {printf "%f\n",999}
999.000000
```

Formatted output

To print out the student names and their serial numbers, I want the names to be left justified; the string that prints them will be 15 characters long, followed by the serial numbers. Note that the \n newline feed is put in after the last specifier. This output will automatically align the two columns,

```
$ awk {printf "%-15s %s\n", $1,$3}' grade.txt
M.Tansley      48311
J.Lulu         48317
P.Bunny        48
J.Troll        4842
L.Tansley      4712
```

It would be nice to have some text explaining what type of report it is so let's stick a header in. You'll notice that we are using the print for the header, but we could have used printf if we wanted to.

```
$ awk 'BEGIN {print "Name \t\tS.Number"}{printf "%-15s %s\n", $1,$3}'
grade.txt
```

Passing values to awk one-liners

Before we look at awk scripts, let's first see how we can pass variables to awk on the command line.

When you want to give a value to an awk variable before awk is invoked you put the variable on the command line. The general format for this is:

awk commands var = value input-file

(We will find out how to pass variables to awk scripts later on.)

Here we set the variable AGE to 10 on the command line. It is then passed to awk, to see which students are under 10 years of age.

```
$ awk '{if ($5 < AGE) print $0}' AGE=10 grade.txt
M.Tansley   05/99   48311  Green   8    40   44
J.Lulu      06/99   48317  green   9    24   26
```

To do a quick check on my file system space and see if it has reached a certain level I use this awk one-liner. Since the amount of used space that I want to monitor may change you can specify this trigger value on the command line. I pipe df -k through to awk, then grab column 4 which is the space available or free; I make sure I only get the numbers (1024 blocks) and not df's text headers using '$4~/^[0-9]/', then I do a test against the value we have previously specified on the command line 'if($4 < TRIGGER)' which is set to the variable TRIGGER.

```
$ df -k | awk '($4 ~/^[0-9]/) {if($4 < TRIGGER) print $6"\t"$4}'
TRIGGER=56000
/dos    55808
/apps   51022
```

When I use df -k on the system I administer, these are the column numbers.

	Filesystem	1024-blocks	Used	Free	%Used	Mounted on
Column	1	2	3	4	5	6

You may have to change the column numbers for the command to work on your system, if df reports back different report formats.

You can of course use pipe to send values through to awk. Here we use the who command: the first column of the who command always contains the user names that are logged on, so we just print that with a message.

```
$ who | awk '{print $1 " is logged on"}'
louisel is logged on
papam is logged on
```

Awk also allows you to pass environment variables. The following example uses the environment variable LOGNAME, which holds your login name and prints out a message. This information is obtained from piping the who's command output through to awk.

```
$ who | awk '{if ($1 == user) print $1" you are connected to
"$2}'user=$LOGNAME
```

Here is the output, if root is indeed logged in.

```
root you are connected to ttyp1
```

awk *script file*

You can stick any awk command(s) in a file and execute it. The commands do not have to be long, though generally this is the reason why you put them in a script file. It is quite acceptable to have one-liners in a script file, after all it saves you retyping the command every time you want to use it. The other advantage of using a file is that you can add comments to it, so you don't forget what the actual program does and what it's for.

We'll use one of our previous examples and convert it to an awk executable script file. Here's one we did earlier. It adds up the columns of the students' points gained in competitions. awk '(tot+=$6); END{print "Club student total points :" tot}' grade.txt.

Let's create a new file, and call it student_tot.awk – it's always a good idea to give all awk programs an awk extension, so you know it's an awk program just by looking at the filename. Now type in the following.

```
!/bin/awk -f
# all comment lines must start with a hash '#'
# name: student_tot.awk
# to call: student_tot.awk grade.txt
# prints total and average of club student points

#print a header first
BEGIN{
print "Student    Date  Member No.  Grade  Age   Points   Max"
print "Name       Joined                         Gained   Point Available"
print "===================================================================="



}
```

```
# let's add the scores of points gained
(tot+=$6)

# finished processing now let's print the total and average point
END{print "Club student total points  :" tot
  print "Average Club Student points:" tot/NR}
```

The first line contains !/bin/awk -f. This is important – without this line the self-contained script will not run. The line tells the script where to find awk on the system. You can see that by spacing out the commands it's a lot easier to read, and you can also have blank lines between your commands. I've added a header and an average score at the end, but in essence, this is a one-liner put into a file.

When we run the script we supply the input file after the script name, but first we need to give the script file execute permission.

```
$ chmod u+x student_tot.awk
$ student_tot.awk grade.txt
Student     Date        Member No. Grade  Age  Points   Max
Name        Joined                             Gained   Point Available
======================================================================
M.Tansley   05/99       48311   Green    8     40       44
J.Lulu      06/99       48317   green    9     24       26
P.Bunny     02/99       48      Yellow   12    35       28
J.Troll     07/99       4842    Brown-3  12    26       26
L.Tansley   05/99       4712    Brown-2  12    30       28
Club student total points  :155
Average Club Student points:31
```

An account checking program that runs on one of our systems checks against data input from the data ops people. Unfortunately there is a little bug in this program, or should we say 'an undocumented feature', where if a record is found to contain an error, it should print out the line "ERROR*" only once. But it seems to want to print the error line out quite a few times. This irritates the accounts people, so here's an awk script that filters out the many occurrences of the error line so that there is only one error line per failed record.

Here's what part of the file looks like before awk does its filtering.

```
...
...
INVALID LCSD 98GJ23
ERROR*
ERROR*
CAUTION LPSS ERROR ON ACC NO.
ERROR*
ERROR*
ERROR*
ERROR*
ERROR*
PASS FIELD INVALID ON LDPS
ERROR*
ERROR*
```

```
PASS FIELD INVALID ON GHSI
ERROR*
CAUTION LPSS ERROR ON ACC NO.
ERROR*
ERROR*
```

Here's the awk script that does the filtering.

```
#!/bin/awk -f
# error_strip.awk
# to call: error_strip.awk <filename>
# strips out the ERROR* lines if there are more than one
# ERROR* lines after each failed record.

BEGIN { error_line="" }
# tell awk the whole is "ERROR*"
{ if ($0 == "ERROR*" && error_line == "ERROR*")

# go to next line
next;
   error_line = $0; print }
```

And here's the output after awk has filtered it:

```
$ strip.awk strip
INVALID LCSD 98GJ23
ERROR*
CAUTION LPSS ERROR ON ACC NO.
ERROR*
PASS FIELD INVALID ON LDPS
ERROR*
PASS FIELD INVALID ON GHSI
ERROR*
CAUTION LPSS ERROR ON ACC NO.
ERROR*
```

Using the FS variable in awk scripts

If you are scanning a file that has a non-space as a field separator (FS), such as a #
or a :, doing one-liners is easy because you can specify the FS on the command line
like this:

```
$ awk -F: 'awk {print $0}' input-file
```

When using awk scripts remember always to put the FS variable in the BEGIN part.
If you don't awk will get confused and not know what the field separator is.

Here's a short script on how to specify the FS variable. The script just pulls
off the first and fifth fields from the /etc/passwd file; the passwd file fields are

separated by a colon (:); the first field is the login name and the fifth is the name holder of the account.

```
$ pg passwd.awk
!/bin/awk -f
# to call: passwd.awk /etc/passwd
# print out the first and fifth fields
BEGIN{
FS=":"}
{print $1,"\t",$5}
```

```
$ passwd.awk /etc/passwd
root        Special Admin login
xdm         Restart xdm Login
sysadm      Regular Admin login
daemon      Daemon Login for daemons needing permissions
```

Passing values to awk scripts

Passing values to awk scripts is done much in the same way as when we pass values to one-liners. The format is:

awk script-file var = value input-file

The following little script will check the number of fields in a file against the number you supply it, a neat little check using the NF variable. MAX holds the field numbers that you want to check. Use double quotes to enclose the field separator even if it is a space.

```
$ pg fieldcheck.awk
#!/bin/awk -f
# check on how many fields in a file
# name:fieldcheck.awk
# to call: fieldcheck MAX=n FS=<separator> filename
#
NF!=MAX{
print("line " NR " does not have" MAX " fields")}
```

If I wanted to run it against the /etc/passwd file (the passwd file has seven fields) I would give the following parameters:

```
$ fieldcheck.awk MAX=7 FS=":" /etc/passwd
```

Using a previous one-liner example, we'll convert it to an awk script. Here it is:

```
$ pg name.awk
#!/bin/awk -f
# name: age.awk
# to call: age.awk AGE=n grade.txt
# prints ages that are lower than the age supplied on the comand line
{if ($5 < AGE)
  print $0}
```

My comments take up more than the actual commands, but it doesn't matter; by looking at these comments I know exactly what it does and how to call it.

Don't forget to make the script executable for yourself, then run it by putting the variable and its value on the command line after the script name, but before the input file.

```
$ age.awk AGE=10 grade.txt
M.Tansley    05/99    48311   Green   8    40   44
J.Lulu       06/99    48317   green   9    24   26
```

You can also pass values using the pipe command as we discovered earlier. Here's an awk script that takes the output from the du command, and presents the output in blocks and bytes.

```
$ pg duawk.awk
#!/bin/awk -f
# to call: du | duawk.awk
# prints file/direc's in bytes and blocks
BEGIN{
OFS="\t" ;
print "name" "\t\t","bytes","blocks\n"
print "=============================="}
{print $2,"\t\t",$1*512,$1}
```

To run this script, just use du and pipe it through to the awk script.

```
$ du | awkdu.awk
name                          bytes     blocks
=============================================
./profile.d                   2048      4
./X11                         135680    265
./rc.d/init.d                 27136     53
./rc.d/rc0.d                  512       1
./rc.d/rc1.d                  512       1
```

9.2.13 awk arrays

When we covered the split function earlier on, we saw how it can be used to load elements into arrays. Here's that example again.

```
$ awk 'BEGIN {print split("123#456#678", myarray, "#")}'
3
```

In the previous example, split returns the number of indexes for the array called myarray. The array myarray would then look like this internally:

Myarray[1] = "123"
Myarray[2] = "456"
Myarray[3] = "678"

When using arrays, they do not have to be declared beforehand nor do you have to specify how many elements are in the array. To access an array the for loop is generally used. Here's the basic construction of one of the types of for loops:

For (element in array) Print array[element]).

Using our example of the record "123#456#678", let us use the split function again to load it up, then use a for loop to print it out. Here's the script that does the loading and printing:

```
$ pg arraytest.awk
#!/bin/awk -f
# name: arraytest.awk
# prints out an array
BEGIN{
record="123#456#789";
split(record, myarray,"#") }
  END { for (i in myarray) {print myarray[i]}}
```

To run the script we use /dev/null as the input file. This tricks awk into thinking it has an input file; if we didn't awk would just sit there and wait for our input.

```
$ arraytest.awk  /dev/null
123
456
789
```

Arrays and records

The above example showed you how to use arrays using the split function, but you can also predefine an array and use this array to test against fields. In the next example a more day-to-day use of arrays is shown.

Below is part of a download from the karate database containing grades of students and whether they are adults or juniors. There are only two fields and the field separator is the hash symbol (#). Here's the file:

```
$ pg grade_student.txt
Yellow#Junior
Orange#Senior
Yellow#Junior
Purple#Junior
Brown-2#Junior
White#Senior
Orange#Senior
Red#Junior
Brown-2#Senior
Yellow#Senior
Red#Junior
Blue#Senior
Green#Senior
Purple#Junior
White#Junior
```

Our task is to read the file and output the following information.

1.   How many Yellow, Orange and Red belt grades there are in the club.

2.   How many juniors and seniors there are in the club.

Looking at the text file, you could probably guess the answer in about 30 seconds –
fine. But what about if I told you that the full file is over 60 records long? Not so
easy now is it? Well, it is with awk.
     Look at the script first and we'll go through it after the listing.

```
$ pg belts.awk
!/bin/awk -f
# name: belts.awk
# to call: belts.awk grade2.txt
# loops through the grade2.txt file and counts how many
# belts we have in (yellow, orange, red)
# also count how many adults and juniors we have
#
# start of BEGIN
# set FS and load the arrays with our values
BEGIN{FS="#"
# load the belt colours we are interested in only
belt["Yellow"]
belt["Orange"]
belt["Red"]
# end of BEGIN
# load the student type
student["Junior"]
student["Senior"]
}
```

```
# loop thru array that holds the belt colours against field-1
# if we have a match, keep a running total
  {for (colour in belt)
    {if ($1==colour)
    belt[colour]++}}
# loop thru array that holds the student type against
# field-2 if we have a match, keep a running total
  {for (senior_or_junior in student)
    {if ($2==senior_or_junior)
    student[senior_or_junior]++}}


# finished processing so print out the matches..for each array
END{ for (colour in belt) print "The club has", belt[colour], colour,
"Belts"

for (senior_or_junior in student) print "The club
has",student[senior_or_junior]\
,senior_or_junior, "students"}
```

The BEGIN part sets the FS to the hash #, which is our field separator, as we want to find the belts (Yellow, Orange and Red). We then set up the array index manually in the script, and the same goes for the student. Notice at this stage these are the indices or elements; we are adding no reference to the array name itself as yet. All our initializing is done, so that's the end of BEGIN. Remember no file processing is carried out in the BEGIN part.

Now we can process the file. Here we give the array its name 'colour', and use a for loop to test if field-1 (that's the belts column) is equal to any of the array 'colour' elements (Yellow, Orange or Red). If there is a match, keep a running total in the array against each matched element.

The same process is then carried out on the 'senior_or_junior' array. If a match is found when scanning field-2, a running total is kept on the matched array elements of junior or senior.

The END part takes care of printing out the results of the scan. Here a for loop is used to go through each array and print them out.

You'll notice a backslash '\' at the end of one of the print statements. This is used to tell awk (or any script for that matter) that the command continues on the next line. This is used when you have a long single command and you want to break it up over a few lines. Before running the script don't forget to make it executable.

```
$ belts.awk grade_student.txt
The club has 2 Red Belts
The club has 2 Orange Belts
The club has 3 Yellow Belts
The club has 7 Senior students
The club has 8 Junior students
```

9.3 Conclusion

The awk language can be a complex language to learn, but to use it for one-liners or small scripts, the learning curve is not very steep. Throughout this chapter I have tried to introduce you to awk at its most basic. I have not gone into the awk language in too much depth; I believe that we have covered the essentials for awk. Awk is an important tool in shell programming, but you do not need to be a guru at it to use its powerful text processing abilities, in the shell or with shell programs.

CHAPTER 10

Using sed

Sed is a non-interactive text stream editor for editing a copy of text from a file or from standard input. Standard input can be text entered from the keyboard, a file redirection, a string or a variable, or by a pipe. So what would you use sed for? After all, vi is also a text editor. Well, sed allows you to edit small or large files on the fly; you can supply a series of sed commands to edit or delete and off it goes and does the job. Sed does all the changes in one pass, thus making it efficient and, most importantly to the user, fast.

In this chapter we will cover:

- extracting fields;

- matching with regular expressions;

- comparing fields;

- adding, appending and substitution; and

- basic sed one-liners and scripts.

You supply sed commands on the command line or put the commands in a file and then call sed, much as you do with awk. One important thing to remember when using sed is that it will not touch your original file, no matter what commands you give it. Sed takes a copy of it first, and all changes are then directed to the screen, unless you redirect the output to a file.

Because sed is a non-interactive editor, you specify the lines of text you want changed either by using line numbers or regular expressions.

This chapter will introduce you to sed and its capabilities. We'll be doing mostly one-liners and small scripts, because that's how you'll use sed to begin with until you get better experience with it and venture out to create long cryptic sed scripts yourself.

Like grep and awk, sed is an invaluable text-filtering tool, either by using one-liners or with combinations of grep and awk using pipes.

10.1 **How** sed **reads data**

Sed will read a line of text from a file or from other forms of standard input, and copy it into an editing buffer area. It will then read the first command from either the command line or a script, and using these commands, will find the pattern or address line and edit it. It will then repeat this procedure until there are no more commands left.

10.2 **Calling** sed

You can invoke sed in three ways: by typing the commands on the command line; by inserting sed commands in a script file then calling sed; or by inserting sed commands in a script file and making the script executable.

To use sed from the command line for one-liners use:

sed [options] 'sed-commands' input-file(s)

Remember when using sed commands on the command line to surround the actual commands with single quotes, although sed will tolerate double quotes.

To use a sed script file use this format:

sed [options] -f sed-script-file input-file(s)

To use a sed script file that has the sed command interpreter line as the first line of the script file use this format:

sed-script-file [options] input-file(s)

Whether you are running a sed script file or sed commands from the shell, if you do not specify an input file sed will take its input from the standard input. This is generally either from the keyboard or from a redirection.

The sed options are as follows:

-n   No print please; sed will not write the edited lines to the standard output. The default is to print 'all' (edited and non-edited) lines. The p command (more on this later) can be used to print the edited lines.

-e   The next command is an editing command. This option is used if you are using multiple edits. If you are using only one sed command this option is not necessary, but if you specify it sed will not complain.

-f   Use this if you are calling a sed script file. It lets sed know a script file will hold all the sed commands. Here's an example: sed -f myscript.sed input-file, where myscript.sed is the file holding the sed commands.

10.2.1 Saving sed output

If the original file is not touched, and you want to save the contents of the changes simply redirect the output to a file. The following example redirects all output from the sed commands to a file called 'myoutfile'. Use this method when you are happy with the results you are getting.

```
$ sed 'some-sed-commands' input-file > myoutfile
```

10.2.2 Ways to find text in a file using sed

When sed scans an input-file, it will start by default at the first line. There are two ways to locate text:

1. Using line numbers. These can be either a single number, or a range of line numbers.

2. Using regular expressions. See Chapter 7 for more information on how these patterns are constructed.

Table 10.1 gives some of the ways to locate text using sed.

Table 10.1 *Ways to locate text in a file using* sed

x	When x is a line number, e.g. 1
x,y	Address a range of lines from x to y, e.g. 2,5 from line 2 to line 5
/pattern/	Find lines containing a pattern, e.g. /disk/ or /[a-z]/
/pattern/pattern/	Find lines containing these two patterns, e.g. /disk/disks/
/pattern/,x	Find lines containing a pattern on the given line number, e.g. /ribbon/,3
x,/pattern/	Find matching lines by line number and a pattern, e.g. 3./vdu/
x,y!	Find lines except those specified by x and y line numbers, e.g. 1,2!

10.2.3 Basic sed editing commands

Table 10.2 Sed*'s editing commands*

p	Print the matched lines
=	Display the line number of the file
a\	Append the text after the addressed line
i\	Insert new text after the addressed line

Table 10.2 Sed*'s editing commands* (cont.)

d	Delete addressed lines
c\	Replace addressed text with new text
s	Substitute pattern with replacement pattern
r	Read text from another file
w	Write text to file
q	Quit after first pattern has been matched, or just quit
l	Show control characters in their octal ASCII page equivalent
{}	Group a series of commands to be performed only on addressed lines
n	Read the next line of text from another file and append it
g	Paste the contents of pattern2 into pattern1
y	Translate characters
n	Append next input line; this allows pattern matching across two lines

Below is a text file called `quote.txt` that we will use as we go through the sed examples, unless otherwise stated.

```
$ pg quote.txt
The honeysuckle band played all night long for only $90.
It was an evening of splendid music and company.
Too bad the disco floor fell through at 23:10.
The local nurse Miss P.Neave was in attendance.
```

10.3 sed **and regular expressions**

Sed will recognize any of the basic regular expressions and patterns and its rules for matching lines. Remember one of these rules is that if you wish to address a special character you must first escape it with a backslash (\), as this disables the meaning of the special character. Refer back to Chapter 7 on regular expressions if you need to; all expressions we covered in that chapter are quite legal in sed.

10.4 **Basic** sed **editing examples**

Let's see some of sed's editing capabilities in action using examples.

10.4.1 Displaying lines using p(rint)

The format for the print command is [address[,address]p. To display a line of text you can supply sed with a line number and sed will display it for you.

```
$ sed '2p' quote.txt
The honeysuckle band played all night long for only $90.
It was an evening of splendid music and company.
Too bad the disco floor fell through at 23:10.
The local nurse Miss P.Neave was in attendance.
```

What went wrong there? We said we wanted line 2 and issued the p to print that line only, but it's printed all the lines in the file. To fix this we use the -n option to explicitly print addressed (matched) lines.

```
$ sed -n '2p' quote.txt
It was an evening of splendid music and company.
```

10.4.2 Range printing

We can also specify a range of lines; let's print lines 1 to 3. You separate ranges with a comma.

```
$ sed -n '1,3p' quote.txt
The honeysuckle band played all night long for only $90.
It was an evening of splendid music and company.
Too bad the disco floor fell through at 23:10.
```

10.4.3 Pattern printing

Suppose we want to match the word Neave and print that line, here's how we do it. We use the '/pattern/' format, so for our example it would be '/Neave/'.

```
$ sed -n '/Neave/'p quote.txt
The local nurse Miss P.Neave was in attendance.
```

10.4.4 Searching using a pattern and line number

When you're scanning a text file for a certain word to edit on, and sed returns a whole lot of lines containing the word you want, how can you then be more specific on the pattern match you want returned? Well, you can mix the line number and the pattern together. Here's an example. Suppose we want to change the word 'The' on the last line of text from the quote.txt file. Using sed we can see that the search on 'The' returned two lines.

```
$ sed -n '/The/'p quote.txt
The honeysuckle band played all night long for only $90.
The local nurse Miss P.Neave was in attendance.
```

To home in on the first line we can mix a line number with a pattern. Here's the format: 'line-number,/pattern/'. The comma separates the line and the start of the pattern. So to print out the word 'The' we can now use, `'4,/The/'`, which means look at only line 4 for the pattern 'The'. Here's the command.

```
$ sed -n '4,/The/'p quote.txt
The local nurse Miss P.Neave was in attendance.
```

10.4.5 Matching a metacharacter

To match the $ sign which is a metacharacter, we must first escape it with a backslash, which takes away the special meaning of the $ sign. Here's the pattern: `'/\$/'p`.

```
$ sed -n '/\$/'p quote.txt
The honeysuckle band played all night long for only $90.
```

10.4.6 Displaying the whole file

To be able to print the whole file we can simply supply a range from the first line to the end line '1,$'. The '$' means the last line of the file.

```
$ sed -n '1,$p' quote.txt
The honeysuckle band played all night long for only $90.
It was an evening of splendid music and company.
Too bad the disco floor fell through at 23:10.
The local nurse Miss P.Neave was in attendance.
```

10.4.7 Any characters

If we wanted to match any letter, followed by zero or more occurrences of any letter, but ending in 'ing' this pattern would do it: `'/.*ing/'`. We can use this pattern to search for any words ending in 'ing'.

```
$ sed -n '/.*ing/'p quote.txt
It was an evening of splendid music and company.
```

10.4.8 First line

To print the first line in a file use the line number:

```
$ sed -n '1p' quote.txt
The honeysuckle band played all night long for only $90.
```

10.4.9 Last line

To print the last line in a file use the '$', which is the metacharacter for the last line.

```
$ sed -n '$p' quote.txt
The local nurse Miss P.Neave was in attendance.
```

10.4.10 Printing line numbers

To print line numbers we use the equals sign '='. To be able to print the line number of a pattern match, use this format: '/pattern/='.

```
$ sed  -e '/music/=' quote.txt
The honeysuckle band played all night long for only $90.
2
It was an evening of splendid music and company.
Too bad the disco floor fell through at 23:10.
The local nurse Miss P.Neave was in attendance.
```

The whole file has been printed out with the line number printed above the matched line. If you are concerned only about the actual line number, use the -e instead like this:

```
$ sed  -n '/music/=' quote.txt
2
```

If you want to print the line number and then only the matched line, you must use two sed commands, using the '-e' option. The first command prints the pattern match, the second will print the line number using the = option. The format now becomes sed -n -e '/pattern/p' -e '/pattern/='.

```
$ sed -n -e '/music/p' -e '/music/=' quote.txt
It was an evening of splendid music and company.
2
```

10.4.11 Appending text

To append text we use the a\ symbol, which will append one or more lines of given text to the addressed line. If you do not supply an address on where to put the text, sed will by default put it on each line. When using append you cannot specify a range. You are only allowed one address pattern. When text is appended, it goes to the standard output (screen etc.), so be aware that it then cannot be edited. This is because when sed is first invoked it copies text from the file into a buffer area. This area is where all the sed edits are carried out – remember sed never works on the original file, because the text goes straight to the standard output, and sed has no copy of it.

To be able to edit after an append, you must first save the file then run another sed command to edit it, so the file's contents are moved to the buffer area.

The format for the append is:

[address]a\
text\
text\
. . .
text

The address can specify either a pattern or line number to which the new text should be appended. The \a tells sed to actually append the text following the 'a\' sign. Looking at the format, please note that there is a backslash after each text line. This backslash preserves the new line, and when sed sees the backslash, it will create a new line then insert the next line of text. The last line does not need a backslash, since sed will assume that that is the end of the append commands.

When appending or inserting text or keying in a few sed commands you can take advantage of the secondary shell prompt that lets you enter multi-line commands from the shell prompt. We won't do that here, since it leaves users open for typos, and it is better to do it in a script file. That's what we'll do now. Besides, scripts let you have blank lines in them and comment lines that make for better readability of the script.

10.4.12 Creating a sed script file

Create a new file called append.sed and stick the following commands in it:

```
$ pg append.sed
#!/bin/sed -f
/company/ a\
Then suddenly it happened.
```

Now save it. We first have to make it executable:

```
$ chmod u+x append.sed
```

Now run it.

```
$ append.sed quote.txt
The honeysuckle band played all night long for only $90.
It was an evening of splendid music and company.
Then suddenly it happened.
Too bad the disco floor fell through at 23:10.
The local nurse Miss P.Neave was in attendance.
```

If you get an error saying 'file not found', try putting a forward slash in front of the script, like this.

```
$ ./append.sed quote.txt
```

Let's go through what the actual script does. The first line is the sed command interpreter line; this is where the script looks for sed to run the commands. Mine is located in /bin, as yours should be.

The second line starts with /company/; this is where we want the append to start from. The a\ tells sed it's an append and a new line should be inserted first. The third line of the script is the actual text we want appended to the copy of the text.

The output show the results of our append. If we wanted to save this output, we would simply redirect it like this:

```
$ append.sed quote.txt>myfile
```

10.4.13 Inserting text

The insert command is much the same as the append, except it inserts before the address line. Like the append it will accept only one address. Here's the general format of the insert. The address is the pattern or line number you want to match.

```
[address]i\
text\
text\
. . .
text
```

We'll insert the following piece of text 'Utter confusion followed.' before the line that ends with 'attendance'. Here's the script.

```
$ pg insert.sed
#!/bin/sed -f
/attendance/ i\
Utter confusion followed.
```

When we run it, we get:

```
$ insert.sed quote.txt
The honeysuckle band played all night long for only $90.
It was an evening of splendid music and company.
Too bad the disco floor fell through at 23:10.
Utter confusion followed.
The local nurse Miss P.Neave was in attendance.
```

We could have used line numbers to specify where to insert the text. Because the insert goes before the pattern or line number specified we use line 4. Here's the script:

```
#!/bin/sed -f
4 i\
Utter confusion followed.
```

10.4.14 Changing text

The change command will replace the addressed line that is matched in the pattern space with the new text. Here's the format:

```
[address[,address] c\
text\
text\
text\
...
text
```

To change the first line 'The honeysuckle band played all night long for only $90.' to 'The Office Dibble band played well.' all we need to do is match any part of the first line. We'll use the pattern '/Honeysuckle/'; the sed script is called change.sed. Here's the script:

```
$ pg change.sed
#!/bin/sed -f
# change.sed
/honeysuckle/ c\
The Office Dibble band played well.
```

To run it, don't forget to first make the script executable with chmod u+x change.sed.

```
$ change.sed quote.txt
The Office Dibble band played well.
It was an evening of splendid music and company.
Too bad the disco floor fell through at 23:10.
The local nurse Miss P.Neave was in attendance.
```

Like the insert, I could have used a line number instead of a pattern, which would have done the job just as well.

```
#!/bin/sed -f
3 c\
The Office Dibble band played well.
```

You can mix and match changes, appends and inserts on the same file all in one script that affects the original lines.

Here is an example script with comments.

```
$ pg mix.sed
#!/bin/sed -f
# this is a comment line, all comment starts with a #
# name: mix.sed


# this is the change on line 1
1 c\
The Dibble band were grooving.
# let's now insert a line
/evening/ i\
They played some great tunes.
# change the last line, a $ means last line
$ c\
Nurse Neave was too tipsy to help.
# stick in a new line before the last line
3 a\
Where was the nurse to help?
```

Now let's run it and see the changes.

```
$ mix.sed quote.txt
The Dibble band were grooving.
They played some great tunes.
It was an evening of splendid music and company.
Too bad the disco floor fell through at 23:10.
Where was the nurse to help?
Nurse Neave was too tipsy to help.
```

10.4.15 Deleting text

To delete text using sed use this format:

[address[,address]]d

The address can be a range of lines or a pattern. Let's look at some examples.
This will delete the first line; 1d means delete line 1.

```
$ sed '1d' quote.txt
It was an evening of splendid music and company.
Too bad the disco floor fell through at 23:10.
The local nurse Miss P.Neave was in attendance.
```

This deletes lines 1 to 3:

```
$ sed '1,3d' quote.txt
The local nurse Miss P.Neave was in attendance.
```

This will delete the last line:

```
$ sed '$d' quote.txt
The honeysuckle band played all night long for only $90.
It was an evening of splendid music and company.
Too bad the disco floor fell through at 23:10.
```

You can also delete by using regular expressions. This will delete the line containing 'Neave':

```
$ sed '/Neave/d' quote.txt
The honeysuckle band played all night long for only $90.
It was an evening of splendid music and company.
Too bad the disco floor fell through at 23:10.
```

10.4.16 Substituting text

The substitute command substitutes the addresses pattern with a replacement pattern. The format is:

[address[,address]] s/pattern-to-find/replacement-pattern/[g p w n]

The s tells sed that a replacement command is coming and should search for 'pattern-to-find' and if successful replace it with 'replacement-pattern'.
The substitute options are as follows:

g	By default only the first occurrence of the pattern is substituted. Using the 'g' option will make it global and all occurrences are substituted.
p	By default sed writes all lines substituted to standard output. Use the 'p' option which will override the '-n' option, which prints no results out.
w filename	Use this option to append the output to a filename.

Let's look at some examples using the substitute command. To change night into NIGHT, we can do the following. What the following command is saying is find the pattern 'night' then replace it with the text 'NIGHT'.

```
$ sed 's/night/NIGHT/' quote.txt
The honeysuckle band played all NIGHT long for only $90.
```

To delete the '$' sign from $90 (remember it's a special character, so we escape it with a backslash) do not put any pattern in the 'replacement-pattern' part of the substitute command. This is how you delete words in sed; just leave the replacement pattern part blank, but still enclose it with the forward-slash.

```
$ sed 's/\$//' quote.txt
The honeysuckle band played all night long for only 90.
```

To make the substitute global, which means search and replace on all occurrences of the pattern, just add a 'g' on the end of the command. This example replaces all occurrences of the word 'The' to 'Wow!'.

```
$ sed 's/The/Wow!/g' quote.txt
Wow! honeysuckle band played all night long for only $90.
It was an evening of splendid music and company.
Too bad the disco floor fell through at 23:10.
Wow! local nurse Miss P.Neave was in attendance.
```

To write the results of a substitution to a file use the 'w' option. To write the results of this substitution which replaces 'splendid' with 'SPLENDID' to a file called sed.out we can do this:

```
$ sed s/splendid/SPLENDID/w sed.out' quote.txt
```

Remember to enclose the filename within sed's single quotes. To see the results of the file:

```
$ pg sed.out
It was an evening of SPLENDID music and company.
```

10.5 Modifying strings with substitute (&)

If you want to be able to append or modify a string, you can use the ampersand (&) command. The ampersand stores the pattern found so that you can recall it and then place it in the replacement string. That was a bit of a mouthful; here's the layout on the modifier. Give it a normal substitute pattern to search for, then a pattern you want to append the first pattern with, followed by an ampersand. When the modifier is placed it is placed before the matched pattern. For instance, this sed statement 's/nurse/"Hello" &/p' will produce the following output:

```
$ sed -n 's/nurse/"Hello" &/p' quote.txt
The local "Hello" nurse Miss P.Neave was in attendance.
```

based on the following input line of text, 'The local nurse Miss P.Neave was in attendance.'

Remember to use spacing in the pattern as you want it to appear in the text.

Here's another example.

```
$ sed -n 's/played/from Hockering &/p' quote.txt
The honeysuckle band from Hockering played all night long for only $90.
```

Looking at the original line 'The honeysuckle band played all night long for only $90.' it becomes clearer how the modifier works.

10.6 **Writing to a file within** sed

As well as using the '>' file redirection to send output to a file, you can send the results from a sed command to a file. The format for this is a little like the write using substitutes. Here's the format:

[address[,address]] w filename

where 'w' lets sed know it's going to write the results to a file, and 'filename' is the filename is self-explanatory. It's straightforward; here are a couple of examples.

```
$ sed '1,2 w filedt' quote.txt
```

Here the file is sent to the screen, and the pattern range, which is lines 1 and 2, is sent to the file called filedt.

```
$ pg filedt
The honeysuckle band played all night long for only $90.
It was an evening of splendid music and company.
```

In this example we search for the pattern 'Neave', and the result of that match is written to the file filedht.

```
$ sed '/Neave/ w dht' quote.txt

$ pg dht
The local nurse Miss P.Neave was in attendance.
```

10.7 Reading text from a file

When processing a file, sed allows you to read from another file and append the text from that file to the current file, placing it after the line with the pattern match. The format is:

address r filename

where 'r' lets sed know it's going to read from another file source and 'filename' is the name of that file.

Let's create a small file called `sedex.txt`. Here are the contents of the file:

```
$ pg sedex.txt
Boom boom went the music.
```

We are now going to append the file `sedex.txt` to the current working copy of our `quote.txt` file. We'll put the contents of the file after the line where the pattern `/company/` is matched, which is line 3. Please note that the filename we want to read stays enclosed by the single quotes.

```
$ sed '/company./r sedex.txt' quote.txt
The honeysuckle band played all night long for only $90.
It was an evening of splendid music and company.
Boom boom went the music.
Too bad the disco floor fell through at 23:10.
The local nurse Miss P.Neave was in attendance.
```

10.8 Quitting after a match

Occasionally you want to be able to quit sed as soon as you have matched the first occurrence of a pattern, so you can carry on with some other script processing etc. The format of the quit command is:

address q

Here's an example. Suppose we wish to search for the following pattern `/.a.*/` which means any letter, followed by an 'a', followed by any letter matched zero or more times. Looking at our text file this will bring up the following word on the following lines:

Line 1. band
Line 2. bad
Liner3. was
Line 4. was

To be able to find the first pattern (band) then quit all we need to do is put the q at the end of the sed statement.

```
$ sed '/.a.*/q' quote.txt
The honeysuckle band played all night long for only $90.
```

10.9 Displaying control characters in a file

When downloading files from other systems, you sometimes get control characters (non-printable characters) spread all over the file. Capturing an application screen output from a menu can sometimes cause control characters to be put in a file. How can you tell if there are any in a file? If you do 'cat -v filename', and the screen bleeps and spurts rubbish everywhere, then be assured you've got control characters in that file. If you get funny looking characters being displayed then be pretty sure that they are control characters as well.

On some systems you can do just a 'cat filename' instead of cat -v to see all those non-printable characters.

The sed format is:

[address,[address]]l

where the 'l' means list.

Generally you'll want to list the whole file, instead of pattern matching, so use '1' for line 1 and the $ for the last line. The pattern range '1,$' means the first line to the last line of the file.

If I cat a file we get an indication that there are in fact control characters in the file.

```
$ cat -v func.txt
This is is the F1 key:^[OP
This is the F2 key:^[OQ
```

Now let's run sed over the file and see what it says.

```
$ sed -n '1,$l' func.txt
This is is the F1 key:\0330P$
This is the F2 key:\0330Q$
```

Sed has found and displayed a couple of control characters. The \033 is the escape key, OP is the value of the F1 key, after the escape sequence, and so on for the second line.

Your values may be different if you try your function key; it depends on how it's mapped (i.e. using terminfo or termcap). If you want to insert the control character of the F1 key into a text file using vi to see what sequence it returns do the following:

Load vi up.
Go into insert mode.
Hold down the <Ctrl> and then the <v> key.   (a ˆ will appear)
Now release both keys.
Hit the F1 key.   ([OP will appear)
Hit the <Esc> key.   (the value F1 sends will now be displayed)

10.10 Using sed **on the system**

We have now gone over the basics of sed, but what you really use sed for in your scripts or on the shell line is changing or deleting text from strings or files. That's what we will look at next, using what we have learnt in the previous section.

10.10.1 Dealing with control characters

One task for which you'll use sed a lot will be stripping off control characters from files that have been downloaded from another system.

Here's a part of a file (dos.txt) that has been transferred. We've got to get rid of all the suspect characters so the accounts department can use the file.

```
$ pg dos.txt
12332##DISO##45.12^M
00332##LPSO##23.11^M
01299##USPD##34.46^M
...
```

Here's what has got to be done:

1. Replace all the hash symbols (##) with a single space.

2. Delete all leading zeros (00) from the first field.

3. Delete all the carriage returns (^M) from the end-of-lines.

On some systems that I have had to convert, I have seen ^@ and ^L as carriage returns, so don't worry if you see weird characters as long as they are all the same and on the end of each line.

We'll carry out each task to make sure we get the required results before moving on to the next task. We will keep using the original dos.txt file as input.

Task 1. To delete all the hash symbols is easy; just do a global substitute command, stating that two or more hash symbols must be replaced with a space.

```
$ sed 's/##*//g' dos.txt
12332 DISO 45.12^M
00332 LPSO 23.11^M
01299 USPD 34.46^M
```

Task 2. To delete all leading zeros, we use the ^ sign to say the pattern must start at the beginning of the line. We'll use '^0*' to trap any number of leading zeros. Here's the pattern: 's/^0*//g'. We use nothing in the replacement part of the substitution, because this will in effect delete the pattern, which is what we want.

```
$ sed 's/^0*//g' dos.txt
12332##DISO##45.12^M
332##LPSO##23.11^M
1299##USPD##34.46^M
```

Task 3. OK then, to get rid of the '^M' at the end of the lines we'll need to do a global substitution. We will not put anything in the replacement pattern part. Here's the pattern: 's/^M//g'. Be careful now on the '^M', since it's a control character.

To generate the control character (^M) we need to follow the same process as when we generated the F1 key sequences earlier on. So, to get the ^M, do the following: type sed 's/; now hold down the <Ctrl> key then the v key, now release the v key and hit the ^ key whilst still holding down the <Ctrl> key; now release both keys, and finally hit the <return> key. This command will now get rid of the ^Ms at the end of the lines.

```
$ sed 's/^M//g' dos.txt
```

Showing you each task on how to get rid of all the unwanted characters helps you to understand the whole picture. It is important that you test each step before moving on to the next one when dealing with sed, because if not you'll leave yourself open to some weird and unexpected results.

Now we have tested each task we can put all these commands together. We cat the file into a series of sed commands using pipes. The sed commands are exactly the same ones we have been doing in each of the steps to filter out the characters.

```
$ cat dos.txt | sed 's/^0*//g' | sed 's/^M//g' | sed 's/##*/ /g'
12332 DISO 45.12
332 LPSO 23.11
1299 USPD 34.46
```

Now the file is ready for the accounts department.

We could have stuck the commands in one file and then run it. Here's the one-liner converted into a script.

```
$ pg dos.sed
#!/bin/sed -f
# name: dos.sed
# to call: dos.sed dos.txt

# get rid of the hash marks
s/##//g

# now get rid of the leading zeros
s/^0*//g
```

```
# now get rid of the carriage return
# the ^M is generated like we did for the F1 key.
s/\^M//g
```

You can even make the command line shorter, by specifying only one sed command instead of three. We'll see how when we use sed in our scripts later on in the book.

10.10.2 Dealing with report output

When you are dealing with statement outputs from databases and you are grabbing the results of the statement so your script can do further processing, you generally need to do some tidying up first. Here's a statement from an sql query.

Database	Size (MB)	Date Created
GOSOUTH	2244	12/11/97
TRISUD	5632	8/9/99

(2 rows affected)

In order to use the information on this output for further automatic script processing, we need all the database names, so we need to do the following tasks:

1. Delete the dotted line using 's/–*//g'.

2. Delete all blank lines using '/^$/d'.

3. Delete the last line using '$d'.

4. Delete the first line '1d'.

5. Print out the first column using awk '{print $1}'.

Here are the commands. Again I use cat and pipes to get the desired result.

```
$ cat sql.txt | sed 's/--*//g' | sed '/^$/d' | sed '$d' | sed '1d' | awk
'{print $1}'
GOSOUTH
TRISUD
```

Now the script has the database names, it can go to be used for other processing.

10.10.3 Getting rid of numbers at the beginning of a line

Our task in this next file download is to get rid of all the numbers at the start of each line. Each record should begin with either a UNH or UND, and not the numbers in front of the codes UNH or UND. Here's the file:

```
$ pg UNH.txt
12345UND SPLLFC 234344
9999999UND SKKLT    3423
1UND SPLLY   434
. . .
```

Using a basic regular expression will do the job here; we can use '[0-9]' which means any numbers that are at the beginning of the line, making sure we delete the numbers by putting no pattern in the replacement pattern part of the substitute command.

```
$ sed 's/^[0-9]//g' UNH.txt
UND SPLLFC 234344
UND SKKLT    3423
UND SPLLY   434
```

10.10.4 Appending text

When accounts have finished validating a file, the accounts department wants a piece of text appended to each account number saying so. Here's a portion of a similar file:

```
$ pg ok.txt
AC456
AC492169
AC9967
AC88345
```

The task here is to append a string containing 'passed' at the end of each account number.

This task is relatively easy when you use the '&' command to modify each field. All we need to make sure is that we match at least two or more occurrences of numbers so all the account numbers will be caught in the pattern match.

```
$ sed 's/[0-9][0-9]*/& Passed/g' ok.txt
AC456 Passed
AC492169 Passed
AC9967 Passed
AC88345 Passed
```

10.10.5 Passing values from the shell to sed

To pass variables to sed from the command line, all you need to remember is to use double quotes, otherwise it will not work.

```
$ NAME="It's a go situation"
$ REPLACE="GO"
$ echo $NAME | sed "s/go/$REPLACE/g"
It's a GO situation
```

10.10.6 Assigning a shell variable from sed output

To assign shell variables from sed output is a simple case of substitution. Using the above example, let's create a shell variable called NEW_NAME to hold the output from the above sed example.

```
$ NAME="It's a go situation"
$ REPLACE="GO"
$ NEW_NAME=`echo $NAME | sed "s/go/$REPLACE/g"`
$ echo $NEW_NAME
It's a GO situation
```

10.11 Quick one-liners

Here's a small collection of one-liners ([] means a space and [ ] means a tab).

's/\.$//g'	Delete all lines ending with a period
'-e /abcd/d'	Delete lines containing abcd
's /[][][]*/[]/g'	Delete two or more spaces and replace with a single space
's/^[][]*//g'	Delete one or more spaces at the beginning of a line
's/\.[][]*/[]/g'	Delete a full stop followed by two or more spaces and replace with a space
'/^$/d'	Delete all blank lines
's/^.//g'	Delete the first character
's/COL\(...\)//g'	Delete three characters following the letters COL
's/^\///g'	Delete the leading slash from a pathname
's/[]/[ ]/g'	Delete all spaces and replace with a tab
's/^[ ]//g'	Delete all tabs from the beginning of the line
's/[ ]*//g'	Delete all tabs

Let's see some quick one-liner examples in action before we close this chapter.

Removing leading slash of a pathname

Echo the current working directory to sed and delete the leading slash.

```
cd /usr/local
$ echo $PWD| sed 's/^\///g'
$ usr/local
```

Appending/inserting text

Echo the string "Mr Willis" to sed and append the string "Bruce" after "Mr".

```
$ echo "Mr Willis" | sed 's/Mr /& Bruce/g'
Mr Bruce Willis
```

Deleting the first character

Echo the string "accounts.doc" to sed and remove the first character.

```
$ echo "accounts.doc" | sed 's/^.//g'
$ ccounts.doc
```

Deleting a filename extension

Echo the string "accounts.doc" to sed and delete the filename extension '.doc'.

```
$ echo "accounts.doc" | sed 's/.doc//g'
accounts
```

Adding a filename extension

Echo the string "accounts" to sed and append the string ".doc" to "accounts".

```
$ echo "accounts" | sed 's/$/.doc/g'
accounts.doc
```

Substituting a series of characters

If variable x contained this string:

```
$ x="Department+payroll%Building G"
$ echo $x
$ Department+payroll%Building G
```

and you wanted to convert the following characters

```
    + to 'of'
    % to 'located'
```

this sed command would do it:

```
$ echo $x | sed 's/\+/ of /g' | sed 's/\%/ Located at /g'
Department of payroll Located Building G
```

10.12 Conclusion

Sed is a powerful tool in text filtering; using sed allows you to pick apart a string or file and keep the bits you want. You don't have to write big scripts to get the required information from a file, as we have found out. We have just touched on the basics of sed in this chapter, but from what we have learnt we can carry out many tasks using sed.

If you have to carry out filtering on a file using sed, break the problem down into small steps, assign each step a task and test the results as you go along. From experience, this is the most productive way of carrying out tasks.

CHAPTER 11

Merge and divide

A few years ago, I used to look after a collection of UNIX boxes that had PICK running on top. Most of the time that I spent in the actual PICK applications was for carrying out sort and join routines – sort this, join that. I was glad I wasn't a full-time PICK operator.

Quite a few tools deal mainly with text file sorting, merging and dividing. We will look at some of these tools in this chapter.

In this chapter we will cover:

- useful sorts;
- uniq;
- join;
- cut;
- paste; and
- split.

11.1 Using sort

The sort command enables you to sort on many different fields (sort keys) in different column orders. You'll find sort will come in very handy when going over log files, or rearranging the text columns for downloaded files for another user. In fact, when you use other UNIX tools it assumes the files to be worked on have been previously sorted. Anyway, it makes more sense to have a file sorted than unsorted.

11.1.1 A word to the wise

The sort utility that comes with UNIX/LINUX is very powerful, though care has to be taken when using different combinations of the sort options as they can lead to unexpected results. The options for sort are very long, and even I have trouble sometimes working out what the different switches actually do compared to the results I get. I reckon that there is definitely some ambiguity when combining the different options in sort.

I will not go into the discussions on the different sort methods (but you can't beat a good bubble sort; it's slow, very slow, but fun watching the numbers interchange) or what all the different combination of switches do. This chapter will deal with the main sort options, using lots of examples. Other commands that work seamlessly with sort are uniq, join, cut and paste, which will also be covered, along with split.

As mentioned above, the options of the sort command are very long. Here are the options we'll be using in this chapter.

11.1.2 sort options

This is the general format of the sort command:

> **Sort -cmu -o output-file [other options] + pos1 + pos2 input-files**

Let's now go over the sort parameters:

-c   Test to see if the file is already sorted
-m   Merge two sorted files
-u   Delete all duplicate lines
-o   Name of an output file, for the sort results

Other options:

-b   Ignore any leading blanks, when using fields to sort on
-n   Specify that this sort is to be a numerical sort on this field(s)
-t   Field separator; the fields are separated by non-blanks or a tab
-r   Reverse the sort order or comparisons
+n   Where n is a field number, start sorting using this field number
-n   Where n is a field number, ignore this field for sorting comparisons, usually used in conjunction with +n
Pos1   Transforms to m.n where m is the field number and .n is how many characters in to start the sort; for example, 4,6 means start the sort on field 5, starting seven characters in

11.1.3 Saving output

Use the '-o' option to save the results from your sort. However, you can use the redirection method to save the output. The following example saves the results to a file called `results.out`:

```
$ sort video.txt >results.out
```

11.1.4 How `sort` starts

By default, `sort` expects the separator to be a blank space, or series of blank spaces. If you have fields separated by other means, use the -t option to set it.

When `sort` is invoked it looks to see if the '-t' option has been set for the field separator; if so it will use this to divide the fields into field 0, field 1, etc. If '-t' has not been set, `sort` uses the blank(s) as field separators. By default, `sort` will order the whole line unless you specify field numbers.

Below is a listing of a file called `video.txt`, which contains 'top video rentals' of the local video shop for the last quarter. The fields are (1) video title, (2) supplier area code, (3) rentals this quarter, and (4) rentals this year. The field separator is the colon. Because it's a colon we use the '-t:' option on all our `sort` examples for the video file. Here's the file:

```
$ pg video.txt
Boys in Company C:HK:192:2192
Alien:HK:119:1982
The Hill:KL:63:2972
Aliens:HK:532:4892
Star Wars:HK:301:4102
A Few Good Men:KL:445:5851
Toy Story:HK:239:3972
```

11.1.5 How `sort` references fields

One other important thing to remember about `sort` is that it references the first field as field 0, then uses field 1 for the second field and so on. Sort can also use the whole line to sort on. Confusing – you bet it is. So using our video file, the fields should be referenced by the user and `sort` as:

Field 0	Field 1	Field 2	Field 3
Star Wars	HK	301	4102
A Few Good Men	KL	445	5851

Sort will address the fields, and so should we really, as field 0 as sort key 0, field 1 as sort key 1 and so on.

11.1.6 Is the file already sorted?

How can you tell if a file is already sorted? Just looking at it is fine if it's only 30 lines or so, but what if it's, say, 400 lines? Use 'sort -c' to tell you if sort thinks the file is sorted in some order.

```
$ sort -c video.txt
sort: disorder on video.txt
```

According to sort it's not sorted, so let's get it sorted and try again:

```
$ sort -c video.txt
$
```

It's returned to the prompt, so it's sorted. However, it would be even better if sort could return an informative message line when the test is successful.

11.1.7 Basic sort

The most basic sort on any file is 'sort filename'. This sorts on the first field (sort key 0), and in reality it is comparing each field along the line as it reads the file. It returns the sort based on the first field, which is what you'd expect.

```
$ sort -t: video.txt
Alien:HK:119:1982
Aliens:HK:532:4892
Boys in Company C:HK:192:2192
A Few Good Men:KL:445:5851
Star Wars:HK:301:4102
The Hill:KL:63:2972
Toy Story:HK:239:3972
```

11.1.8 Reverse sort

If you wish to sort in reverse, use the -r option. Using the reverse sort is handy when you're hacking through large log files. Here the reverse is again sorted on field 0.

```
$ sort -t: -r video.txt
Toy Story:HK:239:3972
The Hill:KL:63:2972
Star Wars:HK:301:4102
A Few Good Men:KL:445:5851
Boys in Company C:HK:192:2192
Aliens:HK:532:4892
Alien:HK:119:1982
```

11.1.9 Sorting on a specific field

Sometimes it makes sense to sort purely on the second field (sort key one). If we wanted to arrange our supplier codes in preparation for a report, we would use '+1', which means sort on the first `sort` key field. In the following example all the supplier codes have been sorted using `sort` key 1; notice the second and third `sort` key fields have also been sorted.

```
$ sort -t: +1  video.txt
Alien:HK:119:1982
Boys in Company C:HK:192:2192
Toy Story:HK:239:3972
Star Wars:HK:301:4102
Aliens:HK:532:4892
A Few Good Men:KL:445:5851
The Hill:KL:63:2972
```

11.1.10 Numeric field sorting

No surprise here; to sort on the third `sort` key field use '+3'. But because we are dealing with numbers, and we want a numerical `sort`, use the '-n' option. Here's the command to see all the yearly rental figures sorted:

```
$ sort -t: +3n  video.txt
Alien:HK:119:1982
Boys in Company C:HK:192:2192
The Hill:KL:63:2972
Toy Story:HK:239:3972
Star Wars:HK:301:4102
Aliens:HK:532:4892
A Few Good Men:KL:445:5851
```

Let's see what happens if you do not specify the '-n'. We'll sort on the third field to see who's got the best quarter rental figures, and because it's `sort` key field two we reference it as '+2':

```
$ sort -t: +2 video.txt
Alien:HK:119:1982
Boys in Company C:HK:192:2192
Toy Story:HK:239:3972
Star Wars:HK:301:4102
A Few Good Men:KL:445:5851
Aliens:HK:532:4892
The Hill:KL:63:2972
```

Look, it's been sorted but not as we expected, since the third field contains numbers. Surely they would be in some type of order. The video *The Hill* should be at the top. Here's what's happened: the `sort` has looked at the very first digit of each number for each field containing the quarter figures and sorted that first. It has then looked at the second digit of each number and sorted that.

Remember when doing sorts based on numeric data to use the '-n' option to get the right results.

```
$ sort -t: +2n video.txt
The Hill:KL:63:2972
Alien:HK:119:1982
Boys in Company C:HK:192:2192
Toy Story:HK:239:3972
Star Wars:HK:301:4102
A Few Good Men:KL:445:5851
Aliens:HK:532:4892
```

Now that's better; we can now see our top-selling video for the quarter which is *Aliens*. We could have used the '-r' option to reverse the sort, and this would have put *Aliens* at the top of the file.

11.1.11 Unique sorting

There are times when you have a raw file which contains duplicate lines. Using '-u' for unique (no duplicates please) we can get rid of these. The entry for the video *Alien* has been entered twice. Here's the file with a duplicate; Alien has been inserted twice:

```
$ pg video.txt
Boys in Company C:HK:192:2192
Alien:HK:119:1982
The Hill:KL:63:2972
Aliens:HK:532:4892
Star Wars:HK:301:4102
A Few Good Men:KL:445:5851
Alien:HK:119:1982
```

To get rid of the duplicates just use the '-u' option. There is no need for other options here; let sort do it all by itself.

```
$ sort -u video.txt
Alien:HK:119:1982
Aliens:HK:532:4892
Boys in Company C:HK:192:2192
A Few Good Men:KL:445:5851
Star Wars:HK:301:4102
The Hill:KL:63:2972
```

11.1.12 Other sort methods using -k

Sort has other methods for how you can specify the sort key. Using the '-k' option, the first field/sort key starts at '1'; now don't get confused. I actually use this option the most, because I'm used to the first field being number one, so it makes sense to reference them by the same number when using sort. There are other options you can specify using '-k', mainly on how many characters in from the start of the field you want to start the sort on.

To sort on field 4 we can use '-k4'. This will order the yearly rental figures.

```
$ sort -t: -k4  video.txt
Alien:HK:119:1982
Boys in Company C:HK:192:2192
The Hill:KL:63:2972
Star Wars:HK:301:4102
Aliens:HK:532:4892
A Few Good Men:KL:445:5851
```

11.1.13 Order of sort keys using -k

You can also specify the order of the sort keys. To specify that we sort the fourth then the first field use this command '-k4 -k1'. We'll also stick in a reverse so we get the top rentals over the year at the top of the file, as follows:

```
$ sort -t: -r -k4 -k1 video.txt
A Few Good Men:KL:445:5851
Aliens:HK:532:4892
Star Wars:HK:301:4102
The Hill:KL:63:2972
Boys in Company C:HK:192:2192
Alien:HK:119:1982
```

11.1.14 Specifying sort sequences

You can tell sort which sort key fields to search on and in what order, and you can also specify what sort keys not to search on by using the '-n' option. Let's look at the following sort command:

sort +0 -2 +3

This sort command means start sorting on field 0, ignore field 2, but carry on using field 3 with the sort.

11.1.15 Using pos

The other method where you can specify the position in a field to start sorting on is by using this format:

sort +field_number .characters_in

which means start the sort at field_number, but beginning . characters in from the start of that field.

Here's an example. The video file now has area codes suffixing the supplier code; here's the file:

```
$ pg video.txt
Boys in Company C:HK48:192:2192
Alien:HK57:119:1982
The Hill:KL23:63:2972
Aliens:HK11:532:4892
Star Wars:HK38:301:4102
A Few Good Men:KL87:445:5851
Toy Story:HK65:239:3972
```

To sort the file using just the supplier codes, the command '+1.2' will use the first field (supplier code) starting at character 3 from the leftmost side of the field, which is the start of the area codes. Here's a breakdown of that:

	Field 0	Field 1	Field 2	Field 3
	Aliens	H K 1 1	532	4892
Characters in:		0 1 2 3		

```
$ sort -t: +1.2 video.txt
Aliens:HK11:532:4892
The Hill:KL23:63:2972
Star Wars:HK38:301:4102
Boys in Company C:HK48:192:2192
Alien:HK57:119:1982
Toy Story:HK65:239:3972
A Few Good Men:KL87:445:5851
```

11.1.16 Sort output using head and tail

When sorting you don't always have to display the whole file or page to look at the top or bottom of the file containing the sort results. To display only the highest rental of the year, we can sort it by the fourth field '-k4', reverse the sort and then use pipe to display the first line only of the sort output. The head command takes care of this. You specify how many lines you want to see; we're only concerned with the first line so it's 'head -1':

```
$ sort -t: -r -k4 video.txt | head -1
A Few Good Men:KL:445:5851
```

To see only the lowest rental of the year, we can use tail, which is the opposite of head. Tail displays the end of a file, line 1 being the end, line 2 being the second line from the end and so on. The command to see the last line is 'tail -1'. Using the same sort command as above in conjunction with tail displays the lowest rental of the year.

```
$ sort -t: -r -k4 video.txt | tail -1
Alien:HK:119:1982
```

You can use head or tail to view any large text files. Use head to view the top of files. The basic format for head is:

head [how_many_lines_to_display] file_name

Use tail to view the end of files. The basic format of tail is:

tail [how_many_lines_to_display] file_name

If you omit the number of lines you want displayed when using head or tail, it will display ten lines by default.

To see only the first 20 lines of a text file:

```
$ head -20 file_name
```

To see only the last seven lines of a text file:

```
$ tail -7 file_name
```

11.1.17 Using sort output with awk

When sorting data, especially for other users, it's reasonable to assume that they would like a little message with their sort results. Using awk, this is easily done. Taking our last example of the lowest rental, all we need to do is pipe the results through to awk, not forgetting to use a colon as the field separator, and display a message along with the title and actual data.

```
$ sort -t: -r -k4 video.txt|tail -1 | awk -F: '{print "Worst rental
",$1,"has been rented "$3}'

Worst rental Alien has been rented 119
```

11.1.18 Merging two sorted files

To merge two files together, they must first be sorted. Merged files are used in transaction processing or updating of any kind. In this example, we have forgotten to put a couple of video titles in our file, so they've been stuck in a separate file. Now it's time to merge them into one file. The format for a sort merge is 'sort -m sorted_file1 sorted_file2'. Here's the file containing those two new titles; it's already been sorted:

```
$ pg video2.txt
Crimson Tide:134:2031
Die Hard:152:2981
```

To merge against our existing video file, which has been sorted and is now called 'video.sort', we can use '-m +0'. To sort on the titles field, you do not really need the '+0' in this case but best to be safe then sorry.

```
$ sort -t: -m +0 video2.txt video.sort
Alien:HK:119:1982
Aliens:HK:532:4892
Boys in Company C:HK:192:2192
Crimson Tide:134:2031
Die Hard:152:2981
A Few Good Men:KL:445:5851
Star Wars:HK:301:4102
The Hill:KL:63:2972
```

11.2 `sort` **on the system**

`Sort` can be used to sort the usernames from the `/etc/passwd` file. All we need to do is sort on field 1, which is the login name field, then pass the output using a pipe to `awk`, and let `awk` print the first field.

```
$ cat passwd | sort -t: +0 | awk -F":" '{print $1}'
adm
bin
daemon
...
...
```

`Sort` can also be used on the `df` command to print the usage column in desending order. Here's a normal `df` output.

```
$ df
Filesystem   1024-blocks Used    Available Capacity Mounted on
/dev/hda5    495714      291027 179086    62%      /
/dev/hda1    614672      558896 55776     91%      /dos
```

Now using -b option, which ignores any leading blanks when sorting, we use field 4 (+4), which is the 'capacity' column. Reversing the sort gives a clearer picture of the free space on the file systems.

```
$ df | sort -b -r +4
Filesystem   1024-blocks Used    Available Capacity Mounted on
/dev/hda1    614672      558896 55776     91%      /dos
/dev/hda5    495714      291027 179086    62%      /
```

I keep a copy of all my IP addresses in a flat file, since it's easier this way to see which addresses I have allocated. Sometimes I need to sort this file when I'm in 'administration mode'. To be able to sort the IP addresses into some sort of numerical order from the file I need to specify a dot (.) as the field separator. Now the only segment of the IP address that I need to worry about is the last part of the address construct, so the sort should start from that field, which is field 3. Here's the unsorted file.

```
$ pg iplist
193.132.80.123   dave tansley
193.132.80.23    HP printer 2nd floor
193.132.80.198   JJ. Peter's scanner
193.132.80.38    SPARE
193.132.80.78    P.Edron
```

Making sure I start on field 3, the file gets sorted:

```
$ sort -t. +3n iplist
193.132.80.23    HP printer 2nd floor
193.132.80.38    SPARE
193.132.80.78    P.Edron
193.132.80.123   dave tansley
193.132.80.198   JJ. Peter's scanner
```

11.3 Using uniq

The purpose of uniq is to strip or suppress duplicate lines from a text file. Uniq assumes the file has been sorted to get the correct results, though this is not set in stone: you can use any type of unordered text and you can even compare ordinary lines of text if you wish.

You may think that this is a bit like the unique option in the sort command. Well, it is in a way, but with one important difference. The sort's uniq option gets rid of all duplicates, whereas the uniq command does not get rid of all duplicates. What is a repeated line then? In uniq's case it means any line that is continuously repeated without a break. Here's an example.

```
$ pg myfile.txt
May Day
May Day
May Day
Going Down
May Day.
```

Uniq sees the first three 'May Day' lines as duplicates, but because there is a break in the fourth line with different text it does not acknowledge that the fifth line is a duplicate continuation of 'May Day'. Uniq will leave that line in.

Here's the general format for the command:

uniq -u d c   -f input-file output-file

Let's go over the options.

-u   Display only the lines that are not repeated

-d   Display only the repeated lines and one copy of each of those lines

-c   Print only a count of each line occurrence

-f   Where n is a number, the first n fields in are ignored

On some systems the '-f' option is not recognised, so if the '-f' does not work on your system use '-n' instead.

Using the text at the beginning of this section, we'll create a file containing that text for the examples, and start off by running uniq against the file.

```
$ uniq myfile.txt
May Day
Going Down
May Day
```

Note that the fifth line stays in which is the last line 'May Day'. If we had run 'sort -u' on the file it would only have returned 'May Day' and 'Going Down'.

11.3.1 Occurrences

Using the '-c' option displays the line numbers, the number of hits per repeated line found. Here uniq has found that there were three occurrences of the line 'May Day'.

```
$ uniq -c myfile.txt
      3 May Day
      1 Going Down
      1 May Day
```

Not unique

To see the lines that were not unique use the '-d' option:

```
$ uniq -d myfile.txt
May Day
```

Testing on specific fields

To test uniqueness on only part of a line, use '-n'. For example, '-5' means please ignore until after the fifth field; the fields start at number one.

To ignore the first field and only test for uniqueness on the second, use '-n2'. Here's a little file containing part-numbers with group codes as a second field:

```
$ pg parts.txt
AK123 OP
DK122 OP
EK999 OP
```

If we were to run uniq on this file we would get all lines returned, because each full line is different.

```
$ uniq -c parts.txt
      1 AK123 OP
      1 DK122 OP
      1 EK999 OP
```

Now if we were to specify that the test should only be carried out after the first field, the results will now be different. Uniq compares OP against OP against OP, all duplicates, so it will return only one line.

```
$ uniq -f2 parts.txt
AK123 OP
```

If the '-f' option returns errors, don't forget to use the following instead:

```
$ uniq -n2 parts.txt
AK123 OP
```

11.4 Using join

Join lets you join lines together from two sorted text files. The join command may be familiar to you if you are into SQL.

Here's how join works. You have two files, file1 and file2, sorted of course. Both files have a common element in them that relates to the other file. Using this relationship, the join 'folds' the two files together. It's a bit like updating a master file, or updating any file that holds elements that are common to both files.

The fields within the text files are normally separated by tabs or spaces, but you can specify another field separator if you like. Some systems say you should not have more than 20 fields in a file when using join; to be honest, if you've got more than 20 fields anyway you should be using a DBMS system.

To use join effectively, you first need to pre-sort any input files.

Here's the general format:

join [options] input-file1 input-file2.

Let's go over some of the more useful options.

-an   Where 'n' is a number. Use this to display unmatched pairs when joining. For example, -a1 means show unmatched pairs from the first file, -a2 means from the second file.

-o n.m   Where n means the file number and m means the field number. To display only the third field from file1 use 1.3. Each of these 'n.m' options must be separated by a comma, for example 1,3, 2,1.

-j n m   Where n means the file number and m is the field number. Use this if you wish to use other fields as join field.

-t   Field separator. Use this if the fields are not separated by a tab or space. For example, to specify a colon as the field separator use -t:

Let's create two text files, one containing names and street addresses called names.txt, the other containing the names and towns called town.txt.

```
$ pg names.txt
M.Golls 12 Hidd Rd
P.Heller The Acre
P.Willey 132 The Grove
T.Norms 84 Connaught Rd
K.Fletch 12 Woodlea

$ pg town.txt
M.Golls Norwich NRD
P.Willey Galashiels GDD
T.Norms Brandon BSL
K.Fletch Mildenhall MAF
```

11.4.1 Joining two files

The task is to join the two files together, so that the names hold the right addresses; for example, M.Golls' record states that the address is 12 Hidd Rd. The join key that will make this work is the names field which is field 0. As they are both the same, join will assume that's the field to use:

```
$ join names.txt town.txt
M.Golls  12 Hidd Rd Norwich NRD
P.Willey 132 The Grove Galashiels GDD
T.Norms  84 Connaught Rd Brandon BSL
K.Fletch 12 Woodlea Mildenhall MAF
```

Excellent, it worked. By default join will delete or suppress the second occurrence of the join key, which in our case is the names field.

Unmatched joins

Now what happens if one file has an entry with no match in the other file. You cannot tell if you use the join with no options, so always specify the '-a' option for both files to tell you. The following example says, please display if any file has an unmatched field.

```
$ join -a1  -a2 names.txt town.txt
M.Golls  12 Hidd Rd Norwich NRD
P.Heller The Acre
P.Willey 132 The Grove Galashiels GDD
T.Norms  84 Connaught Rd Brandon BSL
K.Fletch 12 Woodlea Mildenhall MAF
```

The output shows that P.Heller is unmatched in one of the files. Just run the command again but specifying only one file to see which file has the added entry. Like this:

```
$ join -a1 names.txt town.txt
```

Selective joins

To select the fields that you want joined, use the '-o' option. Suppose you wanted to create a file that had just the names and towns of the people. Join would still do the matching, but would display only the fields you specify. Here's how it's done.

To display only the first file and first field in that file, use 1.1; to display only the second field in the second file, use 2.2. Both options are separated by commas. The command is:

```
$ join  -o 1.1,2.2 names.txt town.txt
M.Golls Norwich
P.Willey Galashiels
T.Norms Brandon
K.Fletch Mildenhall
```

To create a new file with this information, simply redirect it to a new file, as follows:

```
$ join  -o 1.1,2.2 names.txt town.txt >towns.txt
```

You may wish to use other fields to join on; if so you can use the 'jn m' option. To use field 3 in file1 and field 2 in file2 as the join key you could use this command:

join -j1 3 -j2 2 file1 file2

Let's see an example of using different join fields. Here are two files:

```
$ pg pers
P.Jones Office Runner   ID897
S.Round UNIX admin      ID666
L.Clip  Personl Chief   ID982


$ pg pers2
Dept2C  ID897   6 years
Dept3S  ID666   2 years
Dept5Z  ID982   1 year
```

The file 'pers' contains names, job titles and personal IDs. The file 'pers2' contains their departments, personal IDs and completed worked years at the firm. We want to be able to join using field 4 of the file pers; this join should match field 2 of the file pers2. Here's the command and result.

```
$ join -j1 4 -j2 2 pers pers2
ID897 P.Jones Office Runner Dept2C 6 years
ID666 S.Round UNIX admin Dept3S    2 years
ID982 L.Clip Personl Chief Dept5Z  1 year
```

When using join, be careful about which field you are accessing. You may think you are accessing, say, field 4, but as far as join is concerned it may be field 5, and as a result join may not return any results. If you are not getting any results back, use awk to check the number of fields. For example, type $ awk '{print $4}' filename, to see if it matches up with how many fields you think there are.

11.5 Using cut

Cut allows you to cut columns or fields of text from text files or from standard input. When you have cut some text, you can then paste it to a text file. We'll look at paste in the next section. The general format of cut is:

cut [options] file1 file2

Let's look at some of the available options.

-c list	Use this to specify how many characters to cut.
-f fields	Use this to specify how many fields to cut.
-d	Use this to specify a different field separator, than a space or tab.

Using '-c' you can specify ranges or parts thereof.

-c1,5-7	Means cut characters one and then five to seven.
-c1-50	Means cut the first fifty characters.

Using the '-f' option is the same format:

-f 1,5 Means cut the fields one and five.

-f1 10-12 Means cut field one then fields ten to twelve.

Using one of the files 'pers' from the previous section, let's cut some text from the file. The file now has a colon (:) as the field separator.

```
$ pg pers
P.Jones:Office Runner:ID897
S.Round:UNIX admin:ID666
L.Clip:Personl Chief:ID982
```

11.5.1 Using the field separator

Because the fields in the file are separated by a colon (:), we use the field separator '-d' to specify the colon, i.e. '-d:'. As we are interested in the third field we can then type '-f3'. To extract the ID field, use the following command:

```
$ cut -d: -f3 pers
ID897T
ID666
ID982
```

11.5.2 Cutting specific fields

To cut other fields using the cut command you separate the field option with a comma. So, to cut fields 1 and 3 , which are the names and ID numbers, use:

```
$ cut -d: -f1,3 pers
P.Jones:ID897
S.Round:ID666
L.Clip:ID982
```

To cut the login names and their home directories from /etc/passwd we need to extract fields 1 and 6:

```
$ cut -d: -f1,6 /etc/passwd
gopher:/usr/lib/gopher-data
ftp:/home/ftp
peter:/home/apps/peter
dave:/home/apps/dave
...
```

If you are using cut with absolute numbers use the '-c' option. When using this method, make sure you know which character to start at and end on. Generally I do not use this option except on fixed field lengths or filenames.

When message files come into my system, I look at part of the filename to identify the source of the file. To get this information I need to extract the last three characters of the file name. Based on this I know which directory to save the files in. Here is a sample listing of the filenames followed by the cut command I would use.

```
2231DG
2232DP
2236DK

$ ls 223*|cut -c4-6
1DG
2DP
6DK
```

Using part of an ls -l output, and a different example, let's see how using the '-c' option would work:

-rw-r--r--	1 dave	admin	56 Apr 26 20:40 tr2.txt
-rw-r--r--	1 dave	admin	71 Apr 26 21:20 trpro.txt

To be able to cut characters, we first need to count how many characters in the ls -l listings we want. To show permissions use cut -c1-10. However, it can be rather slow using this method, so use other tools first to get the information out. To cut user information about who is on the system use:

```
$ who -u| cut -c1-8
root
dave
peter
```

11.6 **Using** paste

Using cut you extract columns or fields of data from a text file or standard input. With paste you can then use this data to paste the contents of the file together. When pasting data from two different sources, it pays to sort them first; you should also make sure that the two files have an equal number of lines.

Paste puts the text together in a row by row method. By default, when paste joins, it converts all the new lines into tabs or spaces unless the '-d' option is specified, then this will become the field separator.

The format for paste is:

paste -d -s - file1 file2

Let's look at the options.

-d   Tells paste to use a different field delimiter, rather then a tab or space; for
       example, to separate the fields using an '@', use -d@.

-s   Merge the lines rather than paste row by row.

-      Use the standard input for each dash. For example, `ls -l|paste` means
       to display output in a one-column format only.

Using the following two files from a previous cut, we will now paste them.

```
$ pg pas1
ID897
ID666
ID982

$ pg pas2
P.Jones
S.Round
L.Clip
```

The basic `paste` pastes the two columns of text side by side:

```
$ paste pas1 pas2
ID897    P.Jones
ID666    S.Round
ID982    L.Clip
```

11.6.1 Specifying columns

You can choose which column to paste first by just switching the filenames around:

```
$ paste pas2 pas1
P.Jones ID897
S.Round ID666
L.Clip  ID982
```

11.6.2 Using a different field separator

To create a file with a different field separator instead of the tabs or spaces use '-d'.
Here we paste the contents, but use the colon (:) as the separator.

```
$ paste -d: pas2 pas1
P.Jones:ID897
S.Round:ID66
```

To merge the two lines, instead of using a row by row method use the '-s' option. Here we paste the names followed by the ID numbers on the following line.

```
$ paste -s pas2 pas1
P.Jones S.Round L.Clip
ID897   ID666   ID982
```

11.6.3 Piping into a `paste` command

A useful option of the `paste` command is the hyphen (-), which allows you to read from standard input for each hyphen. Using a space as the field separator, you can display a listing of a directory in a four-column format.

```
$ pwd
$ /etc
$ ls | paste -d" " - - - -
init.d rc rc.local rc.sysinit
rc0.d rc1.d rc2.d rc3.d
rc4.d rc5.d rc6.d
```

Alternatively, you can display the output in just a one-column format.

```
$ ls | paste -d"" -
init.d
rc
rc.local
rc.sysinit
rc0.d
rc1.d
...
```

11.7 Using `split`

`Split` allows you to divide large text files into smaller files. It's surprising how quickly files can grow and, when you need to transfer files, it's sometimes easier to split them up first. When using `vi` or other tools such as `sort`, you can have problems if the file is too big for the working buffer so sometimes you are not given a choice; you have to create smaller chunks out of the file.

Here is the general format of the split command:

split -output-file-size input-filename output-filename

where output-file-size is the number of lines you want the file to be split by. When `split` looks at the file output-file-size option specified it will try to divide the files into 1 000 lines each. If we had a file containing 2 800 lines, then three files would be created, containing 1 000, 1 000 and 800 lines respectively. Each created filename would be in the format x[aa] to x[zz], where x is the first letter of the filename and [aa] [zz], are the sequential character combinations of the rest of the filename. The following example helps to explain this.

Assuming we used split for our 2 800-line file called `bigone.txt`, `split` would generate the following files:

```
$ split bigone.txt
xaa
xab
xac
```

The file sizes would be:

Size	Filename
1000	xaa
1000	xab
800	xac

We will now use the output-file-size option to split up a file. Here's our big file of six lines length.

```
$ pg split1
this is line1
this is line2
this is line3
this is line4
this is line5
this is line6
```

Now to split the file up into chunks of two lines per file, use

```
$ split -2 split1
```

Let's see what `split` has produced.

```
$ ls -lt |head
total 205
-rw-r--r--   1 dave      admin        28 Apr 30 13:12 xaa
-rw-r--r--   1 dave      admin        28 Apr 30 13:12 xab
-rw-r--r--   1 dave      admin        28 Apr 30 13:12 xac
    ...
```

The file contained six lines, and we wanted to split it using two lines for each file. Split has done this, and named each file in character sequence order. To make sure the file is OK, let's have a look at the contents of xac, one of the new files.

```
$ pg xac
this is line5
this is line6
```

11.8 Conclusion

We have looked at tools that deal primarily with dividing and merging text files. The tools that allow us to carry out these tasks are `sort`, `join`, `split`, `uniq`, `cut` and `paste`. We have looked at each one using different examples, and seen how using these tools enables you to be more productive in your work. Now when you have to hack around a raw text file, you know what tools you need to turn the data into more meaningful information.

CHAPTER 12

Using tr

12.1 About tr

Tr is a utility that lets you translate characters by substitution or deletion from standard input. Tr is used mainly for stripping off control characters from files or doing character case conversions. When you use tr you generally pass it two strings: string1 is what you are searching for and string2 is what you want done with the translation. When tr is initially invoked, the characters in string1 are mapped across into the characters of string2; the conversion will then begin.

In this chapter we will cover:

- converting lower to upper case;
- stripping files of control characters; and
- deleting blank lines.

The formats of the tr command with its most used options are:

tr -c -d -s ["string1_to_translate_from"] ["string2_to_translate_to"] input_file

where

   -c   replaces the set of characters in string1 with a complement of itself, so
         long as the characters are in the ASCII range

   -d   deletes all input characters of string1

   -s   removes all but the first in a sequence of repeated characters; it squeezes
         the repeating characters into one.

Input_file is the name of the file you want translated. Although you can take the input from other forms, this is the most widely used method.

12.1.1 Character ranges

When using tr you can specify ranges or lists of characters as patterns that make up your strings. These look like regular expressions, but in fact they are not. With tr you can only use ranges and lists or individual characters when specifying string1 or string2 contents.

[a-z]	A string of characters within a-z.
[A-Z]	A string of characters within A-Z.
[0-9]	A string of numbers.
/octal	A three-digit octal number representing any valid ASCII character.
[O*n]	Means the character 'O' occurring as many times as specified by 'n'. So [O*2] would mean OO. Any string up to and including 00.

Most tr variants support character classes and shorthand control character notion. The character class format of [:class], includes amongst others, alnum, alpha, blank, upper, lower, cntrl, space, digit, graph etc. Table 12.1 contains the shorthand way of representing some of the more widely used control characters instead of using the three-digit octal notation, which is also listed.

When replacing a string or range of characters with a single character, please note that the character does not go inside the square brackets ([ ]). Some systems are tolerant of using the square brackets; for instance you can get away with either ["\012"] or "\012". Tr is quite forgiving in the use of quotes as well, so don't be surprised if it still works when you use single instead of double quotes.

Like most system tools, tr is not immune to special characters, so if you want to match one of these then you should first escape it with a backslash. For example,

Table 12.1 *Different ways of specifying control characters using* pr

Shorthand	Meaning	Octal
\a	Control-G the bell sound	\007
\b	Control-H the backspace key	\010
\f	Control-L the formfeed	\014
\n	Control-J the new line	\012
\r	Control-M the carriage return key	\015
\t	Control-I the tab key	\011
\v	Control-X	\030

to specify the left curly bracket ({) you must type \{, to disable the curly bracket's special meaning.

12.1.2 Saving output

If you wish to save the output of your results, you have to redirect them to a file. The example below redirects output to a file called results.txt. The input file is oops.txt.

```
$ tr -s "[a-z]"< oops.txt >results.txt
```

Let's now look at some examples.

12.1.3 Getting rid of repeated characters

Looking at the file below, it contains some typing errors. This is easily done, of course – how many times have you been in the vi editor and accidentally kept a key depressed?

```
$ pg oops.txt
And the cowwwwws went homeeeeeeee
Or did theyyyy
```

If we wanted to get rid of the recurring letters or squeeze the duplicated letters together, we can use the '-s' option. We'll use [a-z] as they are all alpha characters. The input file is redirected into tr.

```
$ tr -s "[a-z]"< oops.txt
And the cows went home
Or did they
```

All the duplicate characters have now been 'squeezed' into one, so to speak. I could have piped the file oops.txt using cat if I wanted to; the results are still the same.

```
$ cat oops.txt | tr -s "[a-z]"
And the cows went home
Or did they
```

12.1.4 Deleting blank lines

To delete blank lines, we 'squeeze' them out of a file. Here's a file called plane.txt containing some blank lines between text.

```
$ pg plane.txt
987932  Spitfire


190992  Lancaster


238991  Typhoon
```

We'll use '-s' which means squeeze the blank lines. The octal value for new lines is \012. Here's the command.

```
$ tr -s "[\012]" < plane.txt
987932  Spitfire
190992  Lancaster
238991  Typhoon
```

Alternatively we could have used the shorthand notion for the new line which is '\n'. We can use single or double quotes (double quotes is usual though).

```
$ tr -s ["\n"] < plane.txt
987932  Spitfire
190992  Lancaster
238991  Typhoon
```

12.1.5 Upper to lower case

Using tr to change character cases must be one of its most widely used options, after control character deletes. To convert, all we need to do is specify lower case '[a-z]' in what we're translating from and upper case '[A-Z]' in what we are translating to.

In the first example a string is echoed into tr containing a mixed set of characters.

```
$ echo "May Day, May Day, Going Down.." | tr "[a-z]" "[A-Z]"
MAY DAY, MAY DAY, GOING DOWN..
```

Alternatively, I could have used the character classes [:lower:] and [:upper:].

```
$ echo "May Day, May Day, Going Down.." | tr "[:lower:]" "[:upper:]"
MAY DAY, MAY DAY, GOING DOWN..
```

To translate a text file from upper to lower case and place it in a new file use this format:

cat file-to-translate | tr "[A-Z]" "[a-z]" > new-file-name

where 'file-to-translate' holds the file you want translated and 'new-file-name' is what you want the new file to be called. For example:

cat myfile | tr "[A-Z]" "[a-z]" > lower_myfile

12.1.6 Lower to upper case

Converting lower to upper case is just the reverse of the previous section. Here are a couple of examples.

```
$ echo " Look for the route, or make the route" | tr "[a-z]" "[A-Z]"
 LOOK FOR THE ROUTE, OR MAKE THE ROUTE

$ echo "May Day, May Day, Going Down.." | tr "[:upper:]" "[:lower:]"
may day, may day, going down..
```

To translate a text file from lower to upper case and place it in a new file use this format:

cat file-to-translate | tr "[a-z]" "[A-Z]" > new-file-name

where 'file-to-translate' holds the file you want translated and 'new-file-name' is what you want the new file to be called. For example:

cat myfile | tr "[a-z]" "[A-Z]" > upper_myfile

12.1.7 Deleting certain characters

Occasionally, you may need to delete columns from a downloaded file that may contain only letters or numbers. To be able to do this you need to use the '-c' and '-s' options together.

The file below contains part of a diary for a week. The task is to get rid of all the numbers and just leave the days of the week. You'll see the week days are in both upper and lower case format, so we have to use both character ranges, [a-z] and [A-Z]. The command 'tr -cs "[a-z][A-Z]" "[\012*]"', will take all the file contents that are not in [a-z] or [A-Z] (all alpha characters) held in string1, and convert them to new lines. Using the '-s' option tells tr to 'squeeze' all the new lines. Using the '-c' keeps all the alpha characters intact. Here's the file holding the diary info, followed by the tr command.

```
$ pg diary.txt
monday 10:50
Tuesday 15:30
wednesday 15:30
thurday 10:30
Friday 09.20
```

```
$ tr -cs "[a-z][A-Z]" "[\012*]" < diary.txt
monday
Tuesday
wednesday
thurday
Friday
```

12.1.8 Translating control characters

Tr's no. 1 use is translating control characters, especially during DOS to UNIX downloads, when you have forgotten to set the ftp option on carriage returns to linefeed conversion.

Below is a text file that's been deliberately transferred with no transfer options set. It's part of a stationery request. Here are the control characters displayed using cat -v.

```
$ cat -v stat.tr
Boxes paper^^^^^^12^M
Clips metal^^^^^^50^M
Pencils-meduim^^^^^^10^M
^Z
```

We have suspect tabs '^^^^^^'; each line is terminated with control-M and control-Z at the end-of-file. Here's how to remedy this.

We are going to have to use the '-s' squeeze option. Looking at the ASCII chart, the octal code for '^' is 136. The value for ^M is '015', the value for a tab is '011', and the ^Z is '032'. We'll complete this task in steps.

To replace the '^^^^^^' with tabs the command is "\136" "[\011*]". The results are then redirected to a temporary worker file called stat.tmp.

```
$ tr -s "[\136]" "[\011*]" < stat.tr  >stat.tmp
Boxes paper 12^M
Clips metal 50^M
Pencils-medium 10^M
^Z
```

To replace all the ^Ms at the end of each line with new lines, and get rid of that ^z use \n. Remember we are now taking the input from our temporary file stat.tmp.

```
$ tr -s "[\015\032]" "\n" < stat.tmp
Boxes paper     12
Clips metal     50
Pencils-medium  10
```

All control characters have now gone, and the file is now ready for use.

12.1.9 Quick conversions

If you have a file that just needs the ^Ms removed and replaced with new linefeeds use this command:

```
$ tr -s "[\015]" "\n" < input_file
```

Alternatively, you can use this command – it will do the same translation:

```
$ tr -s "[\r]" "[\n]" < input_file
```

Alternatively, this command will do the same translation again:

```
$ tr -s "\r" "\n" < input_file
```

Another general DOS to UNIX converter is this command:

```
$ tr -s "[\015\032]" "[\012*]" < input_file
```

which deletes all ^Ms and ^Zs and replaces them with linefeeds.

This command will delete all tabs and replace them with spaces.

```
$ tr -s "[\011]" "[\040*]" < input_file
```

To replace all the colons in the passwd file with tabs to make it more readable, enclose the colon in quotes and specify the octal tab value which is '011' in the replacement string. Here's the passwd file first, then the tr command to do the job.

```
$ pg passwd
halt:*:7:0:halt:/sbin:/sbin/halt
mail:*:8:12:mail:/var/spool/mail:
news:*:9:13:news:/var/spool/news:
uucp:*:10:14:uucp:/var/spool/uucp:

$ tr -s "[:]" "[\011]" < passwd
halt    *    7      0      halt    /sbin    /sbin/halt
mail    *    8      12     mail    /var/spool/mail
news    *    9      13     news    /var/spool/news
uucp    *    10     14     uucp    /var/spool/uucp
```

Alternatively, the following will get the same results; we specify the shorthand notation of the tab key:

```
$ tr "[:]" "[\t]" < passwd
```

12.1.10 Matching more than one character

To match more than one character use the [character*n] format. Below is a listing from the hard disks on one of my systems. The file contains disks that have been registered or have not been recognized by the system. The first column contains numbers. If that column does not contain all zeros, then the corresponding disk in column 2 has been registered.

Looking at all zeros gets boring sometimes, so I like to replace them with a character that catches the eye, so I know instantly which disks are 'in' and which disks are 'out'. Here's part of the file.

```
$ pg hdisk.txt
1293 hdisk3
4512 hdisk12
0000 hdisk5
4993 hdisk12
2994 hdisk7
```

By looking at the file I can see that I have one hard disk that is not registered, so to change all the zeros to, say, an asterisk, we can use the pattern [0*4], which means match at least four zeros. The replacement string just contains the asterisk. Here's the command and result of the filter:

```
$ tr "[0*4]" "*" <hdisk.txt
1293 hdisk3
4512 hdisk12
**** hdisk5
4993 hdisk12
2994 hdisk7
```

Now from looking at the file, I can tell straightaway which disk is not registered.

12.2 Conclusion

Tr is used mainly for character conversions, or stripping out control characters. All of the functions used in this chapter can be accomplished using sed, but some people prefer to use tr. Tr is quick and easy, and does the job.

## PART 3

The login environment

CHAPTER 13

The login environment

When you log in to the system, before you are even presented with the command prompt, a couple of tasks happen. After you have typed in your login name and password, the system checks that you are indeed a valid user. It does this by checking the /etc/passwd file. If your login name is OK and the password you entered is valid, the next process can begin, which is your login environment.

In this chapter we will cover:

- the process of logging in;

- the /etc/profile;

- the $HOME.profile; and

- customizing your $HOME.profile.

Before we look at the next process let's first look at the /etc/passwd file, which is a text file. You can alter any of the text fields including the password fields, so be careful. The passwd file contains seven fields, each of which is separated by a colon. Below is a partial listing of a passwd file. I have put column numbers at the top, so you can easily identify each field.

```
[ 1 ][      2         ][ 3 ][ 4 ][    5    ][       6        ][  7  ]
kvp:JFqMmk9.uRioA:405:413:K.V.Pally:/home/sysdev/kvp:/bin/sh
dhw:hi/G4U1CUd9aI,B/0J:407:401:D.Whitely:/home/dept47/dhw:/bin/sh
aec:ILgHtxJ9kXtSc,B/GI:408:401:A.E.Cloody:/b_user/dept47/aec:/bin/sh
gdw:iLFu9BB8RNjpc,B/MK:409:401:G.D.Wilcom:/b_user/dept47/gdw:/bin/sh
```

Let's look at some of the fields. The first field is the login name The second field is the encrypted password. The fifth field is the user's full name. The sixth field is the user's home directory. The seventh field is the shell that is to be used by the user. In this case '/bin/sh' means the default shell which is by convention the Bourne shell.

There are other types of passwd files around; one version is where the actual passwd field is held in another file. The above is the most common format.

After a successful login, two environment files are then executed. The first is a file called /etc/profile and the second is a file called .profile, located in your $HOME (home) directory.

There are other initializing files that are processed, but we are only concerned with the profile files.

13.1 The /etc/profile

The profile file located in /etc is read automatically by everyone when they log in. This file will generally contain:

- global or local environment variables;

- PATH information;

- terminal settings;

- security commands; and

- message of the day or disclaimer information.

Here's a brief explanation of the above points.

Certain *global environment variables* are set so that users and their shell processes and applications can have access to them.

PATH holds the location of directories containing executable, library, or just plain files so that you locate them quickly.

Terminal settings lets the system know about the more general characteristics of your terminal.

Security commands will include file creation modes, or double login prompts for sensitive areas.

Message of the day is a text file holding any forthcoming events for users to see when they log in, or any disclaimer messages.

Here is an /etc/profile, which will be discussed after the listing.

```
$ pg /etc/profile
#!/bin/sh
#
trap "" 2 3
```

```
#  Set LOGNAME
export LOGNAME


# set additional MAN paths.
MANPATH=/usr/opt/sybase/man
export MANPATH


#  Set TZ.
if [ -f /etc/TIMEZONE ]
then
.  /etc/TIMEZONE
fi


#  Set TERM.
if [ -z "$TERM" ]
then
  TERM=vt220      # for standard async terminal/console
  export TERM
fi


  #  Allow the user to break the Message-Of-The-Day only.
  trap "trap "2"  2
  if [ -f /usr/bin/cat ] ; then
    cat -s /etc/motd
  fi
  trap "" 2
  if [ -f /usr/bin/mail ] ; then
    if mail -e ; then
      echo "Hey guess what? you have mail"
    fi
  fi
  ;;
esac


#  set the umask for more secure operation
umask 022
fi
#  set environments
SYSHOME=/appdvb/menus
ASLBIN=/asl_b/bin
UDTHOME=/dbms_b/ud
UDTBIN=/dbms_b/ud/bin
PAGER=pg
NOCHKLPREQ=1
PATH=$PATH:$UDBIN:$ASLBIN
export PATH UDTHOME UDTBIN PAGER NOCHKLPREQ SYSHOME


trap  2 3
```

```
# Set variable SAVEDSTTY so that it can be used to recover the
# stty settings on coming out of the audit system.
SAVEDSTTY=`stty -g`
export SAVEDSTTY


# log all connections to syslog
logger -p local7.info -t login  $LOGNAME `tty`
trap 'logger -p local7.info -t logout $LOGNAME `tty`' 0


# suppress creation of core dumps
ulimit -c 0
#
# check if users are logged in more than twice apart from...
case $LOGNAME in
idink | psalon | dave)
    ;;
  *)
    PID=${$};export PID
    Connected=`who | awk '{print $1}' | fgrep -xc ${LOGNAME}`
    if [ "$Connected" -gt  2 ]
    then
        echo
        echo 'You are logged in more than twice.'
        echo
        who -u | grep $LOGNAME
        echo
        echo 'Enter <CR> to exit \c'
        read FRED
        kill -15 $PID
    fi
    ;;
esac
# set the prompt to hold the user id
PS1="$LOGNAME >"
```

Do not worry if you do not understand some of the commands; they are
all covered later in the book. You can then refer to this listing as and when you
like.

The first line traps a couple of signals, which stop users from using the QUIT
or <CTRL-C> key to break out of the file execution.

Next we export the LOGNAME. I have added extra man pages in the system.
MANPATH will add these on to the existing man pages search list.

Check the time zone file and source it if it is present. Set the emulation to
vt220.

Reset the trap so that users can break out of the message of the day file, but
reset it afterwards.

Set up the mail message (that's the message you get when you have new
mail).

Set the umask value, which enables file creation, with certain permission bits set by default.

Initialize environment variables. Set the path up and export it so they are available to everyone.

Reset the trap to catch signals, <CTRL-C> and QUIT.

Save the default stty setting now, so that we can reinitialize the terminal settings when the users come out of the audit system.

Log all connections to /var/adm/messages, which is my default syslog file.

Using the ulimit command, you can limit the number of core dumps or hex dumps.

A little code segment allows users to log in twice only concurrently, apart from three people (idink, psalom, dave). Kick the others out if they try to log in more than twice.

Finally set the command prompt to their login name.

Your environment is now set for global use. Now let's customize it a bit with our own profile.

13.2 Your $HOME .profile

When the /etc/profile has been executed, you are then put into your own $HOME directory. Looking back at the passwd file, this location is the second from the last field.

You may regard this as your home, as this is where you keep all your private stuff.

If there is a .profile present the system will source this file. To source means not to create another shell for this process, thus keeping all your existing environments (/etc/profile) intact from any changes the file (.profile) would make otherwise. When you create another process, your local shell variables, for all intents and purposes, are overwritten.

Back to the .profile. Generally when an account is set up, a skeleton profile is always present. One important thing to remember is that you can override the settings made in the /etc/profile by making a new entry in your .profile with a different value or by using the unset command. It's up to you if you want to customize the file, so let's look at a standard .profile file.

```
$ pg .profile
#.profile
set -a
MAIL=/usr/mail/${LOGNAME:?}
PATH=$PATH
export PATH
#
```

Let's now tailor the file.

We want to set up a couple of environment variables, like EDITOR, so cron and other applications know about the editor we are using. I do not like using vt220, so I'll stick to vt100. We'll use that for our TERM variable.

We can also create a bin directory and add it to our path. It's always a good idea to have a bin directory, as this is where you can keep all your scripts and, by adding it to your PATH, you do not have to type the full path name of the script to execute it, just type the script name.

Who wants to have a command prompt showing their own login name? You'd be surprised. I don't. I would rather have the current directory path as my prompt, or maybe the hostname of the system that I am using. Here's how to set the hostname.

```
$ PS1="`hostname`>"
dns-server>
```

Or for the current directory you are in:

```
$ PS1="\`pwd\`>"
/home/dave>
```

If the above prompt returns 'pwd', use this instead:

```
PS1='$PWD >';
```

For my secondary prompt (this gets used when you are doing a multi-line command at the command prompt) I like to have the copyright sign ©. The ASCII character value for that is the octal number 251; in decimal it is 169.

```
$ PS2="`echo "\251"`:"
/home/dave> while read line
©:do
©:echo $line
©:done
```

If it's LINUX, then...

To use an octal value in an echo command use

```
$ PS2="`echo -e "\251"`:"
```

I also have access to our admin area, located in /usr/admin, so let's add that as an environment variable, so I can easily cd to the directory.

```
ADMIN=/usr/adm
```

I also like to know how many users are on the system as soon as I log in. You can use the who and wc command to do this.

```
$ echo "`who|wc -l` users are on today"
```

19 users are on today.

Let's add the above to our .profile file. For any changes in the .profile or /etc/profile to take effect, you either have to log out then back in again or source the file. To source a file the format is:

. /pathname/filename

To source the .profile file just type

```
$. .profile
```

and if the above does not work, try

```
$. ./profile
```

Here's our newly amended .profile file.

```
$ pg .profile
#.profile
MAIL=/usr/mail/${LOGNAME:?}
PATH=$PATH:$HOME:bin
#
EDITOR=vi
TERM vt100
ADMIN=/usr/adm
PS1="`hostname`>"
PS2="`echo "\0251"`:"
export EDITOR TERM ADMIN PATH PS1
echo "`who|wc -l` users are on to-day"
```

13.3 Using stty

Stty is a command that lets you set up your terminal characteristics. To find out what your current stty options are, use stty -a.

```
$ stty -a
speed 9600 baud; rows 24; columns 80; line = 0;
intr =^C; quit =^\; erase =^?; kill =^U; eof =^D; eol =<undef>;
eol2 =<undef>; start =^Q; stop =^S; susp =^Z; rprnt =^R; werase = ^W;
lnext =^V; flush =^O; min =1; time =0;
```

```
-parenb -parodd cs8 -hupcl -cstopb cread -clocal -crtscts
-ignbrk -brkint -ignpar -parmrk -inpck -istrip -inlcr -igncr icrnl ixon
-ixoff -iuclc -ixany -imaxbel
opost -olcuc -ocrnl onlcr -onocr -onlret -ofill -ofdel nl0 cr0 tab0 bs0
vt0 ff0 isig icanon iexten echo echoe echok -echonl -noflsh -xcase
-tostop -echoprt echoctl echoke
```

One of the most common problems when setting up a terminal is that the backspace key does not work, i.e. it is not destructive. My stty command reports that it is using ^? for the backspace key; well it isn't working. Using <CTRL-H> will probably backspace and destroy any previous characters so let's use stty to sort that out. The general format to set an stty option on the command line is:

stty name character.

Here's how to set the backspace to ^H:

```
$ stty erase '\^H'
```

You may have problems using the above stty command to work in the .profile file, because stty may expect an actual 'control H' sequence. To fix that use the following format when you are in vi.

Hold the control key down with the v key, then release the v key, and then hit the H key.

The most common stty names you will come into contact with are:

Name	Key	Meaning
intr	^C	terminate a process
echo		turn echo on
-echo		turn echo off
eof	^D	end-of-file, log out
kill	^Y	delete a line
start	^Q	scroll text of screen
stop	^S	stop scrolling text on screen

A very useful stty option is:

stty -g

This option allows you to save the current contents of stty in a readable format, so that it can be assigned back to stty later on, just like we saw in the /etc/profile earlier. All you have to do is put the contents of stty -g into a variable, do any stty changes you require then read it back to stty when you have finished.

A good case for using this is when you are changing `stty` values and you accidentally mess up your terminal; you can then easily restore the original setting. Below is an example of saving then restoring the current settings of `stty`. We use `stty -g` to turn the echo off then restore the original setting at the end of the script.

```
$ pg password
#!/bin/sh
# password
# show use of the restoring stty environment
SAVEDSTTY=`stty -g`
stty -echo
echo "\nGive me that password :\c"
read PASSWD
echo "\nyour password is $PASSWD"
stty $SAVEDSTTY


$ sttypass
Give me that password :
your password is bong
```

If it's LINUX, then...

To let LINUX know you are going to use escape characters in strings, the `echo` command should start 'echo -e'

```
SAVEDSTTY=`stty -g`
stty -echo
echo "\nGive me that password :\c"
read PASSWD
echo "\nyour password is $PASSWD"
stty $SAVEDSTTY
```

The `stty` command allows you to tweak your terminal, printers or modems; it is very versatile. Be careful though when using `stty`; do not use a key that is already in use, or it will not work.

13.4 Creating a `.logout` file

One of the drawbacks of using the Bourne shell is that unlike other shells, it does not have a `.logout` file. This file holds commands that you want executed just before your session is terminated when you issue an `exit` command.

But by using the `trap` command (more on `trap` and signals later in the book), the Bourne shell can have its own `.logout` file. Here's how to do it. Edit your .profile file and put the following command on the last line of your .profile file, then save and exit the file.

trap "$HOME/.logout" 0

Now create a .logout file and enter any commands you want executed. You can put in anything you like.

```
$ pg .logout
rm -f $HOME/*.log
rm -f $HOME/*.tmp
echo "Bye...bye $LOGNAME"
```

The .logout file is called when the user exits. When a user exits from a shell a signal 0 is sent, which means exit from the current shell. The line in the .profile will trap this signal, and execute the file .logout, before control is passed back to the shell, to continue the log off process.

13.5 Conclusion

You can customize your $HOME .profile to suit your needs. This chapter has showed you how you can override system-wide settings to suit your preference. There are many ways you can customize your environment, from greetings messages to terminal characteristics.

CHAPTER 14

Environment and shell variables

To make your time in the shell more productive, you have shell variables at your disposal. Shell variables are names that hold values. A value can be a path name, a filename, or maybe a number, the shell treats any assignment as a string of text.

There are two types of variables, local and environment. Strictly speaking there are four, but the other two are read-only and are considered special variables used in passing parameters to shell scripts.

In this chapter we will cover:

- shell variables;
- environment variables;
- variable substitution;
- exporting variables;
- special variables;
- passing information to scripts; and
- using positional parameters on system commands.

14.1 What is a shell variable?

Variables let you customize your working environment. You use variables to hold information that you want to use yourself, to let the system know more about you. Variables are also used to hold constant information. For instance, there is a variable called EDITOR. Now there are not that many editors around, but which is your favourite? Assign this name to the EDITOR variable, and that's what you'll use all the time if you use cron or other applications that require you to use an editor. The system looks for the value held in the variable EDITOR, and will use that as your default editor.

Here's an example. Our audit system has logs that need to be edited. When I select this option from the menu, the application looks for my EDITOR variable; it sees the value is vi, and then knows to use this editor.

Here's another example; to log in to my sybase system, I would have to type this command:

```
$ isql -Udavet -Pabcd -Smethsys
```

where the -S is the server name I'm connecting to. Now I have a variable that holds the server name called DSQUERY. I assign the server name to DSQUERY; now when I log in if I do not supply a server name with '-S', the application looks for the DSQUERY variable, and uses that value as the server name. All I need to do now to log in is type

```
$ isql -Udavet -Pabcd
```

This is how most applications work

14.2 Local variables

Local variables are what you would use in a script for your current shell lifetime, then discard. For instance, a local variable called file_name may have the value loops.doc. This value is important to you but only for the lifetime of your current shell; you do not keep that value if you start another process in your shell or log out. This is good news because you cannot make this type of variable available to other shells or processes.

Table 14.1 contains various variable modes of action.

When using variables some users like to enclose them in curly brackets, which stops the shell from misinterpreting the value of the variable. You do not have to, but this can be useful.

To assign a local variable the format is:

$variable_name = value or **${variable_name = value}**

Notice that there are spaces either side of the = sign. If the value contains a space then enclose the whole value with double quotes. You can use lower or upper case letters for shell variables.

Table 14.1 *Different modes of variable assignments*

Variable_name = value	Assign a value to variable_name
Variable_name + value	If variable_name is set, assign value to variable_name
Variable_name:?value	If variable_name is not set, display defined user error message
Variable_name?value	If variable_name is not set, display a system error message
Variable_name: = value	If variable_name is not set, assign value to variable_name
Variable_name:-value	As above, but value is not assigned to variable_name – it can be substituted

14.2.1 Displaying a variable

To display a value of a single variable use the `echo` command and prefix the variable name with a $. Here are some examples.

```
$ GREAT_PICTURE="die hard"
$ echo ${GREAT_PICTURE}
die hard

$ DOLLAR=99
$ echo ${DOLLAR}
99

$ LAST_FILE=ZLPSO.txt
$ echo ${LAST_FILE}
ZLPSO.txt
```

You can also combine variables. Here we assign an error message and the environment variable `LOGNAME` to the variable `error_msg`.

```
$ ERROR_MSG=" Sorry this file does not exist user $LOGNAME"
$ echo ${ERROR_MSG}
Sorry this file does not exist user dave
```

In the above example, the shell first displays the text, then sees the variable $LOGNAME; then it expands the variable to display the value of the variable.

14.2.2 Clearing a variable

To take a value away from a variable, use the `unset` command:

unset variable_name

```
$ PC=enterprise
$ echo ${PC}
enterprise
$ unset PC
$ echo ${PC}
$
```

14.2.3 Displaying all local shell variables

To see all your locally defined shell variables use the set command.

```
$ set
...
PWD=/root
SHELL=/bin/sh
SHLVL=1
TERM=vt100
UID=7
USER=dave
dollar=99
great_picture=die hard
last_file=ZLPSO.txt
```

The output from set can be quite long; when you look at the output you'll see that the shell has set some up for you to make your working environment easier.

14.2.4 Variable values together

You can join variables together by daisy-chaining the variables:

echo ${variable_name}${variable_name} ...

```
$ FIRST="Bruce "
$ SURNAME=Willis
$ echo ${FIRST}${SURNAME}
Bruce Willis
```

14.2.5 Testing if a variable is set (substitution)

Occasionally you will want to test if a variable has been set or initialized. If it hasn't, you will want to use another value. The format for this is:

${variable:-value}

which means use the variable if it is set, if not use value instead. Here's an example.

```
$ COLOUR=blue
$ echo "The sky is ${COLOUR:-grey} today"
The sky is blue today
```

A variable called 'colour' has the value of 'blue'. When `echo` prints the variable colour, it will test to see if the variable has been set previously. It has, so it will use that value. Now let's clear that value and see what happens.

```
$ COLOUR=blue
$ unset COLOUR
$ echo "The sky is ${COLOUR:-grey} today"
The sky is grey today
```

The above example does not assign the actual value to the variable; to do this we need to use the format

   ${variable: = value}

A more useful example follows. It asks for a time to run a payroll, and what type of payroll should be run. Hitting `enter` on both the value's time and type will mean that these two variables have not been set by the user; the new default values (03:00 and Weekly), will then be used. The values are then passed on to the `at` command to submit the job to run later.

```
$ pg vartest
#!/bin/sh
# vartest
echo  "what time do you wish to start the payroll [03:00]:"
read TIME
echo " process to start at ${TIME:=03:00} OK"
echo  "Is it a monthly or weekly run [Weekly]:"
read RUN_TYPE
echo "Run type is ${RUN_TYPE:=Weekly}"
at -f $RUN_TYPE $TIME
```

Here's what the output looks like when you run it hitting `enter` on both fields.

```
$ vartest
what time do you wish to start the payroll [03:00]:
 process to start at 03:00 OK
Is it a monthly or weekly run [Weekly]:
Run type is Weekly

warning: commands will be executed using /bin/sh
job 15 at 1999-05-14 03:00
```

You can also test to find out if a variable has a value set, and then exit with a system error message. The following example tests if the variable file has a value.

```
$ echo "The file is ${FILES:?}"
sh: files: parameter null or not set
```

The above was not very informative, but you can make it more user-friendly by adding your own message instead.

```
$ echo "The file is ${FILES:?" sorry cannot locate the variable files"}"

sh: files:  sorry cannot locate the variable files
```

To test if a variable contains a value, but in case it does not, return (nothing) an empty string, use the following:

${variable: + value}

If you want to initialize a variable with an empty string use this method:

variable = ""

```
$ DESTINATION=""
```

14.2.6 Using variables to hold arguments for system commands

You can also use variables to hold information that you can then use to substitute arguments for system commands. In the next example we use variables to hold filename information to copy a file. The variable source holds the path to the passwd file and dest holds the destination of that file to be used in the cp command.

```
$ SOURCE="/etc/passwd"
$ DEST="/tmp/passwd.bak"
$ cp ${SOURCE} ${DEST}
```

In this example, the variable device holds the tape device path, which we then use in the mt command to rewind a tape.

```
$ DEVICE="/dev/rmt/0n"
$ mt -f ${DEVICE} rewind
```

14.2.7 Making a variable read-only

When you assign a variable, you may not want the value to be changed. To accomplish this you have to make the variable read-only. If you or anybody else then tries to change the value an error message will be generated, telling the user it's a read-only variable. The format for this is:

variable_name = value
readonly variable_name

In the following example, I set the variable `tape_dev` to a device path of one of the system's tape devices. I then make it read-only. Trying to change the value throws up an error message.

```
$ TAPE_DEV="/dev/rmt/0n"
$ echo ${TAPE_DEV}
/dev/rmt/0n
$ readonly TAPE_DEV
$ TAPE_DEV="/dev/rmt/1n"
sh: TAPE_DEV: read-only variable
```

To see all the variables that are set to read-only, just issue the command `readonly`.

```
$ readonly
declare -r FILM="Crimson Tide"
declare -ri PPID="1"
declare -r TAPE_DEV="/dev/rmt/0n"
declare -ri UID="0"
```

14.3 Environment variables

An environment variable is made available to all your processes (which are often called child processes). When you log in this is called the father process, and other processes that you invoke from your shell are called child processes. Unlike local variables, which can be accessed only by your current shell, environment variables are available to all your child processes. This may include, amongst others, editors, scripts and applications.

Environment variables can be set on the command line, but these values will be lost when you log out, so it's best to put them in your .profile. The system administrator will probably have set some environments up already in your /etc/profile. Putting them in the profile files means that they will be initialized every time you log in.

By convention all environment variables are in upper case. To make the variable available to all your processes you must use the export command. The assigning of the environment variables is done in the same way as with the local shell variables.

14.3.1 To assign an environment variable

VARIABLE_NAME = value; export VARIABLE_NAME

The semicolon between the two commands is just a command separator. The following would have done the same thing:

VARIABLE_NAME = value
export VARIABLE_NAME

14.3.2 Displaying environment variables

Displaying an environment variable is again the same as in the local shell variables. Here are some examples.

```
$ CONSOLE=tty1; export CONSOLE
$ echo $CONSOLE
tty1

$ MYAPPS=/usr/local/application; export MYAPPS
$ echo $MYAPPS
/usr/local/application
```

To see all your globally defined environment variables use the env command.

```
$ env
HISTSIZE=1000
HOSTNAME=localhost.localdomain
LOGNAME=dave
MAIL=/var/spool/mail/root
TERM=vt100
HOSTTYPE=i386
PATH=/sbin:/bin:/usr/sbin:/usr/bin:/usr/X11R6/bin:/root/bin:
CONSOLE=tty1
HOME=/home/dave
ASD=sdf
SHELL=/bin/sh
PS1=$
USER=dave
. . .
```

14.3.3 Clearing environment variables

To clear a variable, again use the unset command.

```
$ unset MYAPPS
$ echo $MYAPPS

$
```

14.3.4 Built-in shell variables

The Bourne shell has some names reserved for environment variables. You cannot use these variable names for anything else. They are generally set up in your /etc/profile, but not always, so it's up to you to set a value to them. Here is a list of the built-in shell variables.

CDPATH

The change directory path variable holds a series of pathnames separated by a colon. It is used in conjunction with the cd command. If CDPATH is set, when you cd, the CDPATH is searched first. If the directory is located within CDPATH, this becomes the new working directory. Here's an example.

```
$ CDPATH=:/home/dave/bin:/usr/local/apps; export CDPATH
```

Now if you wanted to

```
$ cd apps
```

the cd command would search through the directory listings given in CDPATH. If it is found, this would become your current working directory.

EXINIT

The EXINIT variable holds initialization options when using the vi editor. For example, to have all the lines numbered and set the tab to 10 spaces when using vi, use

```
$ EXINIT='set nu  tab=10'; export EXINIT
```

HOME

The HOME directory, usually located in the second from last field in the passwd file, is where you keep all your personal files. When set, you can use the shortcut to cd back to your HOME directory.

```
$ HOME=/home/dave; export HOME
$ pwd
$ /usr/local
$ cd
$ pwd
$ /home/dave
```

You can also use

```
$ cd $HOME
```

IFS

The IFS is used by the shell as the default field separator. The internal field separator can be set to anything, but by default is generally set to a space, new line or tab. IFS is quite useful in separating fields in files or variables. Setting IFS to a colon and then echoing the PATH variable will give a more readable directory-separated path.

```
$ export IFS=:
$ echo $PATH
/sbin /bin /usr/sbin /usr/bin /usr/X11R6/bin /root/bin
```

To set it back to its original setting use:

```
$ IFS=<space><tab>; export IFS
```

where <space><tab> means hit the space and tab keys.

LOGNAME

This variable holds your login name. This should really be set by default, but if it isn't you can set it with this command.

```
$ LOGNAME=`whoami`; export LOGNAME
$ echo $LOGNAME
dave
```

MAIL

The MAIL variable holds the pathname and file of your mailbox. By default this is /var/spool/mail/<login name>. The shell will check periodically for new mail. If you have mail a message will be displayed on your command line. If you have a different route to your mail box, set it with MAIL:

```
$  MAIL=/usr/mail/dave; export MAIL
```

MAILCHECK

The MAILCHECK default for checking for new mail is 60 seconds. But if you like your mail checked less often, say every 2 minutes, use this command:

```
$ MAILCHECK=120; export MAILCHECK
```

MAILPATH

Use MAILPATH if you have more than one mailbox. This variable set will override the variable MAIL:

```
$  MAILPATH=/var/spool/dave:/var/spool/admin; export MAILPATH
```

In the above example, MAIL will now check the two mailboxes dave and admin.

PATH

The search PATH variable holds the order of directories you want to be searched for a command or script. It is important to get this order right, because it saves you time when trying to execute a command. You do not want to search in a directory where you know the command will not be. Generally speaking, it's best to put your HOME directory first, followed by a list of directories starting from the most used to the least used. If you want your current working directory searched, no matter where that is, use a period. Each directory is separated by a colon. Here's an example.

```
$ PATH=$HOME/bin:.:/bin:/usr/bin; export PATH
```

Using the above example my HOME/bin directory would be searched first, followed by my current working directory, then /bin, followed by /usr/bin.

The PATH would be set up in /etc/profile for the system directories. To use this PATH and stick on your own search PATH at the end use a semi-colon (:).

```
$ PATH=$PATH:/$HOME/bin:. ; export PATH
```

Here we have used the already defined PATH variable from /etc/profile, and stuck on the $HOME/bin and current working directory. Generally speaking it's not a good idea to use your current working directory as the first search path, as this can be exploited by other users.

PS1

The primary prompt holds your shell prompt. By default it's a # for root and $ for everybody else. You can use whatever you like in your prompt. Here are a couple of examples.

```
$ PS1="star trek:"; export PS1
star trek:
$ PS1="->" ; export PS1
->
```

PS2

This is the secondary prompt, which by default is a > sign. The secondary prompt comes into play when you do a multi-line command, or when a command exceeds a line length.

```
$ PS2="@:"; export PS2
$ for loop in *
@:do
@:echo $loop
...
```

SHELL

The SHELL contains your default shell, usually picked up from /etc/passwd, but you can override it you feel you need to use another shell.

```
$ echo $SHELL
/bin/sh
```

TERMINFO

The terminal initialization variable holds the location of your terminal configuration files. Usually this is in either /usr/lib/terminfo or /usr/share/terminfo.

```
$  TERMINFO=/usr/lib/terminfo; export TERMINFO
```

TERM

The TERM variable holds the name of your terminal type. This is used so that applications know what type of control sequences your terminal understands for the screen and keyboard. The most common terminal types are vt100, vt220, vt220-8, wyse etc.

```
$ TERM=vt100; export TERM
```

TZ

The time zone variable holds the time zone value. It is the system administrator's job to do this. But as you may wish to change it for your shell, here are a couple of examples:

```
$ echo $TZ
GMT2EDT
```

The value returned means that we are using Greenwich Mean Time, with 0 local time difference from GMT, and Eastern Daylight Saving is in operation.

14.3.5 Other environment variables

There are other environment variable names that are reserved; other system or commands applications will pick these up. Here are the most common ones. Remember the values may not have been set; it's up to you to set them.

EDITOR

Set this variable to the editor you like using the most.

```
$ EDITOR=vi; export EDITOR
```

PWD

Contains the pathname of your current directory. Generally set using the cd command.

PAGER

Holds the screen pager command, for instance pg, more. The system uses this variable if set when you view man pages.

```
$ PAGER='pg -f -p%d'; export PAGER
```

MANPATH

Holds the directories that contain man pages on the system. Each directory should be separated by a colon.

```
$ MANPATH=/usr/apps/man:/usr/local/man; export MANPATH
```

LPDEST *or* PRINTER

Holds the name of your default printer. It saves you specifying the printer name when you print jobs.

```
$ LPDEST=hp3si_systems
```

14.3.6 Using the set command

When setting environment variables in your $HOME .profile, there is another method for exporting them. Use the set command with the '-a' option. Using 'set -a' says that all variables should be exported straightaway. Do not use this method in /etc/profile, only in your $HOME .profile file.

```
$ pg .profile
#.profile
set -a
MAIL=/usr/mail/${LOGNAME:?}
PATH=$PATH:$HOME:bin
#
EDITOR=vi
TERM vt220
ADMIN=/usr/adm
PS1="`hostname`>"
```

14.3.7 Exporting variables to child processes

One of the problems new users to shell have is with the concept of exporting variables to child processes. As we have already discussed how environment variables work, let's now put that into practice with a script that calls another script, which in effect creates a child process.

Below is a listing of two short scripts called father and child.

The father script sets a variable called 'film' with the value 'A Few Good Men'. It echoes out that variable, then calls another script called 'child'. This script displays the variable film from the first script. The variable film then has its value changed to 'Die Hard', before being displayed on the screen. Control is then returned back to the father script, and the variable is then displayed again.

```
$ pg father
#!/bin/sh
# father script.
echo "this is the father"
FILM="A Few Good Men"
echo "I like the film :$FILM"
# call the child script
child
echo "back to father"
echo "and the film is :$FILM"

$ pg child
#!/bin/sh
# child
echo "called from father..i am the child"
echo "film name is :$FILM"
FILM="Die Hard"
echo "changing film to :$FILM"
```

Let's see what the script displays.

```
$ father
this is the father
I like the film :A Few Good Men
called from father..i am the child
film name is :
changing film to :Die Hard
back to father
and the film is :A Few Good Men
```

Because we did not export the variable film in the father script, the child script could not give back the variable film.

Now, if we add an export command to the father script, so that the child script knows all about the film variable, this should work.

```
pg father
#!/bin/sh
# father script.
echo "this is the father"
FILM="A Few Good Men"
echo "I like the film :$FILM"
# call the child script
# but export variable first
export FILM
child
echo "back to father"
echo "and the film is :$FILM"

$ father2
this is the father
I like the film :A Few Good Men
called from father..i am the child
film name is :A Few Good Men
changing film to :Die Hard
back to father
and the film is :A Few Good Men
```

Now we have the export command in the script we can run off as many processes as we like, and they will all know about the variable film.

You cannot export variables from child processes back to the father process; however, with a little bit of redirection it is possible to get around this.

14.4 Positional variable parameters

At the beginning of this chapter, I said that there were four types of variables, local and environment, plus two other types considered special because they are read-only. These are positional and special variable parameters. Let's look at the positional variables.

When you want to pass information to a shell script, you can access this information using positional parameters. A number references each parameter passed to a script. You can pass as many arguments as you like but you can only access the first nine parameters, though you can get around this limitation using the command shift. We will see shift in action later on in the book. The parameters start at one and finish at nine; each parameter you wish to access should be prefixed by a dollar '$'. The first parameter which is zero is reserved to hold the actual script name; this value can be used whether there are parameters to the script or not.

If you want to pass the following string 'Did You See The Full Moon', to a script, the following table demonstrates how each parameter would be accessed.

$0	$1	$2	$3	$4	$5	$6	$7	$8	$9
Script name	Did	You	See	The	Full	Moon			

14.4.1 Using positional parameters in scripts

Let's use the above example in the following script.

```
$ pg param
#!/bin/sh
# param
echo "This is the script name       : $0"
echo "This is the first parameter    : $1"
echo "This is the second parameter   : $2"
echo "This is the third parameter    : $3"
echo "This is the fourth parameter   : $4"
echo "This is the fifth parameter    : $5"
echo "This is the sixth parameter    : $6"
echo "This is the seventh parameter  : $7"
echo "This is the eighth parameter   : $8"
echo "This is the ninth parameter    : $9"


$ param Did You See The Full Moon
This is the script name       : ./param
This is the first parameter    : Did
This is the second parameter   : You
This is the third parameter    : See
This is the fourth parameter   : The
This is the fifth parameter    : Full
This is the sixth parameter    : Moon
This is the seventh parameter  :
This is the eighth parameter   :
This is the ninth parameter    :
```

As we only passed six parameters, the seventh, eighth and ninth are blank, and this is what we would expect. Notice the first parameter pulls off the script name. This can be used to good effect when you are dealing with error messages from your script. Here's another example that just returns the name of the script.

```
$ pg param2
#!/bin/sh
echo "Hello world this is $0 calling"


$ param2
Hello world this is ./param2 calling
```

You will notice that the $0 also returns the path from the current directory. If you just want the script name, prefix the $0 with the command basename. You will then get just the script name.

```
$ pg param2
#!/bin/sh
echo "Hello world this is `basename $0` calling"

$ param2
Hello world this is param2 calling
```

14.4.2 Passing parameters to system commands

You can pass parameters to a system command within a script. In the following example we use the find command, using the parameter $1 to specify the filename we wish to find.

```
$  pg findfile
#!/bin/sh
# findfile
find / -name $1 -print

$ findfile passwd
/etc/passwd
/etc/uucp/passwd
/usr/bin/passwd
```

Here's another example, passing a user-id to grep in the form of $1; grep uses this to search the passwd file for the user's full name.

```
$ pg who_is
#!/bin/sh
# who_is
grep $1 passwd | awk -F: {print $4}'

$ who_is seany
Seany Post
```

14.4.3 Special variable parameters

Now that we know how to access and use parameters to shell scripts, it would be useful to have a bit more information about them. You really need to have a bit more control in what the script is going to do with them. That's where special variables come in. There are seven special variables in all. Let's look at them (*see* Table 14.2).

Table 14.2 *Special shell variables*

$#	The number of arguments passed to the script.
$*	Shows in a single string all the arguments passed to the script. The parameters for this option can exceed nine, unlike the positional variables.
$$	The current PID of the script running.
$!	The PID of the last process that was put in the background.
$@	Really the same as $#, but when used with quotes, returns each argument in quotes.
$-	Shows the current options in the shell; same as using set.
$?	Shows the exit status of the last command. 0 is no errors, any other value is an error.

Let's amend our `param` script and substitute in some special variables, and rerun the script with different passing text.

```
$ pg param
#!/bin/sh
# allparams
echo "This is the script name          : $0"
echo "This is the first parameter       : $1"
echo "This is the second parameter      : $2"
echo "This is the third parameter       : $3"
echo "This is the fourth parameter      : $4"
echo "This is the fifth parameter       : $5"
echo "This is the sixth parameter       : $6"
echo "This is the seventh parameter     : $7"
echo "This is the eighth parameter      : $8"
echo "This is the ninth parameter       : $9"
echo "The number of arguments passed    :$œ"
echo "Show all arguments                : $*"
echo "Show me my process ID             : $$"
echo "Show me the arguments in quotes   :" "$@"
echo "Did my script go with any errors  :$?"
```

```
$ param Merry Christmas Mr Lawrence
This is the script name          :./param
This is the first parameter      : Merry
This is the second parameter     : Christmas
This is the third parameter      : Mr Lawrence
This is the fourth parameter     :
This is the fifth parameter      :
This is the sixth parameter      :
This is the seventh parameter    :
This is the eighth parameter     :
This is the ninth parameter      :
```

```
The number of arguments passed    :3
Show all arguments                : Merry Christmas Mr Lawrence
Show me my process ID             : 630
Show me the arguments in quotes   : "Merry" "Christmas" "Mr Lawrence"
Did my script go with any errors  :0
```

The output of the special variables tells you a lot more information about your script. We can check how many arguments are passed, and the process-ID of our script, in case we want to kill our script.

14.4.4 Last exit status

Notice the $? returns 0. You can use this on any command or script to tell you if the last command was successful. Based on this information you can then take further action in your scripts. 0 returned means ok; 1 returned means errors.

Here's an example. We first copy a file to /tmp and check the result, using $?.

```
$ cp ok.txt /tmp
$ echo $?
0
```

Now we try to copy a file to a non-existent directory:

```
$ cp ok.txt /usr/local/apps/dsf
cp: cannot create regular file '/usr/local/apps/dsf': No such file or
directory

$ echo $?
1
```

Using $? to check the return status we can see this is 1, so we know we have a problem. But you can see the system 'cp:cannot...' error, so there is no need to check the last exit status. In your scripts you will do some form of processing using system commands, and you do not want the output from the commands messing up your screen, so you will probably redirect the all output to /dev/null, the system's bin. Now how are you going to tell if the last command was successful? That's right, using the last status command. Let's see all that in action using our last example.

```
$ cp ok.txt /usr/local/apps/dsf >/dev/null 2>&1
$ echo $?
1
```

By redirecting all output including errors into the system's bin, we cannot tell if the last command worked. But by using $?, which returns 1, we now know that it failed.

When checking the exit status in scripts, it is good practice to assign the exit value to a meaningful name for the operation you are checking on; besides, this makes the script more readable.

```
$ cp ok.txt /usr/local/apps/dsf >/dev/null 2>&1
$ cp_status=$?
$ echo $cp_status
1
```

14.5 Conclusion

Variables can make your life easier in the shell; they can save you typing and improve your productivity. A shell variable can contain almost any value. Special variables give your scripts better functionality and more information about which parameters are passed to the scripts.

CHAPTER 15

Quoting

In Chapter 14 we learned how to do variable and substitution operations. When carrying out variable substitutions in your scripts one of the most irritating errors you will come across will be due to misquoting. Quoting is also important on the command line.

In this chapter we'll cover:

- why there is a need to quote;
- double, single and back quotes; and
- escaping using the backslash.

15.1 The need for quoting

We will cover only the basic rules of quoting here, because there are plenty of examples of when to use quoting and what it achieves in the next two parts of the book.

When the shell reads the lines in your scripts, it will try to do its own evaluation of the assignments you have made. You need a way to stop the shell from doing this. The methods available are by using quotes, different kinds of quotes, and using a backslash.

Some users do not bother to use double quotes when echoing strings of text. If they did half their quoting problems would go away. I recommend you always to use double quotes when echoing strings of text. Here's an example before we begin on the different quotes.

```
$ echo Hit the star button to exit *

Hit the star button to exit DIR_COLORS HOSTNAME Muttrc X11 adjtime
aliases alias
...
```

The text is echoed, but because we have not used double quotes, the * is evaluated by the shell, and it thinks you want to do a wildcard listing. Enclosing it with double quotes gives:

```
$ echo "Hit the star button to exit *"
Hit the star button to exit *
```

so there's no misinterpretation on the quotes. Table 15.1 shows the different types of quotes.

Table 15.1 *Quotes of the shell*

" "	Double quotes
' '	Single quotes
` `	Grave or back quote
\	Backslash

15.2 Double quotes

Use the double quotes to take literally everything except the following characters: $, `, \. That's a dollar, back quote and backslash; these characters keep their special meanings to the shell. If we assigned a string to a variable using double quotes to echo it, we see that there is no difference when echoing the variable.

```
$ STRING="MAY DAY, MAY DAY, GOING DOWN"
$ echo "$STRING"
MAY DAY, MAY DAY, GOING DOWN

$ echo $STRING
MAY DAY, MAY DAY, GOING DOWN
```

Now suppose we want to assign the system's date output to a variable called mydate:

```
$ MYDATE="date"
$ echo $MYDATE
date
```

Because the shell is taking everything 'as is' inside the string, the date has no special significance, therefore will hold just the word date.

When you want to search for a string of text that contains spaces, always use double quotes. Here we use grep to extract the name "Davey Wire". Because we have not used quotes, grep thinks that "Davey" is the string to search and the file is "Wire".

```
$ grep "Davey Wire" /etc/passwd
grep: Wire: No such file or directory
```

To fix this, just double quote the string, which informs the shell to ignore the spaces. You should always use double quotes when using strings, whether they are single or multi-words.

```
$ grep "Davey Wire" /etc/passwd
davyboy:9sdJUK2s:106:Davey Wire:/home/ap
```

You can use double quotes to include a variable inside an echoed line of text. In the next example the shell echoes the line of text, but sees the '$' and acknowledges it as a variable, then substitutes the variable $BOY with the value boy.

```
$ BOY="boy"
$ echo " The $BOY did well"
 The boy did well

$ echo " The "$BOY" did well"
 The boy did well
```

15.3 Single quotes

The single quote is very similar to the double quote except it tells the shell to ignore any type of value evaluation; in other words, to treat everything inside the quotes as if it was disabling its special meaning – a case of what you type between the single quotes is what you get. Using the sample example as in the double quote:

```
$ GIRL='girl'
$ echo "The '$GIRL' did well"
The 'girl' did well
```

15.4 Back quote

The back quote is the one to use when you want to assign output from system commands to variables. It tells the shell to take whatever is between the back quotes as a system command and execute its output. Using these methods you can then substitute the output into a variable. You can also combine quotes, as we shall see in a moment.

In the following example, the shell has tried to evaluate and substitute the word hello; because there is no command or script called hello, it responds with an error.

```
$ echo `hello`
sh: hello: command not found
```

Now let's try again with the `date` command.

```
$ echo `date`
Sun May 16 16:40:19 GMT 1999
```

This time the command is valid, and the shell can evaluate it correctly.

Let's now assign the output of the date command to a variable called `mydate`. Here's the format of the date:

```
$ date +%A" the "%e" of "%B" "%Y
Sunday the 16 of May 1999
```

Now assign it to `mydate`, and display it.

```
$ mydate=`date +%A" the "%e" of "%B" "%Y`
$ echo $mydate
Sunday the 16 of May 1999
```

Of course I could have just assigned the whole output of date to `mydate`:

```
$ mydate=`date`
$ echo $mydate
Sun May 16 16:48:16 GMT 1999
```

Here's another example, but here we embed back quotes within double quotes:

```
$ echo "The date today is `date`"
The date today is Sun May 16 16:56:53 GMT 1999
```

Let's print a little message showing how many users are on the system.

```
$ echo "There are `who | wc -l` users on the system"
There are   13    users on the system
```

In the above example, the string is printed, and the shell sees the back quote and knows to take everything inside the back quotes and evaluate it, which means to execute it.

15.5 Backslash

The backslash stops the shell from misinterpreting the next character if it has special meaning to the shell. The following characters may have special meaning: & * = ^ $ ` " | ?.

Issuing the `echo` command with an * causes a listing of the whole current directory in a squashed up format, instead of echoing just the asterisk.

```
$ echo *
```

```
conf.linuxconf conf.modules cron.daily cron.hourly cron.monthly
cron.weekly crontab csh.cshrc default dosemu.conf dosemu.users exports
fdprm fstab gettydefs gpm-root.c
onf group group- host.conf hosts hosts.allow hosts.deny httpd inetd
...
```

To disable the special meaning of the asterisk, use a backslash.

```
$ echo \*
*
```

The same thing goes for the $$ command which the shell interprets as your current PID (process ID number). To disable it and just echo the $$ put a backslash in front.

```
$ echo $$
284
$ echo \$$
$$
```

To include octal characters when echoing, you must precede them with the backslash, otherwise the shell will just think they are ordinary numbers.

```
$ echo " This is a copyright 251 sign"
 This is a copyright \251 sign
$ echo  " This is a copyright \251 sign"
 This is a copyright © sign
```

If it's Linux then...

Remember to use the '-e' for control characters.

```
$ echo -e "This is a copyright \251 sign"
 This is a copyright © sign
```

When using the command `expr`, if you try to multiply using the * it will return an error. Put a backslash before the * sign, and this will work.

```
$ expr 12 * 12
expr: syntax error
```

```
$ expr 12 \* 12
144
```

To include any of the metacharacters within an echo statement, you must escape them with a backslash. In the following example, the price $19.99 is to be displayed, but because we have not escaped it the shell, the shell will treat it differently.

```
$ echo "That video looks a good price for $19.99"
That video looks a good price for 9.99
```

Now if we escape the dollar sign we get a better result.

```
$ echo "That video looks a good price for \$19.99"
That video looks a good price for $19.99
```

15.6 Conclusion

Getting tripped up with quoting is a common problem. I use these two rules when using quotes:

1.   Always use double quotes to echo strings; do not use the echo by itself.

2.   If you do not get the desired results using a quote, try another one; after all there are only three different types of quotes.

## PART 4

Basic shell programming

CHAPTER 16

Introduction to shell scripts

A shell script may contain one or contain several commands; there is no rule. Then why use a script for a couple of commands? You don't have to if you don't want to.

In this chapter we will cover:

- reasons for using a shell script;
- basic components of a shell script; and
- how to run a shell script.

16.1 Reasons for using a shell script

Shell scripts can save you time in automating repetitive or long tasks and are very powerful. After all, why have a list of commands that does a certain task, where you have to enter the commands manually then look at the output, then decide if it's the right output you expected? If it is, great, carry on with the next task. If it isn't, look back to the list to see what to do next. A task can be anything including sorting a file, inserting text into files, migrating files, deleting certain lines from a file, cleaning up old files around the system, doing general administrative work on the system. Creating a script using variables, conditional, arithmetic and iteration constructs, with a touch of system commands, enables you to rapidly create a script that does the job thus saving yourself hours of work compared to if you had carried it out manually. The shell can take information from one command and use it for input in another command. Even with the different UNIXs and LINUXs around, using a shell script will require little altering to run on all of them. In fact shell portability is not the problem but rather system command portability is.

16.1.1 Try out new ideas

When you create a script, do not be afraid if it doesn't do exactly as you thought it would; just remember that no matter what unexpected damage the script does you can restore it. Now you do have backups don't you? The point I'm trying to make is do not be afraid to try out new things. If you don't you will not be doing yourself justice and most importantly you will not learn.

16.2 What a script contains

This book is not about good scripting design techniques, but good reusable code. You do not have to make the script complicated when it can achieve the same results through solid understandable code. If I wrote a book that way, I might impress you, but it would take a lot longer for you to get to grips with the code. This is not my goal; my code works and it works using basic scripting techniques, which you will learn more quickly. You will then be able to impress your friends more quickly!

A script is not a compiled program: it is interpreted, line by line. The first line of the script should always start with

#!/bin/sh

This lets the shell know where the Bourne shell interpreter is to be found on the system.

Any script can have comments; to put comments into your script, the first character of the line should be a hash (#), and the interpreter will ignore these lines. It is good practice to include the name of the script as the second line down as a comment.

A script is read from top to bottom. To be able to run a script, it must first be made executable. Make sure your path is set up properly, so your scripts can be run by supplying only the file name.

16.3 Running a script

Here's an example of what we have just discussed. Here is a file called cleanup.

```
$ pg cleanup
#!/bin/sh
# name: cleanup
# this is a general cleanup script
echo "starting cleanup...wait"
rm /usr/lcoal/apps/log/*.log
tail -40 /var/adm/mesages >/tmp/messages
```

```
rm /var/adm/messages
mv /tmp/messages /var/adm/messages
echo "finished cleanup"
```

The above script cleans up var/adm/ messages by truncating the file, and deletes all log files in /usr/local/apps/log.

To make the script executable we use the chmod command:

```
$ chmod u+x cleanup.
```

Now to run the script, just type the script name

```
$ cleanup
```

If you get an error back like this:

```
$ cleanup
sh: cleanup: command not found
```

try this:

```
$./cleanup
```

If you have to type a pathname before your script will run, or the shell reports that it cannot find the command you really need to include your bin directory in your .profile PATH. Make sure you are in your $HOME bin directory by typing

```
$ pwd
$ /home/dave/bin
```

If the last part of the pwd command is bin, then you need to add this to your path. Edit your .profile and add the bin directory $HOME/bin to your .profile, as follows:

PATH = $PATH:$HOME/bin

If you have no bin directory, create one; first make sure you are in your home directory.

```
$ cd $HOME
$ mkdir bin
```

Now add the bin directory to your PATH variable in your .profile, then reinitialize the .profile

```
$. ./profile
```

This should now work.

If you still have problems, see Chapters 2 and 13. There is plenty of information there that should get you up and running.

Throughout this book you will find listings of scripts. The listings are all complete. To run these scripts type the commands into a file, save and exit, then use the `chmod` command to set execute permission. You are then in business.

16.4 Conclusion

This chapter has been a very quick primer in the introduction of shell scripts. I am sure you do not want me to go on about the theory of scripts' functionality, shell I/O etc. You will pick these up quickly as you read the chapters throughout this book. The aim of this chapter is just to show you what you need to do in order to run shell run scripts.

CHAPTER 17

Conditional testing

When scripting, you will probably want to be able to test whether a string is equal to another, or maybe check on a file status or even a numeric test. Based on the results of the test you can take further action. The `test` command can be used to test for strings, file status and numbers. It also fits in very well with the conditional `if`, `then`, `else` construct, as you'll see in the next chapter.

In this chapter we will cover:

- using the `test` command on files, strings and numbers; and

- using the `expr` command on numbers and strings.

The `expr` tests and performs numeric output. Both `test` and `expr` will return 0 for true and 1 for false using the last exit status command $?.

17.1 Testing for a file status

There are two general formats of the `test` and you can use either:

test condition

or

[condition]

Please note the use of a space each side of the condition when using square brackets.

The conditions to which you can test the file's status are quite long, but Table 17.1 lists the most common ones.

Table 17.1 *File status tests*

-d	This is a directory
-f	This is a regular file
-L	This is a symbolic link
-r	This file is readable
-s	This file has a size greater than zero, not empty
-w	This file is writeable
-u	This file has the `suid` bit set
-x	This is executable

We will use both test methods to test if the file `scores.txt` is writeable. We will use the last status command to test it. Remember a zero status is OK, anything else is an error.

```
$ ls -l scores.txt
-rw-r--r--   1 dave    admin   0 May 15 11:29 scores.txt
$ [ -w scores.txt ]
$ echo $?
0

$ test -w scores.txt
$ echo $?
0
```

Both statuses returned zero, so we know it is writeable. Now let's see if it's executable.

```
$ [ -x scores.txt ]
$ echo $?
1
```

No, which is what we would expect, by looking at the permission listing of the file `scores.txt`.

The next example tests for the presence of a directory called `appsbin`.

```
drwxr-xr-x  2 dave  admin    1024 May 15 15:53 appsbin
$ [ -d appsbin ]
$ echo $?
0
```

Yes, the directory `appsbin` is present.

To test if a file has the `suid` bit set.

```
-rwsr-xr--  1 root  root    28 Apr 30 13:12 xab
```

```
$ [ -u xab ]
$ echo $?
0
```

We can see from the above that the suid bit is set.

17.2 Using logical operators with tests

Testing for a file's status is OK, but in some instances you'll want to compare one file's status against another. The shell offers three types of logical operators for you to accomplish this:

-a   Logical AND, true, if both sides of the operator are true

-o   Logical OR, true, if either sides of the operator can be true

!   Logical NOT, true, if the condition is false

Let's now compare using these files.

```
-rw-r--r--   1 root   root     0 May 15 11:29 scores.txt
-rwxr-xr--   1 root   root     0 May 15 11:49 results.txt
```

The following example tests whether both files are readable.

```
$ [ -w results.txt -a -w scores.txt ]
$ echo $?
0
```

It finds out that they are.
    To test if either of the files is executable use the logical OR operator.

```
$ [ -x results.txt -o -x scores.txt ]
$ echo $?
0
```

Scores.txt is not, but results.txt is.
    To test if the file results.txt is both writeable and executable.

```
$ [ -w results.txt -a -x results.txt ]
$ echo $?
0
```

Yes, it is.

17.3 Testing strings

Testing strings is an important part of error trapping, especially when you need to test users input, or compare any variables. To test strings you have the choice of five formats.

> **test "string"**
> **test string_operator "string"**
> **test "string" string_operator "string"**
> **[string_operator string]**
> **[string string_operator string]**

where the string_operator can be:

=	The two strings are equal
!=	The two strings are not equal
-z	This string is null
-n	This string is not null

To test if the environment variable EDITOR is empty:

```
$ [ -z $EDITOR ]
$ echo $?
1
```

No, it isn't. Is it set to vi?

```
$ [ $EDITOR = "vi" ]
$ echo $?
0
```

Yes it is. Let's verify that with an echo.

```
$ echo $EDITOR
vi
```

To test if the variable tape is equal to the variable tape2:

```
$ TAPE="/dev/rmt0"
$ TAPE2="/dev/rmt1"
$ [ "$TAPE" = "$TAPE2" ]
$ echo $?
1
```

No, it isn't. There is no rule stating you have to use the double quotes when assigning variables, but you must do so when comparing strings.

To test if the variable tape is 'not' equal to `tape2`.

```
$ [ "$TAPE" != "$TAPE2" ]
$ echo $?
0
```

They are not equal.

17.4 Testing numbers

To test for numbers a different sort of operators are at our disposal. The general format is:

"number" **numeric_operator** "number"

or

["number" **numeric_operator** "number"]

where the `numeric_operator` can be:

-eq   The two numbers are equal

-ne   The two numbers are not equal

-gt   The first number is greater than the second number

-lt   The first number is less than the second number

-le   The first number is less than or equal to the second number

-gt   The first number is greater than or equal to the second number

Both the following examples returns the same result. To test if a number is equal to another number (in this case is 130 equal to 130):

```
$ NUMBER=130
$ [ "$NUMBER" -eq "130" ]
$ echo $?
0
```

Phew! I'm glad that one returned true.

Here we change the second number, and the test reports a failure, a status of 1. (130 is not equal to 100.)

```
$ [ "$NUMBER" -eq "100" ]
$ echo $?
1
```

To test if a number (130) is greater than 100:

```
$ [ "$NUMBER" -gt "100" ]
$ echo $?
0
```

It is, of course.

You can test two variable integer values as well. Here the variable source_count is tested to see if dest_count is greater, which it is.

```
$ SOURCE_COUNT=13
$ DEST_COUNT=15
$ [ "$DEST_COUNT" -gt "$SOURCE_COUNT" ]
$ echo $?
0
```

You do not have to have the integer values wrapped in a variable; just use the numbers themselves, but use quotes:

```
$ [ "990" -le "995" ]
$ echo $?
0
```

You can also combine and test for two expressions using the logical operators. You still only need one pair of square brackets – do not use two, or you will get the generic error message 'too many arguments':

```
$ [ "990" -le "995" ] -a [ "123" -gt "33" ]
sh:[: too many arguments
```

In the next example, we test two expressions. If both are true then the result is true, which it is. Here's the correct way to do it.

```
$ [ "990" -le "995"  -a  "123" -gt "33" ]
$ echo $?
0
```

17.5 Using expr

The expr command is used mostly for integer values, but can be used for strings as well. Its general format is:

expr argument operator argument

Expr is a handy command line calculator as well:

```
$ expr 10 + 10
20
```

```
$ expr 900 + 600
1500

$ expr 30 / 3
10

$ expr 30 / 3 / 2
5
```

When using the multiply sign, you will have to escape it with a backslash, because the shell might misinterpret the asterisk '*':

```
$ expr 30 \* 3
90
```

17.5.1 Incrementing counters

Expr does the incrementing of values when using loops. First the loop is initialized to zero. Then one is added to the variable loop. The use of the quotes means command substitution, which basically means take the output from the command (expr) and put it in the variable loop.

```
$ LOOP=0
$ LOOP='expr $LOOP + 1'
```

17.5.2 Testing for a number

You can also use expr to test for a number. If you try to do a calculation with a non-integer, it will return an error like this:

```
$ expr rr + 1
expr: non-numeric argument
```

so all we need to do is pass it a variable (it does not matter what it contains), do any arithmetic operation and direct all the output to /dev/null. Then test the status of the last command. If it's zero then it is a number; anything else, it's not a number.

```
$ VALUE=12
$ expr $VALUE + 10 > /dev/null 2>&1
$ echo $?
0
```

It's a number.

```
$ VALUE=hello
$ expr $VALUE + 10 > /dev/null 2>&1
$ echo $?
```

2

It's not a number.

Expr will also return its own exit status; unfortunately it's the opposite of the value from the system's last exit command. Expr will return one for OK, and anything else is invalid or means an error. Here's an example of that testing two strings for equality. It tests to see if "hello" is equal to "hello"!

```
$ VALUE=hello
$ expr $VALUE = "hello"
1
$ echo $?
0
```

Expr has returned one. Do not get confused, it's OK. Now we check it with the last exit status: zero is returned so the test is successful, "hello" is indeed equal to "hello".

17.5.3 Pattern matching

Expr also has pattern matching capabilities. You can count the characters in a string using expr, by specifying the colon option. The '.*' means any character zero or more times.

```
$ VALUE=accounts.doc
$ expr $VALUE : October 8, '.*'
12
```

You can also use string matching in expr; here we use the pattern '.doc', to extract the rest of the filename.

```
$ expr $VALUE : '\(.*\).doc'
accounts
```

17.6 Conclusion

We have covered the basics of test and expr, and we know how to test on file status and string evaluation. Using other conditional statements such as 'if then else' and 'case' you will be able to do robust testing and take some form of action on the results of the test.

CHAPTER 18

Control flow structures

All functional scripts need to have the ability to make decisions. They must also be able to process lists based on certain conditions. That's what this chapter is all about; the building and implementation of control structures in scripts.

In this chapter we will cover:

- exit statuses;
- the while, for and until loops;
- if then else statements;
- making decisions in scripts; and
- menus.

18.1 Exit statuses

Before we get into some proper scripting, here is a quick word about exit statuses in general. Any command that is run will return an exit status. If you want to see that exit status you can use the last status command:

```
$ echo $?
```

There are four main types of exit statuses. We have already met two of them and they are the last command exit status $? and the control order commands (&&, ||). The other two are to do with exiting from a shell script or shell and exit status or return codes from a function. We will look at functions and their return codes later when we deal with functions in Chapter 19.

To exit from a current process the shell provides the command exit. The general format is:

exit n

where n is a number.

If you just type exit from the command prompt, you will exit from the shell, assuming you have not created another shell within your current session. If you type exit by itself, the shell will then try to (and usually does) return the value of the last command. There are many exit code values but most importantly there are two exit values with regard to scripts and general system commands. These are:

exit status 0   Good exit, no errors

exit status 1   Bad exit, errors occurred somewhere

You can supply your own exit codes in shell scripts, which will exit the script, and I encourage you to do so. Why? Because another shell script or returning function may want to pick up the exit code from your script. Besides, I believe it's good programming practice to leave your script with an exit code. You can exit after a bad response from user input, from an unrecoverable error, or at the end of normal processing if you wish.

Note:
From now on throughout the book all the scripts you will see have some comment lines in them. Comment lines are just what they sound like, comments to help you remember or understand parts of your scripts. You are free to put these lines in wherever you wish, as they are ignored by the interpreter. A comment line must begin with a hash (#) character.

18.2 Control structures

With very few exceptions, nearly all scripts have some type of flow control in them. What is flow control? Well, suppose you had a script containing a few commands like this:

```
#!/bin/sh
# make a directory
mkdir /home/dave/mydocs
# copy all doc files
cp *.docs /home/dave/docs
# delete all doc files
rm *.docs
```

The above is a script; it does a job – what's the problem? The problem is what happens if the directory cannot be created. What happens if the directory can be created but fails when the copy tries to copy the files? What if you need to cp different files from different directories. We need to make informed decisions before the command takes place or more likely on the outcome of the last command. The shell comes to our rescue here in providing a series of command statements that can help you take appropriate action when a command succeeds or fails, or if you need to process a list. These command statements fall into two categories:

Iteration

and

Flow control

18.2.1 Flow control

if, then, else statements provide conditional tests. The test can be based on a variety of things, like the size or permissions of a file, or comparing values or strings. These tests return either a true (0) or a false (1) value, and based on this result you then take further action. We have seen some of these tests already when we dealt with conditional testing.

case statements let you match up patterns, words or values. Once this pattern or value is matched, you can then do other statements based purely on this matched condition.

18.2.2 Iteration

Iteration or looping is the process of executing repeatedly a series of commands. There are three looping statements at our disposal:

for loop Will process all information once in a list until that information is exhausted.

until loop The least used of the looping statements, the until loop will loop continuously waiting for a condition to be true. The test part is at the end of the loop.

while loop The while loop will loop until a certain condition is met. The test part is at the top of the loop.

Any of the iteration of flow control statements can be nested. For example you can have a for loop within a for loop.

Now we know a bit about iteration and control flow let's do some scripts.

From now on all the echo statements in the scripts will use the LINUX or BSD version. That is to say we will use this method of echo 'echo -e -n', which keeps the new line at the end of the echo from being executed. To implement a universal echo command that works on both types of UNIX (System V and BSD), see Chapter 19 on shell functions.

18.3 if then else **statements**

The if statement lets you test for a condition. Based on the true (0) or false (1) return of a test, a series of statements can then be performed. The construct of the if statement makes it ideal for error checking. Here's the format of the if statement:

```
if condition1
then
    commands1
elif condition2
then
    commands2
else
    commands3
fi
```

Let's break down this if statement to see what's really going on.

if condition1	If condition1 is true
then	then
commands1	do the commands1
elif condition2	if condition1 is not met
then	then
commands2	do the commands2
else	if condition1 or condition2 is not met
commands3	then do commands3
fi	finish

The if statement must be terminated with the word fi. Leaving out the closing fi on an if statement will be one of your most common errors. I know I still sometimes forget to put the fi in myself.

The elif and else are optional. If your statement does not have a elif then it does not require an else. The if statement can also be used with many elif parts. The most basic if statement is the if then fi construct.

Let's do some examples.

18.3.1 Simple if **statements**

The most basic if statement is:

if condition
then
   commands
fi

When using the if statement you must put the `then` part on a new line; if you do not an error will be generated. There are ways round this though using the command separator. This is what we will use throughout the rest of this book. So our simple if statement now becomes:

if condition; then
   commands
fi

   Notice how the statement is indented. You do not have to do this to your statements, but I strongly advise you to do so, since it makes for better reading and you can follow through the flow of the conditions and actions more easily.
   The following example uses the test statement to see if '10' is less then '12'. This condition will of course return true, and because this condition is true the statements following the then part are executed, in this case just a simple echo. If the condition returned false, then the script would exit, as there is no `else` part to this statement.

```
$ pg iftest
#!/bin/sh
# iftest
# this is a comment line, all comment lines start with a #
if [ "10" -lt "12" ]
then
   # yes 10 is less than 12
   echo "Yes, 10 is less than 12"
fi
```

18.3.2 Testing values of variables

You can also test to see if a user has entered information by testing the variable you have assigned to read the input. Here, we test to see if the variable NAME holds any information, after the user has pressed `return`.

```
$ pg iftest2
#!/bin/sh
# if test2
echo -n "Enter your name :"
read NAME
# did the user just hit return ????
if [ "$NAME" = "" ] ; then
   echo "You did not enter any information"
fi
```

```
$ iftest2
Enter your name :
You did not enter any information
```

18.3.3 Checking the output of grep

You are not restricted to variable or numeric tests; you can test to see if a system command has completed successfully.

You can use the if statement with grep, to find out whether grep was successful or not. In this example grep is used to see if 'Dave' is in the file data.file. Note the use of 'Dave\>' for an exact match.

```
$ pg grepif
#!/bin/sh
# grepif
if grep 'Dave\>' data.file > /dev/null 2>&1
then
   echo "Great Dave is in the file"
else
   echo "No Dave is not in the file"
fi

$ grepif
No Dave is not in the file
```

In the above example the output of grep is directed to the system dustbin, and grep will return a 0 for success if the match was successful. You just embed the grep command inside an if statement; if grep was successful the if part will be true.

18.3.4 Testing the output of grep on a variable

As we saw earlier, you can use grep on a string. In the following script, a user inputs a list of names; grep then searches the variable holding the names for a person called Peter.

```
$ pg grepstr
#!/bin/sh
# grepstr
echo -n "Enter a list of names:"
read list
if echo $list | grep "Peter" > /dev/null 2>&1
then
   echo "Peter is here"
   # could do some processing here..
else
   echo "Peter's not in the list. No comment!"
fi
```

Here's the output, with some names entered.

```
$ grepstr
Enter a list of names:John Louise Peter James
Peter is here
```

18.3.5 Checking the outcome of a file copy

Here we test to see if a file copy went OK. If the cp command did not copy the file myfile to myfile.bak then an error message is printed. Notice in the error message the command 'basename $0', this prints the script name.

   If any of your scripts exit with an error, it's considered good practice to show the script name as well as directing it to standard error. After all, the user will want to know the script name that threw out the error.

```
$ pg ifcp
#!/bin/sh
# ifcp
if cp myfile myfile.bak; then
  echo "good copy"
else
  echo "`basename $0`: error could not copy the files" >&2
fi

$ ifcp
cp: myfile: No such file or directory
ifcp: error could not copy the files
```

   Notice that the file could not be found and the system generated its own error message as well. These types of errors can mess up your output; the script has already displayed the error so we know it has failed; do we need to be told twice? To get rid of the system-generated errors and system output simply use redirection of the standard error and output. Amending the script thus: > /dev/null 2>&1, we now have:

```
$ pg ifcp
#!/bin/sh
# ifcp
if cp myfile myfile.bak >/dev/null 2> then
  echo "good copy"
else
  echo "`basename $0`: error could not copy the files" >&2
fi
```

   When the script is run all the output including errors will be directed to the system's dustbin.

```
$ ifcp
ifcp: error could not copy the files
```

18.3.6 Testing for current directory

When you run certain administrative scripts, you may want these run from the root directory. Especially if you are doing any kind of global file movement or permission changes, a simple test can tell you if it is being run from the root directory. In the next script the variable DIRECTORY uses command substitution to hold the current directory. A comparison is then made from the value of this variable to a string that holds the value "/" (which is the root directory). If the variable DIRECTORY and string are not equal, the user is exited from the script. The exit status is 1, which means an error.

```
$ pg ifpwd
#!/bin/sh
# ifpwd
DIRECTORY=`pwd`
# grab the current directory

if [ "$DIRECTORY" != "/" ]; then
# is it the root directory ?
# no, the direct output to standard error, which is the screen by default.
   echo "You need to be in the root directory not $DIRECTORY to run this
        script" >&2
# exit with a value of 1, an error
   exit 1
fi
```

18.3.7 Testing for file permissions

You can also test file permissions; here a simple test is used to see if the file test.txt, which has been reassigned to the variable LOGFILE, can be written to.

```
$ pg ifwr
#!/bin/sh
# ifwr
LOGFILE=test.txt
echo $LOGFILE
if [ ! -w "$LOGFILE" ]; then
   echo " You cannot write to $LOGFILE " >&2
fi
```

18.3.8 Testing for parameters passed to a script

The if statement can be used to test the number of parameters passed to your script. Using the special variable $#, which holds the number of calling parameters, we can test to see if the required number of parameters is equal to the number of calling parameters.

Here a test is made to make sure we have three parameters; if not, then a usage message is echoed to standard error. The script then exits with an error status. If the parameters amount to three then all arguments are echoed.

```
$ pg ifparam
#!/bin/sh
# ifparam
if [ $# -lt 3 ]; then
# less than 3 parameters called, echo a usage message and exit
   echo "Usage: `basename $0`arg1 arg2 arg3" >&2
   exit 1
fi
# good, received 3 params, let's echo them
echo "arg1: $1"
echo "arg2: $2"
echo "arg3: $3"
```

Passing only two parameters, a usage message is echoed and the script exits:

```
$ ifparam cup medal
Usage:ifparam arg1 arg2 arg3
```

Passing three parameters this time:

```
$ ifparam cup medal trophy
arg1: cup
arg2: medal
arg3: trophy
```

18.3.9 Determining if a script is in interactive mode

Occasionally you may want to determine if your script is running interactively (terminal mode) or running non-interactively (cron or at). A script may need to know this information so it can decide where to get its input and where to put its output. This can easily be verified by using the test command with the -t option. If it returns true, you are interacting with a terminal.

```
$ pg ifinteractive
#!/bin/sh
# ifinteractive
if [ -t ]; then
   echo "We are interactive with a terminal"
else
   echo "We must be running from some background process probably
         cron or at "
fi
```

18.3.10 Simple `if else` **statements**

The next form of the `if` statement and probably the most widely used is:

> **if condition**
> **then**
>   commands1
> **else**
>   commands2
> **fi**

   Using the `else` part of the `if` statement enables you to take appropriate action if a condition fails its test.

18.3.11 Testing for set variables

Here we test to see if the environment variable `EDITOR` has been set. If the `EDITOR` variable is empty, we will inform the user that `EDITOR` has not been set. If the `EDITOR` variable is set, echo the type of editor to the screen:

```
$ pg ifeditor
#!/bin/sh
# ifeditor
if [ -z $EDITOR ]; then
# the variable has not been set
   echo "Your EDITOR environment is not set"
else
# let's see what it is
   echo "Using $EDITOR as the default editor"
fi
```

18.3.12 Checking the user who is running a script

In the following example, a environment variable is used to test a condition. Here we test to see if `LOGNAME` holds the value 'root'. This type of statement is a common method to add at beginning of scripts as an added security measure. Of course the `LOGNAME` test can be tested on any valid user.

   If the variable is not equal to the string "root", a message is echoed to the standard error which is the screen. The user will be informed that he or she is not root, and the script then exits with a error value of 1.

   If the string "root" is equal to the `LOGNAME` variable, the statement after the else will be executed.

In practice, the script would then continue normal processing of its task. These statements would then go after the `fi`, because all non-root logins would have been kicked out of the script on the first test part.

```
$ pg ifroot
#!/bin/sh
# ifroot
if [ "$LOGNAME" != "root" ]
# if the user is not root
then
  echo "You need to be root to run this script" >&2
  exit 1
else
# yes it is root
  echo "Yes indeed you are $LOGNAME proceed"
fi
# normal processing statements go here
```

18.3.13 Using script parameters to pass down to a system command

You can pass positional parameters to a script and then test the variable. Here, if the user types a directory name after the script name, the script will reassign the $1 special variable to a more meaningful name, in this case DIRECTORY. As we are going to test if a directory is empty, using the command ls -A will return nothing if the directory is empty. A message is then displayed to that effect.

```
$ pg ifdirec
#!/bin/sh
# ifdirec
# assigning $1 to DIRECTORY variable
DIRECTORY=$1
if [ "`ls -A $DIRECTORY`" = "" ] ; then
# if it's an empty string, then it's empty
  echo "$DIRECTORY is indeed empty"
else
# otherwise it is not
  echo "$DIRECTORY is not empty"
fi
```

We could have used the following, instead of the above example, which would have yielded the same results.

```
$ pg ifdirec2
#!/bin/sh
# ifdirec2
DIRECTORY=$1
if [ -z "`ls -A $DIRECTORY`" ]
```

```
then
    echo "$DIRECTORY is indeed empty"
else
    echo "$DIRECTORY is not empty"
fi
```

18.3.14 Using the `null:` command

So far, the action of the conditional tests has been to execute both the then and else parts. Sometimes you may not care to act if a condition is true or even false.

Unfortunately, you cannot leave parts of the if statement blank – some form of statement has to go there. To solve this the shell provides the null ':' command. The null command will always return true, which is just what we want. Going back to our previous example, we can now just place commands in the then part, if the directory is empty.

```
$ pg ifdirectory
#!/bin/sh
# ifdirectory
DIRECTORY=$1
if [ "`ls -A $DIRECTORY`" = "" ]
then
    echo "$DIRECTORY is indeed empty"
    else :    # do nothing
fi
```

18.3.15 Testing the outcome of a directory creation

Still on the subject of directories, the following script takes in a parameter and tries to create a directory with the value of that parameter. The parameter is passed on the command line and reassigned to the variable name DIRECTORY. A test is carried to see if the variable is null.

if ["$DIRECTORY" = ""]

I could have used

if [$# -lt 1]

instead which is more common for parameter testing.

If the string is null a usage message is displayed and the script exits. If the directory already exists then we do nothing, and just fall through the script.

You are prompted to make sure you want to create the directory. If you input anything other than Y or y using the null command no action is taken. The directory is created.

A test on the success of the creation is carried out using the last command status and reported if the creation failed.

```
$ pg ifmkdir
!/bin/sh
# ifmkdir
# parameter is passed as $1 but reassigned to DIRECTORY
DIRECTORY=$1
# is the string empty ??
if [ "$DIRECTORY" = "" ]
then
   echo "Usage :`basename $0` directory to create" >&2
   exit 1
fi
if [ -d $DIRECTORY ]
then : # do nothing
else
   echo "The directory does exist"
   echo -n "Create it now? [y..n] :"
   read ANS
   if [ "$ANS" = "y" ] || [ "$ANS" = "Y" ]
   then
     echo "creating now"
     # create directory and send all output to /dev/null
     mkdir $DIRECTORY >/dev/null 2>&1
     if [ $? != 0 ]; then
        echo "Errors creating the directory $DIRECTORY" >&2
        exit 1
     fi
   else :      # do nothing
   fi
```

Executing the above script displays:

```
$ ifmkdir dt
The directory does exist
Create it now? [y..n]:y
creating now
```

18.3.16 Another copy

Using another cp example, here the script is passed two parameters (which should be holding filenames). The system command cp then copies the value of $1 to $2, all output goes to /dev/null. If the command was successful, no action is to be taken, so we will use the null command.

On the other hand, if it failed, then we want to know about it before the script exits.

```
$ pg ifcp2
#!/bin/sh
# ifcp2
if cp $1 $2 > /dev/null 2>&1
# successful, great do nothing
then :
else
# oh dear, show the user what files they were.
  echo "`basename $0`: ERROR failed to copy $1 to $2"
  exit 1
fi
```

The script is run with no cp errors:

```
$ cp2 myfile.lex myfile.lex.bak
```

The script is run with cp errors:

```
$ ifcp2 myfile.lexx myfile.lex.bak
ifcp2: ERROR failed to copy myfile.lexx myfile.lex.bak
```

In the next script the sort command is used to sort a file called accounts.qtr. All output is sent to the system dustbin. Who wants to see a 300-line sort page up the screen? If successful, no action please; if failed, then let the user know.

```
$ pg ifsort
#!/bin/sh
# ifsort
if sort accounts.qtr > /dev/null
# sorted. Great
then :
else
# better let the user know
  echo "`basename $0`: Oops..errors could not sort accounts.qtr"
fi
```

18.3.17 More than one if statement

You can have nested if statements; all you need to watch out for is that you match up the corresponding ifs with the fi.

18.3.18 Testing and setting environment variables

Earlier on we used the environment variable EDITOR as an example to see if it was set. Let's now take that a step further and let the user set it if it has not previously been set. Here's the script.

```
$ pg ifseted
#!/bin/sh
# ifseted
# is the EDITOR set ?


if [ -z $EDITOR ] ; then
   echo "Your EDITOR environment is not set"
   echo "I will assume you want to use vi..OK"
   echo -n "Do you wish to change it now? [y..n] :"
   read ANS

   # check for an upper or lower case 'y'
   if [ "$ANS" = "y" ] || [ "$ANS" = "Y" ]; then
     echo "enter your editor type :"
     read EDITOR
     if [ -z $EDITOR ] || [ "$EDITOR" = "" ]; then
       # if EDITOR not set and no value in variable EDITOR,
       # then set it to vi
       echo "No, editor entered, using vi as default"
       EDITOR=vi
       export EDITOR
     fi

     # got a value use it for EDITOR
     EDITOR=$EDITOR
     export EDITOR
     echo "setting $EDITOR"
   fi
else
# user
   echo "Using vi as the default editor"
   EDITOR=vi
   export vi
fi
```

Here's how the script works. We first check to see if the variable has been set. If it has, a message outputs saying use vi as the default editor, vi is set as the editor and the script exits.

If vi is not set, it will prompt the user and ask if he or she wants to set it. A check is made for either a lower or upper case response of y. If the response is anything else apart from y or Y, the script ends.

The user is prompted to input the editor type. A check is made to see if it is not set and also to check the user did not just hit return by using the test $EDITOR ="". This is actually a better test than the -z $EDITOR, but both are left in to show both methods. If the test fails, a message is echoed to the screen that vi will be used and vi is thus set as the EDITOR.

If the user enters a name into the variable EDITOR, this is then set and exported.

18.3.19 Checking the last command status

Earlier we created a directory by passing the directory name to a script. The script then prompted the user to see if it was to be created. In this next example we also create a directory and copy all *.txt files from the current directory into the new directory. But with this script we check each command was successful with the last status command and inform the user if the commands failed.

```
$ pg ifmkdir2
#!/bin/sh
# ifmkdir2
DIR_NAME=testdirec
# where are we ?
THERE=`pwd`
# send all output to the system dustbin
mkdir $DIR_NAME > /dev/null 2>&1
# is it a directory ?
if [ -d $DIR_NAME ]; then
# can we cd to the directory
   cd $DIR_NAME
   if [ $? = 0 ]; then
   # yes we can
     HERE=`pwd`
     cp $THERE/*.txt $HERE
   else
     echo "Cannot cd to $DIR_NAME"  >&2
     exit 1
   fi
else
   echo "$cannot create directory $DIR_NAME" >&2
   exit 1
fi
```

18.3.20 Adding and checking integer values

In this next example we look at numeric testing. The script holds a set counter value, which the user can change simply by inputting a new number. The script then adds the new value to the constant value of 100. Here's how it works.

The user can change the value by entering a new value, or if he or she hits return nothing is changed. The current value is then echoed, and the script exits.

If the user replies Y or y, the user is prompted for the new value to add on to the counter. If the user hits return, the script echoes that the counter will stay the same value. When the user enters a value, a numeric test is carried out to see if it is a number. If it is then it is added to the value of COUNTER and the new value is then displayed.

```
$ pg ifcounter
#!/bin/sh
# ifcounter
COUNTER=100
echo "Do you wish to change the counter value currently set at $COUNTER ?
      [y..n] :"
read ANS
if [ "$ANS" = "y" ] || [ "$ANS" = "Y" ]; then
# yes user wants to change the value
  echo "Enter a sensible value "
  read VALUE
  # simple test to see if it's numeric, add any number to VALUE,
  # then check out return
  # code
  expr $VALUE + 10 > /dev/null 2>&1
    STATUS=$?
  # check return code of the expr
  if [ "$VALUE" = "" ] || [ "$STATUS" != "0" ]; then
  # send errors to standard error
    echo " You either entered nothing or a non-numeric " >&2
    echo " Sorry now exiting..counter stays at $COUNTER" >&2
    exit 1
  fi
# if we are here, then it's a number, so add it to COUNTER
  COUNTER=`expr $COUNTER + $VALUE`
  echo " Counter now set to $COUNTER"
else
# if we are here then user just hit return instead of entering a number
# or answered n to the change a value prompt
  echo " Counter stays at $COUNTER"
fi
```

Here's how the above script runs.

```
$ ifcount
Do you wish to change the counter value currently set at 100 ? [y..n]:n
Counter stays at 100


$ ifcount
Do you wish to change the counter value currently set at 100 ? [y..n]:y
Enter a sensible value
fdg
 You either entered nothing or a non-numeric
 Sorry now exiting..counter stays at 100


$ ifcount
Do you wish to change the counter value currently set at 100 ? [y..n]:y
Enter a sensible value   250
Counter now set to 350
```

18.3.21 Simple security login script

Here is a framework to add extra security before you launch your applications when a user logs in. It prompts for a username and password; if the username and password match the strings contained in the script then the user is in. If not then the user is exited.

The script works by setting the variables to a false value first – always assume that the user input will be wrong. The current settings of stty are saved, so we can then hide the characters being typed into the password field. The stty settings are then restored.

If the user enters a correct user ID and password (the password is mayday) the variables INVALID_USER and INVALID_PASSWD are set to 'no' for a invalid user or password. A test is then carried out, and if either of the variables is set to yes, the default, the script will exit the user.

Users with valid IDs and passwords are then let in. This is a pretty basic framework for a type of login script. In this example valid user IDs are dave or pauline.

```
$ pg ifpass
#!/bin/sh
# ifpass
# set the variables to false
INVALID_USER=yes
INVALID_PASSWD=yes
# save the current stty settings
SAVEDSTTY=`stty -g`
echo "You are logging into a sensitive area"
echo -n "Enter your ID name :"
read NAME
# hide the characters typed in
stty -echo
echo "Enter your password :"
read PASSWORD
# back on again
stty $SAVEDSTTY
if [ "$NAME" = "dave" ] || [ "$NAME" = "pauline" ]; then
  # if a valid then set variable
  INVALID_USER=no
fi

if [ "$PASSWORD" = "mayday" ]; then
# if valid password then set variable
INVALID_PASSWD=no
fi
if [ "$INVALID_USER" = "yes" -o "$INVALID_PASSWD" = "yes" ]; then
  echo "`basename $0 :` Sorry wrong password or userid"
  exit 1
fi
# if we get here then their ID and password are OK.
echo "correct user id and password given"
```

When the above script is run giving an invalid password:

```
$ ifpass
You are logging into a sensitive area
Enter your ID name  : dave
Enter your password :
ifpass :Sorry wrong password or userid
```

Now giving a correct login name and password.

```
$ ifpass
You are logging into a sensitive area
Enter your ID name  : dave
Enter your password :
correct user id and password given
```

18.3.22 Using `elif`

The `elif` part of the `if then else` statement is used to test for more than two conditions.

18.3.23 Multiple checks using `elif`

Using a simple example, a test is carried out on usernames entered into a script. The script will first test that the user actually entered a name; if nothing is entered then do nothing. If a name is entered, using `elif` we test to see if the name matches either root, louise or dave. If the name does match any of these values then echo the name anyway, informing the user he or she is not root, louise or dave.

```
$ pg ifelif
#!/bin/sh
# ifelif
echo -n "enter your login name :"
read NAME
# no name entered do not carry on
if [ -z $NAME ] || [ "$NAME" = "" ]; then
  echo "You did not enter a name"
elif
  # is the name root
  [ "$NAME" = "root" ]; then
  echo "Hello root"
elif
  # or is it louise
  [ $NAME = "louise" ]; then
  echo "Hello louise"
```

```
elif
  # or is it dave
  [ "$NAME" = "dave" ]; then
  echo "Hello dave"
else
  # no it's somebody else
  echo "You are not root or louise or dave but hi $NAME"
fi
```

When we run the above script with different information for the login name we get:

```
$ ifelif
enter your login name : dave
Hello dave

$ ifelif
enter your login name :
You did not enter a name

$ ifelif2
enter your login name : peter
You are not root or louise or dave but hi peter
```

18.3.24 Checking multiple file locations

Suppose we want to cat an audit log file. The file is either held in /usr/opts/audit/logs or in /usr/local/audit/logs, depending on who installed it. Before we cat the file we will want to make sure that the file is readable; this is our test part. If we cannot find the file or it is not readable, we will want to echo out an error message. Here's the script:

```
$ pg ifcataudit
#!/bin/sh
# ifcataudit
# locations of the log file
LOCAT_1=/usr/opts/audit/logs/audit.log
LOCAT_2=/usr/local/audit/audit.logs

if [ -r $LOCAT_1 ]; then
  # if it is in this directory and is readable then cat it
  echo "Using LOCAT_1"
  cat $LOCAT_1
elif
  # else it then must be in this directory, and is it readable
  [ -r $LOCAT_2 ]
then
  echo "Using LOCAT_2"
  cat $LOCAT_2
```

```
else
  # not in any of the directories...
  echo "`basename $0`: Sorry the audit file is not readable or cannot be
      located." >&2
  exit 1
fi
```

When we run the above script, if the file is in either of the two directories and the file is readable then you can `cat` it. If not, echo an error and exit. This example fails because our imaginary file is not present.

```
$ ifcataudit
ifcataudit: Sorry the audit file is not readable or cannot be located.
```

18.4 Case statement

The `case` statement is a multiple-choice statement. You use `case` statements to match a value against a pattern. If the match is successful, you can execute commands based purely on this match. Here's the format of the 'case' statement:

case value in
pattern1)
   commands1
   ...
  ;;
pattern2)
   commands2
   ...
  ;;
esac

Here's how `case` works. The word after the value must be 'in', and each pattern must be terminated with a right bracket. The value can be a variable or a constant. When a match is found against a pattern all commands are then executed for that pattern up to the `;;`.

The value will check each pattern for a match. Once a pattern is matched, it will not continue with the other patterns even after it has executed the commands for the matched pattern. If no match is found against the patterns, you can then trap the value by using an asterisk, which will catch any other input.

The pattern part can include metacharacters, the same type of pattern matching we used in filename expansions on the command line, which are as follows:

*   any characters
?   any single character
[..]   any character from a class or range.

Let's do some examples.

18.4.1 Simple case statement

The following script prompts for a number 1 to 5. The number is passed down to the case statement, the variable ANS is assigned to the case value ANS, and ANS is compared against each pattern.

If a match is found, the commands inside the pattern part are executed until it sees the ;;. In this case, it will just echo a command informing the user what selection was made. The execution of the case will then terminate, because a match has been found.

Processing can continue after the case statement.

If a match is not found, it will be trapped by using the *, pattern, which traps anything. The error message is then executed.

```
$ pg caseselect
#!/bin/sh
# caseselect
echo -n "enter a number from 1 to 5   :"
read ANS
  case $ANS in
  1) echo "you select 1"
     ;;
  2) echo "you select 2"
     ;;
  3) echo "you select 3"
     ;;
  4) echo "you select 4"
     ;;
  5) echo "you select 5"
     ;;
  *) echo "`basename $0`: This is not between 1 and 5" >&2
     exit 1
     ;;
  esac
```

When we run this script with different input we get.

```
$ caseselect
enter a number from 1 to 5 : 4
you select 4
```

Using the pattern * traps anything else that does not match:

```
$ caseselect
enter a number from 1 to 5   :pen
caseselect: This is not between 1 and 5
```

18.4.2 Using | with pattern matching

When using case you can also specify the | symbol as an or command. For example, vt100|vt102) will match the patterns vt100 or vt102.

In this example, the user is asked for his or her terminal type. If the user enters vt100 or vt102, a match will occur with the pattern 'vt100|vt102)'. The command to execute is the setting of the TERM variable to vt100. If the user puts in a terminal type that is not matched against the pattern, the * will trap it and set it to vt100 anyway. Finally, outside of the case statement, the TERM is exported. No matter what the user enters, TERM will hold a valid terminal type because we used the * pattern match.

```
$ pg caseterm
#!/bin/sh
# caseterm
echo " choices are.. vt100, vt102, vt220"
echo -n "enter your terminal type :"
read TERMINAL
  case $TERMINAL in
  vt100|vt102) TERM=vt100
    ;;
  vt220) TERM=vt220
    ;;
  *) echo "`basename $0` : Unknown response" >&2
     echo "setting it to vt100 anyway, so there"
     TERM=vt100
    ;;
  esac
  export TERM
echo "Your terminal is set to $TERM"
```

When the script runs and we input an invalid terminal type we get

```
$ caseterm
 choices are.. vt100, vt102, vt220
enter your terminal type :vt900
caseterm : Unknown response
setting it to vt100 anyway, so there
Your terminal is set to vt100
```

For a correct terminal type we get

```
$ case2
 choices are.. vt100, vt102, vt220
enter your terminal type :vt220
Your terminal is set to vt220
```

Either way, the user is set up with a terminal type.

18.4.3 Prompting for a y or n

A good use of the case is prompting for a response on whether to continue processing. Here the user is prompted to answer either y to continue processing or n to exit. If the user enters either y, Y, yes or Yes then processing will continue as the execution of the script will continue after the case statement. If the user enters n, N, no or some other response the user is exited from the script.

```
$ pg caseans
#!/bin/sh
# caseans
echo -n "Do you wish to proceed [y..n] :"
read ANS
  case $ANS in
  y|Y|yes|Yes) echo "yes is selected"
    ;;
  n|N) echo "no is selected"
    exit 0    # no error so only use exit 0 to terminate
    ;;
  *) echo "`basename $0` : Unknown response" >&2
    exit 1
    ;;
  esac
# if we are here then a y|Y|yes|Yes was selected only.
```

Here's the output if we run the script with an invalid response:

```
$ caseans
Do you wish to proceed [y..n] :df
caseans : Unknown response
```

And with a good response.

```
$ caseans
Do you wish to proceed [y..n] :y
yes is selected
```

18.4.4 Case and passing command parameters

You can also use case to handle passing parameters to scripts.

In the next script, a test is carried out on the special variable $#, which holds the number of arguments passed. If it is not equal to 1 then it will exit with a usage message.

A case statement then traps the following parameters: passwd, start, stop or help. Further coding can then be undertaken for each of these matched patterns. If an unknown value is passed then a usage message is echoed out to standard error.

```
$ pg caseparam
#!/bin/sh
# caseparam
if [ $# != 1 ]; then
  echo "Usage:`basename $0`[start|stop|help]"  >&2
  exit 1
fi
# assign the parameter to the variable OPT
OPT=$1
  case $OPT in
  start) echo "starting..`basename $0`"
    # code here to start a process
    ;;
  stop) echo "stopping..`basename $0`"
    # code here to stop a process
    ;;
  help)
    # code here to display a help page
    ;;
  *) echo "Usage:`basename $0`[start|stop|help]"
    ;;
  esac
```

When the script runs with an invalid parameter passed we get

```
$ caseparam what
Usage:caseparam [start|stop|help]
```

And with a valid parameter passed:

```
$ caseparam stop
stopping..caseparam
```

18.4.5 Trapping input with no pattern commands

You do not have to put commands after the pattern match part if you do not want to; not doing this is generally a good way of filtering out unwanted responses before carrying out further processing.

If we wanted to run a account report for an accounts department, it would be a good idea first to make sure that the user has input the correct department number before determining what type of report to run. This is easily accomplished by pattern matching all the possible values that we require; anything else is not valid.

In the following script, if the user inputs a department number that is not 234, 453, 655 or 454, the user is exited with a usage statement. Once we have a valid department number, we can then apply the same technique for the type of report. At the end of the case statement what is left is the validated department numbers and a report type. Here's the script.

```
$ pg casevalid
!/bin/sh
# casevalid
TYPE=""
echo -n "enter the account dept No: :"
read ACC
  case $ACC in
    234);;
    453);;
    655);;
    454);;
  *) echo "`basename $0`: Unknown dept No:"  >&2
     echo "try..234,453,655,454"
     exit 1
     ;;
  esac

# if we are here, then we have validated the dept no
echo " 1 . post"
echo " 2 . prior"
echo -n "enter the type of report: "
read ACC_TYPE
  case $ACC_TYPE in
  1)TYPE=post;;
  2)TYPE=prior;;
  *)  echo "`basename $0`: Unknown account type." >&2
     exit 1
     ;;
  esac

# if we get here then we are validated!
echo "now running report for dept $ACC for the type $TYPE"
# run the command report..
```

For a valid input we get:

```
$ casevalid
enter the account dept No: :234
 1 . post
 2 . prior
enter the type of report:2
now running report for dept 234 for the type  prior
```

For an invalid department number input we could get:

```
$ casevalid
enter the account dept No: :432
casevalid: Unknown dept No:
try..234,453,655,454
```

Or for an invalid report type we get:

```
$ casevalid
enter the account dept No: :655
 1 . post
 2 . prior
enter the type of report:4
casevalid: Unknown account type.
```

18.4.6 Default variable values

If the user just hits return on a read variable, the script does not always have to exit. A test can determine if the variable is set, and if it isn't then a value can be assigned.

In the following script, a user is asked to input a day to run a report. If the user just hits return, the default day is used, which is Saturday. That day is assigned to the variable WHEN.

If the user inputs another day, this day is validated with a case statement for valid days to run, which are Saturday, Sunday and Monday. Notice that different abbreviations of the days have been included to trap all 'most probable' combinations of the days.

Here's the script.

```
$ pg caserep
#!/bin/sh
# caserep
echo "     Weekly Report"
echo -n "What day do you want to run report [Saturday] :"

# if just a return is hit then except default which is Saturday
read WHEN
echo "validating..${WHEN:="Saturday"}"
  case $WHEN in
  Monday|MONDAY|mon)
    ;;
  Sunday|SUNDAY|sun)
    ;;
  Saturday|SATURDAY|sat)
    ;;
  *) echo " Are you nuts!, this report can only be run on " >&2
    echo " on a Saturday, Sunday or Monday" >&2
    exit 1
    ;;
  esac
echo "Report to run on $WHEN"
# command here to submitted actual report run
```

For a correct input we get:

```
$ caserep
      Weekly Report
What day do you want to run report [Saturday] :
validating..Saturday
Report to run on Saturday
```

For an incorrect input we could get:

```
$ caserep
      Weekly Report
What day do you want to run report [Saturday] :Tuesday
validating..Tuesday
 Are you nuts!, this report can only be run on
 on a Saturday, Sunday or Monday
```

You may have concluded that the case statement can do the same task as several
if then else statements. You would be correct in this assumption.

18.5 for **loop**

The general format of the for loop is:

for variable_name in list
do
   command1
   command...
done

The for loop processes all the information once for each value contained in list.
To access each value in list use variable_name. The commands can be any valid
shell command or statement. Variable_name can be any word you want.

     The use of in list is optional; if you do not include it, the for loop uses the
positional parameters from the command line.

     The in list can contain substitution, strings and filenames. Let's look at
some examples.

18.5.1 Simple for **loop**

This loop simply echoes out the list, which is '1 2 3 4 5'. To access each variable the
variable_name loop is used.

```
$ pg for_i
#!/bin/sh
# for_i
```

```
for loop in 1 2 3 4 5
do
   echo $loop
done
```

Running the above script outputs:

```
$ for_i
1
2
3
4
5
```

18.5.2 Printing out a string list

Here is a for loop where the list contains a string which holds the values "orange red blue grey". The command for each variable is echo, the variable_name is loop. The echo command echoes out each value of the list using $loop until the list is empty.

```
$ pg forlist
#!/bin/sh
# forlist
for loop in "orange red blue grey"
do
   echo $loop
done

$ forlist
orange red blue grey
```

You can also combine strings with the variable_name which in our case is loop.

```
echo " this is the fruit $loop"
```

This would give

```
This is the fruit orange red blue grey
```

18.5.3 Using ls with the for loop

This loop evaluates the shell's ls command and prints out each file in the current directory.

```
$ pg forls
```

```
#!/bin/sh
# forls
for loop in `ls `
do
   echo $loop
done

$ forls
array
arrows
center
center1
center2
centerb
```

18.5.4 Using parameters with a for loop

When you omit the in list with the for loop, it will take the command line positional parameters as its arguments. This is really the same as stating:

for params in "$@"

or

for params in "$*"

Here's an example of not using the in list. The for loop will now look to the special parameter $@ or $* to get the arguments form the command line.

```
$ pg forparam2
#!/bin/sh
# forparam2
for params
do
   echo "You supplied $params as a command line option"
done
   echo $params
done

$ forparam2 myfile1 myfile2 myfile3
 You supplied myfile1 as a command line option
 You supplied myfile2 as a command line option
 You supplied myfile3 as a command line option
```

The following script includes the in "$@", which produces the same output as the above script.

```
$ pg forparam3
#!/bin/sh
# forparam3
for params in "$@"
do
   echo "You supplied $params as a command line option"
done
   echo $params
done
```

Taking the above a step further, if you wanted to find a series of files, you could use the find command with the for loop, taking advantage of the command line parameter, to pass all the files down to find.

```
$ pg forfind
#!/bin/sh
# forfind
for loop
do
   find / -name $loop -print
done
```

When the script gets executed it takes its values from the command line parameter, and uses these values to form the -name part of the find command.

```
$ forfind passwd LPSO.AKSOP
/etc/passwd
/etc/pam.d/passwd
/etc/uucp/passwd
/usr/bin/passwd
/usr/local/accounts/LPSO.AKSOP
```

18.5.5 Pinging servers with a for loop

As the for loop can process each word in a list, let's set up a variable that holds the names of some servers on a network, and use the for loop to ping each one.

```
$ pg forping
#!/bin/sh
# forping
HOSTS="itserv dnssevr acctsmain ladpd ladware"
for loop in $HOSTS
do
   ping -c 2 $loop
done
```

18.5.6 Backing up files using a `for` loop

You can use the `for` loop to backup all files, simply by appending a variable to the destination argument of the `cp` command. Here we have a variable called `.BAK`, which is appended to each destination filename as it goes through the loop using the `cp` command. The list is the shell command `ls`.

```
$ pg forcp
#!/bin/sh
# forcp
BAK=".bak"
for loop in `ls `
do
   echo "copying $loop to $loop$BAK"
   cp $loop $loop$BAK
done

$ forcp
copying array to array.bak
copying arrows to arrows.bak
copying center to center.bak
copying center1 to center1.bak
. . .
```

18.5.7 Multiple translation

To match all files that begin with LPSO and convert them to upper case, the `ls` and `cat` commands are used; `ls` gets the files and `cat` is used to pipe them through to `tr`. The destination files are all given the extension '.UC'. Notice the use of the back quote when using the `ls` command in the for loop.

```
$ pg forUC
#!/bin/sh
# forUC
for files in `ls LPSO*`
do
   cat $files |tr "[a-z]" "[A-Z]" >$files.UC
done
```

18.5.8 Multiple `sed` deletes

In the next example, `sed` is used to delete all empty lines, directing the output to a new files with the extension `.HOLD`. `mv` then moves the files back to their original filename.

```
$ pg forsed
```

```
#!/bin/sh
# forsed
for files in `ls LPSO*`
do
   sed -e "/^$/d" $files >$files.HOLD
   mv $files.HOLD $files
done
```

18.5.9 Counting iterations

When we discussed `expr` previously, I stated that this is the command to use when you want to have counters in your loops. Here it is, using an `ls` listing and counting each file as it goes through the for loop.

```
$ pg forcount
#!/bin/sh
# forcount
counter=0
for files in *
do
   # increment
   counter=`expr $counter + 1`
done
   echo "There are $counter files in `pwd` we need to process"

$ forcount
There are 45 files in /apps/local we need to process
```

Alternatively the same result could have been obtained with the `wc` command.

```
$ ls |wc -l
   45
```

18.5.10 `for` loops and here documents

You can combine any commands you like in a `for` loop. In this example, a variable holds all the current users that are logged on. This is obtained by using the `who` command, with a bit of `awk`. Next, a `for` loop loops round all these usernames, and mails each user a message. The mail message part is accomplished using a 'here' document.

```
$ pg formailit
#!/bin/sh
# formailit
WHOS_ON=`who -u | awk '{print $1}'`
```

```
for user in $WHOS_ON
do
mail $user << MAYDAY
Dear Colleagues,
It's my birthday today, see you down the
club at 17:30 for a drink.

See ya.
$LOGNAME
MAYDAY
Done
```

Here's the output of the mail message to the about script.

```
$ pg mbox
Dear Colleagues,
It's my birthday today, see you down the
club at 17:30 for a drink.

See ya.
dave
```

18.5.11 Nested `for` loops

To nest loops, you put a `for` loop inside another for loop:

for variable_name in list
do
   for variable_name2 in list2
   do
     command1
     ...
   done
done

The following script is a nested `for` loop. We have two lists, APPS and SCRIPTS, the first of which contains the path to applications on a server, and the second administrative scripts that are to be run on each application. For each application in the list APPS a script name held in the list SCRIPTS will be run against it. The scripts actually get run in the background using `&`. The script also puts an entry to a log file, using `tee`, so the output goes to the screen as well as a file. Look at the output to see how the `for` nest uses the list SCRIPTS to perform processing on the list APPS.

```
$ pg audit_run
#!/bin/sh
# audit_run
APPS="/apps/accts /apps/claims /apps/stock /apps/serv"
SCRIPTS="audit.check report.run cleanup"
```

```
LOGFILE=audit.log
MY_DATE=`date +%H:%M" on "%d/%m%Y`


# outer loop
for loop in $APPS
do
  # inner loop
  for loop2 in $SCRIPTS
  do
    echo "system $loop now running $loop2 at $MY_DATE" | tee -a $LOGFILE
    $loop $loop2 &

  done
done


$ audit_run
system /apps/accts now running audit.check at 20:33 on 23/051999
system /apps/accts now running report.run at 20:33 on 23/051999
system /apps/accts now running cleanup at 20:33 on 23/051999
system /apps/claims now running audit.check at 20:33 on 23/051999
system /apps/claims now running report.run at 20:33 on 23/051999
system /apps/claims now running cleanup at 20:34 on 23/051999
system /apps/stock now running audit.check at 20:34 on 23/051999
system /apps/stock now running report.run at 20:34 on 23/051999
system /apps/stock now running cleanup at 20:34 on 23/051999
system /apps/serv now running audit.check at 20:34 on 23/051999
system /apps/serv now running report.run at 20:34 on 23/051999
system /apps/serv now running cleanup at 20:34 on 23/051999
```

18.6 `until` **loop**

The until loop lets you execute a series of commands until a condition is true. The until loop is really the opposite of the while loop in its processing. The while loop should always be preferred to the until loop, but in some cases – and it's only a few – the until loop does the job better.

The format of the until loop is:

until condition
    command1
    ...
done

The condition is any valid test condition. The test takes place at the end of the loop, therefore it will always loop once – be aware of that please.

Here are a few examples.

18.6.1 Simple until loop

This script continuously greps the who command for the user root. The variable IS_ROOT holds the result of the grep.

If root is found, the loop finishes processing. A mail message is then sent to user simon telling him that root has logged in. Notice the use of the sleep command, which gets used quite a lot with the until loop, because you have to have some command in place, and what better than sleeping for a few seconds.

```
$ pg until_who
#!/bin/sh
# until_who
IS_ROOT=`who | grep root`
until [ "$IS_ROOT" ]
do
   sleep 5
done
echo "Watch it. roots in " | mail simon
```

18.6.2 Monitoring for a file presence

In this example, the until loop hangs around doing 'sleep 1' until a file called /tmp/monitor.LCK is deleted. When it is deleted the script carries on with normal processing.

```
$ pg until_lck
!/bin/sh
# until_lck
LOCK_FILE=/tmp/process.LCK
until  [ !  -f $LOCK_FILE ]

do
   sleep 1
done
echo "file deleted "
# normal processing now, file is present
```

The above is one method on how scripts can work together when processing.

Here's one way how scripts can communicate. Suppose another script, let's call it process_main, is used to collect information from all the machines on the local network and put the information into a report file.

When the script process_main runs it creates a LCK file (lock file). The above script has to take the information that process_main has gathered, but it is no good trying to process a file if the script process_main is still updating the report file.

To overcome these problems the script process_main will create a LCK file when it starts and delete it when it finishes.

The above script will hang around waiting for the LCK file to be deleted. When it has been deleted the script then can process the contents of the report file.

18.6.3 Monitoring disk space

The until loop is also very useful for monitoring conditions. Suppose we wanted to monitor a filesystem capacity, and to mail root when it hits a certain level.

The next script monitors the filesystem /logs. It continuously pulls off information from the variable $LOOK_OUT, which holds the capacity of /logs, using awk and grep.

If the capacity goes above 90%, the command part is triggered, root is mailed, and the script exits. The exit is needed because if we did not exit and the condition remained true (for example, it always remained above 90%), root would be mailed continuously.

```
$ pg until_mon
#!/bin/sh
# until_mon
# get percent column and strip off header row from df
LOOK_OUT=`df |grep /logs | awk '{print $5}'| sed 's/%//g'`
echo $LOOK_OUT
until [ "$LOOK_OUT" -gt "90" ]
do
   echo "Filesystem..logs is nearly full" | mail root
   exit 0
done
```

18.7 while **loop**

The while loop is used conditionally to execute a series of commands. It is also used to read data from a input file. The format of the while loop is:

while command
do
    commands1
    commands2
    ...
done

Several commands can be placed between the while and do, though generally only one is used, and the command is usually a test condition.

The commands after the do and up to the done will be executed only if the exit status of the command is zero; if the exit status is anything else, the loop will terminate.

When the commands have been executed, control is returned back to the top of the loop to start all over again until the condition of the test is a non-zero.

18.7.1 Simple `while` loop

Here's a basic `while` loop. The test condition is if 'COUNTER is less than 5' then the condition will remain true. The COUNTER starts at zero and is incremented each time the loop is processed.

```
$ pg whilecount
#!/bin/sh
# whilecount
COUNTER=0
# does the counter = 5 ?
while [ $COUNTER -lt 5 ]
do
   # add one to the counter
   COUNTER=`expr $COUNTER + 1`
   echo $COUNTER
done
```

Running the above script will echo out the numbers 1 to 5, then terminate.

```
$ whilecount
1
2
3
4
5
```

18.7.2 Using the `while` loop to read from the keyboard

The `while` loop can be used to read information from the keyboard. In the following example, information entered is assigned to the variable FILM. Typing <CTRL-D> will terminate the loop.

```
$ pg whileread
#!/bin/sh
# whileread
echo " type <CTRL-D> to terminate"
echo -n "enter your most liked film :"
while read FILM
do
   echo "Yeah, great film the $FILM"
done
```

When the script is run, the input could be:

```
$ whileread
enter your most liked film: Sound of Music
Yeah, great film the Sound of Music
<CTRL-D>
```

18.7.3 Using the `while` loop to read data from files

The most common use of the while loop is to read data in from a file, so the script can process the information.

Suppose we want to read information from the following personnel file that contains employee names, departments and their employee IDs.

```
$ pg names.txt
Louise Conrad:Accounts:ACC8987
Peter James:Payroll:PR489
Fred Terms:Customer:CUS012
James Lenod:Accounts:ACC887
Frank Pavely:Payroll:PR489
```

We can use a variable to hold each line of data. The condition will be true until there is no more data to be read. The `while` loop uses the redirection of input to read in the file. Notice the whole line is assigned to the single variable $LINE.

```
$ pg whileread
#!/bin/sh
# whileread
while read LINE
do
   echo $LINE
done < names.txt

$ whileread
Louise Conrad:Accounts:ACC8987
Peter James:Payroll:PR489
Fred Terms:Customer:CUS012
James Lenod:Accounts:ACC887
Frank Pavely:Payroll:PR489
```

18.7.4 Reading files using `IFS`

To get rid of the colon field separators when outputting use the `IFS` variable, simply save the current settings of the `IFS` before it is changed, and then restore the settings after the script has finished with them. Using `IFS` we can now change the field separator to a colon instead of the default white space or tab. As we know there are three fields we can assign to a separate variable: `NAME`, `DEPT` and `ID`.

To make it even more presentable, we can use tabs with the echo command to spread the fields out a bit. Here's the script.

```
$ pg   whilereadifs
#!/bin/sh
# whilereadifs
# save the setting of IFS
SAVEDIFS=$IFS
# assign new separator to IFS
IFS=:
while read NAME DEPT ID
do
   echo -e "$NAME\t $DEPT\t $ID"
done < names.txt
# restore the settings of IFS
IFS=$SAVEDIFS
```

When the script runs we get a better output:

```
$ whilereadifs
Louise Conrad      Accounts    ACC8987
Peter James        Payroll     PR489
Fred Terms         Customer    CUS012
James Lenod        Accounts    ACC887
Frank Pavely       Payroll     PR489
```

18.7.5 Processing a file with conditional tests

Most while loops have some sort of test statement in them to decide what to do next.

Here we read in the employee file and echo out all details to a hold file until the employee "James Lenod" is found, then the script exits. The echo of the details before the test ensures that "James Lenod" gets added to the hold file.

Notice how all the variables are set at the top of the script. This will save you time and typos when you have to do small amendments to the variables. All your editing stays at the top of the script, instead of messing around through the whole script.

```
$ pg whileread_file
#!/bin/sh
# whileread_file
# initialise variables
SAVEDIFS=$IFS
IFS=:
HOLD_FILE=hold_file
NAME_MATCH="James Lenod"
INPUT_FILE=names.txt

# create a new HOLD_FILE each time, in case script is continuously run
>$HOLD_FILE
```

```
while read NAME DEPT ID
do
  # echo all information into holdfile with redirection
  echo $NAME $DEPT $ID >>$HOLD_FILE
  # is it a match ???
  if [ "$NAME" = "$NAME_MATCH" ]; then
    # yes then nice exit
    echo "all entries up to and including $NAME_MATCH are in $HOLD_FILE"
    exit 0
  fi
done < $INPUT_FILE
# restore IFS
IFS=$SAVEDIFS
```

We could take this a step further and list how many employees belong to each department. We keep the same reading in format, assigning each field to a variable name. Using a `case` statement we then simply use `expr` to add up each match. Any unknown department found is just echoed to the standard error; there is no need to abort if an invalid department is found.

```
$ pg whileread_cond
!/bin/sh
# whileread_cond
# initialise variables
ACC_LOOP=0; CUS_LOOP=0; PAY_LOOP=0;

SAVEDIFS=$IFS
IFS=:
while read NAME DEPT ID
do
  # increment counter for each matched dept.
  case $DEPT in
  Accounts) ACC_LOOP=`expr $ACC_LOOP + 1`
    ACC="Accounts"
    ;;
  Customer) CUS_LOOP=`expr $CUS_LOOP + 1`
    CUS="Customer"
    ;;
  Payroll) PAY_LOOP=`expr $PAY_LOOP + 1`
    PAY="Payroll"
    ;;
  *) echo "`basename $0`: Unknown department $DEPT" >&2
    ;;
  esac
done < names.txt
IFS=$SAVEDIFS
echo "there are $ACC_LOOP employees assigned to $ACC dept"
echo "there are $CUS_LOOP employees assigned to $CUS dept"
echo "there are $PAY_LOOP employees assigned to $PAY dept"
```

Running the script outputs:

```
$ whileread_cond
there are 2 employees assigned to Accounts dept
there are 1 employees assigned to Customer dept
there are 2 employees assigned to Payroll dept
```

18.7.6 Running totals

A fairly common task is to read in a file and keep a running total of some columns containing numbers. A file below contains the number of items sold by the departments STAT and GIFT.

```
$ pg total.txt
STAT    3444
GIFT     233
GIFT     252
GIFT     932
STAT     212
STAT     923
GIFT     129
```

Our task is to provide a total for all items sold for the department GIFT. To keep running totals we use expr. Looking at the following expr statement below, the variables LOOP and TOTAL are initially assigned a zero value outside of the loop. As the script loops the ITEMS are added to the TOTAL. The first iteration of the loop will contain only the first item but, as the process continues, the ITEMS will be added to the cumulating TOTAL.

The next expr statement increments the counter.

```
LOOP=0
TOTAL=0
...
while...
TOTAL=`expr $TOTAL + $ITEMS`
ITEMS=`expr $ITEMS + 1`
done
```

A common mistake to make when using expr is forgetting to initialize your variables first.

```
LOOP=0
TOTAL=0
```

If you do forget to initialize you will get expr errors creeping up your screen.

You can initialize the variable inside the loop if you wish:

```
TOTAL=`expr ${TOTAL:=0} + ${ITEMS}`
```

The above will assign zero to the variable TOTAL if the variable does not contain a value. You will find the first example of initializing variables with expr is more common. Also, remember to echo out the final total value outside of the loop.

Here's the script.

```
$ pg $total
#!/bin/sh
# total
# init variables
LOOP=0
TOTAL=0
COUNT=0

echo "Items  Dept"
echo "_____"
while read DEPT ITEMS
do
   # keep a count on total records read
   COUNT=`expr $COUNT + 1`
   if [ "$DEPT" = "GIFT" ]; then
     # keep a running total
     TOTAL=`expr $TOTAL + $ITEMS`
     ITEMS=`expr $ITEMS + 1`
     echo -e "$ITEMS\t$DEPT"
   fi
   #echo $DEPT $ITEMS
done < total.txt
echo "============"
echo $TOTAL
echo "There were $COUNT entries altogether in the file"
```

When we run the script, we get:

```
$ total
Items  Dept
_____
234     GIFT
253     GIFT
933     GIFT
130     GIFT
============
1546
There were 7 entries altogether in the file
```

18.7.7 Reading a pair of records at a time

At some point you may wish to process two records at a time, perhaps to compare different fields from both records. Reading in two records at a time is fairly straightforward, all we need to do after the first 'while' read is put a 'do' after it with another read. When using this technique it helps that here are indeed an even amount of records to read, so don't forget to check that.

Here's a file containing six records, record 1, record 2 etc.

```
$ pg record.txt
record 1
record 2
record 3
record 4
record 5
record 6
```

We will read in two records at a time, no actual testing is done on the records in this example.

Here's the script that does the work.

```
$ pg readpair
#!/bin/sh
# readpair
# first record
while read rec1
do
  # second record
  read rec2
  # further processing/testing goes here to test or compare both records
  echo "This is record one of a pair :$rec1"
  echo "This is record two of a pair :$rec2"
  echo "--------------------------"
done < record.txt
```

Let's first check that we do have an even amount of records, using the wc command.

```
$ cat record.txt | wc -l
      6
```

We have six records so let's process.

```
$ readpair
This is record one of a pair :record 1
This is record two of a pair :record 2
----------------------------
This is record one of a pair :record 3
This is record two of a pair :record 4
----------------------------
This is record one of a pair :record 5
This is record two of a pair :record 6
----------------------------
```

18.7.8 Ignoring the # character

While reading text files you may want to ignore or disregard any comment lines you come across. Here's a typical example.

Suppose you wish to read in a configuration file using a normal while loop. You would pick up every line, which is what you want in most cases.

However, to ignore certain lines that start with a certain character you need to use the case statement. As the # sign is a special character, it's best to escape it with a backslash first; we then put an asterisk after the hash sign, to include any characters after the hash.

Here's a typical configuration file.

```
$ pg config
# THIS IS THE SUB SYSTEM AUDIT CONFIG FILE
# DO NOT EDIT!!!!.IT WORKS
#
# type of admin access
AUDITSCM=full
# launch place of sub-systems
AUDITSUB=/usr/opt/audit/sub
# serial hash number of product
HASHSER=12890AB3
# END OF CONFIG FILE!!!
```

And here's the script that ignores the hash signs:

```
$ pg ignore_hash
#!/bin/sh
# ignore_hash
INPUT_FILE=config
if [-s $INPUT_FILE ]; then
  while read LINE
  do
    case $LINE in
    \#*) ;;     # ignore any hash signs
    *) echo $LINE
      ;;
    esac
  done <$INPUT_FILE
else
  echo "`basename $0` : Sorry $INPUT_FILE does not exist or is empty"
  exit 1
fi
```

When it runs we get:

```
$ ignore_hash
AUDITSCM=full
AUDITSUB=/usr/opt/audit/sub
HASHSER=12890AB3
```

18.7.9 Processing formatted reports

Getting unwanted lines out of the way is a common task when you want to read report files. Below is part of a report from a stationery stock level listing. The items of interest here are the columns containing the item reorder level and the current level.

Here's the report.

```
$ pg order
########  RE-ORDER REPORT #########
  ITEM              ORDERLEVEL      LEVEL
####################################
Pens                  14              12
Pencils               15              15
Pads                   7               3
Disks                  3               2
Sharpeners             5               1
####################################
```

Our task is to read in the values and determine what items need reordering. If a reorder is necessary then the reorder should be twice the reorder level for that item. The output should also report how many items need reordering, and the total of all reorders taking place.

We already know how to ignore the lines beginning with certain characters, so there is no problem there. We need first to read in the file, ignoring all the lines that begin with # and the header line that starts with 'ITEM'; as we read in the file it gets echoed out to a temporary file. To make sure that we do not have any empty lines sed then deletes all empty lines. What we are actually doing is filtering the text file. Here's the code that does that part.

```
$ pg whileorder
#!/bin/sh
# whileorder
INPUT_FILE=order
HOLD=order.tmp

if [ -s $INPUT_FILE ]; then
  # zero the output file, we do not want to append!
  >$HOLD
  while read LINE
  do
    case $LINE in
    \#*|ITEM*) ;;      # ignore any # or the line with ITEM

    *)
      # redirect the output to a temp file
      echo $LINE >>$HOLD
      ;;
    esac
  done <$INPUT_FILE
```

```
# use to sed to delete any empty lines, if any
sed -e '/^$/d' order.tmp >order.$$
mv order.$$ order.tmp
else
  echo "`basename $0` : Sorry $INPUT_FILE does not exist or is empty"
fi
```

Here is the output;

```
$ pg order.tmp
Pens        14 12
Pencils     15 15
Pads         7  3
Disks        3  2
Sharpeners   5  1
```

Now all we have to do is simply read the temp file in with another while loop and do some maths on the figures using expr.

Here's the script.

```
$ pg whileorder2
#!/bin/sh
# whileorder2
# init the variables
HOLD=order.tmp
RE_ORDER=0
ORDERS=0
STATIONERY_TOT=0
if [ -s $HOLD ]; then
  echo "=========== STOCK RE_ORDER REPORT ==============="
  while read ITEM REORD LEVEL
  do
    # are we below the reorder level for this item??
    if [ "$LEVEL" -lt "$REORD" ]; then
      # yes, do the new order amount
      NEW_ORDER=`expr $REORD + $REORD`
      # running total of orders
      ORDERS=`expr $ORDERS + 1`
      # running total of stock levels
      STATIONERY_TOT=`expr $STATIONERY_TOT + $LEVEL`
      echo "$ITEM need reordering to the amount $NEW_ORDER"
    fi
  done <$HOLD
  echo "$ORDERS new items need to be ordered"
  echo "Our reorder total is $STATIONERY_TOT"
else
else
  echo "`basename $0` : Sorry $HOLD does not exist or is empty"
fi
```

Here's the output run against our order file.

```
$ whileorder
============ STOCK REORDER REPORT ================
Pens need reordering to the amount 28
Pads need reordering to the amount 14
Disks need reordering to the amount 6
Sharpeners need reordering to the amount 10
4 new items need to be ordered
Our reorder total is 18
```

It would be no trouble at all to combine the two scripts into one; in fact the original script was one script, but for our purposes it was broken down into two.

18.7.10 The `while` loop and file descriptors

When we looked at file descriptors in Chapter 5, I said that you really need a `while` loop to read data into a file. Using file descriptors 3 and 4, the following script makes a backup of the file `myfile.txt` to `myfile.bak`. Notice the test at the begining of the script to make sure that the file is present. The script will terminate immediately if the file is not present or has no data in it. Also notice the null command (:) with the `while` loop. It will loop forever, because null always returns true. Trying to read past the end of file will return an error. That is how the script terminates.

```
$ pg copyfile
#!/bin/sh
# copyfile
FILENAME=myfile.txt
FILENAME_BAK=myfile.bak
if [ -s $FILENAME ]; then
  # open FILENAME for writing
  # open FILENAME for reading
  exec 4>$FILENAME_BAK
  exec 3<$FILENAME

# loop forever until no more data and thus an error so we are at end of
file
  while :
  do
    read LINE <&3
    if [ "$?" -ne 0 ]; then
      # errors then close up
      exec 3<&-
      exec 4<&-
      exit
    fi
```

```
   # write to FILENAME_BAK
   echo $LINE>&4
   done
else
   echo "`basename $0` : Sorry, $FILENAME is not present or is empty" >&2
fi
```

18.8 **Controlling loops using** break **and** continue

Occasionally when processing you may need to break out or skip certain iterations based on some form of criteria. To help you achieve this the shell provides two commands:

- break

- continue.

18.8.1 break

The break command allows you to break out of loops. Breaks are usually used to quit a loop or case statement after some form of processing. If you are inside a nested loop, you can specify how many loops you should break out of: for instance if you are in a loop within a loop (that's two loops down), then issue break 2 to come right out.

18.8.2 Breaking out of a case statement

Here's an example. This script will loop forever until the user inputs a number above the number 5. To break out of this loop and come back to the shell prompt, the command break is issued.

```
$ pg breakout
#!/bin/sh
# breakout
# while : means loop forever
while :
do
   echo -n "Enter any number [1..5] :"
   read ANS
   case $ANS in
      1|2|3|4|5) echo "great you entered a number between 1 and 5"
      ;;
    *) echo "Wrong number..bye"
      break
      ;;
   esac
done
```

18.8.3 `continue`

The `continue` command is quite similar to the `break` command except for one important difference; it will not exit the loop, but will only skip the current iteration of the loop.

18.8.4 Skipping lines of files

Here is a listing of the personnel file we used previously, but now the file has some header information.

```
$ pg names2.txt
------LISTING OF PERSONNEL FILE-----
--- TAKEN AS AT 06/1999 -----
Louise Conrad:Accounts:ACC8987
Peter James:Payroll:PR489
Fred Terms:Customer:CUS012
James Lenod:Accounts:ACC887
Frank Pavely:Payroll:PR489
```

We need to process the above file, and we know by looking at the file that the first two lines hold no personnel information. We should therefore skip those lines.

Also we should not process the employer Peter James. This person has left the company, but has not yet been taken off the employee file.

To take care of the header information, we simply count how many lines we are reading; we will only process when the line count is greater than two. If the name we are about to process is Peter James, we should skip this record.

Here is the script that does this task.

```
$ pg whilecontinue
#!/bin/sh
# whilecontinue
SAVEDIFS=$IFS
IFS=:
INPUT_FILE=names2.txt
NAME_HOLD="Peter James"
LINE_NO=0

if [ -s $INPUT_FILE ]; then
  while read NAME DEPT ID
  do
    LINE_NO=`expr $LINE_NO + 1`
    if [ "$LINE_NO" -le 2 ]; then
      # skip if the count is less than 2
      continue
    fi
```

```
   if [ "$NAME" = "$NAME_HOLD" ]; then
     # skip if the name in NAME_HOLD is Peter James
     continue
   else
     echo " Now processing...$NAME $DEPT $ID"
     # all the processing goes here
   fi
 done < $INPUT_FILE
IFS=$SAVEDIFS
else
 echo "`basename $0 ` : Sorry file not found or there is no data in the
file" >&2
 exit 1
fi
```

Running the above script gives:

```
$ whilecontinue
Louise Conrad Accounts ACC8987
Fred Terms Customer CUS012
James Lenod Accounts ACC887
Frank Pavely Payroll PR489
```

18.9 Menus

When creating menus, the `null` command comes in very handy with the `while` loop. A `while` and `null` combined mean loop forever, which is what we want for a menu, unless of course the user selects exit or a valid option.

To create a menu you need only a `while` loop and a `case` statement to catch all the patterns the user inputs. If an invalid input is given then sound the bell, echo a error message and then carry on with the loop until the user has finished his processing and selected the `exit` option.

A menu should also be friendly; the user should not have to guess what to do. The main screen would also look good with the hostname and date on it, coupled with the name of the user who is running the menu. For our test purposes, all the options will use system commands.

Here's how our menu is going to look when displayed.

```
_____

User: dave              Host:Bumper              Date:31/05/1999
_____
                   1 :  List files in current directory
                   2 :  Use the vi editor
                   3 :  See who is on the system
                   H :  Help screen
                   Q :  Exit Menu
_____
              Your Choice [1,2,3,H,Q] >
```

First, we'll use command substitution to assign the date, hostname and user. For the date the format will be DD/MM/YYYY. The parameter to get this format is:

```
$ date +%d/%m/%Y
32/05/1999
```

For the hostname you may have to use the -s option to pull off just the hostname part. The hostname will sometimes append its fully qualified domain name to it. Of course, you may want your fully qualified hostname on the screen; that's OK.

Giving the variables a more meaningful name:

MYDATE = `date +%d/%m/%Y`
THIS_HOST = `hostname -s`
USER = `whoami`

For the while loop we just put the null command directly after the word 'while'. Here's the format to loop forever.

while :
do
   commands..
done

To take care of the displaying of the actual screen, do not waste time using lots of single echo statements, or you will be forever adjusting them. We have already met the here document, where the input is taken after the delimiter until the delimiter is located again. In case you have forgotten, here's the format again:

command < <WORD
any input
WORD

This is what we will use for the menu screen. We will also use it for the help screen. My help screen is a bit sparse I'm afraid.

To handle the user choices, a case statement will do the job. The choices in the menu are:

1 : List files in current directory
2 : Use the vi editor
3 : See who is on the system
H: Help screen
Q: Exit Menu

Our case statement should handle all these patterns, not forgetting to put lower case with the upper case patterns, just in case the user has the CAPS LOCK on or off. As the menu script is in a continuous loop, the user needs to exit gracefully, so if the user selects the Q or q key, the script should exit with a value of zero.

If the user selects any invalid input, the bell should sound with a warning message. Although I said at the beginning of this chapter that I will only be using the LINUX BSD echo statements from now on, here's what to use if you have got the System V version to ring the bell:

echo "\007 the bell rang"

A simple echo and read statement takes care of halting the screen until the user hits enter, so any messages or command output can be viewed.

We also need to clear the screen. Using the tput command should do it (we will discuss tput later on) but if not try just the clear command. That's about all we need, so here's the script.

```
$ pg menu
#!/bin/sh
# menu
# set the date, user and hostname up
MYDATE=`date +%d/%m/%Y`
THIS_HOST=`hostname -s`
USER=`whoami`
# loop forever !
while :
do
  # clear the screen
  tput clear
  # here documents starts here
  cat <<MAYDAY
```

User: $USER	Host:$THIS_HOST	Date:$MYDATE
	1 : List files in current directory	
	2 : Use the vi editor	
	3 : See who is on the system	
	H : Help screen	
	Q : Exit Menu	

```
MAYDAY

# here document finished
echo -e -n "\tYour Choice [1,2,3,H,Q] >"
read CHOICE
  case $CHOICE in
  1) ls
    ;;
  2) vi
    ;;
  3) who
    ;;
  H|h)
```

```
    # use a here document for the help screen
    cat <<MAYDAY
    This is the help screen, nothing here yet to help you!
    MAYDAY
      ;;
    Q|q) exit 0
      ;;
    *) echo -e "\t\007unknown user response"
      ;;
    esac
  echo -e -n "\tHit the return key to continue"
  read DUMMY
done
```

18.10 Conclusion

At the heart of any reasonable script there is some form of flow control. If you want scripts to be intelligent, they must be able to make decisions.

In this chapter you have learnt how flow control can make the difference between an OK script and a robust script and you have also learnt how to process lists or loop until a condition is true or false.

CHAPTER 19

Shell functions

All the code in the scripts so far in this book has been executed from top to bottom. This approach is OK, but you may have noticed that some segments of the code we have covered in our examples has been duplicated further on in the same script.

The shell allows you to group a set of commands or statements into a reusable block. These blocks are called shell functions.

In this chapter we will cover:

- defining functions;
- using functions from within a script;
- using functions from a functions file; and
- function examples.

A function is made up of two parts:

The function label
The function body

The label is the function name and the body is the set of commands inside the function. The label name should really be unique; if not you will get confusing results, as the script will first hunt around the shell for the function before looking at your calling script.

Here is the format for defining functions:

```
function_name( )
{
command1
...
}
```

or

```
function_name( ) {
command1
...
}
```

Both ways are acceptable. You can also include the word `function` before the function_name if you wish; this is up to you.

```
function function_name( )
{
...
}
```

You can think of functions as a sort of script within a script, but there is one main difference. When you execute a function, it stays in the current shell and stays in memory. On the other hand if you execute or call a script from within a script then a separate shell is created, thus wiping out all your existing variables that were declared in your previous script.

Functions can be placed in the same file as your scripts, or in a separate file containing only functions. A function does not have to contain many statements or commands – it could just contain a single echo statement, it's up to you.

19.1 Declaring functions in a script

Here is a simple function:

```
hello ()
{
echo "Hello there today's date is `date`"
}
```

All functions have to be declared before you use them. What this means is that you must put all your functions at the top of the script. You cannot reference a function until the shell interpreter has seen it first. To call a function you simply call it by its name. In the above example, the function name is 'hello'; the function's body contains a echo statement containing today's date.

19.2 Using functions in a script

Now we have created a function let's see it being used in a script.

```
$ pg func1
#!/bin/sh
# func1
hello ()
{
echo "Hello there today's date is `date`"
}

echo "now going to the function hello"
hello

echo "back from the function"
```

When the above script is run, we get:

```
$ func1
now going to the function hello
Hello there today's date is Sun Jun  6 10:46:59 GMT 1999
back from the function
```

In the above example, the function is declared at the top of the script. To reference the function we called it by its name which was 'hello'. When the function has finished, control returns to the next statement following the function call, which is the echo statement 'back from the function'.

19.3 Passing parameters to a function

Parameters are passed to function just like in a normal script using the special variables $1, $2 ... $9. When the function gets arguments passed to it, it will replace the arguments originally passed to the shell script, if any, so it's always a good idea to reassign the variables when the function gets them. This is a good idea anyway; if there are any bugs in the function, they can quickly be tracked down by the localized variable names. The convention for calling arguments (variables) inside a function is to start each variable name with a underscore (_), like this: _FILENAME or _filename.

19.4 Returning from a called function

When a function has finished processing or you wish the function to finish based on a conditional statement, you can do one of two things:

1.   Let the function fall through naturally to the end of the function, thus returning control back to the part of the script that called it.

2.   Use the word 'return', which will return from the function to the next statement of your script from whence it was called. A value can be used with the return; this is optional, and is 0 for non-errors and 1 for errors, pretty much the same as the last status command reports. The format is:

> **return**   will return from the function, use the last status command to determine status
>
> **return 0**   for non-errors
>
> **return 1**   for errors

19.5 Testing the values returned by a function

To test a value returned by a called function you can use the last status command directly after the function is called from your script. For example:

```
check_it_is_a_directory $FILENAME    # this is the function call and check
if [ $? = 0 ]     # use the last status command now to test
then
  echo "All is OK"
else
  echo " Something went wrong!"
fi
```

A much better way is to use an if statement when testing on either a return 0 or a return 1 value. Enclosing the function call with an if statement makes better logical reading. For example:

```
if check_it_is_a_directory $FILENAME; then
  echo "All is OK"
  # do something ??
else
  echo "Something went wrong !"
  # do something ??
fi
```

If the function is going to echo out output from a result of some test then use substitution to grab the result. The format for using substitution with function calls is:

variable_name = `function_name`

The output from the function `function_name` is assigned to the variable `variable_name`.

Shortly we will see lots of different functions and different ways of using the return values and output from a function.

19.6 Using functions in the shell

When you have collected a few functions that you use regularly you can put them in a function file and load the file into the shell. This method is called sourcing a file or using the dot command.

The file should contain the #!/bin/sh at the top of the file. The file can be called anything you like, but be sure to call it something meaningful to its task, for example 'functions.main'.

Once the file is loaded into the shell, you can call the functions from the command line or your script. To see all your defined functions use the set command. The output will contain all the functions that have been loaded into the shell.

To make changes to any of your functions first use the unset command to delete the function from the shell. Unset deletes the function so that it is no longer available to call from your scripts or the shell – the actual function is not physically deleted. Make your changes to the function file then reload the file. Some shells will recognize the change and you may not need to use unset, but to be safe always use the unset command when you want to make changes to shell functions.

19.7 Creating a function file

Let's create a function file that holds one function. We will load it into the shell, test it, make a change then reload it.

Create a file called functions.main and type in the following:

```
$ pg functions.main
#!/bin/sh
# functions.main
#
# findit: this is front end for the basic find command
findit() {
# findit
if [ $# -lt 1 ]; then
  echo "usage :findit file"
  return 1
fi
find / -name $1 -print
```

The above is a script used previously in the book, but now it has been turned into a function. It's a front end to a basic find command. If no argument is passed to it, a return with a value of 1 is executed meaning errors have occurred. Notice on the error statement that the actual function name is shown, because if we had used $0, the shell would simply return a sh- message. The reason you get this message is because the file is not a script file. Either way this type of message is not very helpful to the user.

19.8 Sourcing the file

To source a file the format is:

. /pathname/filename

Now the file is created, let's load the file into the shell (source it). Type the following:

```
$. functions.main
```

If the above returns a 'file not found' message then try the following instead:

```
$. /functions.main
```

That's a `<dot><space><forward slash><filename>`. The file should now be loaded into the shell. If you still get an error, make sure you supply your full pathname to the file instead.

19.9 Checking the loaded functions

To make sure that the functions have been sourced, use the `set` command, which will display all the loaded functions available to the shell.

```
$ set
USER=dave
findit=()
{
if [ $# -lt 1 ]; then
  echo "usage :findit file";
  return 1;
fi;
find / -name $1 -print
}
...
```

19.10 Executing shell functions

To execute the function, simply type the function name, which is `findit`, with an argument, which should be a file located somewhere on the system.

```
$ findit groups
/usr/bin/groups
/usr/local/backups/groups.bak
```

19.10.1 Deleting shell functions

Let's now make a small change to the function. First delete the function, so it is no longer available to the shell. Do this using the unset command. The format for using the unset command when removing functions is:

unset function_name

```
$ unset findit
```

If you type set now, you will find that the function is no longer displayed.

19.10.2 Editing shell functions

Now edit the file functions.main and add a for loop to the function, so the script can read in more than one parameter from the command line. The function will now look like this:

```
$ pg functions.main
#!/bin/sh
findit()
{
# findit
if [ $# -lt 1 ]; then
   echo "usage :findit file"
   return 1
fi
for loop
do
   find / -name $loop -print
done
}
```

Now source the file again:

```
$. /functions.main
```

Using the set command to see that it is indeed loaded, you will notice that the shell has correctly interpreted the for loop to take in all parameters.

```
$ set
findit=()
{
if [ $# -lt 1 ]; then
   echo "usage :`basename $0` file";
   return 1;
fi;
```

```
for loop in "$@";
do
  find / -name $loop -print;
done
}
...
```

Now to execute the changed `findit` function. Supplying a couple of files to find:

```
$ findit LPSO.doc passwd
/usr/local/accounts/LPSO.doc
/etc/passwd
...
```

19.10.3 Function examples

Now you have a grasp of functions let's see how you can make them work for you. Once you have a function it can save you lots of coding time because a function is reusable.

Validating input

Here is a small script that asks for a first name then a second name:

```
$ pg func2
#!/bin/sh
# func2
echo -n "What is your first name :"
read F_NAME
echo -n "What is your surname :"
read S_NAME
```

The task is to make sure that the characters entered in both variables contain letters only. To do this without functions would duplicate a lot of code. Using a function cuts this duplication down. To test for characters only, we can use awk. Here's the function to test if we only get upper or lower case characters.

```
char_name()
{
# char_name
# to call: char_name string
# assign the argument across to new variable
_LETTERS_ONLY=$1
# use awk to test for characters only !
_LETTERS_ONLY=`echo $1|awk '{if($0~/[^a-z A-Z]/) print "1"}'`
if [ "$_LETTERS_ONLY" != "" ]
then
  # oops errors
  return 1
```

```
else
  # contains only chars
  return 0
fi
}
```

We first assign the $1 variable to a more meaningful name. Awk is then used to test if the whole record passed contains only characters. The output of this command, which is 1 for non-letters and null for OK, is held in the variable _LETTERS_ONLY.

A test on the variable is then carried out. If it holds any value then it's an error, but if it holds no value then it's OK. A return code is then executed based on this test. Using the return code enables the script to look cleaner when the test is done on the function on the calling part of the script.

To test the outcome of the function we can use this format of the `if` statement if we wanted:

```
if char_name $F_NAME; then
  echo "OK"
else
  echo "ERRORS"
fi
```

If there is an error we can create another function to `echo` the error out to the screen:

```
name_error()
# name_error
# display an error message
{
echo " $@ contains errors, it must contain only letters"
}
```

The function `name_error` will be used to echo out all errors disregarding any invalid entries. Using the special variable $@ allows all arguments to be echoed. In this case it's the value of either F_NAME or S_NAME. Here's what the finished script now looks like, using the functions:

```
$ pg func2
!/bin/sh
char_name()
# char_name
# to call: char_name string
# check if $1 does indeed contain only characters a-z,A-Z
{
# assign the argurment across to new variable
_LETTERS_ONLY=$1
_LETTERS_ONLY=`echo $1|awk '{if($0~/[^a-zA-Z]/) print "1"}'`
if [ "$_LETTERS_ONLY" != "" ]
```

```
then
  # oops errors
  return 1
else
  # contains only chars
  return 0
fi
}

name_error()
# display an error message
{
echo " $@ contains errors, it must contain only letters"
}

while :
do
  echo -n "What is your first name :"
  read F_NAME
  if char_name $F_NAME
  then
    # all ok breakout
    break
  else
    name_error $F_NAME
  fi
done

while :
do
  echo -n "What is your surname :"
  read S_NAME
  if char_name $S_NAME
  then
    # all ok breakout
    break
  else
    name_error $S_NAME
  fi
done
```

Notice a while loop for each of the inputs; this makes sure that we will continue prompting until a correct value is input, then we break out of the loop. Of course, on a working script, an option would be given for the user to quit this cycle, and proper cursor controls would be used, as would checking for zero length fields.

Here's what the output looks like when the script is run:

```
$ func2
What is your first name :Davi2d
 Davi2d contains errors, it must contain only letters
What is your first name :David
```

```
What is your surname :Tansley1
Tansley1 contains errors, it must contain only letters
What is your surname :Tansley
```

The echo *problem*

There have been references to which type of echo statement to use depending on whether you are using a LINUX, BSD or System V throughout this book. We will create a function that will determine what type of echo statement to use.

When an echo is used the prompt can be kept at the end of the echo, awaiting further input from a read command.

LINUX and BSD use the -n option of the echo command to do this.

Here's an example of a LINUX (BSD) echo, where the prompt is kept at the end:

```
$ echo -n "Your name :"
Your name : {{?}}
```

System V uses \c to keep its prompts at the end:

```
$ echo "Your name :\c"
Your name : □
```

To echo control characters LINUX also requires the -e option at the beginning of the echo statement. Other systems can just use the backslash to let the shell know about the presence of a control character.

There are two ways to test which type of echo statement to use. We will look at both methods, and then you can choose which one to use.

The first method involves testing the control character inside the echo statement. If we type echo \007 and a bell sounds, it's a System V. If just the string \007 is displayed then it's LINUX.

Here is the first function that tests for control characters.

```
uni_prompt ()
# uni_prompt
# universal echo
{
if [ `echo "\007"` = "\007" ] >/dev/null 2>&1
# does a bell sound or are the characters just echoed??
then
  # characters echoed, it's LINUX /BSD
  echo -e -n "$@"
else
  # it's System V
  echo "$@\c"
fi
}
```

Notice again the use of the special variable $@ to echo the string. To call the above function in a script we could use:

```
uni_prompt "\007There goes the bell, What is your name :"
```

which will sound a bell and echo out 'What is your name', with the prompt hanging on the end of the line.

To test using the presence of a new line, we can echo out any character using the System V echo \c version. If the character hangs on to the end of line, then it's a System V version; if not, it must be LINUX/BSD.

The second method tests whether the letter Z is hanging on the end of the line using the System V \c.

```
uni_prompt ()
# uni_prompt
# universal prompt
{
if [ `echo "Z\c"` = "Z" ] >/dev/null 2>&1
# echo any chracter out, does it hang on to the end of line ???
then
   # yes, it's System V
   echo "$@\c"
else
   # No, it's LINUX, BSD
   echo -e -n "$@"
fi
}
```

To call the above function in a script you could use the following:

```
uni_prompt "\007 There goes the bell, What is your name :"
```

Using any one of the above functions with the following snippet of code

```
uni_prompt "\007 There goes the bell, What is your name :"
read NAME
```

will yield the following output:

```
There goes the bell, What is your name :
```

Reading a single character

When navigating menus, one of the most frustrating tasks is having to keep hitting the return key after every selection, or when a 'press any key to continue' prompt appears. A command that can help us with not having to hit return to send a key sequence is the dd command.

The dd command is used mostly for conversions and interrogating problems with data on tapes or normal tape archiving tasks, but it can also be used to create fixed length files. Here a 1-megabyte file is created with the filename myfile.

```
dd if=/dev/zero of=myfile count=512 bs=2048
```

The dd command can interpret what is coming in from your keyboard, and can be used to accept so many characters. In this case we only want one character. The command dd needs to chop off the new line; this control character gets attached when the user hits return. dd will also send out only one character. Before any of that can happen the terminal must first be set into raw mode using the stty command. We save the settings before dd is invoked and then restore them after dd has finished.

Here's the function:

```
read_a_char()
# read_a_char
{
# save the settings
SAVEDSTTY=`stty -g`
# set terminal raw please
    stty cbreak
  # read and output only one character
    dd if=/dev/tty bs=1 count=1 2> /dev/null
  # restore terminal and restore stty
    stty -cbreak
stty $SAVEDSTTY
}
```

To call the function and return the character typed in, use command substitution. Here's an example.

```
echo  -n "Hit Any Key To Continue"
character=`read_a_char`
echo " In case you are wondering you pressed $character"
```

Testing for the presence of a directory

Testing for the presence of directories is a fairly common task when copying files around. This function will test the filename passed to the function to see if it is a directory. Because we are using the return command with a succeed or failure value, the if statement becomes the most obvious choice in testing the result.

Here's the function.

```
is_it_a_directory()
{
# is_it_a_directory
# to call: is_it_a_directory directory_name
```

```
if [ $# -lt 1 ]; then
  echo "is_it_a_directory: I need an argument"
  return 1
fi
# is it a directory ?
_DIRECTORY_NAME=$1
if [ ! -d $_DIRECTORY_NAME ]; then
  # no it is not
  return 1
else
  # yes it is
  return 0
fi
}
```

To call and test the result, we could use:

```
echo -n "enter destination directory :"
read DIREC
if is_it_a_directory $direc;
then :
else
  echo "$DIREC does not exist, create it now ? [y..n]"
  # commands go here to either create the directory or exit
  . . .
  . . .
fi
```

Prompting for a Y or N

Many scripts prompt for a response before continuing with a process. A prompt could be to do any of the following:

Create a directory
Do you wish to delete this file
Run the backup now
Confirm to save a record

The list can be pretty long.

The following function is a generic prompt. You supply the message to be displayed, as well as the default answer. The default answer is used in case the user just hits return at the prompt. The case statement is used to catch the answers.

```
continue_prompt()
# continue_prompt
to call: continue_prompt "string to display" default_answer
{
_STR=$1
_DEFAULT=$2
```

```
# check we have the right params
if [ $# -lt 1 ]; then
  echo "continue_prompt: I need a string to display"
  return 1
fi
# loop forever
while :
do
  echo -n "$_STR [Y..N] [$_DEFAULT]:"
  read _ANS
  # if user hits return set the default and determine the return value,
  # that's a : then a <space> then $
  :   ${_ANS:=$_DEFAULT}
  if [ "$_ANS" = "" ]; then
    case $_ANS in
    Y) return 0 ;;
    N) return 1 ;;
    esac
  fi
  # user has selected something
  case $_ANS in
  y|Y|Yes|YES)
    return 0
    ;;
  n|N|No|NO)
    return 1
    ;;
  *) echo "Answer either Y or N, default is $_DEFAULT"
    ;;
  esac
  echo $_ANS
done
}
```

To call the above function, you can either supply the message to be displayed in double quotes or call it with an argument, $1, or with a variable containing a string. A default answer in the form of Y or N must also be passed.

Here are a couple of ways the function continue_prompt could be called.

```
if continue_prompt "Do you want to delete the var filesytem" "N"; then
  echo "Are you nuts!!"
else
  echo "Phew !, what a good answer"
fi
```

Using the above code in a script you could give it the following input

```
Do you really want to delete the var filesystem [Y..N] [N]:
phew !!
```

```
Do you really want to delete the var filesystem [Y..N] [N]:y
are you nuts..
```

Now you know why the function has a default answer that you can specify!

Here is another way to call the function:

```
if continue_prompt "Do you really want to print this report" "Y"; then
  lpr report
else:
fi
```

Alternatively, it could be called like this, with $1 containing a string:

```
if continue_prompt $1 "Y"; then
  lpr report
else:
fi
```

Getting information from a login ID

When you are on a big system, and you want to contact one of the users who is logged in, don't you just hate it when you have forgotten the person's full name? Many a time I have seen users locking up a process, but their user ID means nothing to me, so I have to grep the passwd file to get their full name. Then I can get on with the nice part where I can ring them up to give the user a telling off.

Here's a function that can save you from greping the /etc/passwd file to see the user's full name.

On my system the user's full name is kept in field 5 of the passwd file; yours might be different, so you will have to change the field number to suit your passwd file.

The function is passed a user ID or many IDs, and the function just greps the passwd file.

Here's the function:

```
whois()
# whois
# to call: whois userid
{
# check we have the right params
if [ $# -lt 1 ]; then
  echo "whois : need user id's please"
  return 1
fi

for loop
do
  _USER_NAME=`grep $loop /etc/passwd | awk -F: '{print $4}'`
```

```
    if [ "$_USER_NAME" = "" ]; then
      echo "whois: Sorry cannot find $loop"
    else
      echo "$loop is $_USER_NAME"
    fi
  done
}
```

The whois function can be called like this:

```
$ whois dave peters superman
dave is David Tansley - admin accts
peter is Peter Stromer - customer services
whois: Sorry cannot find superman
```

Line numbering a text file

When you are in vi you can number your lines which is great for debugging, but if you want to print out some files with line numbers then you have to use the command nl. Here is a function that does what nl does best – numbering the lines in a file. The original file is not written to.

Here's the function.

```
number_file()
# number_file
# to call: number_file filename
{
_FILENAME=$1
# check we have the right params
if [ $# -ne 1 ]; then
  echo "number_file: I need a filename to number"
  return 1
fi

loop=1
  while read LINE
  do
    echo "$loop: $LINE"
    loop=`expr $loop + 1`
  done < $_FILENAME
}
```

To call the number_file function just supply the filename to be numbered as an argument to the function, or from the shell supplying a filename. For example,

```
$ number_file myfile
```

or to call it from a script you can use the above example or use

```
number_file $1
```

The output could look like this:

```
$ number_file /home/dave/file_listing
1: total 105
2: -rw-r--r--   1 dave     admin        0 Jun  6 20:03 DT
3: -rw-r--r--   1 dave     admin      306 May 23 16:00 LPSO.AKS
4: -rw-r--r--   1 dave     admin      306 May 23 16:00 LPSO.AKS.UC
5: -rw-r--r--   1 dave     admin      324 May 23 16:00 LPSO.MBB
6: -rw-r--r--   1 dave     admin      324 May 23 16:00 LPSO.MBB.UC
7: -rw-r--r--   1 dave     admin      315 May 23 16:00 LPSO.MKQ
...
...
```

String to upper case

You may need to convert text from lower to upper case sometimes, for example to create directories in a filesystem with upper case only, or to input data into a field you are validating that requires the text to be in upper case.

Here is a function that will do it for you. No points for guessing it's `tr`.

```
str_to_upper ()
# str_to_upper
# to call: str_to_upper $1
{
_STR=$1
# check we have the right params
if [ $# -ne 1 ]; then
   echo "number_file: I need a string to convert please"
   return 1
fi
echo $@ |tr '[a-z]' '[A-Z]'
}
```

The variable UPPER holds the newly returned upper case string. Notice the use again of using the special parameter $@ to pass all arguments. The `str_to_upper` can be called in two ways. You can either supply the string in a script like this:

```
UPPER=`str_to_upper "documents.live"`
echo $upper
```

or supply an argument to the function instead of a string, like this:

```
UPPER=`str_to_upper $1`
echo $UPPER
```

Both of these examples use substitution to get the returned function results.

is_upper

The function `str_to_upper` does a case conversion, but sometimes you only need to know if a string is upper case before continuing with some processing, perhaps to write a field of text to a file. The `is_upper` function does just that. Using an if statement in the script will determine if the string passed is indeed upper case.

Here is the function.

```
is_upper()
# is_upper
# to call: is_upper $1
{
# check we have the right params
if [ $# -ne 1 ]; then
  echo "is_upper: I need a string to test OK"
  return 1
fi
# use awk to check we have only upper case
_IS_UPPER=`echo $1|awk '{if($0~/[^A-Z]/) print "1"}'`
if [ "$_IS_UPPER" != "" ]
then
  # no, they are not all upper case
  return 1
else
  # yes all upper case
  return 0
fi
}
```

To call the function `is_upper` simply send it a string argument. Here's how it could be called.

```
echo -n "Enter the filename :"
read   FILENAME
if is_upper $FILENAME; then
  echo "Great it's upper case"
  # let's create a file  maybe ??
else
  echo "Sorry it's not upper case"
  # shall we convert it anyway using str_to_upper ???
fi
```

To test if a string is indeed lower case, just replace the existing awk statement with this one inside the function `is_upper` and call it `is_lower`.

```
_IS_LOWER=`echo $1|awk '{if($0~/[^a-z]/) print "1"}'`
```

String to lower case

Now I've done it. Because I have shown you the str_to_upper, I'd better show you its sister function str_to_lower. No guesses here please on how this one works.

Here's the function.

```
str_to_lower ()
# str_to_lower
# to call: str_to_lower $1
{
# check we have the right params
if [ $# -ne 1 ]; then
  echo "str_to_lower: I need a string to convert please"
  return 1
fi
echo $@ |tr '[A-Z]' '[a-z]'
}
```

The variable LOWER holds the newly returned lower case string. Notice the use again of using the special parameter $@ to pass all arguments. The str_to_lower can be called in two ways. You can either supply the string in a script like this:

```
LOWER=`str_to_lower "documents.live"`
echo $LOWER
```

or supply an argument to the function instead of a string, like this:

```
LOWER=`str_to_upper $1`
echo $LOWER
```

Length of string

Validating input into a field is a common task in scripts. Validating can mean many things, whether it's numeric, character only, formats, or the length of the field.

Suppose you had a script where the user enters data into a name field via an interactive screen. You will want to check that the field contains only a certain number of characters, say 20 for a person's name. It's easy for the user to input up to 50 characters into a field. This is what this next function will check. You pass the function two parameters, the actual string and the maximum length the string should be.

Here's the function:

```
check_length()
# check_length
# to call: check_length string max_length_of_string
{
_STR=$1
_MAX=$2
```

```
# check we have the right params
if [ $# -ne 2 ]; then
  echo "check_length: I need a string and max length the string should be"
  return 1
fi
# check the length of the string
_LENGTH=`echo $_STR |awk '{print length($0)}'`
if [ "$_LENGTH" -gt  "$_MAX" ]; then
  # length of string is too big
  return 1
else
  # string is ok in length
  return 0
fi
}
```

You could call the function check_length like this:

```
$ pg test_name
# !/bin/sh
# test_name
while :
do
  echo -n "Enter your FIRST name :"
  read NAME
  if check_length $NAME 10
  then
    break
    # do nothing fall through condition all is ok
  else
    echo "The name field is too long 10 characters max"
  fi
done
```

The loop will continue until the data input into the variable NAME is less than the MAX characters permitted which in this case is ten; the break command then lets it drop out of the loop.

Using the above piece of code this is how the output could look.

```
$ val_max
Enter your FIRST name :Pertererrrrrrrrrrrrrrrr
The name field is too long 10 characters max
Enter your FIRST name :Peter
```

You could use the wc command to get the length of the string, but beware: there is a glitch when using wc in taking input from the keyboard. If you hit the space bar a few times after typing in a name, wc will almost always retain some of the spaces as part of the string, thus giving a false length size. Awk truncates end of string spaces by default when reading in via the keyboard.

Here's an example of the wc glitch (or maybe it's a feature):

```
echo -n "name :"
read NAME
echo $NAME | wc -c
```

Running the above script segment (where □ is a space)

name :Peter□□
　　6

chop

The chop function chops off characters from the beginning of a string. The function chop is passed a string; you specify how many characters to chop off the string starting from the first character. Suppose you had the string MYDOCUMENT.DOC and you wanted the MYDOCUMENT part chopped, so that the function returned only .DOC. You would pass the following to the chop function:

MYDOCUMENT.DOC   10

Here's the function chop:

```
chop()
# chop
# to call:chop string how_many_chars_to_chop
{
_STR=$1
_CHOP=$2
# awk's substr starts at 0, we need to increment by one
# to reflect when the user says (ie) 2 chars to be chopped it will be 2
chars off
# and not 1
CHOP=`expr $_CHOP + 1`

# check we have the right params
if [ $# -ne 2 ]; then
  echo "check_length: I need a string and how many characters to chop"
  return 1
fi
# check the length of the string first
# we can't chop more than what's in the string !!
_LENGTH=`echo $_STR |awk '{print length($0)}'`
if [ "$_LENGTH" -lt "$_CHOP" ]; then
  echo "Sorry you have asked to chop more characters than there are in
        the string"
  return 1
fi
```

```
echo $_STR |awk '{print substr($1,'$_CHOP')}'
}
```

The returned string newly chopped is held in the variable CHOPPED. To call the function chop, you could use:

```
CHOPPED=`chop "Honeysuckle" 5`
echo $CHOPPED
suckle
```

or you could call this way:

```
echo -n "Enter the Filename :"
read FILENAME
CHOPPED=`chop $FILENAME 1`
# the first character would be chopped off !
```

Months

When generating reports or creating screen displays, it is sometimes convenient to the programmer to have a quick way of displaying the full month. This function, called months, will accept the month number or month abbreviation and then return the full month.

For example, passing 3 or 03 will return March. Here's the function.

```
months()
{
# months
_MONTH=$1
# check we have the right params
if [ $# -ne 1 ]; then
   echo "months: I  need a number 1 to 12 "
   return 1
fi

case $_MONTH in
1|01|Jan)_FULL="January" ;;
2|02|Feb)_FULL="February" ;;
3|03|Mar)_FULL="March";;
4|04|Apr)_FULL="April";;
5|05|May)_FULL="May";;
6|06|Jun)_FULL="June";;
7|07|Jul)_FULL="July";;
8|08|Aug)_FULL="August";;
9|10|Sep|Sept)_FULL="September";;
10|Oct)_FULL="October";;
11|Nov)_FULL="November";;
12|Dec)_FULL="December";;
```

```
*) echo "months: Unknown month"
   return 1
   ;;
esac
echo $_FULL
}
```

To call the function `months` you can use either of the following methods.

```
months 04
```

The above method will display the month April; or from a script:

```
MY_MONTH=`months 06`
echo "Generating the Report for Month End $MY_MONTH"
. . .
```

which would output the month June.

19.10.4 Putting it all together

The functions we have covered so far in this chapter were in no particular order. The aim of the example functions was to show you that a function does not have to be lengthy or reserved for complicated coding.

Many of my functions do pretty ordinary stuff – they do not break any new ground in scripting, they just save you from retyping the same bits of code and that's really what a function should do; anything else is a benefit.

At the beginning of the chapter, we looked at how functions were used in the shell. When I first got into using functions, it took a while to get my head around the values being returned by a function.

The examples we have seen incorporate different methods of calling and testing the returned function values so, if you have any problems, just check out the examples to see how the functions can be returned and the values tested.

Here is a tip for you. When testing a function, test it as a script first; when you are happy with the results then turn it into a function. You will save a lot of testing time by doing it that way.

19.11 Calling functions

Let's finish this chapter with two different ways of using functions: calling the functions from a source file and using functions that are already placed in your scripts.

19.11.1 Calling functions inside a script

To use a function in a script, create the function, and make sure it is above the code that calls it. Here's a script that uses a couple of functions. We have seen the script before; it tests to see if a directory exists.

```
$ pg direc_check
!/bin/sh
# function file
is_it_a_directory()
{
# is_it_a_directory
# to call: is_it_a_directory directory_name
_DIRECTORY_NAME=$1
if [ $# -lt 1 ]; then
  echo "is_it_a_directory: I need a directory name to check"
  return 1
fi
# is it a directory ?
if [ ! -d $_DIRECTORY_NAME ]; then
  return 1
else
  return 0
fi
}
#------------------------------------------------
error_msg()
{
# error_msg
# beeps; display message; beeps again!
echo -e "\007"
echo $@
echo -e "\007"
  return 0
}
}

### END OF FUNCTIONS

echo -n "enter destination directory :"
read DIREC
if is_it_a_directory $DIREC
then :
else
  error_msg "$DIREC does not exist...creating it now"
  mkdir $DIREC > /dev/null 2>&1
  if [ $? != 0 ]
  then
    error_msg "Could not create directory:: check it out!"
    exit 1
```

```
    else :
    fi
fi # not a directory
echo "extracting files..."
```

In the above script two functions are declared at the top of the script and called from the main part of the script. All functions should go at the top of the script before any of the main scripting blocks begin. Notice the error message statement; the function error_msg is used, and all arguments passed to the function error_msg are just echoed out with a couple of bleeps.

19.11.2 Calling functions from a function file

We have already seen how to call functions from the command line; these types of functions are generally used for system reporting utilities.

Let's use the above function again, but this time put it in a function file. We will call it functions.sh, the sh meaning shell scripts.

```
$ pg functions.sh
#!/bin/sh
# functions.sh
# main script functions
is_it_a_directory()
{
# is_it_a_directory
# to call: is_it_a_directory directory_name
#
if [ $# -lt 1 ]; then
   echo "is_it_a_directory: I need a directory name to check"
   return 1
fi
# is it a directory ?
DIRECTORY_NAME=$1
if [ ! -d $DIRECTORY_NAME ]; then
   return 1
else
   return 0
fi
}

#------------------------------------------------

error_msg()
{
echo -e "\007"
echo $@
echo -e "\007"
   return 0
}
```

Now let's create the script that will use functions in the file functions.sh. We can then use these functions. Notice the functions file is sourced with the command format:

. / < path to file >

A subshell will not be created using this method; all functions stay in the current shell.

```
$ pg direc_check
!/bin/sh
# direc_check
# source the function file functions.sh
# that's a <dot><space><forward slash>
. /home/dave/bin/functions.sh

# now we can use the function(s)

echo -n "enter destination directory :"
read DIREC
if is_it_a_directory $DIREC
then :
else
   error_msg "$DIREC does not exist...creating it now"
   mkdir $DIREC > /dev/null 2>&1
   if [ $? != 0 ]
   then
      error_msg "Could not create directory:: check it out!"
      exit 1
   else :
   fi
fi # not a directory
echo "extracting files..."
```

When we run the above script we get the same output as if we had the function inside our script:

```
$ direc_check
enter destination directory :AUDIT
AUDIT does not exist...creating it now
extracting files...
```

19.12 Sourcing files is not only for functions

To source a file, it does not only have to contain functions – it can contain global variables that make up a configuration file.

Suppose you had a couple of backup scripts that archived different parts of a system. It would be a good idea to share one common configuration file. All you need to do is to create your variables inside a file then when one of the backup scripts kicks off it can load these variables in to see if the user wants to change any of the defaults before the archive actually begins. It may be the case that you want the archive to go to a different media.

Of course this approach can be used by any scripts that share a common configuration to carry out a process. Here's an example. The following configuration contains default environments that are shared by a few backup scripts I use. Here's the file.

```
$ pg backfunc
#!/bin/sh
# name: backfunc
# config file that holds the defaults for the archive systems
_CODE="comet"
_FULLBACKUP="yes"
_LOGFILE="/logs/backup/"
_DEVICE="/dev/rmt/0n"
_INFORM="yes"
_PRINT_STATS="yes"
```

The descriptions are clear. The first field _CODE holds a code word. To be able to view this and thus change the values the user must first enter a code that matches up with the value of _CODE, which is "comet".

Here's the script that prompts for a password then displays the default configuration:

```
$ pg readfunc
#!/bin/sh
# readfunc

if [ -r backfunc ]; then
  # source the file
  . /backfunc
else
  echo "$`basename $0` cannot locate backfunc file"
fi

echo -n "Enter the code name :"
# does the code entered match the code from backfunc file ???
if [ "${CODE}" != "${_CODE}" ]; then
  echo "Wrong code...exiting..will use defaults"
  exit 1
fi

echo " The environment config file reports"
echo "Full Backup Required           : $_FULLBACKUP"
echo "The Logfile Is                 : $_LOGFILE"
echo "The Device To Backup To is     : $_DEVICE"
echo "You Are To Be Informed by Mail : $_INFORM"
echo "A Statistic Report To Be Printed: $_PRINT_STATS"
```

When the script is run, you are prompted for the code. If the code matches, you can view the defaults. A fully working script would then let the user change the defaults.

```
$ readback
Enter the code name :comet

 The environment config file reports
Full Backup Required          : yes
The Logfile Is                : /logs/backup/
The Device To Backup To is    : /dev/rmt/0n
You Are To Be Informed by Mail : yes
A Statistic Report To Be Printed: yes
```

19.13 Conclusion

Using functions will greatly reduce the time you spend scripting. Creating useable and reuseable functions makes good sense; it also makes your main scripts less maintenance-prone.

When you have got a set of functions you like, put them in a functions file, then other scripts can use the functions as well.

CHAPTER 20

Passing parameters to scripts

We have already seen how to pass parameters to scripts by using the special variables $1..$9. Using $# can tell us how many parameters have been passed. We also know how to construct a usage statement, which is when we need to inform the user on how to call a script or function with its proper calling parameters.

In this chapter we will cover:

- shift;

- getopts; and

- shift and getopts examples.

To recap, here's a framework of a script that handles the parameters start and stop. The script requires two parameters. If it does not get two parameters then a usage statement is produced. Notice we use the case statement to process the different parameters coming into the script.

```
$ pg opt
#!/bin/sh
# opt

usage()
{
echo "usage:'basename $0' start|stop process name"
}

OPT=$1
PROCESSID=$1
if [ $# -ne 2 ]
then
  usage
  exit 1
fi
```

```
case $OPT in
start|Start) echo "Starting..$PROCESSID"
  #  some process to go here
  ;;
stop|Stop) echo "Stopping..$PROCESSID"
  # some process to go here
  ;;
*) usage
  ;;
;;
esac
```

When executed, with the following input, we get:

```
$ opt start named
Starting..named

$ opt start
usage:opt start|stop process name
```

Any UNIX or LINUX command takes the general format:

command options files

The options part can contain up to 12 different values. Looking at our example script opt, a lot of coding is going to have to be put in place if we had to handle different command options. At the moment it handles only two options, start and stop.

Fortunately the shell provides the shift command, to help us shift through the different options. Using shift takes away the limitation of using only the special variables $1 to $9 for passing parameters.

20.1 The shift command

When parameters are passed to a script a method is required that will help us shift through each parameter so that we can process the options. This is what the shift command does. It shifts positional arguments one place to the left. To explain how this works let's first look at a simple script using a while loop to echo out all the arguments passed to a script.

```
$ pg opt2
#!/bin/sh
# opt2
loop=0
while [ $# -ne 0 ]    # while there are still arguments
do
  echo $1
done
```

You may think that the script above will process until there are no more arguments left on the command line. Wrong, I'm afraid. Because there is no way to shift to the next parameter inside the script, it will just keep echoing out the first argument. Here's how it looks when executed:

```
$ opt2 file1 file2 file3
file1
file1
file1
...
```

20.1.1 Simple use of `shift`

To be able to process each argument passed we need to use the `shift` command. Here's the modified script:

```
$ pg opt2
#!/bin/sh
# opt2
loop=0
while [ $# -ne 0 ]      # while there are still arguments
do
   echo $1
   shift
done
```

Now when we execute it, we get a better result:

```
$ opt2 file1 file2 file3
file1
file2
file3
```

20.1.2 Last parameter supplied on the command line

Though we haven't covered the `eval` command yet, if your script needs to know the last parameter supplied on the command line (which is generally a filename) you have two choices. Using eval you can use **eval echo \$$#**; using `shift` you can use: **shift `expr $# - 2`.**

20.1.3 Using `shift` to process file conversions

Seeing how `shift` works makes the job of handling command line options easier. Let's construct a case conversion script, that will use `tr` to convert files to either upper case or lower case.

The options to the script will be:

-l   **for lower case**

-u   **for upper case**

Using the shift command we can now start to put together a script that will handle the options -l and -u. Here's the first draft of the script.

```
$ pg tr_case
!/bin/sh
# tr_case
# case conversion
usage()
{
# usage
echo "usage:`basename $0` -[l|u] file [files]" >&2
exit 1
}

if [ $# -eq 0 ]; then
  # no parameters passed !
  usage
fi

while [ $# -gt 0 ]
do
   case $1 in
    -u|-U) echo "-u option specified"
     # do any settings of variables here for lowercase then shift
     shift
     ;;
    -l|-L) echo "-l option specified"
     # do any settings of variables here for uppercase then shift
     shift
     ;;
   *) usage
    ;;
   esac
done
```

We first check that there are arguments to the script. If not, a usage statement is printed. While there are arguments to be processed, using a case statement trap each option passed, and when we have finished with each option use shift to collect the next option on the command line. If any non-matching options are found, print a usage statement.

Here's how the output looks from the script, when a couple of invalid arguments are passed to the script.

```
$ tr_case -u -l -k
-u option specified
-l option specified
usage:tr_case -[l|u] file [files]
```

The next step is to handle the files that come in after the options have been trapped with the case statement. To do this, a slight change is required in the case statement. The catch any pattern '*' of the case statement should be changed to '-*', to allow for invalid options being passed, for example -p or -q.

The '*' pattern will be where we collect all the filenames that are passed so we can process each file later on with a for loop. We will also check that the filenames given are present, using the -f option.

So our amended case statement will now look like this:

```
case
...
-*) usage
  ;;
*)  if [ -f  $1 ]; then
      FILES=$FILES" " $1   # assign the filenames to a variable
    else
       echo "`basename $0` cannot find the file $1"
    fi
  shift  # get next one !
  ;;
esac
```

We also need to specify some variable settings depending on which option (-l, -u) is passed. The variables will be:

TRCASE	holds the case conversion type (upper or lower).
EXT	all files that are being converted will have either .UC for upper case or .LC for lower case. The original file will not be touched.
OPT	set to yes if options are given otherwise it is set to no. Just in case no options are given, we can trap it and echo out a message.

The only other bit of code left is the actual conversion process, which is the tr command. This will be put at the end of the script again using a case statement with the for loop to read in the filenames to process.

Here's the full script:

```
$ pg tr_case
!/bin/sh
# tr_case
# convert files to either upper or lower case
```

```
FILES=""
TRCASE=""
EXT=""
OPT=no


# gets called when a conversion fails
error_msg()
{
_FILENAME=$1
echo "`basename $0`: Error the conversion failed on $_FILENAME"
}


if [ $# -eq 0 ]
then
  echo "For more info try `basename $0` --help"
  exit 1
fi
while [ $# -gt 0 ]
do
  case $1 in
  # set the variables based on what option was used
  -u) TRCASE=upper
    EXT=".UC"
    OPT=yes
    shift
    ;;
  -l) TRCASE=lower
    EXT=".LC"
    OPT=yes
    shift
    ;;
  -help) echo "convert a file(s) to uppercase from lowercase"
         echo "convert a file(s) from lowercase to uppercase"
         echo "will convert all characters according to the"
         echo " specified command option."
         echo " Where option is"
         echo " -l Convert to lowercase"
         echo " -u Convert to uppercase"
         echo " The original file(s) is not touched. A new file(s)"
         echo "will be created with either a .UC or .LC extension"
         echo "usage: $0 -[l|u] file [file..]"
    exit 0
    ;;
  -*) echo "usage: `basename $0` -[l|u] file [file..]"
    exit 1
    ;;

  *) # collect the files to process
    if [ -f $1 ]
```

```
    then
      # add the filenames to a variable list
      FILES=$FILES" "$1
    else
      echo "`basename $0`: Error cannot find the file $1"
    fi
    shift
    ;;
  esac

done
# no options given ... help the user
if [ "$OPT" = "no" ]
then
  echo "`basename $0`:Error you need to specify an option. No action taken"
  echo " try `basename $0` --help"
  exit 1
fi

# now read in all the file(s)
# use the variable LOOP, I just love the word LOOP
for LOOP in $FILES
do
  case $TRCASE in
  lower) cat $LOOP|tr "[a-z]" "[A-Z]" >$LOOP$EXT
    if [ $? != 0 ]
    then
      error_msg $LOOP
    else
      echo "Converted file called $LOOP$EXT"
    fi
    ;;
  upper) cat $LOOP|tr "[A-Z]" "[a-z]" >$LOOP$EXT
    if [ $? != 0 ]
    then
      error_msg $LOOP
    else
      echo "Converted file called $LOOP$EXT"
    fi
    ;;
  esac
done
```

When the above script is run with different options of input we get the following.

Passing a file that does not exist:

```
$ tr_case -k cursor
usage: shift1 -[l|u] file [file..]
```

Passing the incorrect options:

```
$ tr_case cursor
tr_case:Error you need to specify an option. No action taken
 try tr_case -help
```

Just type the filename, in the hope that the script will give a pointer to more help. (It does.)

```
$ tr_case
For more info try tr_case -help
```

Supplying two valid files and a third that does not exist:

```
$ tr_case -l cursor sd ascii
tr_case: Error cannot find the file sd
Converted file called cursor.LC
Converted file called ascii.LC
```

Using the above script we can convert many files to the same case. To be able to code a script that can handle different command line options will take a lot of coding, and would be a maintenance headache.

Suppose we had a script that had to handle these different command line options:

command -l -c 23 -v file1 file2

The `shift` command is not up to it; we need to use the `getopts` command.

20.2 getopts

Getopts allows you to write code that can easily handle multiple command line arguments. Getopts is used to bring some form of standard in command line processing. After all, scripts should have the ability to conform to the standard format of command options files.

20.2.1 An example getopts script

Getopts is better understood with an example. Here is a simple getopts script that will take the following options or arguments.

-a	Set the variable ALL to true
-h	Set the variable HELP to true
-f	Set the variable FILE to true
-v	Set the variable VERBOSE to true

As with all variable settings we always assume the worst so initially set the variables to their false state:

```
$ pg getopt1
!/bin/sh
#getopt1

# set the vars
ALL=false
HELP=false
FILE=false
VERBOSE=false

while getopts ahfgv OPTION
do
  case $OPTION in
  a)ALL=true
    echo "ALL is $ALL"
    ;;
  h)HELP=true
    echo "HELP is $HELP"
    ;;
  f)FILE=true
    echo "FILE is $FILE"
    ;;
  v)VERBOSE=true
    echo "VERBOSE is $VERBOSE"
    ;;
  esac
done
```

The general format of getopts is:

getopts option_string variable

Using the code from our example:

```
while getopts ahfgv OPTION
```

we can see that a while loop is used to read in the command line. The option_string is our five options that we specified (-a, -h, -f, -g, -v), and the variable in our example is called OPTION. Notice we do not have to specify each single option with a hyphen.

If we run our example script with valid and non-valid options we get:

```
$ getopt1 -a -h
ALL is true
HELP is true
```

```
$ getopt1 -ah
ALL is true
HELP is true

$ getopt1 -a -h -p
ALL is true
HELP is true
./getopt1: illegal option -- p
```

Notice how we can now combine the different options.

20.2.2 How getopts works

Getopts reads the option_string, and knows that these are valid options to be used in the script.

Getopts will look for all arguments starting with a hyphen. It knows that these are the options. When it gets an option it compares this against the option_string. If a match is found then the variable is set to OPTION; if no match is found the variable is set to '?'. This process is repeated until there are no more options left.

When getopts has finished getting all the arguments it returns a non-zero status, which means all is OK with the arguments passed. A variable called OPTIND holds the last argument processed. We shall see in a minute how this can help in processing.

20.2.3 Specifying values using getopts

Sometimes it may be appropriate for your scripts to include an actual value with one of the command line options. Getopts provides a way to do this. All you need to do is put a colon after the option letter in the option_string. For example:

getopts ahfvc: OPTION

The above states that option a, h, f, v can be passed with no values, but option c must have a value. When you use a value you must use the variable OPTARG to hold the values. If you try and pass it without a value, you will get an error message. The error message is an unfriendly one, so to suppress this error and use your own, do the following:

Put a colon at the start of the option_string.

```
while getopts :ahfgvc: OPTION
```

Create a usage statement within the case statement using '?' to trap the error.

```
case
...

...
\?)    # usage statement
   echo "`basename $0` -[a h f v] -[c value] file"
   ;;
esac
```

Here's the modified getopt1 script:

```
$ pg getopt1
#!/bin/sh
#getopt1

# set the vars
ALL=false
HELP=false
FILE=false
VERBOSE=false
COPIES=0    # the value for the -c option is set to zero

while getopts :ahfgvc: OPTION
do
   case $OPTION in
   a)ALL=true
      echo "ALL is $ALL"
      ;;
   h)HELP=true
      echo "HELP is $HELP"
      ;;
   f)FILE=true
      echo "FILE is $FILE"
      ;;
   v)VERBOSE=true
      echo "VERBOSE is $VERBOSE"
      ;;
   c) COPIES=$OPTARG
      echo "COPIES is $COPIES"
   \?)    # usage statement
      echo "`basename $0` -[a h f v] -[c value] file" >&2
      ;;
   esac
done
```

Running the above script with no value for the -c option, we get an error, but now a usage is displayed:

```
$ getopt1 -ah -c
ALL is true
HELP is true
getopt1 -[a h f v] -[c value] file
```

Now with all legal options:

```
$ getopt1 -ah -c 3
ALL is true
HELP is true
COPIES is 3
```

20.2.4 How values can be accessed

One of the common uses of getopts is to run backup scripts, so the user can have the option to specify different tape devices to back up the data. Here is a framework using getopts for that very task.

```
$ pg backups
#!/bin/sh
# backups
QUITE=n
DEVICE=awa
LOGFILE=/tmp/logbackup
usage()
{
echo "Usage: `basename $0` -d [device] -l [logfile] -q"
exit 1
}
if [ $# = 0 ]
then
  usage
fi

while getopts :qd:l: OPTION
do
  case $OPTION in
  q) QUIET=y
    LOGFILE="/tmp/backup.log"
    ;;
  d) DEVICE=$OPTARG
    ;;
  l) LOGFILE=$OPTARG
    ;;
  \?) usage
    ;;
  esac
done
echo "you chose the following options..I can now process these"
echo "Quite= $QUITE $DEVICE $LOGFILE"
```

In the above script a value is required if the option d is specified. The value is the path to a tape device. The user can also specify whether to have a backup where all output goes to a log file. Running the above script with the following input gives:

```
$ backups -d/dev/rmt0 -q
you chose the following options..I can now process these
Quite= y /dev/rmt0 /tmp/backup.log
```

When getopts has finished checking, the values assigned from OPTARG can then be used in any normal processing. Of course, once you have the options, it's up to you to further process and validate the option values.

That's all you really need to know about getopts to provide a framework for command line passing.

To actually process the files we use a for loop, just like we did in our tr_case script using the shift command to work through the options.

Using getopts greatly reduces the amount of coding required if you compare it to using the shift method.

20.2.5 Using getopts to process file conversions

Let's now use the tr_case script and turn it into a getopts version with what we have learnt. The only difference in the command line options using the getopts method to the shift method is a VERBOSE option.

The variable VERBOSE by default holds a 'no', but when selected with the command line option the case statement traps it and assigns 'yes' to VERBOSE. The echoing of the commands is a simple if statement.

```
if [ "VERBOSE" = "on" ]; then
  echo "doing upper on $LOOP..newfile called $LOOP$EXT"
fi
```

If you were using a wrapper for other system commands that always echoed out their actions, simply redirect its output including any errors to /dev/null like this.

command > /dev/null 2 > &1

By default VERBOSE is off (no display). To turn it on use the -v option. For example, to convert a series of myfiles to lower case with the VERBOSE use:

tr_case -l -v myfile1 myfile2...

or

tr_case -v -l myfile1 myfile2...

Probably the first thing you will notice is the reduction in code using the getopts method. The code used for the processing of the files is the same though as the shift version.

Here's the script:

```
$ pg tr_case2
#!/bin/sh
#tr_case2
# convert case, using getopts
EXT=""
TRCASE=""
FLAG=""
OPT="no"
VERBOSE="off"


while getopts :luv OPTION
do
   case $OPTION in
   l) TRCASE="lower"
      EXT=".LC"
      OPT=yes
      ;;
   u) TRCASE="upper"
      EXT=".UC"
      OPT=yes
      ;;
   v) VERBOSE=on
      ;;
   \?) echo "usage: `basename $0`: -[l|u] --v file[s]"
      exit 1 ;;
   esac
done
# next argument down only please
shift `expr $OPTIND - 1`
# are there any arguments passed ???
if [ "$#" = "0" ] || [ "$OPT" = "no" ]
then
   echo "usage: `basename $0`: -[l|u] -v file[s]" >&2
   exit 1
fi
for LOOP in "$@"
do
   if [ ! -f $LOOP ]
   then
     echo "`basename $0`: Error cannot find file $LOOP" >&2
     exit 1
   fi
   echo $TRCASE $LOOP
   case $TRCASE in
   lower) if [ "VERBOSE" = "on" ]; then
             echo "doing..lower on $LOOP..newfile called $LOOP$EXT"
          fi
```

```
        cat $LOOP | tr "[a-z]" "[A-Z]" >$LOOP$EXT
        ;;
    upper) if [ "VERBOSE" = "on" ]; then
            echo "doing upper on $LOOP..newfile called $LOOP$EXT"
        fi
        cat $LOOP | tr "[A-Z]" "[a-z]" >$LOOP$EXT
        ;;
    esac
  done
```

When specifying command line options for your scripts, it is a good idea to try and keep a naming convention that is in tune with UNIX or LINUX. The following is a table with some common options and their meanings.

Option	Meaning
-a	append
-c	counter, copy
-d	directory, device
-e	execute
-f	filename, force
-h	help
-i	ignore case
-l	logfile
-o	full output
-q	quite
-p	path
-v	verbose

20.3 Conclusion

Being able to correctly handle command line options makes your scripts look professional; to the user they appear just like any other system command. This chapter has shown two methods of handling command line options, using shift and using getopts. The amount of checking code required in using getopts is far less than if you were to use the shift method.

Shift also overcomes the limitation of the $1..$9 parameters you can pass to your scripts. Using shift your script can simply shift its way up through all the arguments called, so the script can then get on with some processing.

CHAPTER 21

Creating screen output

Creating professional-looking screens for interactive use can be accomplished using shell scripts. All you need is a colour monitor and the `tput` command on your system.

In this chapter we will cover:

- the `tput` command;

- using escape sequences and generating control codes; and

- using colour.

Whilst writing this book I came across three different variants of `tput`. By far the best was GNU `tput`. If you haven't got this version, download it and install it on your system. Tput uses your `/etc/terminfo` or `/etc/termcap` file so you can use most commands that your terminal supports in your shell scripts.

Tput does not recognize colour settings, but we can take care of that using control characters.

21.1 `tput`

Before using `tput` you need to initialize your terminal using the `tput` command either inside your scripts or on the command line.

```
$ tput init
```

Tput can produce three different kinds of output: string, numeric and Boolean (true/false). We will cover the most useful capabilities of each.

21.1.1 String output

Here are the most common strings:

Name	Meaning
bel	Ring the bell
blink	Blinking mode
bold	Double intensity
civis	Hide the cursor
clear	Clear the screen
cnorm	Unhide the cursor
cup	Move cursor to x, y position on screen
el	Clear to the end of line
ell	Clear to the beginning of line
smso	Start stand out mode
rmso	End stand out mode
smul	Start underline mode
rmul	End underline mode
sc	Save current cursor position
rc	Restore cursor to last saved position
sgr0	Normal screen
rev	Reverse video

21.1.2 Numeric output

Here is the most common numeric output.

Name	Meaning
cols	Number of columns
it	Width of tab settings
lines	Number of lines on screen

21.1.3 Boolean output

There are not many Boolean operators in `tput`.

Name	Meaning
chts	Cursor is hard to see
hs	Has a status line

21.2 **Using** tput

Now we have gone over the most common names of tput that you will probably use, let's see how we can use tput in scripts.

21.2.1 Assigning tput commands

We can use the output of all tput names and store them inside more meaningful variable names. The format to do this is:

variable_name = `tput name`

21.2.2 Using Boolean output

To use the Boolean tput output use the if statement:

```
STATUS_LINE='tput hs'
if $STATUS_LINE; then
   echo "your terminal has a status line"
else
   echo "your terminal has NO status line"
fi
```

21.2.3 Using tput in your scripts

Here's a script that has assigned the tput bel and cl to more meaningful variable names.

```
$ pg tput1
#!/bin/sh
BELL=`tput bel`
CLEAR=`tput cl`

echo $BELL
echo $CLEAR
```

The following script changes a couple of video attributes and turns the cursor off and on:

```
$ pg tput2
#!/bin/sh
BOLD=`tput bold`
REV=`tput rev`
NORMAL=`tput sgr0`
CURSOR_OFF=`tput civis`
```

```
CURSOR_ON=`tput cnorm`
tput init

#turn cursor off, highlight text, reverse some text, cursor on
echo $CURSOR_OFF
echo "${BOLD} WELCOME TO THE PIZZA PLACE${NORMAL}"
echo -e "\n${REV} WE ARE OPEN 7 DAYS A WEEK${NORMAL}"
echo $CURSOR_ON
```

21.2.4 Generating escape sequences

Please note that if you are using an emulator, you may have problems making the cursor invisible. This could be because:

1. Some emulators do not trap the control character that makes the cursor invisible. I had to ask the author of the software emulator that I am using to make amendments to his source code so the cursor could be turned off.

2. Some older versions of the `tput civis` command in my opinion do not seem to work properly.

The control character for turning the cursor off is ?25l (that's the letter l). The character for turning it back on is ?25h.

All control characters start with an escape sequence, usually the escape key followed by [, then the actual sequence to turn some terminal attribute on or off.

You can use two different methods to generate escape sequences. The following table lists both methods depending on what system you have. The third method will work no matter what UNIX or LINUX variation you have got because the control sequence is embedded in the `echo` statement. This third method is the one we will use in the book.

To send an escape sequence to turn the cursor off:

LINUX/BSD	`echo -e "\033[?25l"`
System V	`echo "\033[?25l"`
Generic method	`echo "<CTRL-V><ESCAPE>[?25l"`

The `\033` is the value for the escape key. The '\' tells the `echo` command an octal value follows next. For instance to echo out the @ character, I could just use

```
echo "@"
```

or I could instead use the octal value of that character which is 100 to echo out the character.

```
echo -e "\100"
```

For System V use

```
echo "\100"
```

The results are the same.

The command clear clears the screen and sends the cursor to the top left-hand side of the screen, more commonly called home. The sequence it sends to do this on a VT terminal range is ESC[2J – you can send this sequence using an echo statement.

| System V | `echo "\033[2J"` |
| LINUX/BSD | `echo -e "\033[2J"` |

As with any control characters that are embedded in text files, do not try to cut and paste, as you will lose the characters' special meaning. To insert control characters, for example, to turn on the cursor do this:

echo ' < CTRL-V > hit the < ESCAPE > key then [?25h'

That's <CTRL-V>, then hit the escape key, then the characters [?251

If your cursor does not go off when you issue a tput civis and you are sure it's not the emulator, then use this little script to turn it on and off. I will leave it up to you to turn it into a function, or you could turn a couple of pages and find it already done.

```
$ pg cursor
#!/bin/sh

# cursor  on|off
# turns the cursor on or off for the vt100, 200, 220, meth220
# note : will work on normal tty connec.. if'ie on some win emulations
# check TERM env for your type !
_OPT=$1
if [ $# -ne 1 ]; then
  echo "Usage:`basename $0` cursor [on|off]"
  exit 1
fi

case "$_OPT" in
on|ON|On)
  # turn it on (cursor)
  ON=`echo ^[[?25h`
  echo $ON
  ;;
off|OFF|Off)
  # turn it off (cursor)
  OFF=`echo ^[[?251`
  echo $OFF
  ;;
 ;;
```

```
*) echo "Usage: cursor on|off"
   exit 1
   ;;
esac
```

21.2.5 Cursor position

We can also use `tput` to place the cursor anywhere on the screen. The format for this is:

cup r c

where `r` is the row (line) number down the screen and `c` is the column number across the screen.

It's best to use this as a function, then you can pass it the row and column values.

```
xy()
{
#_R= row, _C=column
_R=$1
_C=$2
tput cup $_R $_C
}

clear
xy 1 5
echo -n "Enter your name :"
read NAME
xy 2 5
echo -n "Enter your age   :"
read AGE
```

Of course it would be just as appropriate to pass it a string to display as well; here's the slightly amended function that will do this.

```
xy()
{
#_R= row, _C=column
_R=$1
_C=$2
_TEXT=$3
tput cup $_R $_C
echo -n  $_TEXT
}
```

This could be called like this:

```
xy 5 10 "Enter your password :"
read CODE
```

21.2.6 Centring text on the screen

It would not be too much trouble to centre text on the screen. All we need to do is get the columns from `tput` and then work out the length of the string supplied, take that value away from `tput` columns and divide the answer by two. All that is left is to supply the row number where we want the string to be displayed.

Here's the piece of code that does the job. Only a slight change would be needed to read lines from a file and centre all the text on the screen.

Enter some characters, hit `return` and the text is displayed in the middle of screen at row 10.

```
echo -n "input string :"
read STR
# quick way of getting length of string
LEN=`echo $STR | wc -c`
COLS=`tput cols`
NEW_COL=`expr \($COLS - $LEN \) / 2`
xy 10 $NEW_COL
echo $STR
```

For the above function to be more flexible you will probably want to call it with some text and a row number as well. This function will do that.

```
centertxt()
{
_ROW=$1
_STR=$2
# quick way of getting length of string
LEN=`echo $_STR | wc -c`
COLS=`tput cols`
_NEW_COL=`expr \($COLS -- $LEN \) / 2`
xy $_ROW $_NEW_COL
echo   $_STR
}
```

You could call the above function like this:

```
centertxt 15 "THE MAIN EVENT"
```

or like this, with the string as a argument:

```
centertxt 15 $1
```

21.2.7 Finding out your terminal attributes

Here's a script that will interrogate `terminfo` via `tput` to display some terminal escape codes on some of the `tput` commands we have met.

```
$ pg termput
#!/bin/sh
# termput

#init tput for your terminal
tput init

clear

echo " tput <> terminfo"
infocmp -1 $TERM | while read LINE
do
  case $LINE in
  bel*)   echo "$LINE: sound the bell" ;;
  blink*) echo "$LINE: begin blinking mode" ;;
  bold*)  echo "$LINE: make it bold" ;;
  el*)    echo "$LINE: clear to end of line" ;;
  civis*) echo "$LINE: turn cursor off" ;;
  cnorm*) echo "$LINE: turn cursor on " ;;
  clear*) echo "$LINE: clear the screen ";;
  kcuu1*) echo "$LINE: up arrow ";;
  kcub1*) echo "$LINE: left arrow ";;
  kcuf1*) echo "$LINE: right arrow ";;
  kcud1*) echo "$LINE: down arrow ";;
  esac
done
```

The command `infocmp`, extracts information about your terminal from the `terminfo` database. If you want to see the complete listing of your terminal definition file use the command:

```
$ infocmp $TERM
```

Here's the output from my terminal using the `termput` script:

```
$ termput
tput <> terminfo
bel=^G,: sound the bell
blink=E[5m,: begin blinking mode
bold=E[1m,: make it bold
civis=E[?25l,: turn cursor off
clear=E[HE[J,: clear the screen
cnorm=E[?25h,: turn cursor on
el=E[K,: clear to end of line
el1=E[1K,: clear to end of line
kcub1=E[D,: left arrow
kcud1=E[B,: down arrow
kcuf1=E[C,: right arrow
kcuu1=E[A,: up arrow
```

21.2.8 Using function keys with your scripts

You can see what control sequence any of the special keys (F1, up arrow etc.) are sending by using the cat command. Type cat -v then press any control key to see what your terminal is sending down the line. When you have finished just press <CTRL-C> to quit.

In the following example cat is invoked. The keys pressed are F1 (^[OP), F2 (^[OQ) and the up arrow key (^[[A).

```
$ cat -v
^[OP^[OQ^[[A
<CTRL-C>
```

Once you have this information you can then insert these characters into your scripts as additional methods of user selection.

The following script recognizes keys F1, F2 and the arrow keys. Your values may be different so use the cat command to see what values your terminal control keys send first.

```
$ pg control_keys
#!/bin/sh
# control_keys
# to insert use '<CTRL-V><ESCAPE>sequence'
uparrowkey='^[[A'
downarrowkey='^[[B'
leftarrowkey='^[[D'
rightarrowkey='^[[C'
f1key='^[OP'
f2key='^[OQ'

echo -n " Press a control key then hit return"
read KEY

case $KEY in
$uparrowkey) echo "UP Arrow"
  ;;
$downarrowkey) echo "DOWN arrow"
  ;;
$leftarrowkey) echo "LEFT arrow"
  ;;
$rightarrowkey) echo "RIGHT arrow"
  ;;
$f1key) echo "F1 key"
  ;;
$f2key) echo "F2 key"
  ;;
*) echo "unknown key $key"
  ;;
esac
```

21.2.9 Using colours

Using colours on fields can make your data input screen look more professional. The colours we are going to use are ANSI standard. Not all colours work on all systems so here are the most common colours.

Foreground colours

Number	Colour
30	black foreground
31	red foreground
32	green foreground
33	yellow (or brown) foreground
34	blue foreground
35	purple foreground
36	cyan foreground
37	white (or grey) foreground

Background colours

Number	Colour
40	black background
41	red background
42	green background
43	yellow (or brown) background
44	cyan background
45	blue background
46	cyan background
47	white (or grey) background

The format to use for displaying background and foreground colours is:

< ESCAPE >[background_number ; foreground_number m

21.2.10 Generating colours

To generate a colour we will embed the control characters into the `echo` statement, because this method works on any system with a colour terminal. But again, as in control characters, you can generate colours using escape sequences inside an `echo` statement.

To generate a black background with a green foreground:

LINUX/BSD	`echo -e "\033[40;32m"`
System V	`echo "\033[40;32m"`
Generic method	`echo "<CTRL-V><ESCAPE>[40;32m"`

For the generic method that's `<CTRL-V>`, hit the `<ESCAPE>` key then `[40;32m`. The generic method is the one we will use in the book.

You will probably find it best to put your colour `echo` statements in a case statement then enclose it inside a function. Here's my case colour function.

```
colour()
{
# format is background;foregroundm
case $1 in
black_green)
  echo '^[[40;32m'
  ;;
black_yellow)
  echo '^[[40;33m'
  ;;
black_white)
  echo '^[[40;37m'
  ;;
black_cyan)
  echo '^[[40;36m'
  ;;
red_yellow)
  echo '^[[41;32m'
  ;;
black_blue)
  echo '^[[40;34m'
  ;;
esac
}
```

To call the colours `red_yellow` (that's a red background and yellow foreground) all I need to do is

```
colour red_yellow
```

To use colours in your scripts the action is this:

colour what_ever
echo something
 # now change to a different colour
colour what_ever
echo something

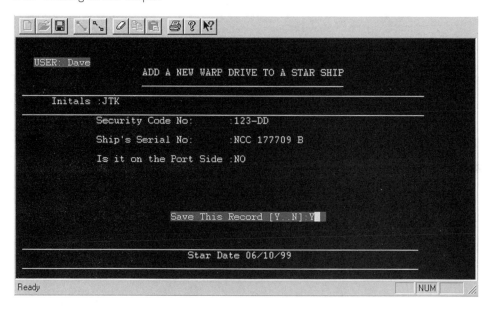

Figure 21.1 *A screenshot from the following script code using colours and the* tput *command*

My terminal default screen colour is black and white, but I like using a black background on a green foreground. To fix this I simply insert an echo statement that generates this combination in my .profile file.

Figure 21.1 shows a basic input screen with some colours added to it. It looks a lot more interesting in colour!

Here's the code for the screen shown in Figure 21.1.

```
$ pg colour_scr
#!/bin/sh
# colour_scr
tput init
MYDATE=`date +%D`
colour()
{
# format is background;foregroundm
case $1 in
black_green)
   echo '^[[40;32m'
   ;;
black_yellow)
   echo '^[[40;33m'
   ;;
black_white)
   echo '^[[40;37m'
   ;;
```

```
black_cyan)
  echo '^[[40;36m'
  ;;
black_red)
  echo '^[[40;31m'
  ;;
esac
}

xy()
# xy
# to call: xy row, column, "text"
# goto xy screen co-ordinates
{
#_R= row, _C=column
_R=$1
_C=$2
_TEXT=$3
tput cup $_R $_C
echo -n $_TEXT
}

center()
{
# center
# centers a string of text across screen
# to call: center "string" row_number
_STR=$1
_ROW=$2
# crude way of getting length of string
LEN=`echo $_STR | wc -c`

COLS=`tput cols`
HOLD_COL=`expr $COLS - $LEN`
NEW_COL=`expr $HOLD_COL / 2`
tput cup $_ROW $NEW_COL
echo -n $_STR
}

tput clear
colour red_yellow
xy 2 3 "USER: $LOGNAME"
colour black_cyan
center "ADD A NEW WARP DRIVE TO A STAR SHIP" 3
echo -e "\f\f"
center "_____" 4

colour black_yellow
xy 5 1  "_____"
xy 7 1  "_____"
xy 21 1 "_____"
```

```
center "Star Date $MYDATE " 22
xy 23 1 "_____"

colour black_green
xy 6 6 "Initials :"
read INIT
xy 8 14
echo -n "Security Code No:        :"
read CODE
xy 10 14
echo -n "Ship's Serial No:        :"
read SERIAL
xy 12 14
echo -n "Is it on the Port Side :"
read PORT

colour red_yellow
center " Save This Record [Y..N]: " 18
read ans

#reset to normal
colour black_white
```

As you can see, the script has no validation. That's OK, because the aim of the script is to show you how to paint your screen.

21.2.11 Creating better menus

Remember the menu we created when we covered while loops? Let's now improve on the menu script. The menu will now have the following options:

1 : ADD A RECORD
2 : VIEW A RECORD
3 : PAGE ALL RECORDS
4 : CHANGE A RECORD
5 : DELETE A RECORD
P : PRINT ALL RECORDS
H : Help screen
Q : Exit Menu

We will use our read_char function, so that the user does not have to hit return when selecting menu options. The trap command (more on traps later in the book) will also be used to ignore signals 2, 3 and 15. This will stop the user from trying to break out of the menu.

The menu will also have some form of control access. Certain privileged users will be able to change or delete records. The rest of the defined users will only be able to add, view or print records. A list of valid users with their access levels is held in a file called priv.user.

If a user tries to run the menu and their name is not present in the file, they will be informed that they cannot run this application and be exited.

For display purposes only, system commands will replace the actual behind the scenes options. Have a look at Chapter 22 if you want to see data validation on file updates.

Here's the `priv.user` file that contains usernames of who can and cannot delete or change records. At a glance we can see that root, dave and matty cannot make changes to the database files, but peter and louise can.

```
$ pg priv.user
# prov.user access file for apps menu
# edit this at your own risk !!!!
# format is USER AMEND/DELETE records
# example root yes means yes root can amend or delete recs
#       "    dave no  means no dave cannot amend or delete recs
root no
dave no
peter yes
louise yes
matty no
```

To check user accesses we first read the file in, ignoring comment lines and redirecting any other lines to a temp file.

```
user_level()
{
while read LINE
do
  case $LINE in
  \#*);;
  *) echo $LINE >>$HOLD1
    ;;
  esac
done < $USER_LEVELS

FOUND=false
while read MENU_USER PRIV
do
  if [ "$MENU_USER" = "$USER" ];
  then
    FOUND=true
    case $PRIV in
    yes|YES)
      return 0
      ;;
    no|NO)
      return 1
      ;;
    esac
```

```
    else
      continue
    fi
  done <$HOLD1
    if [ "$FOUND" = "false" ]; then
    echo "Sorry $USER you have not been authorised to use this menu"
    exit 1
    fi
}
```

The next step is to read in the newly formatted file. The variable FOUND is set to false. The temp file now holds just the names and privilege levels; variables are assigned to the user and privilege level. A test is carried out to see if the name in the file matches the USER; the value of USER is taken from the command whoami at the beginning of the script. If no match is found, the else comes into play and we continue with the next iteration of processing, using the command continue.

This process carries on until all names have been read in and compared. If after reading in the whole file no matches have been found, the test statement at the end of the code checks the variable FOUND. If it is set to false the user is kicked out.

If a match is found during the while loop, the variable FOUND is set to true. The case statement then traps the privilege levels and will either return 1 for normal level access or 0 for high level access.

When a user selects to either change or delete a record, a test is carried out based on the return code of the above function. In this example script the passwd file is sorted or a directory is listed

```
  if user_level; then
    sort /etc/passwd
  else
    restrict
  fi
```

Restrict is a function that simply echoes out a violation prompt.

The above testing could have been done in one loop, but I think the code looks clearer using the two-file method, and it's certainly a lot easier to debug.

Figure 21.2 shows user dave who has normal permission trying to change a record and is being prompted that he does not have the authorization to do so.

To exit the menu the user selects q or Q, and a function is called to clean up. When a user exits any large script, it's a good idea to call a function to carry out this task. This allows for any growth in the commands you may want to run when a user exits, plus greater ease of readability of the code.

Here's the script.

```
$ pg menu2
#!/bin/sh
# menu2
```

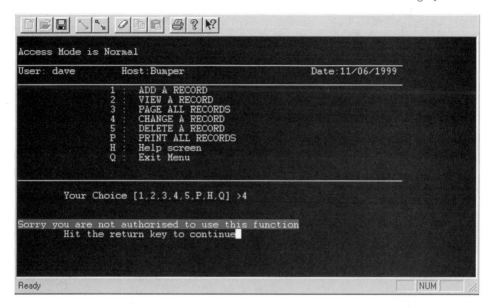

Figure 21.2 *A screenshot of the menu with access restrictions*

```
# MAIN MENU SCRIPT
# ignore CTRL-C and QUIT interrupts
trap "" 2 3 15
MYDATE=`date +%d/%m/%Y`
THIS_HOST=`hostname -s`

USER=`whoami`

# user level file
USER_LEVELS=priv.user

# hold file
HOLD1=hold1.$$

# colour function
colour()
{
# format is background;foregroundm
case $1 in
black_green)
  echo '^[[40;32m'
  ;;
black_yellow)
  echo '^[[40;33m'
  ;;
```

```
black_white)
   echo '^[[40;37m'
   ;;
black_cyan)
   echo '^[[40;36m'
   ;;
red_yellow)
   echo '^[[41;33m'
   ;;
esac
}

# just read a single key please
get_char()
{
# get_char
# save current stty settings
SAVEDSTTY=`stty -g`
   stty cbreak
   dd if=/dev/tty bs=1 count=1 2> /dev/null
   stty -cbreak
# restore stty
stty $SAVEDSTTY
}

# turn the cursor on or off
cursor()
{
# cursor
#turn cursor on/off

_OPT=$1
   case $_OPT in
   on) echo '^[[?25h'
     ;;
   off) echo '^[[?25l'
     ;;
   *) return 1
     ;;
   esac
}

# check what privilege level the user has
restrict()
{
colour red_yellow
echo -e -n "\n\n\007Sorry you are not authorised to use this function"
colour black_green
}
```

```
user_level()
{
# user_level
# read in the priv.user file
while read LINE
do
  case $LINE in
  # ignore comments
  \#*);;
  *) echo $LINE >>$HOLD1
    ;;
  esac
done < $USER_LEVELS

FOUND=false
while read MENU_USER PRIV
do
  if [ "$MENU_USER" = "$USER" ];
  then
    FOUND=true
    case $PRIV in
    yes|YES)
      return 0
      ;;
    no|NO)
      return 1
      ;;
    esac
  else
  # no match found read next record
    continue
  fi
done <$HOLD1
if [ "$FOUND" = "false" ]; then
  echo "Sorry $USER you have not been authorised to use this menu"
  exit 1
fi
}

# called when user selects quit
my_exit()
{
# my_exit
# called when user selects quit!
colour black_white
  cursor on
  rm *.$$
  exit 0
}
tput init
```

```
# display their user levels on the screen
if user_level; then
  ACCESS="Access Mode is High"
else
  ACCESS="Access Mode is Normal"
fi


tput init
while :
do
tput clear
colour black_green
cat <<MAYDAY
$ACCESS
```

```
User: $USER          Host:$THIS_HOST                    Date:$MYDATE
```

```
              1 :   ADD A RECORD
              2 :   VIEW A RECORD
              3 :   PAGE ALL RECORDS
              4 :   CHANGE A RECORD
              5 :   DELETE A RECORD
              P :   PRINT ALL RECORDS
              H :   Help screen
              Q :   Exit Menu
```

```
MAYDAY
colour black_cyan
echo -e -n "\tYour Choice [1,2,3,4,5,P,H,Q] >"
œread CHOICE
CHOICE=`get_char`
  case $CHOICE in
  1) ls
    ;;
  2) vi
    ;;
  3) who
    ;;
  4) if user_level; then
       ls -l |wc
     else
       restrict
     fi
     ;;
  5) if user_level; then
       sort /etc/passwd
     else
       restrict
     fi
     ;;
```

```
    P|p) echo -e "\n\nPrinting records......."
     ;;
    H|h)
    tput clear
    cat <<MAYDAY
    This is the help screen, nothing here yet to help you!
    MAYDAY
     ;;
    Q|q) my_exit
     ;;
    *) echo -e "\t\007unknown user response"
     ;;
    esac
  echo -e -n "\tHit the return key to continue"
  read DUMMY
  done
```

This type of menu could be called from a `profile` file with the `exec` command. The users would not be able to break out; they would be kept in the menu or the application(s) that the menu kicks off. This is fairly common practice for users who use only UNIX or LINUX applications and who are not bothered about the shell.

21.3 Conclusion

Using the `tput` command can greatly enhance the look of, and the control you can have over, your scripts. Using colours gives that slight professional edge to them. Beware of overdoing the colours; they may look good to you, but not to a user who has to keep looking at your screen when using your script. Being able to use and read control characters can give your scripts more flexibility, especially on user input by key selection.

CHAPTER 22

Creating screen input

Screen input or data input is the ability to take input (from the keyboard in our case) then validate the input. If it's OK accept it, if not throw it back out.

We have seen functions that test for certain conditions; for example the length of a string; whether a string is either numeric or character based. We will be using these functions amongst others in this chapter.

In this chapter we will cover:

- validating input;
- adding, deleting, amending and viewing records; and
- working file update scripts.

This chapter may be a bit heavy going at the first read, so you may want to scan it first, then come back later. Validation can be fairly code-intensive, but to catch all possible errors, the code has to test for at least the most probable errors.

Let's go through each task that is involved in creating a general file update system; namely adding, deleting, amending and viewing records. We will create a personal file update system. The records in our file called DBFILE will hold the following information.

Field	Length	Allow only	Description
Staff number	10	Numeric	Employee staff number
First name	20	Character	Employee's first name
Second name	20	Character	Employee's second name
Department	–	Accounts IT Services Sales Claims	Employee's department

Each field is separated by a colon ':'. For example:

< Staff number > : < First name > : < Second name > : < Department >

Each task is presented as a complete script. Some small parts of the code are duplicated in a couple of the scripts presented. This is intentional, and the object of this chapter is to show you how a file update system is updated. When I first started scripting, one of the most frustrating things was the lack of clear documentation on putting a file update or database system together.

A live running script would have a menu connecting up the different tasks or module, or most probably a suite of functions contained in a file with one menu script. Each script contains the trap command; signals 2, 3 and 15 are ignored.

22.1 Adding records

The tasks involved in adding a record to a file are the following:

1.   Validate the input.

2.   Write the record(s) to a file.

The first task we need to do is put some functions together that can tell us whether the fields are numeric or character based and the length of the fields. This will be our data input validation, which will be used with records that are added as well as amended. Luckily we already have some of these functions at hand.

Function to check the length of a string:

```
length_check()
{
# length_string
# $1=string, $2= length of string not to exceed this number
_STR=$1
_MAX=$2
_LENGTH=`echo $_STR |awk '{print length($0)}'`
if [ "$_LENGTH" -gt "$_MAX" ]; then
  return 1
else
  return 0
fi
}
```

Function to check whether a string contains all numeric data:

```
a_number()
#a _number
# $1= string
{
_NUM=$1
_NUM=`echo $1|awk '{if($0~/[^0-9]/) print "1"}'`
```

```
if [ "$_NUM" != "" ]
then
   return 1
else
   return 0
fi
}
```

Function to check a string contains only characters:

```
characters()
# characters
# $1 = string
{
_LETTERS_ONLY=$1
_LETTERS_ONLY=`echo $1|awk '{if($0~/[^a-zA-Z]/) print "1"}'`

if [ "$_LETTERS_ONLY" != "" ]
then
   return 1
else
   return 0
fi
```

When the fields are read in, we can simply call the appropriate function and then test against their return codes.

We also need a prompt to hold messages on the screen until the user presses a key to erase them. The following function uses read_a_char.

```
continue_promptYN()
{
# continue_prompt
echo -n "Hit any key to continue.."
DUMMY=`read_a_char`
}
```

When we get the user's input for the employee number, we want to make sure that the number does not already exist; this field must be unique. This task can be carried out in several ways, but we will use grep. Grep will search for the employee number, which is contained in the string _CODE. If awk returns nothing, then there are no duplicates, and the function will return with a 0 status. Here's the function (Note that we are using "$_CODE\>" in grep for an exact match. We use double quotes to protect the variable, if we had used single quotes nothing would be returned):

```
check_duplicate()
{
# check_duplicate
# check for employee number duplicate
```

```
_CODE=$1
MATCH=`grep "$_CODE\>" $DBFILE`
echo $_CODE
if [ "$MATCH" = "" ]; then
  return 0  # no duplicate
else
  return 1 # duplicate found
fi
}
```

Here's the piece of code for checking the employee number. I will describe what's going on after the listing.

```
while :
do
echo -n "Employee Staff Number :"
read NUM
# check for input
if [ "$NUM" != "" ]; then
  if a_number $NUM; then
  # number OK
    NUM_PASS=0
  else
    NUM_PASS=1
  fi
  if length_check $NUM 10; then
  # length OK
    LEN_PASS=0
  else
    LEN_PASS=1
  fi
  # now check for duplicates...

  if check_duplicate $NUM; then
  # no duplicates
    DUPLICATE=0
  else
    DUPLICATE=1
    echo "Staff Number: There is already an employee with this number"
    continue_prompt
  fi
  # check all three variables now, they must all be true
  if [ "$LEN_PASS" = "0"  -a  "$NUM_PASS" = "0" -a "$DUPLICATE" = "0" ]
  then
    break
  else
    echo "Staff Number: Non-Numeric or Too Many Numbers In Field"
    continue_prompt
  fi
```

```
else
  echo "Staff Number: No Input Detected, This Field Requires a Number"
  continue_prompt
fi

done
```

We keep everything enclosed inside a `while` loop (in fact each data entry field is enclosed inside a separate while loop), so if there is an invalid entry, the prompt will return to its original read place.

After reading in the staff number, we check that there is actually some data in the field with

if ["$NUM" != ""]

The then part of the `if` statement will not be executed if the field contains no input. The else part is at the end of this field's code validation, which displays the following message:

`Staff Number: No Input Detected, This Field Requires a Number`

The then part encompasses all the validation checks carried out on the field input. Assuming that there is input, the function `a_number` gets called. This function's task is to test if the string passed is a number; if it is then the function returns a 0, if not it returns a 1. Based on the returned values, the flag `NUM_PASS` is set to either 0 for a good return (it's numeric) or 1 for a bad return (it's non-numeric).

The function `length_check` is then called, passing not only the string but the maximum number of characters the string should contain, in this case ten. It will return 0 if the length of characters is less than or equal to this maximum number; otherwise it will return 1. The flag `LEN_PASS` is set to either 0 for a good return (length did not exceed the maximum length) or 1 for a bad return (if it did exceed the maximum length).

We now check for any duplicate employee numbers. The function `check_duplicate` does this. If there are no duplicates found, the flag `DUPLICATE` is set to 1. Now all we need to do is test that all three flag values are 0 (non-errors), and we use the AND test for this. All sides of the equation must be true, if the then part is to be executed.

If the test passes, we now have a validated field. Because we are in a continuous while loop all we need to do is break out of it with the command `break`.

**if ["$LEN_PASS" = "0" -a "$NUM_PASS" = "0" -a "$DUPLICATE" = "0"
]; then
break**

If any part of the validation fails either on the length or numeric only test, an error message will be displayed at the bottom of the screen.

```
Staff Number: Non-Numeric or Too Many Numbers In Field
```

And that's it; one field validated.

To validate the second and third fields, the process is the same. The validation part is kept inside another continuous while loop. The function `characters` is called this time, which checks that the field contains characters only. Here's the piece of code that does the first name validation:

```
while :
do
echo -n  "Employee's First Name :"
read F_NAME
if [ "$F_NAME" != "" ]; then
  if characters $F_NAME; then
    F_NAME_PASS=0
  else
    F_NAME_PASS=1
  fi
  if length_check $F_NAME 20; then
    LEN_PASS=0
  else
    LEN_PASS=1
  fi
  if [ "$LEN_PASS" = "0"  -a  "$F_NAME_PASS" = "0" ]; then

    break
  else
    echo "Staff First Name: Non-Character or Too Many Characters In Field"
    continue_prompt
  fi
else
  echo "Staff First Name: No Input Detected, This Field Requires
        Characters"
  continue_prompt
fi
done
```

To validate the department (see the listing below) I have used a `case` statement, as the company only has five departments and the field must contain one of these departments. Notice the three different pattern matches for each of the departments; this is to catch differently typed department names by the user. If a pattern is matched, the user breaks out of the `case` statement. Any other input is caught, with the list of valid departments being displayed.

```
while :
do
echo -n  "Company Department    :"
read DEPART
```

```
    case $DEPART in
    ACCOUNTS|Accounts|accounts) break;;
    SALES|Sales|sales)break;;
    IT|It|it) break;;
    CLAIMS|Claims|claims)break;;
    SERVICES|Services|services)break;;
    *) echo "Department: Accounts,Sales,IT,Claims,Services";;
    esac
  done
```

When all the fields have been validated a prompt is displayed to the user to ask if he or she wants this record saved. To take care of that we will use the function continue_promptYN. We have met this function before; it deals with getting a Y or N response. We can also pass a default answer in case the user just hits return.

If the user selects N, they fall through the if statement code blocks and exit the script. If the user is inputting a lot of records then you would encase the function that does the adding of records within a while loop. This way they would not keep returning to the menu or exiting after adding a record.

If the user selects Y, the record is saved. The code that appends the record to a file is

echo "$NUM:$F_NAME:$S_NAME:$DEPART" > > $DBFILE

A message is displayed informing the user that the record is saved to file; the sleep command sleeps for one second, just long enough to let the user see the message.

The field separator is a colon. The file is then sorted on the surname field, and the output goes to a temp file. The file is then moved back to the original file DBFILE. A last status test is carried out on both of these file movements, and if there are any problems the user is informed.

Here's what the output looks like when we add a record:

```
    ADD A RECORD

          Employee Staff Number :23233

          Employee's First Name :Peter

          Employee's Surname    :Wills

          Company Department    :Accounts

    Do You wish To Save This Record  [Y..N] [Y]:
    saved
```

Here's what our DBFILE looks like after some records have been added:

```
$ pg DBFILE
32123:Liam:Croad:Claims
2399:Piers:Cross:Accounts
239192:John:Long:Accounts
98211:Simon:Penny:Services
99202:Julie:Sittle:IT
```

```
23736:Peter:Wills:Accounts
89232:Louise:Wilson:Accounts
91811:Andy:Wools:IT
```

Here's the complete script to add a record:

```
$ pg dbase_add
#!/bin/sh
# dbase_add
# add a record
#ignore signals
trap ""  2 3 15
# temp hold files
DBFILE=DBFILE
HOLD1=HOLD1.$$

read_a_char()
{
# read_a_char
# save the settings
SAVEDSTTY=`stty -g`
  stty cbreak
  dd if=/dev/tty bs=1 count=1 2> /dev/null
  stty -cbreak
stty $SAVEDSTTY
}

continue_promptYN()
#to call: continue_prompt "string to display" default_answer
{
# continue_prompt
_STR=$1
_DEFAULT=$2
# check we have the right params
if [ $# -lt 1 ]; then
  echo "continue_prompt: I need a string to display"
  return 1
fi
while :
do
  echo -n "$_STR [Y..N] [$_DEFAULT]:"
  read _ANS
  # if user hits return set the default and determine the return value
  : ${_ANS:=$_DEFAULT}
  if [ "$_ANS" = "" ]; then
    case $_ANS in
    Y) return 0 ;;
    N) return 1 ;;
    esac
  fi
```

```
    # user has selected something
      case $_ANS in
      y|Y|Yes|YES)
        return 0
        ;;
      n|N|No|NO)
        return 1
        ;;
      *) echo "Answer either Y or N, default is $_DEFAULT"
      ;;
      esac
    echo $_ANS
done
}

continue_prompt()
{
# continue_prompt
echo -n "Hit any key to continue.."
DUMMY=`read_a_char`
}

length_check()
{
# length_check
# $1=str to check length $2=max length
_STR=$1
_MAX=$2
_LENGTH=`echo $_STR |awk '{print length($0)}'`
if [ "$_LENGTH" -gt "$_MAX" ]; then
  return 1
else
  return 0
fi
}

a_number()
{
# a_number
# call: a_number $1=number
_NUM=$1
_NUM=`echo $1|awk '{if($0~/[^0-9]/) print "1"}'`
if [ "$_NUM" != "" ]
then
  # errors
  return 1
else
  return 0
fi
}
```

```
characters()
# characters
# to call: char_name string
{
_LETTERS_ONLY=$1
_LETTERS_ONLY=`echo $1|awk '{if($0~/[^a-zA-Z]/) print "1"}'`
if [ "$_LETTERS_ONLY" != "" ]
then
  # oops errors
  return 1
else
  # contains only chars
  return 0
fi
}

check_duplicate()
{
# check_duplicate
# check for employee number duplicate
# to call: check_duplicate string
_CODE=$1
MATCH=`grep "$_CODE\>" $DBFILE`
echo $_CODE
if [ "$MATCH" = "" ]; then
  return 0   # no duplicate
else
  return 1   # duplicate found
fi
}

add_rec()
{
# add_rec
# ==  STAFF NUMBER
while :
do
  echo -n "Employee Staff Number :"
  read NUM
  if [ "$NUM" != "" ]; then
    if a_number $NUM; then
      NUM_PASS=0
    else
      NUM_PASS=1
    fi
    if length_check $NUM 10; then
      LEN_PASS=0
    else
      LEN_PASS=1
    fi
```

```
  # now check for duplicates...
  if check_duplicate $NUM; then
    DUPLICATE=0
  else
    DUPLICATE=1
    echo "Staff Number: There is already a employee with this number"
    continue_prompt
  fi
  if [ "$LEN_PASS" = "0"  -a  "$NUM_PASS" = "0" -a "$DUPLICATE" = "0" ]
  then
    break
  else
    echo "Staff Number: Non-Numeric or Too Many Numbers In Field"
    continue_prompt
  fi
  else
    echo "Staff Number: No Input Detected, This Field Requires a Number"
    continue_prompt
  fi
done

# == First Name
while :
do
  echo -n  "Employee's First Name :"
  read F_NAME
  if [ "$F_NAME" != "" ]; then
    if characters $F_NAME; then
      F_NAME_PASS=0
    else
      F_NAME_PASS=1
    fi
    if length_check $F_NAME 20; then
      LEN_PASS=0
    else
      LEN_PASS=1
    fi
    # both conditons must be true to get out of this loop
    if [ "$LEN_PASS" = "0"  -a  "$F_NAME_PASS" = "0" ]; then
      break
    else
      echo "Staff First Name: Non-Character or Too Many Characters In
          Field"
      continue_prompt
    fi
  else
    echo "Staff First Name: No Input Detected, This Field Requires
        Characters"
    continue_prompt
  fi
```

```
done

# == Surname
while :
do
  echo -n "Employee's Surname    :"
  read S_NAME
  if [ "$S_NAME" != "" ]; then
    if characters $S_NAME; then
      S_NAME_PASS=0
    else
      S_NAME_PASS=1
    fi
    if length_check $S_NAME 20; then
      LEN_PASS=0
    else
      LEN_PASS=1
    fi
    if [ "$LEN_PASS" = "0"  -a  "$S_NAME_PASS" = "0" ]; then
      break
    else
      echo "Staff Surname: Non-Character or Too Many Characters In Field"
      continue_prompt
    fi
  else
    echo "Staff Surname: No Input Detected, This Field Requires Characters"
    continue_prompt
  fi
done

# == Department
while :
do
  echo -n  "Company Department    :"
  read DEPART
  case $DEPART in
    ACCOUNTS|Accounts|accounts) break;;
    SALES|Sales|sales)break;;
    IT|It|it) break;;
    CLAIMS|Claims|claims)break;;
    Services|SERVICES|services)break;;
    *) echo "Department: Accounts,Sales,IT,Claims,Services";;
  esac
done
}

#  main
clear
echo -e "\t\t\tADD A EMPLOYEE RECORD"
```

```
if [ -s $DBFILE ]; then :
else
  echo "Information: Creating new file to add employee records"
  >$DBFILE
fi
add_rec
if continue_promptYN "Do You wish To Save This Record " "Y"; then
  echo "$NUM:$F_NAME:$S_NAME:$DEPART" >>$DBFILE
  echo "record saved"

  sleep 1
  sort +2 -t: $DBFILE >$HOLD1 2> /dev/null
  if [ $? -ne 0 ]; then
    echo "problems trying to sort the file..check it out"
    exit 1
  fi
  mv $HOLD1 $DBFILE
  if [ $? -ne 0 ]; then
    echo "problems moving the temp sort file..check it out"
    exit 1
  fi

else
  echo " record not saved"
  sleep 1
fi
```

22.2 Deleting records

To delete records from a file you must first present the record to the user to make sure that this is the correct record to delete. When this is confirmed you can then proceed to delete the record from the file.

To delete a record we need to be able to do the following tasks:

1. Search for the record.

2. Display the record.

3. Confirm deletion.

4. Update the file.

To search for a record we will use the field surname. Once we have got a surname from the user on which to search we can then proceed. We could use grep or awk, but because our file will have no more than perhaps 100 records we shall read the file in and test for a match.

If your file is going to contain over a couple of hundred records, I advise you to use awk, as it's much faster than reading in a file, and better suited than grep, for splitting up fields into variables.

To use grep or awk we could search the DBFILE like this:

echo "enter the surname to search "
read STR

 # for awk use this
awk -F: '/$STR/' DBFILE

# for grep use this	or
grep "$STR" DBFILE	**grep "$STR\ > "DBFILE**

Notice when using awk, the variable is enclosed with single quotes. If you do not do this you will get no data returned.

To be able to split up the fields so we can assign variables to each field (remember they are colon-separated), we have to change the IFS setting to the colon. If we do not, we would not be able to read the record. When changing the IFS it is always a good idea to save the settings first so you can restore them again when the script has finished.

To save IFS:

SAVEDIFS = $IFS

To change it to a colon:

IFS = :

When we have finished with the IFS we can then simply restore it:

IFS = $SAVEDIFS

The bulk of the search is carried out in one function called get_rec; there are no parameters passed to it.

```
get_rec()
{
# get_rec
clear
echo -n "Enter the employee surname :"
read STR
if [ "$STR" = "q" ]; then
  return 1
fi

REC=0
MATCH=no
if [ "$STR" != "" ]; then
  while read CODE F_NAME S_NAME DEPART
```

```
  do
    REC=`expr $REC + 1`
    tput cup 3 4
    echo -n " searching record.. $REC"
    if [ "$S_NAME" = "$STR" ]; then
      MATCH=yes
      display_rec
      break
    else
      continue
    fi
  done <DBFILE
else
  echo "Enter a surname to search for or q to quit"
fi
if [ "$MATCH" = "no" ]; then
  no_recs
fi
}
```

The user can enter a surname or q to quit the task. Once the surname has been entered a test is carried out to make sure that there is input. Remember it's always better to use this test:

if ["$STR" != ""]; then

then this one:

[-z $STR]

The first test will trap a user just hitting return; the second test will only test for a zero length string which is not the same thing.

Meaningful variable names are used to read in each field from the file. A counter is then used when reading in the records. This is really just cosmetic, to show the user that something is happening when searching for records. If a match is found, another procedure is called to display the fields; the user is then taken out of the loop with the break command. If no match is found the script continues to the next iteration of the loop.

When a match is found the user is asked if he or she wants to delete the record. The default answer is no.

if continue_promptYN "Do You Wish To DELETE This Record" "N"; then
echo "DEL"
grep -v $STR DBFILE >$HOLD1 2> /dev/null
if [$? -ne 0]; then
    echo "Problems creating temp file $HOLD1..check it out"
    exit 1
fi
    ...

The deletion of the record is carried out by using `grep` with the `-v` option, which causes all non-matching fields to be displayed using the string `STR` (which holds the user surname that the user requested to be deleted).

All output from the `grep` command is redirected to a temporary file. The file is then moved back to the original file `DBFILE`. Following a deletion a sort is carried out on the file, the output is redirected to a temporary file, and then moved back to the original file `DBFILE`. The temporary file could have been sorted first, then moved back, instead of doing the move then doing the sort.

Tests using the last status command are carried out on all the file movements. Here is the output when deleting a record:

```
Enter the employee surname :Wilson

     searching record.. 6

 EMPLOYEE NO: 89232
 FIRST NAME : Louise
 SURNAME    : Wilson
 DEPARTMENT : Accounts

Do You Wish To DELETE This Record [Y..N] [N]:
```

Here's the complete listing of deleting a record:

```
$ pg dbase_del
#!/bin/sh
# dbase_del
# delete a record

# trap signals
trap "" 2 3 15

# DATAFILE
DBFILE=DBFILE

# temp files
HOLD1=HOLD1.$$
HOLD2=HOLD2.$$

continue_promptYN()
{
# continue_prompt
_STR=$1
_DEFAULT=$2
# check we have the right params
if [ $# -lt 1 ]; then
  echo "continue_prompt: I need a string to display"
  return 1
fi
while :
do
  echo -n "$_STR [Y..N] [$_DEFAULT]:"
```

```
  read _ANS
  : ${_ANS:=$_DEFAULT}
  if [ "$_ANS" = "" ]; then
    case $_ANS in
    Y) return 0 ;;
    N) return 1 ;;
    esac
  fi
  case $_ANS in
  y|Y|Yes|YES)
    return 0
    ;;
  n|N|No|NO)
    return 1
    ;;
  *) echo "Answer either Y or N, default is $_DEFAULT"
    ;;
  esac
done
}

display_rec()
{
# display_rec
# could use cat << here document
tput cup 5 3
echo  "EMPLOYEE NO: $CODE"
echo  "FIRST NAME : $F_NAME"
echo  "SURNAME    : $S_NAME"
echo  "DEPARTMENT : $DEPART"
echo -e "\n\n"
}

no_recs()
{
# no_recs
echo  -e "\n\nSorry could not find a record with the name $STR"
}

get_rec()
{
# get_rec
clear
echo -n "Enter the employee surname :"
read STR
if [ "$STR" = "q" ]; then
  return 1
fi

REC=0
MATCH=no
```

```
if [ "$STR" != "" ]; then
  while read CODE F_NAME S_NAME DEPART
  do
    REC=`expr $REC + 1`
    tput cup 3 4
    echo -n " searching record.. $REC"
    if [ "$S_NAME" = "$STR" ]; then
      MATCH=yes
      display_rec
      break
    else
      continue
    fi
  done $DBFILE
else
  echo "Enter a surname to search for or q to quit"
fi
if [ "$MATCH" = "no" ]; then
  no_recs
fi
}


SAVEDIFS=$IFS
IFS=:
get_rec
if [ "$MATCH" = "yes" ]; then
  if continue_promptYN "Do You Wish To DELETE This Record" "N"; then
    echo "DEL"
    grep -v $STR DBFILE >$HOLD1 2> /dev/null
    if [ $? -ne 0 ]; then
      echo "Problems creating temp file $HOLD1..check it out"
      exit 1
    fi
    mv $HOLD1 DBFILE
    if [ $? -ne 0 ]; then
      echo "Problems moving temp file..check it out"
      exit 1
    fi
    # sort the file after changes
    sort +2 -t: $DBFILE >$HOLD2 2> /dev/null
    if [ $? -ne 0 ]; then
      echo "problems trying to sort the file..check it out"
      exit 1
    fi
    mv $HOLD2 $DBFILE
    if [ $? -ne 0 ]; then
      echo "problems moving the temp sort file..check it out"
      exit 1
    fi
```

```
   else
     echo "no deletion"
     # no deletion
   fi # if wish to delete
 fi # if match

 # restore IFS settings
 IFS=$SAVEDIFS
```

22.3 Amending records

We have already seen most of the code for amending a record. We saw this code when we looked at record deletion.

When the correct record has been found, we simply assign all the record field variables to a temp variable then, using the default assignment variable:

: {default_variable: = variable}

The user can simply hit return on the fields he or she does not want to change. The default value will then replace the temp variable. Any amendments can be made simply by typing the new values in the adjacent fields.

```
echo  -n -e "EMPLOYEE NO: $CODE\n"

echo  -n "FIRST NAME : [$F_NAME] >"
read _F_NAME
: ${_FNAME:=$F_NAME}
...
```

The actual updating of the file is carried out using grep with the -v option again. All records apart from the one being amended are redirected to a temporary file. The employee's number is used as the grep string:

```
grep -v $CODE $DBFILE >$HOLD1
```

The user is asked if he or she wants to save this record. If the answer is yes, the newly updated record is also appended to the temporary file. The temporary file is then moved to the original file DBFILE.

```
echo "$CODE:$_F_NAME:$_S_NAME:$_DEPART" >> $HOLD1
mv $HOLD1 $DBFILE
```

The file is then sorted with output being redirected to a temporary file, then moved back again to the original file DBFILE. Last status tests are carried out on the file movements, and the user is informed if there are any problems. In a real working script the validation tests that were carried out when we added a record would be carried out here as well. Here is how the output looks when amending a record.

```
Enter the employee surname :Penny

      searching record.. 7

EMPLOYEE NO: 98211
FIRST NAME : Simon
SURNAME    : Penny
DEPARTMENT : Services

Is this the record you wish to amend [Y..N] [Y]:
amending
EMPLOYEE NO: 98211
FIRST NAME : [Simon] >
SURNAME    : [Penny] >
DEPARTMENT : [Services] >Accounts
Ready to save this record [Y..N] [Y]:
```

Here's the full script to amend a record:

```
$ pg dbasechange
# !/bin/sh
# dbasechange
# amend a record

# ignore signals
trap "" 2 3 15

# temp files
DBFILE=DBFILE
HOLD1=HOLD1.$$
HOLD2=HOLD2.$$

continue_promptYN()
{
# continue_prompt
_STR=$1
_DEFAULT=$2
# check we have the right params
if [ $# -lt 1 ]; then
   echo "continue_prompt: I need a string to display"
   return 1
fi
while :
do
   echo -n "$_STR [Y..N] [$_DEFAULT]:"
   read _ANS
   : ${_ANS:=$_DEFAULT}
```

```
    if [ "$_ANS" = "" ]; then
      case $_ANS in
      Y) return 0 ;;
      N) return 1 ;;
      esac
    fi
    case $_ANS in
    y|Y|Yes|YES)
      return 0
      ;;
    n|N|No|NO)
      return 1
      ;;
    *) echo "Answer either Y or N, default is $_DEFAULT"
      ;;
    esac
  done
}

display_rec()
{
# display_rec
# could use cat << as a here document, but I won't
tput cup 5 3
echo  "EMPLOYEE NO: $CODE"
echo  "FIRST NAME : $F_NAME"
echo  "SURNAME    : $S_NAME"
echo  "DEPARTMENT : $DEPART"
echo -e "\n\n"
}

no_recs()
{
# no_recs
echo  -e "\n\nSorry could not find a record with the name $STR"
}

get_rec()
{
# get_rec
clear
echo -n "Enter the employee surname :"
read STR
if [ "$STR" = "q" ]; then
  return 1
fi

REC=0
MATCH=no
```

```
if [ "$STR" != "" ]; then
  while read CODE F_NAME S_NAME DEPART
  do
    REC=`expr $REC + 1`
    tput cup 3 4
    echo -n " searching record.. $REC"
    if [ "$S_NAME" = "$STR" ]; then
      MATCH=yes
      display_rec
      break
    else
      continue
    fi
  done $DBFILE
else
  echo "Enter a surname to search for or q to quit"
fi
if [ "$MATCH" = "no" ]; then
  no_recs
fi
}

# main
SAVEDIFS=$IFS
IFS=:
get_rec
if [ "$MATCH" = "yes" ]; then
  if continue_promptYN "Is this the record you wish to amend" "Y"
  then
    echo "amending"
    # cannot change employee code
    echo  -n -e "EMPLOYEE NO: $CODE\n"

    echo  -n "FIRST NAME : [$F_NAME] >"
    read _F_NAME
    : ${_FNAME:=$F_NAME}

    echo  -n "SURNAME    : [$S_NAME] >"
    read _S_NAME
    : ${_S_NAME:=$S_NAME}

    echo  -n "DEPARTMENT : [$DEPART] >"
    read _DEPART
    : ${_DEPART:=$DEPART}

    grep -v $CODE $DBFILE >$HOLD1
    if [ $? -ne 0 ]; then
      echo "Problems creating temporary file..check it out"
      exit 1
    fi
```

```
    if continue_promptYN "Ready to save this record" "Y"; then
      echo "$CODE:$_F_NAME:$_S_NAME:$_DEPART" >> $HOLD1
      mv $HOLD1 $DBFILE
      if [ $? -ne 0 ]; then
        echo "Problems moving temporary file...check it out"
      fi
      echo " Record Amended"
      # now sort the file after changes,
      # could have been done in one file movement of course
      sort +2 -t: $DBFILE >$HOLD2 2> /dev/null
      if [ $? -ne 0 ]; then
        echo "problems trying to sort the file..check it out"
        exit 1
      fi
      mv $HOLD2 $DBFILE
      if [ $? -ne 0 ]; then
        echo "problems moving the temp sort file..check it out"
        exit 1
      fi


    else #if amend aborted
      echo "Amend aborted"
      exit 0
    fi
  else # if no amend
    echo "no amending"
    # no deletion
  fi # if wish to delete
fi # if match


IFS=$SAVEDIFS
```

22.4 Viewing records

The user can either view all records or just a particular record. If the user wants to see all records then a simple `cat` and `awk` statement does it. If the records contain many fields then a more user-friendly output would be required, but this will suffice for our needs.

```
if [ "$STR" = "all" ]; then
  echo "Surname    Name    Employee Code"
  echo "_____"
  cat $DBFILE |awk -F: '{print $2"\t"$3"\t\t"$1}' | more
  return 0
fi
```

The code to display a single record has already been covered in deletion and amendments. One slight change is the ability to print a record when the user chooses this option. Here's the piece of code that sends a record to the printer:

```
pr  <<- MAYDAY

RECORD No            : $REC
EMPLOYEE NUMBER      : $CODE
EMPLOYEE NAME        : $F_NAME
EMPLOYEE SURNAME     : $S_NAME
EMPLOYEE DEPARTMENT  : $DEPART
MAYDAY
```

Here's how the output looks when viewing a record:

```
Enter the employee surname to view or all for all records:Wilson

      searching record.. 8

EMPLOYEE NO: 89232
FIRST NAME : Peter
SURNAME    : Wilson
DEPARTMENT : IT

Do You Wish To Print This Record [Y..N] [N]:
```

Here's the full script to view a record(s):

```
$ pg dbaseview
#!/bin/sh
# dbaseview
# view records

# ignore signals
trap "" 2 3 15

# temp files
HOLD1=HOLD1.$$
DBFILE=DBFILE

continue_promptYN()
{
# continue_prompt
_STR=$1
_DEFAULT=$2
# check we have the right params
if [ $# -lt 1 ]; then
   echo "continue_prompt: I need a string to display"
   return 1
fi
```

```
while :
do
  echo -n "$_STR [Y..N] [$_DEFAULT]:"
  read _ANS
  : ${_ANS:=$_DEFAULT}
  if [ "$_ANS" = "" ]; then
    case $_ANS in
    Y) return 0 ;;
    N) return 1 ;;
    esac
  fi
  case $_ANS in
  y|Y|Yes|YES)
    return 0
    ;;
  n|N|No|NO)
    return 1
    ;;
  *) echo "Answer either Y or N, default is $_DEFAULT"
    ;;
  esac
done
}

display_rec()
{
# display_rec
# could use cat <<.
tput cup 5 3
echo "EMPLOYEE NO: $CODE"
echo "FIRST NAME : $F_NAME"
echo "SURNAME    : $S_NAME"
echo "DEPARTMENT : $DEPART"
echo -e "\n\n"
}

no_recs()
{
# no_rec
echo -e "\n\nSorry could not find a record with the name $STR"
}

get_rec()
{
# get_rec
clear
echo -n "Enter the employee surname to view or all for all records:"
read STR
if [ "$STR" = "q" ]; then
  return 1
fi
```

```
if [ "$STR" = "all" ]; then
  # view all recs
  echo "Surname    Name    Employee Code"
  echo "_____"
  cat $DBFILE |awk -F: '{print $2"\t"$3"\t\t"$1}' | more
  return 0
fi
REC=0
MATCH=no
if [ "$STR" != "" ]; then
  while read CODE F_NAME S_NAME DEPART
  do
    REC=`expr $REC + 1`
    tput cup 3 4
    echo -n " searching record.. $REC"
    if [ "$S_NAME" = "$STR" ]; then
      # found name
      MATCH=yes
      display_rec
      break
    else
      continue
    fi
  done <$DBFILE
else
  echo "Enter a surname to search for or q to quit"
fi
if [ "$MATCH" = "no" ]; then
  no_recs
fi
}


# main
SAVEDIFS=$IFS
IFS=:
get_rec
if [ "$MATCH" = "yes" ]; then
  if continue_promptYN "Do You Wish To Print This Record" "N"; then
  lpr   <<- MAYDAY

  RECORD No: $REC

  EMPLOYEE NUMBER      : $CODE
  EMPLOYEE NAME        : $F_NAME
  EMPLOYEE SURNAME     : $S_NAME
  EMPLOYEE DEPARTMENT  : $DEPART


  MAYDAY
```

```
    else
       echo "No print of $S_NAME"
       # no print
    fi # if wish to print
 fi # if match

 IFS=$SAVEDIFS
```

22.5 Conclusion

Being able to validate user input is an important and sometimes advanced skill. You may know what your records take as input, but generally users will not.

There's an old saying in the computer industry that goes something like this: 'Garbage in garbage *out* ... who cares, it's too late then'. This means that if you do not test for garbage data coming in through your scripts you are going to output garbage information.

CHAPTER 23

Debugging scripts

One of the most annoying tasks of shell scripting is debugging problems. There are aids to help you but, to prevent most errors before they happen, follow this rule:

Break your proposed script down into tasks or procedures, then code and test each procedure before continuing with the next step.

In this chapter we will cover:

- common errors; and

- introducing the set command.

There really is nothing more irritating than trying to discover an elusive error in your script. However, as you get more experienced in scripting you'll know what to look for.

The most common problems are missing quotes or not having an fi on the end of an if statement.

One important thing to remember is that when the shell reports an error from your script, do not look only at the suspect line but also at the block of code in which it is contained. The shell does not always report the exact location of the error; rather it reports when it is trying to close off a statement.

23.1 Common errors

23.1.1 The loop error

Errors that are reported on the for, while, until or case statements mean the actual statement block is incorrect. You have missed out a reserved word for that construct.

The following error below reports the word 'done', which is a good clue, since you know it is something to do with a `while` statement. Looking back through your code check out the `while` statement for any missing words, like 'do', or the conditional statement you are using.

```
syntax error near unexpected token 'done'
line 31: ' done'
```

23.1.2 The classic missing quote

The second error is the classic missing quote error. Learn to like this one, because you will see a lot of these. The only solution I offer on this type of error is to go through your script making sure that all quotes are paired off.

```
unexpected EOF while looking for '"'
line 36: syntax error
```

When the shell reports the line number with the error, it is usually in tune with `vi`'s `set nu` option, so use that when looking at a file in `vi`. Load `vi` up, then hit `<ESC>` followed by a colon, then type `set nu <return>`. Your lines will now be numbered, so go to the line that the shell reported the error on.

23.1.3 The test error

Another common error is when using the `-eq` statement you forget to use a number value either side of the test condition.

If you get the following error, then it is most certainly due to one of two things; either you need a space between your variables and the square bracket, or you have a missing operator inside the square bracket. I bet it's the first one I mentioned.

```
[: missing ']'
```

23.1.4 Character case

From my experience most errors are due to not keeping the same (character) case when using variables. For instance I will almost certainly start using upper case, then I may reference the variable using lower case, and I wonder why I get no values.

23.1.5 `for` loops

Using the `for` loop I will sometimes forget to put the dollar sign on the list part of the loop, if I am reading it in from a string.

23.1.6 `echo`

One of your most useful tools as an aid to debugging scripts is the `echo` command. Add the `echo` command at important points in your script where you think you may have problems. For instance, use the `echo` command before and after a variable is read or changed.

Use the last status command to determine if the command was successful. One note of caution here; do not use `echo` followed by the last status, since the command will always return true.

23.2 The `set` command

The `set` command can be used as an aid to debugging. Here are `set`'s most useful debugging options.

`set -n`	Read commands but do not execute them
`set -v`	Display all lines as they are read
`set -x`	Display all commands and their arguments

To turn a `set` option off simply substitute the - sign with the +. I always think that it should be the other way round, + to turn it off and - to turn it on, but that's just me.

You can use `set` at the top of your script to enable it and then disable it when the script finishes, or you can stick `set` in just a particular block statement that is giving you problems.

Let's see `set` in action. Here's a little script that holds some names in a variable list. The user inputs a name, a `for` loop then loops through the list to see if there is a match. Notice I have used `set -x` at the top of the script and then disabled it at the bottom.

```
$ pg error
#!/bin/sh
# error
# set set -x
set -x
LIST="Peter Susan John Barry Lucy Norman Bill Leslie"
echo -n "Enter your Name :"
read NAME

for LOOP in $LIST
do
  if [ "$LOOP" = "$NAME" ]; then
    echo "you're on the list, you're in"
    break
  fi
```

```
done
# unset set -x
set +x
```

Let's run the script giving a name that is not present in the list to see what the output looks like.

```
$ error
error
+ error
+ LIST=Peter Susan John Barry Lucy Norman Bill Leslie
+ echo -n Enter your Name :
Enter your Name :+ read NAME
Harry
+ [ Peter = Harry ]
+ [ Susan = Harry ]
+ [ John = Harry ]
+ [ Barry = Harry ]
+ [ Lucy = Harry ]
+ [ Norman = Harry ]
+ [ Bill = Harry ]
+ [ Leslie = Harry ]
```

All the comparisons are displayed as the for loop works its way through the list. Using set in this way is indispensable when you have problems with reading in files or comparing strings or values.

23.3 Conclusion

The best way to track errors is to look at your scripts yourself and using the set command coupled with plenty of echo statements.

CHAPTER 24

Shell built-in commands

We have actually met most of the shell built-ins already. You may be wondering what a shell built-in is; these are commands that are built into the actual Bourne shell instead of residing in the /bin or usr/bin directory. Built-in commands run faster than their equivalent (if any) in the system.

In this chapter we will cover:

• the list of the standard Bourne shell built-in commands.

For instance, we have used cd and pwd, which can be found both in the system and as a shell built-in. To run the system version simply supply the path to the command:

/bin/pwd

24.1 Complete list of shell built-in commands

Table 24.1 shows a complete list of the standard built-ins.

Table 24.1 *Standard built-in commands*

:	Null, will always return true
.	Read files from the current shell
break	Exists from a for, while, until or case statement
cd	Change the current directory
continue	Carry on with the next iteration of the loop
echo	Write output to the standard output
eval	Read the argument and execute the resulting command

Table 24.1 *Standard built-in commands* (cont.)

exec	Execute the command but not in this shell
exit	Exit the shell
export	Export the variables so that they are available to the current shell
pwd	Display the current directory
read	Read a line of text from standard input
readonly	Make this variable read-only
return	Exit the function with a return value
set	Control the display of various parameters to standard input
shift	Shifts the command line arguments one to the left
test	Evaluate a conditional expression
times	Display the user and system times for processes run from the shell
trap	Run a specified command when a signal is received
type	Interpret how the shell will use a name as a command
ulimit	Displays or sets shell resources
umask	Display or set default file creation modes
unset	Remove a variable or function from the shell's memory
wait	Wait until the child process has finished and report its termination

Let's look at some of the commands that we have either not yet covered or, if we have, not in any detail.

24.1.1 pwd

Display the current directory

```
$ pwd
/tmp
```

24.1.2 set

We met the set command when we looked at debugging to turn shell options on and off. Set can also be used to give arguments to a script internally. Here's how it is done. Suppose we wanted a script to handle two parameters, but instead of passing these to the script we set them up in the script. To do this we use the set command.

The format is:

set param1 param2..

The following example sets the parameters to accounts.doc and accounts.bak. The script then loops through the parameters.

```
$ pg set_ex
#!/bin/sh
set accounts.doc accounts.bak

while [ $# != 0 ]
do
   echo $1
   shift
done

$ set_ex
accounts.doc
accounts.bak
```

Using set in this way is great when you are testing a script and it requires parameters, as it saves you having to retype the arguments every time you run the script.

24.1.3 times

The times command informs you how much time the user and any system commands have consumed. The first line reports time consumed by the shell and the second line reports time consumed by any commands that have been run. Here is my output using the times command.

```
$ times
0m0.10s 0m0.13s
0m0.49s 0m0.36s
```

I bet that you will use that command a lot!

24.1.4 type

Use type to find out if a command resides on the system and what type of command it is. Type will report if the command name is valid and where on the system it lives. Here are some examples:

```
$ type mayday
type: mayday: not found
$ type pwd
pwd is a shell builtin
$ type times
times is a shell builtin
$ type cp
cp is /bin/cp
```

24.1.5 `ulimit`

Use `ulimit` to set up display limits that run in the shell. Generally this command is situated in `/etc/profile`, but you can tailor it to your needs from the current shell or your `.profile`. Here's the general format:

ulimit options

There are quite a few options to `ulimit`; here are the most used ones:

Option	Meaning
-a	Show current limits
-c	Limit the size of the core dumps
-f	Limit the size of the output file created by a running process to N blocks

My `ulimit` values are:

```
$ ulimit -a
core file size (blocks)    1000000
data seg size (kbytes)     unlimited
file size (blocks)         unlimited
max memory size (kbytes)   unlimited
stack size (kbytes)        8192
cpu time (seconds)         unlimited
max user processes         256
pipe size (512 bytes)      8
open files                 256
virtual memory (kbytes)    2105343
```

To disable any dumping of core files set it to zero.

```
$ ulimit -c 0
$
$ ulimit -a
core file size (blocks)    0
data seg size (kbytes)     unlimited
file size (blocks)         unlimited
max memory size (kbytes)   unlimited
stack size (kbytes)        8192
cpu time (seconds)         unlimited
max user processes         256
pipe size (512 bytes)      8
open files                 256
virtual memory (kbytes)    2105343
```

24.1.6 `wait`

Use the `wait` command to wait around until one of your child processes has finished. You can specify the `wait` command with a process ID. If you do not, then it will wait around until all child processes have finished.

Wait around until all my child processes have finished:

```
$ wait
```

24.2 Conclusion

We have gone over the shell built-in commands. We had already met most of them before, and have discussed in detail how to use the commands.

## PART 5

Better scripting skills

CHAPTER 25

Going further with here documents

We have already met here (redirection) documents a few times when we dealt with standard input and output and while loops. We learnt how to send mail and how to construct a menu screen, but there are also other uses for here documents.

In this chapter we will cover:

- creating a quick file;
- automatically navigating menus;
- `ftp` transfers; and
- connecting to other application systems.

The format for a here document is:

```
command  < <word
text
word
```

To recap on here documents, this is how they work. When the shell sees the <<, it knows the next word is a delimiter (word). Anything after the word it treats as input until it sees the word again on a line by itself. The delimiter word can be any word you like.

You can use here documents to create a file, print a list of files or maybe to sort a list of files or create screens.

25.1 Creating a quick file

Here's a quick way to create a file with some text in it:

```
$ cat >> myfile <<NEWFILE
```

Now type some text, and when you have finished simply type NEWFILE on a new line and you have got yourself a file called myfile, containing some text.

If you supply a filename that already has some text in it, the contents you type in will append to the original file.

If you use the tab key, please note that some older shell versions do not preserve the meaning of tabs. To overcome this simply use a hyphen after the two left angled brackets, like this.

cat > > myfile < <- NEWFILE
...

25.2 Creating a quick print document

Suppose you wanted to create and print a little message document. You do not have to run vi; you can use this method instead. As soon as you hit return after typing QUICKDOC using this example, the document will be sent to the printer.

```
$ lpr <<QUICKDOC
   **** INVITATION****
 The Star Trek convention is in town
next week. Be there.

Ticket prices: (please phone)
--------------------------------
QUICKDOC
```

25.3 Automating menus

Though here documents are great for creating menu screens you can also use them to automatically navigate a menu, instead of the user having to do it manually to select some process option.

I have a database menu script that takes care of all our database backups and administrative tasks. The database menu is used during the day to back up databases or run other administrative tasks. When it was decided to do all the database backups every night to be run from cron, I did not want to write another script. So

I put together a here document that used its input to navigate the menu script called
syb_backup. Here's how the output of the menu script syb_backup looks.

   I would have to press the following keys to be able to select the option to
back-up all my databases.

Here's the main screen. Selection is 2.

   1: Admin Tasks
   2: Sybase Backups
   3: Maintenance Tasks
   Selection > 2

Here's the second screen. Selection is 3.

   1: Backup A Single Database
   2: Backup Selected Databases
   3: Backup All Databases
   Selection > 3

Here's the third screen. Selection is Y.

   1. dw_levels
   2. dw_based
   3. dw_aggs
   ...
   ...
   Are You Sure You Wish To Backup [Y..N] : Y

So from our menu screen, to backup all the databases I would have to type:

1.   The menu script name, **syb_backup**

2.   followed by **2**

3.   followed by **3**

4.   followed by **Y**.

Here's the script that will automatically set off the database backups using the
above menu script syb_backup:

```
$ pg auto.sybackup
#!/bin/sh
# set the path
PATH=/usr/bin:/usr/sbin:/sybase/bin:$LOCALBIN
export PATH
# set the sybase variable
DSQUERY=COMET; export DSQUERY
```

```
# set the TERM and init it
TERM=vt220; export TERM
tput -T vt220 init
#   keep a log of all output
log_f=/logs/sql.backup.log
#
>$log_f

# here's the code that does all the work !
/usr/local/sybin/syb_backup >> $log_f 2>&1  << MAYDAY
2
3
Y
MAYDAY

chown sybase $log_f
```

The actual redirection bit that does the work is this:

usr/local/sybin/syb_backup > > $log_f 2 > &1 < < MAYDAY
2
3
Y
MAYDAY

Looking at the redirection piece of code, the full path is given to my syb_backup script; the >>$log_f>&1 means all output should go to the file $log_f, which is a variable holding the value /logs/sql.backup.log. This is always a good idea, since you can then capture all output from the menu including all the backup details and any possible errors from the application.

The <<MAYDAY is the start of the here document. What follows are the menu selections that would have to be keyed in manually to run the backups. The here document is also terminated with the word MAYDAY.

And that's it. There is no need to rewrite a script; if you already have a menu script in place, use a here document to automate it for you.

25.4 Automating ftp transfers

One popular use of here documents is to automate ftp transfers. When using ftp, it's nice to give the users a simple interface to work with. The following script uses the username anonymous to make an ftp connection. This is a special username that enables systems to create security-based ftp accounts that hold public directories. Generally speaking, everybody who connects with an anonymous username can only download files from that public directory, but it can be set to upload files.

The password can be anything, but it's considered good practice to use your hostname and your local userid or e-mail address.

The script that is presented here prompts for the following information:

1.   Remote machine you wish to connect to.

2.   Type of file transfer binary or ASCII.

3.   The name of the file to get.

4.   The local directory in which the retrieved file is to be placed.

When the user inputs the remote machine to connect to, a `traceroute` is then executed on the remote host to make sure the local host can actually see it. The script will re-prompt if the `traceroute` fails.

Hitting `return` on the transfer mode will default to binary.

After typing in the downloaded name for the file, the user is prompted for a destination directory of the downloaded file. The default is `/tmp`. If the user gives a different directory and it cannot be found, then `/tmp` is used.

The downloaded file will be the name of the file to get with `.ftp` appended to it.

Finally all these choices are displayed and confirmation is requested before the transfer begins.

Here's how the script looks when run.

```
$ ftpauto
User: dave               05/06/1999                This host: bumper
                   FTP RETRIEVAL / POSTING SCRIPT
                   ==============================
                      Using the ID of anonymous
Enter the host you wish to access :uniware
Wait..seeing if uniware is out there..
bumper can see uniware
What type of transfer / receive mode ?
 1 : Binary
 2 : ASCII
Your choice [1..2] [1]:
   Enter the name of the file to retrieve :gnutar.Z
 Enter the directory where the file is to be placed[/tmp] :
               Host to connect is: uniware
               File to get is     : gnutar.Z
               Mode to use is     : binary
               File to be put in : /tmp/gnutar.Z.ftp
          Ready to get file 'y' or 'q' to quit? [y..q] :
```

Here is the script.

```
$ pg ftpauto
#!/bin/sh
# ftp script
# ftpauto
USER=`whoami`
MYDATE=`date +%d/%m/%Y`
THIS_HOST=`hostname -s`
```

```
tracelog=/tmp/tracelog.$$

while :
do
  # loop forever
  tput clear
  cat <<MAYDAY
User: $USER                    $MYDATE                This host: $THIS_HOST
                    FTP RETRIEVAL SCRIPT
                    =====================
                Using the ID of anonymous
MAYDAY
  echo -n "Enter the host you wish to access :"
  read DEST_HOST
  # is a hostname entered ???
  if [ "$DEST_HOST" = "" ]
  then
    echo "No destination host entered" >&2
    exit 1
  fi
  # can we see the host ???
  echo "Wait..seeing if $DEST_HOST is out there.."
  # use traceroute to test connectivity
  traceroute $DEST_HOST > $tracelog 2>&1

  if grep "unknown host" $tracelog >/dev/null 2> then
    echo "Could not locate $DEST_HOST"
    echo -n "Try another host? [y..n] :"
    read ANS
    case $ANS in
    y|Y) ;;
    *) break;;   # get out of the forever loop
    esac
  else
    echo "$THIS_HOST can see $DEST_HOST"
    break   # get out of the forever loop
  fi
done

# the default is binary
echo  "What type of transfer /receive mode ?"
echo  " 1 : Binary"
echo  " 2 : ASCII"
echo -n -e "\fYour choice [1..2] [1]:"
read $TYPE
case $TYPE in
1) MODE=binary
  ;;
2) MODE=ascii
  ;;
```

```
*) MODE=binary
  ;;
esac

echo -n "    Enter the name of the file to retrieve :"
read FILENAME
if [ "$FILENAME" = "" ]; then
  echo "No filename entered" >&2
  exit 1
fi

# default is tmp
echo -n -e "\f Enter the directory where the file is to be placed[/tmp] :"
read DIREC
cd $DIREC >/dev/null 2>&1
# if we cannot cd to the directory then use tmp
if [ "$DIREC" = "" ]; then
  DIREC=/tmp
fi

if [ $? != 0 ]
then
  echo "$DIREC does not exist placing the file in /tmp anyway"
  DIREC=/tmp
fi

echo -e "\t\tHost to connect is: $DEST_HOST"
echo -e "\t\tFile to get is    : $FILENAME"
echo -e "\t\tMode to use is    : $MODE"
echo -e "\t\tFile to be put in : $DIREC/$FILENAME.ftp"
echo -e -n "\t\tReady to get file 'y' or 'q' to quit? [y..q] :"
read ANS
case $ANS in
Y|y);;
q|Q) exit 0;;
*) exit 0 ;;
esac
echo "ftp.."
ftp -i -n $DEST_HOST<<FTPIT
user anonymous $USER@$THISHOST
$MODE
get $FILENAME $DIREC/$FILENAME.ftp
quit
FTPIT
if [ -s $DIREC/$FILENAME.ftp ]
then
  echo "File is down"
else
  echo "Unable to locate $FILENAME.ftp"
fi
```

The actual here document that deals with the ftp uses the options ftp -i -n, which mean 'do not output any auto login prompts' and 'turn off interactive prompting mode'. This allows the script to log in using the 'user' command. The password is $USER@THISHOST which, when evaluated, comes out as dave@bumper.

If a user downloads the same file from the same host every day, maybe containing sales data from the previous day, the user should not really have to keep typing in the same remote host or filename all the time. You can get on the good side of the user here by setting default values of the fields DEST_HOST and FILENAME. Setting default values saves the user having to keep typing in the same information into the same field.

Below is a piece of the ftpauto script that prompts for the remote hostname, but now it sets a default value for DEST_HOST, which is set to 'my_favourite_-host'. The user can now type in a different remote hostname or hit return at the prompt to load the default value into the variable DEST_HOST.

Notice that you do not now need to check if the user has entered a value, because the default value will now be loaded into the variable DEST_HOST.

```
echo -n "Enter the host you wish to access :"
read DEST_HOST
: ${DEST_HOST:="my_favourite_host"}
echo "Wait..seeing if $DEST_HOST is out there.."
traceroute $DEST_HOST >$tracelog 2>&1
...
```

25.5 Accessing databases

A common task among scripts is to access database systems to retrieve information. This type of process is ideal for here documents. You can do practically anything that you would normally do at the database prompt. This is not an exercise in databases, but to show you how here documents can be used to connect to other applications, and carry out tasks.

On one of our database systems the 'select into' gets turned off when the database is accessed from certain third party products. This means that certain databases cannot be used for any insertion of data or the creation of temporary tables.

To fix this problem a here document is used to connect into the database system, and a for loop will feed the here document with the database names to change. Once connected the here document is used to supply the sql commands to set the options.

Here is the script that sets the options on each database:

```
$ pg set.select
#!/bin/sh
# set.select
# fixes known bug. Sets the select into db option on
```

```
PATH=$PATH:/sybase/bin:/sybase/install
export PATH
SYBASE="/sybase"; export SYBASE
DSQUERY=ACESRV; export DSQUERY
PASSWORD="prilog"
DATABASES="dwbased tempdb aggs levels reps accounts"

for loop in $DATABASES
do
   su sybase -c '/sybase/bin/isql -Usa -P$PASSWORD' << MAYDAY
   use master
   go
   sp_dboption $loop,"select into/bulkcopy/pllsort",true
   go
   use $loop
   go
   checkpoint
   go
   MAYDAY
done
```

Looking at the here document bit, the shell is evaluating the above code when running the above command.

use master
go
sp_dboption dwbased,"select into/bulkcopy/pllsort",true
  go
  use dw_based
  go
  checkpoint
  go

When the shell sees the terminating word MAYDAY, the script starts its next iteration of the for loop, picking up the next database from its list. When run the output is:

```
$ set.select
Database option 'select into/bulkcopy/pllsort' turned ON for database
'dwbased'.
Run the CHECKPOINT command in the database that was changed.
(return status = 0)
Database option 'select into/bulkcopy/pllsort' turned ON for database
'tempdb'.
Run the CHECKPOINT command in the database that was changed.
(return status = 0)
Database option 'select into/bulkcopy/pllsort' turned ON for database
'aggs'.
Run the CHECKPOINT command in the database that was changed.
(return status = 0)
```

25.6 Conclusion

This chapter has shown further examples of how here documents can automate tasks. Here documents can be used for a variety of tasks, especially when connecting to applications or ftping. Once written, you can then run these scripts and continue with another task.

CHAPTER 26

Shell utilities

In this chapter we will cover:

- creating date named filenames and temporary files;
- . signals;
- the `trap` command and how to trap signals;
- the `eval` command; and
- the `logger` command.

26.1 Creating hold files

Any script needs to be able to create temporary or log files. When running scripts that do backups, it is generally good practice to keep a log of the actual backup. These are usually kept in a filesystem for a few weeks and then purged by age.

When developing scripts you will be continuously creating temporary files. Temporary files are also used in normal running scripts which hold information prior to being used for input into another process. One can also use `cat` to display a temporary file to the screen or send it to the printer.

26.1.1 Using `date` to create log files

When you want to create a log file, it is always a good idea to make it unique for that day or even hour. To do this the `date` command comes to our rescue. We can manipulate the `date` command and append it to a filename that will be our log file.

To change the format on how the date is displayed, this format is used:

date option + %format

Using the plus (+) sign allows the current date to be displayed in different formats. The following displays the date in the form day,month,year.

```
$ date +%d%m%y
090699
```

Here are some date formats that might come in handy.

```
$ date +%d-%m-%y
09-06-99
```

```
$ date +%A%e" "%B" "%Y
Wednesday 9 June 1999
```

Show the time in hh:mm format.

```
$ date +%R
10:07
```

```
$ date +%A" "%R" "%p
Wednesday 10:09 AM
```

Show the time in full.

```
$ date +%T
10:29:41
```

```
$ date +%A" "%T
Wednesday  10:31:19
```

Notice the use of double quotes to allow for spacing in the date output.

To use the date as part of a file name it's a simple case of using substitution. Using the variable that holds the newly formatted date, append the variable to the filename that you want the log file to be called.

In the following example two log files are created, one with the date in the form dd,mm,yy, the other in the form dd,hh,mm.

Here's the script.

```
$ pg log
#!/bin/sh
# log
#
MYDATE=`date +%d%m%y`
# append MYDATE to the variable LOGFILE that holds the actual filename of
the log.
LOGFILE=/logs/backup_log.$MYDATE
# create the file
>$LOGFILE

MYTIME=`date +%d%R`
LOGFILE2=/logs/admin_log.$MYTIME
# create the file
>$LOGFILE2
```

When the above script is run we get two log files that are created.

backup_log.090699
admin_log.0910:18

26.1.2 Creating unique temporary files

When we covered special variables earlier on in the book, we came across the variable $$, which holds the process ID or number of the current process you are running. We can use this to create temporary files within the current script we are running, because the process ID will be unique to that script. All we really need to do is create a file and append the $$ on to it. When we are finished we can just delete all files that have an extension of $$. The shell will evaluate the $$ to your current process ID and delete these files but no other process ID appended files.

At the command line type the following.

```
$ echo $$
281
```

This is my process ID, yours will return a different number. Now if I create another logon session and type the same command again, I will get a different number, because I have started a new process.

```
$ echo $$
382
```

Here's a script that creates a couple of temporary files, does some processing and then deletes the files at the end.

```
$ pg tempfiles
#!/bin/sh
# tempfiles
# name the temp files
HOLD1=/tmp/hold1.$$
HOLD2=/tmp/hold2.$$

# do some processing using the files
df -tk >$HOLD1
cat $HOLD1 >$HOLD2
# now delete them
rm /tmp/*.$$
```

When the above script is run, it will create the following two files.

hold1.408
hold2.408

When the command rm /tmp/*.$$ is executed, the shell will actually be doing rm /tmp/*.408.

It's important to remember that the process ID is unique to your current process only. For instance, if I ran the above script again, I would have a new process ID number, because I have created a new process.

Creating date hold files enables you to track when files were created for a specific purpose. It is also easier to purge files based on dates, as you will know at a glance which is the oldest or newest.

Temporary files are quick and easy to create and are unique to your process. When your script has finished processing, the deletion is quick and foolproof.

26.2 Signals

A signal is a type of message sent from the system to inform a command or script that an event has occurred somewhere. The events are usually to do with memory error, access problems or some user trying to stop your process. The signals are actually numbers. Below is a table listing the most used signals and their meaning.

Signal no.	Signal name	Meaning
1	SIGHUP	Hangup or parent process killed
2	SIGINT	Interrupt from keyboard, usually <CTRL-C>
3	SIGQUIT	Quit from the keyboard
9	SIGKILL	Definite kill
11	SIGSEGV	Segmentation (memory) violation
15	SIGTERM	Software termination (default kill)

There is a signal 0, which we have already met when we created a .logout file earlier in the book. This signal is the 'exit from shell' signal. To send a signal 0, just type exit from the command line or use <CTRL-D> on a process or on the command line.

To send a signal use this format:

kill [- signal no:| signal name] process ID

Using the kill command with no signal number or name means that the kill command will default to signal 15.

To see a list of all the signals:

```
$ kill -1
 1) SIGHUP     2) SIGINT    3) SIGQUIT    4) SIGILL
 5) SIGTRAP    6) SIGIOT    7) SIGBUS     8) SIGFPE
 9) SIGKILL   10) SIGUSR1  11) SIGSEGV   12) SIGUSR2
13) SIGPIPE   14) SIGALRM  15) SIGTERM   17) SIGCHLD
```

```
18) SIGCONT    19) SIGSTOP    20) SIGTSTP    21) SIGTTIN
22) SIGTTOU    23) SIGURG     24) SIGXCPU    25) SIGXFSZ
26) SIGVTALRM  27) SIGPROF    28) SIGWINCH   29) SIGIO
30) SIGPWR
```

26.2.1 Killing a process

Sending a signal 1 allows a process to re-read its configuration file. For instance, if you are running the process named the DNS demon, and you make changes to the database files, you do not have to kill the demon and restart it, just send it a kill -1. Named will just re-read its configuration files.

Here's an example of sending a signal 9 (sure kill) to kill a process called mon_web running on my system. First use ps to get the process.

```
$ ps -ef | grep mon_web |grep -v root
157  ?  S     0:00 mon_web
```

If your system does not use ps -ef use ps xa instead. To kill it I can use either:

kill -9 157

or

kill -s SIGKILL 157

On some systems you don't have to supply the -s, for example: kill SIGKILL 157)

The following script will kill a process based on a process name. The name of the process to be killed is supplied as a parameter. A check is performed that there is actually a process to be killed. Grep does the job of finding any matched process names. If successful you are prompted with the processes found and asked if you want to kill them. A kill -9 is used to kill the process.

Here's the script.

```
$ pg pskill
#!/bin/sh
# pskill
HOLD1=/tmp/hold1.$$
PROCESS=$1
usage()
{

# usage
echo "Usage :`basename $0` process_name"
exit 1
}
```

```
if [ $# -ne 1 ]; then
  usage
fi


case $1 in
*)
# grep the process, do not include our script in the output from ps
# extract fields 1 and 6, redirect to a temp file
  ps x | grep $PROCESS | grep -v $0 | awk '{print $1"\t" $6}'>$HOLD1
  # ps -ef |..     if ps x does not work
  ;;
esac


# is the file there??
if [ ! -s $HOLD1 ]; then
  echo "No processes found..sorry"
  exit 1
fi


# read in the contents from the temp file and display the fields
while read LOOP1 LOOP2
do
  echo $LOOP1 $LOOP2
done <$HOLD1
echo -n "Are these the processes to be killed ? [y..n] >"
read ANS


case $ANS in
Y|y) while read LOOP1 LOOP2
     do
        echo $LOOP1
        kill -9 $LOOP1
     done <$HOLD1
  rm /tmp/*.$$
  ;;
N|n);;
esac
```

When run, the above script output could be:

```
$ pskill web
1760 ./webmon
1761 /usr/apps/web_col
Are these the processes to be killed ? [y..n] >y

1760
1761
[1]+  Killed                    webmon
```

And to make sure:

```
$ pskill web
No processes found..sorry
```

26.2.2 Detecting a signal

Some signals can be caught and appropriate action taken. Other signals cannot be caught. For instance, if a command receives a signal 9, you cannot do anything about it.

As far as scripting is concerned we only need to worry about signals 1, 2, 3 and 15. When a script receives a signal, it can do one of three things:

1.   Do absolutely nothing, and let the system take its course.

2.   Catch the signal, but ignore it.

3.   Catch the signal and take some form of action.

Most scripts use number 1. This is the method we have used in all the scripts in the book so far.

To be able to use the other two methods, we must use the trap command.

26.3 trap

The trap command allows you to trap incoming signals to your scripts. The format of the trap command is:

trap name signal(s)

The name is a list of instructions to be performed when the signal is caught. In reality a function should be called that deals specifically with trapped signals. The name should be surrounded by double quotes (" "). The signal(s) are the incoming signals.

When a signal is trapped a script will generally be in the middle of some processing. The most common form of action to take is:

1.   Clean up temporary files.

2.   Ignore the signals.

3.   Ask the user if the script is really to be terminated.

Here's a table of the most common trap usages:

trap " " 2 3	Ignore the signals 2 and 3; user cannot terminate
trap "commands" 2 3	If signals 2 and 3 are caught then execute commands
trap 2 3	Reset the signals 2 and 3; user can terminate the script

You can use single quotes instead of double quotes; the result is the same.

26.3.1 Trapping signals and taking action

Let's create a script that counts up until the user hits <CTRL-C> (signal 2). The script will then echo a message containing the current loop number it is processing before exiting.

The format for this trap is:

trap "do_something" signal no:(s)

Here's the script:

```
$ pg trap1
#!/bin/sh
#trap1
trap "my_exit" 2
LOOP=0
my_exit()
{
echo "You just hit <CTRL-C>, at number $LOOP"
echo " I will now exit "
exit 1
}

while :
do
   LOOP=`expr $LOOP + 1`
   echo $LOOP
done
```

Let's look at the script in more detail.

```
trap "my_exit" 2
```

The trap command is set, so if it receives a signal 2 then whatever is inside the double quotes will be executed; in this case a function called my_exit.

```
my_exit()
{
echo "You just hit <CTRL-C>, at number $LOOP"
echo " I will now exit "
exit 1
}
```

The function `my_exit` is called upon receiving the signal 2; the variable $LOOP is echoed informing the user what number it was processing when <CTRL-C> was hit. This type of function would actually be used to clean up temporary files etc.

When the above script is run we get:

```
$ trap1
1
. . .
. . .
211
212
You just hit <CTRL-C>, at number 213
 I will now exit
```

26.3.2 Catching a signal and taking action

The most common form of action to take is the cleaning up of temporary files.

The next script will continuously append information using the `df` and `ps` commands to temporary files called `HOLD1.$$` and `HOLD2.$$`. Remember `$$` will contain the process ID number. When the user hits <CTRL-C>, the files will be deleted.

```
$ pg trap2
#!/bin/sh
# trap2
# trap only signal 2....<CTRL-C>
trap "my_exit" 2
HOLD1=/tmp/HOLD1.$$
HOLD2=/tmp/HOLD2.$$

my_exit()
{
# my_exit
echo "<CTRL-C> detected..Now cleaning up..wait"
# delete the temp files
rm /tmp/*.$$ 2> /dev/null
exit 1
}

echo "processing...."
# loop forever, do some processing
while :
do
  df >>$HOLD1
  ps xa >>$HOLD2
done
```

When the above script is run, we get:

```
$ trap2
processing....
<CTRL-C> detected..Now cleaning up..wait
```

You may want to give the user a choice when a signal is received, although if you received signals 2 or 3 you can be pretty sure it was done on purpose. But let's err to the safe side, and assume the user hit <CTRL-C> by mistake.

     In our next example the user is given the choice if he or she wants to exit after the script has received a signal 2. A prompt is displayed asking the user if he or she really wants to quit. The case statement is used to determine what action to take.

     If the user wants to exit then he or she selects 1 and a cleanup process begins followed by an 'exit 1' status. If the user does not want to exit then do nothing; let the user fall through the case statement and return to the code from whence they came. Of course any empty fields would be caught in your validation.

     Here's the function that will give the user a choice when a signal is received:

```
my_exit()
{
# my_exit
echo -e "\nReceived interrupt ... "
echo "Do you really wish to exit ???"
echo " 1: Yes"
echo " 2: No"
echo -n " Your choice [1..2] >"
read ANS
case $ANS in
1) # cleanup temp files.. etc..
   exit 1
   ;;
2) # do nothing
3) ;;
esac
}
```

Here's the script.

```
$ pg trap4
#!/bin/sh
# trap4
# trap signal 1 2 3 and 15
trap "my_exit" 1 2 3 15

LOOP=0

# temp files
HOLD1=/tmp/HOLD1.$$
HOLD2=/tmp/HOLD2.$$
```

```
my_exit()
{
# my_exit
echo -e "\nRecieved interrupt..."
echo "Do you wish to really exit ???"
echo " Y: Yes"
echo " N: No"
echo -n " Your choice [Y..N] >"
read ANS
case $ANS in
Y|y) exit 1;;      # exit the script
N|n) ;;            # return to normal processing
esac
}


# a while loop here perhaps for reading in fields
echo -n "Enter your name :"
read NAME
echo -n "Enter your age :"
read AGE
```

When the above script is run, and <CTRL-C> is hit in the middle of an input field (just after typing in the beginning of the name Tan) you get the choice of returning to carry on with normal processing or exiting the script.

```
$ trap4
Enter your name :David Ta
Received interrupt...
Do you really wish to exit ???
 1: Yes
 2: No
 Your choice [1..2] >2

Enter your age :
```

26.3.3 Locking up your terminal

Here's a script that shows another way to trap signals in a running script. The following script, called lockit, locks up your terminal from the command line by putting it in a continuous while loop. The trap command catches the signals 2, 3 and 15. In case a user tries to break out of the running script a message is displayed informing the user that they were unsuccessful.

You are prompted for a password when the script is first invoked. To unlock the terminal, the read is taken from /dev/tty hence there is no prompt to unlock the terminal; simply key in your password and hit return.

If you forget your password you will have to log on to another terminal and kill it. There is no check for the length of a password – I will leave that to you.

If you kill this script from another terminal you may experience terminal setting problems when you return to your terminal; for example, the return key not working. Try the following at the command prompt, it should fix most tty-related problems.

```
$ stty sane
```

Here's the script.

```
$ pg lockit
#!/bin/sh

# lockit
# trap signals 2 3 and 15
trap "nice_try" 2 3 15

# get the device we are running on
TTY=`tty`

nice_try()
{
# nice_try
echo "Nice try, the terminal stays locked"
}

# save stty settings hide characters typed in for the password
SAVEDSTTY=`stty -g`
stty -echo
echo -n "Enter your password to lock $TTY :"
read PASSWORD
clear

while :
do
  # read from tty only !!,
  read RESPONSE < $TTY
  if [ "$RESPONSE" = "$PASSWORD" ]; then
    # password matches...unlocking
    echo "unlocking..."
    break
  fi

  # show this if the user inputs a wrong password
  # or hits return

  echo "wrong password and terminal is locked.."
done

# restore stty settings
stty $SAVEDSTTY
```

Here's the output when the lockit script is run:

```
$ lockit
Enter your password to lock /dev/ttyS1 :
```

The screen clears then. Hitting return or the wrong password the script outputs:

```
wrong password and terminal is locked..
Nice try, the terminal stays locked
wrong password and terminal is locked..
Nice try, the terminal stays locked
wrong password and terminal is locked..
```

Now enter the correct password

```
unlocking...
$
```

You are now back to your command prompt.

26.3.4 Ignoring signals

When a user logs into a system, the /etc/profile is read; root will not want the users to break out of this process; he or she will usually set the trap to ignore signals 1, 2, 3 and 15, but then turn them on again (reset) when the motd (message of the day) gets read. The trap will then be set again to ignore signals 1, 2, 3 and 15.

The same approach can be adopted for scripts. You may have a critical part in your script where it opens many files, and during this process you may not want the script to be interrupted in case damage is caused to the files. Setting trap to ignore certain signals will solve this problem. When the critical processing has finished use trap again to allow signals to be caught.

The format to ignore incoming signals is (apart from signal 9):

trap "" signal no:(s)

Notice that there is nothing between the double quotes. To reset the trap back to allow signals to be caught:

trap "do something" signal no:(s)

To summarize the process of ignoring then not ignoring signals.

trap "" 1 2 3 15   # ignore signals
code that does really critical stuff
trap "my_exit" 1 2 3 15   # let's catch the signals again! with a
                                                        function called my_exit.

Here is a script that does some critical processing, a while loop actually, but it puts the point across very nicely. Trap is set to ignore signals 2, 3 and 15. When this while loop has finished, another while loop kicks off, but this time the trap has been reset to allow for interrupts.

Both while loops count up to six, then there is a sleep command inside the loop, so it should give you plenty of time trying to break out of the script.

Here's the script.

```
$ pg trap_ignore
#!/bin/sh
# trap_ignore
# ignore the signals
trap "" 1 2 3 15

LOOP=0
my_exit()
# my_exit
{
echo "Received interrupt on count $LOOP"
echo "Now exiting..."
exit 1
}

# critical processing, cannot be interrupted....
LOOP=0
while :
do
  LOOP=`expr $LOOP + 1`
  echo "critical processing..$LOOP..you cannot interrupt me"
  sleep 1
  if [ "$LOOP" -eq 6 ]; then
    break
  fi
done

LOOP=0
# critical processing finished, now set trap again but this time allow
interrupts.
trap "my_exit" 1 2 3 15

while :
do
  LOOP=`expr $LOOP + 1`

  echo "Non-critical processing..$LOOP..interrupt me now if you want"
  sleep 1
  if [ "$LOOP" -eq 6 ]; then
    break
  fi
done
```

When the above script is run and we try to hit <CTRL-C> during the first 'critical processing' loop nothing happens because we have set the trap to ignore the signals. When the second 'non-critical processing' loop kicks in, the trap has been reset to allow for interrupts.

```
$ trap_ignore
critical processing..1..you cannot interrupt me
critical processing..2..you cannot interrupt me
critical processing..3..you cannot interrupt me
critical processing..4..you cannot interrupt me
critical processing..5..you cannot interrupt me
critical processing..6..you cannot interrupt me
Non-critical processing..1..interrupt me now if you want
Non-critical processing..2..interrupt me now if you want
Received interrupt on count 2
Now exiting...
```

Using traps enables you to have more control on how your script behaves when it receives a signal. Catching signals and dealing with them is a sign of robust scripting.

26.4 eval

The eval command will evaluate the command line to complete any shell substitutions and will then execute it. Eval is used to expand variables where one pass of the expansion does not do the job; eval makes two passes through a variable to expand it. Variables that require two passes to evaluate are sometimes called complex variables. Take it from me, variables are not complex.

Eval can still be used to echo out simple variables; they do not have to be complex variables.

```
$ NAME=Honeysuckle
$ eval echo $NAME
Honeysuckle
$ echo $NAME
Honeysuckle
```

The best way to explain how eval works is to see it on the command line as it evaluates.

26.4.1 Executing commands held in a string

Let's first create a little file called testf that holds some text. Next, assign the command cat testf to the variable MYFILE, and echo the variable to see if we can cat the file testf.

```
$ pg testf
May Day, May Day
Going Down
```

Let's assign the variable MYFILE that will hold "cat testf".

```
$ MYFILE="cat testf"
```

If we echo it, we should be able to cat the file testf.

```
$ echo $MYFILE
cat testf
```

Let's use eval to evaluate the variable; remember eval will make two passes through the variable MYFILE.

```
$ eval $MYFILE
May Day, May Day
Going Down
```

It has successfully evaluated the variable and cat the file testf. The first pass displays the actual string "cat testf"; the second pass executes what is contained in the string, which is cat testf.

Here's another example. A variable called CAT_PASSWD will hold the string "cat /etc/passwd | more". The job of eval is to execute the contents of that string.

```
$ CAT_PASSWD="cat /etc/passwd | more"
$ echo $CAT_PASSWD
cat /etc/passwd|more
$ eval $CAT_PASSWD
root:HccPbzT5tb00g:0:0:root:/root:/bin/sh
bin:*:1:1:bin:/bin:
daemon:*:2:2:daemon:/sbin:
adm:*:3:4:adm:/var/adm:
...
...
```

The eval command is also good at showing the last parameter passed to a script. We have already looked at the last parameter, but here it is again.

```
$ pg evalit
#!/bin/sh
# evalit
echo " Total number of arguments passed is $#"
echo " The process ID is $$"
echo " Last argument is " $(eval echo \$$#)
```

When we run the above script we get (your process ID will have a different value):

```
$ evalit alpha bravo charlie
 Total number of arguments passed is 3
 The process ID is 780
 Last argument is  charlie
```

In the above script `eval` first evaluates the variable `$$#` to the process ID, and on its second pass it evaluates to the last parameter passed into the variable.

26.4.2 Making a value a variable name

You can also assign a field of data a variable name. Here's what I mean. Suppose you have a file like this:

```
$ pg data
PC      486
MONITOR svga
NETWORK yes
```

You want to make all the first column of text become variable names, and the second column of text to become the first column's value. So you get this:

echo $PC
486

See what I mean? Here's how we can do it, using `eval` of course.

```
$ pg eval_it
#!/bin/sh
#eval_it
while read NAME TYPE
do
   eval `echo "${NAME}=${TYPE}"`
done < data
echo "You have a $PC pc, with a $MONITOR monitor"
echo "and are you network ? $NETWORK"
```

Taking the first piece of data to see how this works, the script reads in PC and 486, which are assigned to the variables `NAME` and `TYPE` respectively. The first pass of `eval` echoes the two values of the variables PC and 486, while the second pass replaces the `NAME` with `PC` and the `TYPE` with `486`.

When we run the above script we get:

```
$ eval_it
You have a 486 pc, with a svga monitor
and are you network ? yes
```

`Eval` is not a command you will see a lot of in scripts, but it's the one to use when you need to evaluate variables more than once.

26.5 `logger` **command**

The system maintains quite a few log files. One of these log files is called `messages`, usually located in `/var/adm` or `/var/log`. Messages that are logged into this file are carried out via a configuration file called `syslog`; the messages are in a strict format. To see how your system is configured for generating messages from programs check out the `/etc/syslog.conf` file. This file holds all the different priorities and facilities that a program can use to send different message types.

We will not go into how UNIX or LINUX logs messages to the file. All you really need to know for now is that there are different levels of messages ranging from informational to critical.

You can send messages to the message file using the `logger` command. You need to check with your man page on the `logger` command, because this command syntax is varied between vendors.

However, as we will only be covering informational messages you should be safe with commands we are going to cover.

You may want to send messages to the message file for any of the following reasons:

Accessing/Logins over a certain period;
Critical processing of one of your scripts failed; or
Monitoring scripts reports.

Here's what my `/var/adm/messages` file looks like. Yours will be slightly different:

```
$ tail /var/adm.messages
Jun 16 20:59:03 localhost login[281]: DIALUP AT ttyS1 BY root
Jun 16 20:59:03 localhost login[281]: ROOT LOGIN ON ttyS1
Jun 16 20:59:04 localhost PAM_pwdb[281]: (login) session closed for user
root
Jun 16 21:58:38 localhost named[211]: Cleaned cache of 0 RRs
Jun 16 21:58:39 localhost named[211]: USAGE 929570318 929566719
Jun 16 21:58:39 localhost named[211]: NSTATS 929570318 929566719
```

The general format of the `logger` command for our purposes is:

logger -p -i message

where:

-p   Means the priority; we are only concerned with `user.notice` which is the default anyway

-i   Log the process ID with each message

26.5.1 Using the `logger` command

From the shell prompt type the following:

```
$ logger -p notice "This is a test message.Please Ignore $LOGNAME"
```

You may have to wait up to a couple of minutes to see the message logged.

```
$ tail /var/adm/messages
...
...
Jun 17 10:36:49 acers6 dave: This is a test message.Please Ignore dave
```

As can be seen, the user who instigated the log of the message is also recorded.

Let's create a little script that logs a message that reports how many users are on the system. This script could be used to gauge system usage over a daily period. All you would have to do is to run it from `crontab` every 30 minutes, approximately.

```
$ pg test_logger
#!/bin/sh
# test_logger
logger -p notice   "`basename $0`:there are currently `who |wc -l` users on
                   the system"
```

Run the script.

```
$ test_logger
```

Now tail the message file.

```
$ tail /var/adm/messages
...
...
Jun 17 11:02:53 acers6 dave: test_script:there are currently 15 users on
the system
```

26.5.2 Using `logger` in your scripts

A more proper use of logging messages is when one of your scripts is terminated unconditionally. To log these types of messages simply include a `logger` command in your exit functions that trap the signals.

In the following cleanup script, if the script receives any of the signals 2, 3 or 15 then a message is logged.

```
$ pg cleanup
# !/bin/sh
# cleanup
```

```
# cleanup system logs
trap "my_exit" 2 3 15

my_exit()
{
# my_exit
logger -p notice " `basename $0`: Was killed whilst cleaning up system
                logs..CHECK OUT ANY DAMAGE"
exit 1
}

tail -3200c /var/adm/utmp > /tmp/utmp
mv /tmp/utmp /var/adm/utmp
>/var/adm/wtmp
#
tail -10 /var/adm/sulog > /tmp/o_sulog
mv /tmp/o_sulog /var/adm/sulog
...
```

When we look at the messages file we can see if there was a problem with the
processing of the script cleanup.

```
$ tail /var/adm/messages
...

...
Jun 17 11:34:28 acers6 dave: cleanup:Was killed whilst cleaning up
systemlogs..         CHECK OUT ANY DAMAGE
```

Apart from using `logger` in various critical script processing, I also use it to log any
users connecting to the system using a modem. Here's a segment of code that logs
any users who have connected into my system using the serial lines `tty0` and `tty02`.
This piece of code comes from one of my `/etc/profile` files.

```
TTY_LINE=`tty`
case $TTY_LINE in
"/dev/tty0")
  TERM=ibm3151
  ;;
"/dev/tty2")
  TERM=vt220
  # checks for allowed users on the modem line
  #
  echo "This is a modem connection"
  # modemf contains login names of valid users
  modemf=/usr/local/etc/modem.users
  if [-s $modemf ]
  then
    user=`cat $modemf| awk '{print $1}' | grep $LOGNAME`
    # if your name is not in the file, you are not coming in
```

```
    if [ "$user" != "$LOGNAME" ]
    then
      echo "INVALID USER FOR MODEM CONNECTION"
      echo " DISCONNECTING,,,,,,"
      sleep 1
      exit 1
    else
      echo "modem connection allowed"
    fi
  fi
  logger -p notice "modem line connect $TTY_LINE..$LOGNAME"
  ;;
*) TERM=vt220
  stty erase '^h'
  ;;
esac
```

Logger is a good tool to use when you want information logged into the system's global message file.

26.6 Conclusion

Understanding signals and traps gives your scripts better scope for a graceful exit. Being able to log messages to the system log file enables you to place useful information for you or the administrator to look at and to decide on any potential problems.

CHAPTER 27

A small collection of scripts

This chapter contains some of my most used scripts. Looking through them you will see that nearly all are fairly short and simple. That's one of the beauties of scripts; they do not have to be long or complex, just so long as it can save you time.

In this chapter we will cover:

- various script examples.

One script under consideration for this chapter was comet which is a general data validation databases script. However, as it's over 500 lines long, I did not think the editor would approve of its inclusion in this book. The comet script started a couple of years ago as a five-liner script, but due to added features, it really has grown. Anyway, the six scripts I present to you are as follows:

pingall	A script that uses the /etc/hosts entries to ping all hosts
backup_gen	A general purpose backup script that loads default settings
del.lines	A sed wrapper that deletes lines from files
access_deny	A utility to deny access to certain users logging in
logroll	A utility to roll over logs if they reach a certain size
nfsdown	A quick way to unmount all nfs directories

27.1 pingall

I wrote pingall quite a few years ago as part of a general reporting script that ran during the night. It pings all the hosts held in the hosts file.

The script cats the /etc/hosts file and greps out all lines that do not begin with a #. A while loop then reads in lines of filtered text. Awk is used to assign the first field of the filtered text to the variable ADDR. Using a for loop, each address is then pinged.

Here's the script.

```
$ pg pingall
#!/bin/sh
# pingall

# grab /etc/hosts and ping each address
cat /etc/hosts| grep -v '^#' | while read LINE
do
  ADDR=`awk '{print $1}'`
  for MACHINE in $ADDR
  do
    ping -s -c1 $MACHINE
  done
done
```

The pingall script can easily expanded to include reporting functions of other network utilities.

27.2 backup_gen

I have included backup_gen not because it shows how to back up directories, but because it is a good example of how to share common settings amongst other scripts.

The backup_gen is a backup script that reads in a default configuration file which is then used for a backup of the system. A user can alter the default settings if he or she wishes. This script is a good example of how different scripts can use the same settings or change them just for the script's run time. When the script executes, it makes sure the source file (backup.defaults) is present. The script will exit if it cannot be found.

A screen header and the default settings are displayed. The user is asked if he or she wants to change any of the default settings. If the reply is yes, they are then prompted to enter a code before they can amend any of the settings. The user has three attempts at entering the correct code; failure at entering the correct code will mean that they will have to use the default settings. Upon entering the correct code, the user may change any of the following settings (the defaults are in square brackets [ ]):

tape device [rmt0]	choices are rmt1 and rmt3
mail admin when the backup has finished [yes]	choices are no
type of backup [full]	choices are normal and sybase

Temporary variables are used to take any of the changed settings. The user can hit return on any of the fields to accept the default settings. The following settings however cannot be changed:

backup log filename
code name.

Any changes are then validated. After the validation process, the temporary variables are reassigned back to the sourced variables. The tape unit is tested before the backup kicks off. The actual backup uses find and cpio incorporating the variables from the settings file or the new values entered by the user.

Here is the script.

```
$ pg backup_run
#!/bin/sh
# backup_run

# script to run the backups
# loads in a setting file for the user to change

SOURCE=/appdva/bin/backup.defaults
check_source()
{
# check_source
# can we load the file
# backup.defaults is the source file containing config/functions
# make sure your path includes this directory you are running from
if [ -r $SOURCE ]; then
  . /$SOURCE
else
  echo "`basename $0`: cannot locate defaults file"
  exit 1
fi
}

header()
{
# header
USER=`whoami`
MYDATE=`date +%A" "%e" of "%B-%Y`
clear
cat << MAYDAY
User : $USER                                              $MYDATE
                    NETWORK SYSTEM BACKUP
                    =====================

MAYDAY
}

change_settings()
{
# change_settings
# let the user see the default settings..
header
echo "Valid Entries Are..."
echo "Tape Device: rmt0, rmt1, rmt3"
echo "Mail Admin: yes, no"
echo "Backup Type: full, normal, sybase "
```

```
while :
do
  echo -n -c "\n\n Tape Device To Be Used For This Backup  [$_DEVICE] :"
  read T_DEVICE
  : ${T_DEVICE:=$_DEVICE}
  case $T_DEVICE in
  rmt0|rmt1|rmt3) break;;
  *) echo "The devices are either ... rmt0, rmt1, rmt3"
    ;;
  esac
done

# if the user hits return on any of the fields, the default value will be
used
while :
do
  echo -n " Mail Admin When Done                   [$_INFORM] :"
  read T_INFORM
  : ${T_INFORM:=$_INFORM}
  case $T_INFORM in
  yes|Yes) break;;
  no|No) break;;
  *) echo "The choices are yes, no"
    ;;
  esac
done

while :
do
  echo -n " Backup Type                            [$_TYPE] :"
  read T_TYPE
  : ${T_TYPE:=$_TYPE}
  case $T_TYPE in
  Full|full) break;;
  Normal|normal)break;;
  Sybase|sybase)break;;
  *) echo "The choices are either ... full, normal, sybase"
  esac
done
# re-assign the temp variables back to original variables that
# were loaded in
_DEVICE=$T_DEVICE; _INFORM=$T_INFORM; _INFORM=$T_INFORM
}


show_settings()
# display current settings
{
cat << MAYDAY
                    Default Settings Are...
```

```
                  Tape Device To Be Used      : $_DEVICE
                  Mail Admin When Done        : $_INFORM
                  Type Of Backup              : $_TYPE
                  Log file of backup          : $_LOGFILE
MAYDAY
}


get_code()
{
# users get 3 attempts at entering the correct code
# _CODE is loaded in from the source file
clear
header
_COUNTER=0
echo " YOU MUST ENTER THE CORRECT CODE TO BE ABLE TO CHANGE
      DEFAULT SETTINGS"
while :
do
  _COUNTER=`expr $_COUNTER + 1`
  echo -n "Enter the code to change the settings  :"
  read T_CODE
  # echo $_COUNTER
  if [ "$T_CODE" = "$_CODE" ]; then
    return 0
  else
    if [ "$_COUNTER" -gt 3 ]; then
      echo "Sorry incorrect code entered, you cannot change the settings.."
      return 1
    fi
  fi
done
}


check_drive()
{
# make sure we can rewind the tape
mt -f /dev/$_DEVICE rewind > /dev/null 2>&1
if [ $? -ne 0 ]; then
  return 1
else
  return 0
fi
}
#========= main==============


# can we source the file
check_source
header
# display the loaded in variables
```

```
  show_settings
  # ask user if he/she wants to change any settings
  if continue_prompt "Do you wish To Change Some Of The System Defaults" "Y";
  then
    # yes then enter code name
    if get_code; then
      # change some settings
      change_settings
    fi
  fi


  #------- got settings.. now do backup
  if check_drive; then
    echo "tape OK...."
  else
    echo "Cannot rewind the tape..Is it in the tape drive ???"
    echo "Check it out"
    exit 1
  fi


  # file system paths to backup
  case $_TYPE in
  Full|full)
    BACKUP_PATH="sybase syb/support etc var bin apps use/local"
    ;;
  Normal|normal)
    BACKUP_PATH="etc var bin apps usr/local"
    ;;
  Sybase|sybase)
    BACKUP_PATH="sybase syb/support"
    ;;
  esac
  # now for backup
  cd /
  echo "Now starting backup......"
  find $BACKUP_PATH -print | cpio -ovB -O /dev/$_DEVICE >> $_LOGFILE 2>&1


  # if the above cpio does not work on your system try cpio below, instead
  # find $BACKUP_PATH -print | cpio -ovB > /dev/$_DEVICE >> $_LOGFILE 2>&1


  # to get more information on the tape change -ovB to -ovcC66536


  if [ "$_INFORM" = "yes" ]; then
    echo "Backup finished check the log file" | mail admin
  fi
```

The source file called backup.defaults holds the default settings as well as the function continue_prompt. Here's the source file.

```
$ pg backup.defaults
#!/bin/sh
# backup.defaults
# configuration default file for network backups
# edit this file at your own risk !!
# name backup.defaults
#---------------------------------
# not necessary for the environments to be in quotes..but hey!
_CODE="comet"
_LOGFILE="/appdva/backup/log.`date +%y%m%d`"
_DEVICE="rmt0"
_INFORM="yes"
_TYPE="Full"
#---------------------------------
continue_prompt()
# continue_prompt
# to call: continue_prompt "string to display" default_answer
{
_STR=$1
_DEFAULT=$2
# check we have the right params
if [ $# -lt 1 ]; then
  echo "continue_prompt: I need a string to display"
  return 1
fi
while :
do
  echo -n "$_STR [Y..N] [$_DEFAULT]:"
  read _ANS
  : ${_ANS:=$_DEFAULT}
    if [ "$_ANS" = "" ]; then
      case $_ANS in
      Y) return 0 ;;
      N) return 1 ;;
      esac
    fi
  # user has selected something
  case $_ANS in
  y|Y|Yes|YES)
    return 0
    ;;
  n|N|No|NO)
    return 1
    ;;
  *) echo "Answer either Y or N, default is $_DEFAULT"
    ;;
  esac
  echo $_ANS
done
}
```

Here's the output when the default settings are displayed, and the user is asked whether he or she wants to change the settings:

```
User : dave                                      Tuesday 15 of June-1999
                         NETWORK SYSTEM BACKUP
                         =========================
                         Default Settings Are...
            Tape Device To Be Used     : rmt0
            Mail Admin When Done       : yes
            Type Of Backup             : Full
            Log file of backup         : /appdva/backup/log.990615
        Do you wish To Change Some Of The System Defaults [Y..N] [Y]:
```

The next output shows the process of changing a value for its default setting. The backup type has been changed, but when the script checks the tape drive, it has found a problem with it. Using the last status command, the script will now exit.

```
User : dave                                      Tuesday 15 of June-1999
                         NETWORK SYSTEM BACKUP
                         =========================
Valid Entries Are...
Tape Device: rmt0, rmt1, rmt3
Mail Admin: yes, no
Backup Type: full, normal, sybase


 Tape Device To Be Used For This Backup  [rmt0] :
 Mail Admin When Done                    [yes] :
 Backup Type                             [Full : Normal
 Cannot rewind the tape..Is it in the tape drive ???
 Check it out
```

27.3 del.lines

This script came about because the developers kept asking me 'what was that sed command to delete blank lines again?' I decided I would knock up a little script for them to use, which would save them the trouble of ringing me up for the command.

The script is really a wrapper for the sed delete command, but it keeps the developers happy, and it gets used a lot.

Shell scripts do not have to be long. If a task can be automated and it saves you time, script it.

del.lines can take a single file or multiple files. Each file is checked for its presence before sed does the work of deleting all blank lines. The output of sed is directed to a temporary file using $$, and the file is then moved back to replace the original file.

Shift is used to gather all the filenames, and a while loop loops until there are no more files present to be processed.

Just type del.lines -help to get a rather sparse help line. I'll let you create a better help statement.

Here's the script.

```
$ pg del.lines
#!/bin/sh


# del.lines
# script takes filename(s) and deletes all blank lines


TEMP_F=/tmp/del.lines.$$

usage()
{
# usage
echo "Usage :`basename $0` file [file..]"
echo "try `basename $0` -help for more info"
exit 1
}

if [ $# -eq 0 ]; then
   usage
fi


FILES=$1
while [ $# -gt 0 ]
do
   echo "..$1"
   case $1 in
   -help)  cat << MAYDAY
     Use this script to delete all blank lines from a text file(s)
     MAYDAY
     exit 0
     ;;
   *)  FILE_NAME=$1

     if [ -f $1 ]; then
        sed '/^$/d' $FILE_NAME >$TEMP_F
        mv $TEMP_F $FILE_NAME

     else
        echo "`basename $0` cannot find this file : $1"
     fi
     shift
     ;;
   esac
done
```

27.4 access.deny

To keep users from logging into the system when you are carrying out live updates, you can use the /etc/nologin method, available on most systems. When you create a file called nologin in /etc usually with the touch command, no users apart from root are allowed to log in.

If your system is one of the few that do not support the nologin method, all is not lost – you can create this function yourself. Here's what to do.

Put the following code in your /etc/profile.

```
if [ -f /etc/nologin ]; then
  if [ $LOGNAME != "root" ]; then
    echo "Sorry $LOGNAME the system is unavailable at the moment"
    exit 1
  fi
fi
```

Now, when you want to stop all users logging in, apart from root that is, use the touch command to create a nologin file in /etc and make sure it is readable by everyone.

touch /etc/nologin
chmod 644 /etc/nologin

When you need to let the users back in just delete the nologin file, as follows:

rm /etc/nologin

The above is great if you want to disable all users apart from root. If you want to disable certain accounts temporarily, you can hack around with the /etc/passwd file and put an *, as the first character in their password field. However, this is very tricky and, unless you know what you are doing, you could have system-wide problems.

LINUX offers a utility where you can put usernames and groups inside a login.access file. This file is used to either grant or deny access to the system.

Here is a slimmed down version of that utility called deny.access. The script, which is run from /etc/profile, reads a file called lockout.user. This file holds usernames that you do not want logging into the system. If the word 'all' is found in the file then everybody apart from root will be denied access.

Here's a sample lockout.user file. The file can contain comment lines.

```
$ pg lockout.users
# lockout.users
# put the user names in this file, that you want
# locked out of the system.
# Remove the user names from this file, to let the users back in.
```

```
# peter is on long holiday back next month
peter
# lulu is off for two weeks, back at the end of the month
lulu
#dave
#pauline
```

The script works like this. First, a trap is set to ignore signals so the user cannot break out of the execution of the script. If the file lock.users is present then the script will continue executing. The first thing it checks for is the word 'all'. If this is present then it will override any usernames you have in this file. Do not use a comment line to comment out the word 'all', it will still pick it up. You may comment out usernames though.

If the entry 'all' is found then all users are locked out apart from root. To make sure an exact pattern match is found the grep pattern 'all\>' is used. A message is echoed to the screen telling the users the system is unavailable at the moment.

The main function is get_users. This reads the file lockout.users, ignoring all lines beginning with the hash sign. It compares names to make sure no one has put the username root in the file, so root is locked out; we cannot have this can we?

The login name of the current user logging in is pulled from the variable LOGNAME and compared against the variable NAMES which holds the current username from the lockout.users file it is reading. If a match is found the LOGNAME is displayed with a message. The user is then exited.

I have this script running on a couple of systems that have up to 40 users, and there is no lack of speed in their logging in process. I use this script to temporarily lock out users who are away for more than a week, and also to lock out certain users during lunch times when I have to update live systems.

You need to put the following line in your /etc/profile. I've got mine at the end of the file, so the users can view the message of the day first for added information.

```
. /apps/bin/deny.access
```

The directory /apps/bin is one of the areas where I keep all my global scripts – yours will probably be different, but make sure everyone has execute on this script and the directory that the scripts live in.

If you get a 'permission denied' error, then you have not given enough permission on the script or directory.

My lockout.users file is in /apps/etc. You will have to change that directory if your structure is different, which it probably is. Because the file is sourced you will be able to see the functions if you use the set command (but not the actual lockout.users file). If this worries you simply use the unset command to delete the function after it has been executed. Put the unset command directly after the call to the script in the /etc/profile. Like this:

```
unset getusers
```

Here is the script:

```
$ pg deny.access
#!/bin/sh
# deny.access

trap "" 2 3
# CHANGE BELOW IF YOU CHANGE THE LOCATION OF LOCKOUT.USERS
LOCKOUT=/apps/etc/lockout.users
MSG="Sorry $LOGNAME, your account has been disabled, ring the
administrator"
MSG2="Sorry $LOGNAME, the system is unavailable at the moment"

check_lockout()
# check_logout
# make sure we have a file containing names to lockout
{
if [ -r $LOCKOUT ] ; then
  return 0
else
  return 1
fi
}

get_users()
# get_users
# read the file, if their LOGNAME matches a name in lockout.users'
# then kick them out!
{
while read NAMES
do
  case $NAMES in
  \#*);;    #do ignore comments
  *)
  # just in case somebody tries to lockout root..not in this script they
  # won't
    if [ "$NAMES" = "root" ]; then
      break
    fi
    if [ "$NAMES" = "$LOGNAME" ]; then
    # let use see message before kicking them out
      echo $MSG
      sleep 2
      exit 1
    else
      # no match next iteration of reading the file
      continue
    fi
    ;;
  esac
```

```
done < $LOCKOUT
}
if check_lockout; then
  if grep 'all\>' $LOCKOUT >/dev/null 2>&1
then
  # first check that 'all' is not present. If it is then
  # keep everybody out apart from root
  if [ "$LOGNAME" != "root" ]; then
    echo $MSG2
    sleep 2
    exit 2
    fi
  fi
  # do normal users, if any
  get_users
fi
```

27.5 `logroll`

A few of the logs on my system grow quite quickly. Having to manually check the size of these logs for file sizes and then roll over the log (usually with a data stamp) gets tedious. Therefore I decided it was time I set up a script to do this automatically. The script would run from `cron`, and if any of the logs reached a certain size, the guilty log would be rolled over and a new log file created.

The script can easily be amended to suit other logs. For my system logs, I use another script, which is run once a week and truncates the log files. If I need to go back over any period I just check my backup; as I run a 16-week cycle this is no problem.

A size limit is defined in the variable `BLOCK_LIMIT`. This figure is the block size, which I have set to eight which is 4K. You can set yours higher if need be. All the logs I want to be checked are held in the variable `LOGS`.

A `for` loop then loops through this variable checking each log file, using the `du` command, and the size of the log is obtained. If the size is greater than `BLOCK_LIMIT`, the log will be copied with a date stamp appended to the file. The original log file is then zeroed, and the files group ownership is changed.

The script is run from `cron` a couple of times per week, creating a backup of the file with a date stamp, which ensures I can back track quickly if there are any problems that I need to check out.

```
$ pg logroll
#!/bin/sh
# logroll
# roll over the log files if sizes have reached the MARK
# could also be used for mail boxes ?
```

```
# limit size of log
# 4096 k
BLOCK_LIMIT=8

MYDATE=`date +%d%m`
# list of logs to check...yours will be different!
LOGS="/var/spool/audlog /var/spool/networks/netlog /etc/dns/named_log"
for LOG_FILE in $LOGS
do
   if [ -f $LOG_FILE ] ; then
     # get block size
     F_SIZE=`du -a $LOG_FILE | cut -f1`
   else
     echo "`basename $0` cannot find $LOG_FILE" >&2
     # could exit here, but I want to make sure we hit all
     # logs
     continue
   fi

   if [ "$F_SIZE" -gt "$BLOCK_LIMIT" ]; then
     # copy the log across and append a ddmm  date on it
     cp $LOG_FILE $LOG_FILE$MYDATE
     # create / zero the new log
     >$LOG_FILE
     chgrp admin $LOG_FILE$MYDATE
   fi
done
```

27.6 nfsdown

If you have nfs on your system you might find this script handy. I look after several
machines and periodically I may have to reboot one of them during normal working
hours. This usually has to be done as quickly as possible.

As I have remote directories mounted all over the place, I do not want to
have to rely on the rebooting process to take care of the nfs unmounting. I would
rather do it myself; besides it's faster than letting the machine do it.

I just run the script (which is on all the machines) and all the nfs mounts get
unmounted, allowing me to do a faster reboot.

The script holds a list of machines that I have nfs mounts on. A for loop
loops around this list, doing a grep of each host through the df command. The nfs
directories that are mounted are in the form of:

machine:remote_directory

This string is held in the variable NFS_MACHINE. This variable is then used in the
umount command.

Here's the script.

```
$ pg nfsdown
#!/bin/sh
# nfsdown
LIST="methalpha accounts warehouse dwaggs"
for LOOP in $LIST
do
  NFS_MACHINE=`df -k | grep $LOOP | awk '{print $1}'`
  if [ "$NFS_MACHINE" != "" ]; then
    umount $LOOP
  fi
done
```

27.7 Conclusion

The scripts I have presented in this chapter are a selection of those that I use most. As I mentioned earlier, scripts do not have to be long and complicated to carry out a time-saving task.

CHAPTER 28

Run level scripts

If you want an application, service or script process to start automatically when the system comes up, or to close down properly when the system is rebooted, you need to create a run level script. All but one of the LINUX variants now have the System V-based run level configuration directories, as do other kinds of UNIX.

As most systems have this type of configuration, this is what we will cover, but if you do not have run level directories, do not worry. You can still start up applications automatically; we will discuss this method later on in this chapter.

In this chapter we will cover:

- run levels;

- how to create rc.scripts;

- how to implement rc.scripts with different run levels; and

- how to start applications from inittab.

Being able to create run level scripts allows you to have more control and flexibility over your system. You need to install a run level script (or more often called an rc.script) when you want to start or stop applications at a certain run level.

Any script that can start and stop an application and is called by using the keywords 'start' or 'stop' is generally regarded as an rc.script. Please note that it's up to the user to ensure that the script that he or she is submitting is an rc.script that works, by ensuring it can stop and start a service properly.

The mechanism behind the run level configuration directories allows the automation of the rc.scripts only during a run level change. It does not check to see if all the particular services in a run level have started or been stopped. That's down to you, the shell programmer.

You can customize run levels to the services you actually need running, but that is beyond the scope of this book.

28.1 How can you tell if you have run level directories?

The directories where the rc.scripts are kept (actually they are links, we'll discuss this later) live in either:

/etc/rcN.d

or

/etc/rc.d/rcN.d

where N is a number. There are usually seven, since the rcN.d directories are numbered 0 to 6, but you might have a couple more on your system such as rcS.d. This does not matter; all we are concerned about are the numbered ones.

```
$ pwd
/etc
drwxr-xr-x   2 root      sys         1024 Dec 22  1996 rc0.d
drwxr-xr-x   2 root      sys         1024 Dec 22  1996 rc1.d
drwxr-xr-x   2 root      sys         1024 Dec 22  1996 rc2.d
drwxr-xr-x   2 root      sys         1024 Dec 22  1996 rc3.d
drwxr-xr-x   2 root      sys         1024 Dec 22  1996 rc4.d
drwxr-xr-x   2 root      sys         1024 Dec 22  1996 rc5.d
drwxr-xr-x   2 root      sys         1024 Dec 22  1996 rc6.d
drwxr-xr-x   2 root      sys         1024 Dec 22  1996 rcS.d
```

If it's LINUX then...

```
$ pwd
/etc/rc.d
$ ls
init.d      rc.local     rc0.d     rc2.d      rc4.d      rc6.d
rc          rc.sysinit   rc1.d     rc3.d      rc5.d
```

If we cd into one of these rcN.d directories, you can see other rc.scripts already linked in.

```
$ pwd
/etc/rc.d/rc2.d
$ ls -l
lrwxrwxrwx   1 root root 16 Dec 3 15:16 K87ypbind -> ../init.d/yd
lrwxrwxrwx   1 root root 17 Dec 3 15:10 K89portmap -> ../init.d/p
lrwxrwxrwx   1 root root 17 Dec 3 15:07 S01kerneld -> ../init.d/d
...
...
```

28.2 Finding out your current run level

This chapter is not about system administration, but as a shell programmer you should be aware what `rc.scripts` are and how they fit into run level configuration directories. By the way, if you need to know what your current run level is:

```
$ who -r
    .           run-level 4  Apr 22 13:26    4    0    3
```

The number after the 'run level' is the current run level. The date following that is the last time the system was rebooted.

If it's LINUX then...

```
$ runlevel
2 3
```

The first column is the level the system was previously on, and the current one is the second column, which is run level 3.

28.3 Bringing you up to speed on `inittab`

A run level directory consists of a collection of scripts that start off services. The word 'services' in this context means a demon, application, servers, subsystems or script process. A process called `init` (`init` is the father of all processes) is invoked during the boot process of the system. Part of its job is to see what services it should start, and what run level it should default to. It gets this information by looking at a text configuration file called `inittab`, located in `/etc`. Init also consults this file for loading specific processes. If you ever need to edit this file, make a backup first. If this file gets corrupted or there are 'degrading' errors the system will not boot normally; you will have to boot to single user mode and fix the file.

The `inittab` file contains fields that have a very strict format. The format of the file is:

id:rstart:action:process

The `id` field is a unique name that identifies the process entry.

The `rstart` contains a number which specifies at what run level the process should be started.

The `action` field tells `init` how to treat this process. There are many action names, but the most common ones are `wait` and `respawn`. To wait means when the process has been started wait for it to terminate. To respawn means to start the process even if it does not yet exist, and if it does exist to restart it as soon as the process dies.

The `process` field contains the actual command to execute. Here's part of an `inittab` file.

```
$ pg /etc/inittab
id:3:initdefault:

# System initialization.
si::sysinit:/etc/rc.d/rc.sysinit
# run level 0
10:0:wait:/etc/rc.d/rc 0
# run level 1
11:1:wait:/etc/rc.d/rc 1
# run level 2
12:2:wait:/etc/rc.d/rc 2
# run level 3
13:3:wait:/etc/rc.d/rc 3
# run level 4
14:4:wait:/etc/rc.d/rc 4
# run level 5
15:5:wait:/etc/rc.d/rc 5
# runlevel 6
16:6:wait:/etc/rc.d/rc 6
#Run gettys in standard runlevels
1:12345:respawn:/sbin/mingetty tty1
2:2345:respawn:/sbin/mingetty tty2
3:2345:respawn:/sbin/mingetty tty3
4:2345:respawn:/sbin/mingetty tty4
5:2345:respawn:/sbin/mingetty tty5
6:2345:respawn:/sbin/mingetty ttyS1 vt100
```

The first line of the file is the run level the system should default to; here it's run level 3 which is no surprise.

The lines that start with the numbers 10 to 16 start or stop all the run level scripts for that particular run level. For instance, the following line

```
15:5:wait:/etc/rc.d/rc 5
```

states that when we are in run level 5 the script /etc/rc.d/rc should be run with its parameter being 5, which means /etc/rc.d/rc will run all scripts in /etc/rc.d/rc/rc5.d.

Looking at the last line of the file, at run levels 2, 3, 4 and 5 the process is to be respawned, which means it never dies; well, not for more than a second probably. The process being continuously kicked off is mingetty on the serial port ttyS1. A parameter to this is the terminal ID, which is vt100.

28.4 Now for the run levels

One of the last tasks init does before the system 'comes up' is to run all the scripts for the default run level. The file that does this calling is either /etc/rc.d/rc or

/etc/rc.init. The role of this script is to first kill processes for that level then start processes for that level.

But how does it know what services to start or stop? The rc or rc.init file will do a kind of for loop executing each rc.script that starts with a K in the rc3.d directory and passing it a parameter of 'stop'. It will then carry out the same process for all rc.scripts starting with an S and passing it a parameter of 'start'. Indeed the same process is carried out when a run level change is invoked but, instead of rc3.d, it will process the directory rcN.d according to which run level N it is changing.

The scripts that are in the rcN.d directory are only links – the real scripts are held elsewhere. They are located in a directory called /usr/sbin/init.d or /etc/init.d.

If it's LINUX then...

```
/etc/rc.d/init.d
```

In this directory there are several scripts that can stop or start a service. It's considered good form to name these scripts rc.<what it does>, rc meaning run command or run control or, as some system admins call them, 'really crucial'.

Here's a listing of some of these files.

```
$ ls
rc.localfs        rc.halt        rc.reboot  rc.syslogd  rc.daemon
...
```

The general format of these rc.scripts must be able to handle being called by the following ways:

rc.name stop   to stop the service

rc.name start   to start the service

Optional calls are restart and status calls. Any other call should be responded to with a usage message on how the rc.script should be called. It should be noted that you can invoke these scripts manually.

Now we know what a script should be able to do upon being called, the next step is to place these scripts in the corresponding rcN.d directories. But before that let's look at the system run levels.

28.4.1 The different run levels

There are seven run levels (*see* Table 28.1). Different systems have a slight variation on some of the levels.

Before you start placing a script in the different run levels, ask yourself at what levels do I want this service (that my script is going to start or stop) started or killed? Once you have decided on this you can then proceed.

Table 28.1 *What the different run levels do*

Run level 0	Stops and halts the entire system
Run level 1	Single-user or admin mode
Run level 2	Multi-user mode; some networking services are started. Some systems use this as the normal operating mode run level, instead of run level 3
Run level 3	Normal operating mode, all network services up
Run level 4	User-defined level; use this level to customize what you want running
Run level 5	Some variants have this level as the default X-windows mode, others use it to bring the system down to maintenance mode
Run level 6	Reboot

28.4.2 Format of a run level script

The scripts in the `rcN.d` directories are all symbolic links, which is to keep duplication of the scripts to a zero level. The format of these links are:

Snnn.script_name

or

Knnn.script_name

where,

S	means to start a process
K	means to kill a process
nn	is a two digit number from 00 to 99, though some systems have three digits 000 to 999. When linking in different directories, keep the same number. For example, if a service is to be started in `rc3.d` and is called `S45.myscript` and you want it started in `rc2.d`, make sure the script is called `S45.myscript` as well.
script_name	is the name of the script, depending on your type of system. It could be in:

```
/usr/sbin/init.d
/etc/rc.d
/etc/init.d
```

When init needs to call the rc.scripts, the kills will start going from highest to lowest K numbers, i.e. K23.myscript K12.named. The starts are called from the lowest to the highest. If you have LINUX, the K numbers will be executed from the highest to the lowest.

28.4.3 Installing a run level script

To install your own rc.script you must:

- write the script, ensuring it actually conforms to the calling standard;

- make sure it can actually stop and start your desired service;

- place the script (depending on your system) into /etc/init.d or /usr/sbin/init.d or /etc/rc.d; and

- create the links in all the appropriate rcN.d directories using the proper naming convention.

Below is a script that will stop or start an audit application, called rc.audit. The service will be started on run levels 3, 5 and 4 and be killed on run levels 6, 2 and 1. Looking at some of the entries in rcN.d directories the number 35 is spare, so we will use this. Actually, there is nothing from stopping you using a number that is already in use.

Here's the script. As can be seen a simple case statement does the job of trapping the stop and start parameters.

```
$ pg rc.audit
#!/bin/sh
# rc.audit start| stop
# script to start or stop zeega's audit application
#
case "$1" in
start)
  echo -n "Starting the audit system...."
  /apps/audit/audlcp -a -p 12
  echo
  touch /var/lock/subsys/rc.audit
  ;;
stop)
  echo -n "Stopping the audit system...."
  /apps/audit/auddown -k0
  echo
  rm -f /var/lock/subsys/rc.audit
  ;;
restart)
  $0 stop
  $0 start
  ;;
```

```
*)
  echo "To call properly..Usage: $0 {start|stop|restart}"
  exit 1
  ;;
esac
exit 0
```

> **If it's LINUX then...**
>
> Some LINUX variants expect a lock file to be created when you start a service.
> If there is not a lock file present then you might have problems with your kill
> scripts working.

The 'start' option calls the audit process that launches the actual audit
system, and the 'stop' option calls a script that kills the audit system. Of course, you
should test your script before installing it in the init.d directory.

```
$ rc.audit
To call properly..Usage:./rc.audit {start|stop|restart}
$ rc.audit start
Starting the audit system....
```

Let's assume the script has been tested. It stops and starts the audit service
with no problems. So let's now link the script into the required run directories.

On the system I'm using, my rcN.d directories are held in /etc/rc.d and my
rc.scripts are held in /etc/rc.d/init.d. Change your paths accordingly if
yours are different.

We'll do the start script first – remember the start scripts begin with an S.

```
$ pwd
/etc/rc.d/rc3.d
$ ln -s../init.d/rc.audit S35rc.audit

$ ls -l
...
lrwxrwxrwx   1 root   root 27 May  8 14:37 S35rc.audit -> ../init.d/
rc.audit
...
```

The link has now been created. The output from ls -l command that shows the
link goes to /etc/init.d/rc.audit. I could have supplied the whole directory
path as part of my link command, but this is not necessary. Now all I need to do is
cd into the rest of the directories where I want the service to start (that's rc4.d and
rc5.d) and just type the same command in.

To do the kill scripts:

```
$ pwd
/etc/rc.d/rc6.d
$ ln -s../init.d/rc.audit K35rc.audit
```

```
$ ls -l
...
lrwxrwxrwx   1 root   root  27 May  8 14:43 K35rc.audit -> ../init.d/
rc.audit
...
```

I can now do the same for the other directories where I want the audit service stopped. Now when the system reboots, it will be stopped; or, when the run levels change to 2 or 1, it will also be started if the run level changes to 4 or 5.

28.5 Using `inittab` to launch applications

There are other ways to start up applications; indeed, you can do this by placing an entry in `inittab`. On a couple of systems I look after, I have entries in `inittab`, not because these systems do not have run level directories, but because I have a few system checker scripts that I want to be run as soon as the system has finished coming up. Inittab is an ideal place to put these.

For this example we'll use one of my disk mirror check scripts that is run as soon as we are in run level 3. First I make sure the script runs properly, then make a backup copy of `inittab`.

```
$ cp /etc/inittab /etc/inittab.bak
```

Next edit `inittab`. I make the following entry at the end of the file.

```
# disk checker script, let's see if any of the mirrors are broken.
rc.diskchecker:3:once:/usr/local/etc/rc.diskchecker > /dev/console 2>&1
```

Now save and exit.

The above entry says:

Rc.diskchecker is the unique ID at run level 3. Run this process once. The script is `/usr/local/etc/rc.diskchecker`; put all its output to the console.

28.6 Other methods of starting and shutting down services

If you do not want to mess around with the `/etc/inittab` file, there is another method open to you. Most systems have an `rc.local` file, located in or around `/etc`. This is a script file that kicks off after all the `inittab` and `rc.scripts` have been started. You can enter any commands in this file if you wish, or add an entry in to call your favourite start-up script.

Some systems also ship a script file called shutdown in /bin though more generally in /usr/sbin. Use this to shut down your favourite services when the shutdown command is issued.

28.7 Conclusion

Run levels are really a system administration area. The objective of this chapter has been to make you aware of the control and flexibility you can have in deciding and implementing the different services or scripts you may want to have started when the system comes up.

It also means you do not have to worry about starting up or stopping a service manually when the system is rebooted.

CHAPTER 29

cgi scripts

Now that nearly everyone has a Web server installed on their PCs, it seemed appropriate that a chapter on cgi scripts should be included as part of this shell programming book.

In this chapter we will cover:

- basic cgi scripts;

- using Server Side Includes;

- the `get` method;

- the `post` method;

- creating an interactive script; and

- a cgi script that automatically reloads a Web page.

You do not need to be on a network to run a Web server; you can run it from your local host. However, here I will assume you have a Web server installed (apache, Cern etc.) and a browser to display the Web pages (Netscape, Internet Explorer, etc.). In addition, the server has been cgi-enabled. By default this is disabled; just comment out the required lines. See later for more information.

It's beyond the scope of this book to tell you how to install and configure a Web server, but it only takes about 20 minutes to get one up and running. The examples used in this chapter were run under the apache Web server, and the browser I used is Netscape.

This chapter will not go into detail about HTML or Web issues, since there are plenty of books on the market about these subjects already. Besides it would take several chapters to discuss HTML.

29.1 What is a Web page?

A Web page or document consists of HTML tags. When a browser connects to your Web page, the document lets the browser know how to display the page. The page can consist of many things including links that allow your pages to connect to other pages, colour, highlighting, character sizes, lines and tables. A page can also consist of pictures and sounds.

There are two types of Web pages: dynamic and static. Static pages are only used to display information or perhaps to download files. Dynamic pages are interactive; they can generate reports for you using information that you give. Dynamic pages are also used to display changing information in real time, such as stock prices or monitoring tasks. To be able to carry out these types of dynamic processes, scripts are required.

For a server to be able to exchange information scripts it must use a protocol called the Common Gateway Interface, more commonly known as cgi.

29.2 cgi

Cgi is the specification that tells the scripts getting information how to transfer the data to and from the server. These scripts or cgi scripts can be written in any scripting language. Perl is the most popular, but it can be done using normal shell scripts, as you will discover.

Figure 29.1 *Browser and server using cgi to exchange information*

29.3 Connecting to a Web server

To connect to a Web server you use a Uniform Resource Locator (URL). The URL contains two pieces of information:

The protocol
The address and data

The protocol can consist of http, ftp, mailto, file, telnet and news. We will only be concerned with http, which stands for hypertext transfer protocol.

The address is usually the DNS name or hostname of the server, but can be the IP address. Other data can also be the actual pathname to the file that you wish to access.

All connections are carried out using the TCP protocol, which defaults to port 80 on your machine.

If you have a Web server set up on your local host, with a main HTML page called index.html, then you would type:

http://localhost/index.html

Generally speaking, the index.html is the file to be loaded by default, which means that as far as your Web server is concerned it's the default page, though this can be changed using the configuration files. Therefore, you could just type:

http://localhost/

29.4 cgi and HTM script

When a browser makes a request to load a page, the Web server looks at the incoming URL. If there is cgi-bin as part of the URL path, the server opens a connection, which is usually a pipe to the requested cgi script. All input and output from the cgi script is sent through this pipe. Now, if the cgi script is to display a formatted Web page it must have HTML tags within the script so that a page can be displayed in a recognized format to the Web server, hence knowledge of some HTML is necessary. The Web server will send this document page to the browser to be displayed for the calling user. Table 29.1 shows some useful HTML tags.

29.4.1 Basic cgi script

All scripts should reside in the cgi-bin directory of your Web server, although this location can be changed; check out your config files, srm.conf and the section ScriptAlias to change directory locations and make the server cgi enabled. All scripts should have a file extension of .cgi. All documents usually reside in your html or htdocs directory with extensions of .html. All scripts should have the following permissions.

chmod 755 script.cgi

By default all connections to a Web page are generally as the user nobody, although this can be changed via the config file httpd.conf. Although I said that this chapter was not about Web configuration, now is a good time to check that the password field of 'nobody' is disabled. This stops anybody trying to connect as user nobody on a physical tty login connection. To disable the password of user nobody, simply insert an asterisk as the first character in their password field, in /etc/passwd.

Table 29.1 *Basic HTML tags to generate HTML pages*

`<HTML> </HTML>`	Opening and closing document tags
`<HEAD> </HEAD>`	Opening and closing information area
`<TITLE> </TITLE>`	Opening and closing title
`<BODY> </BODY>`	Opening and closing the displayed page
`<Hn> </Hn>`	Font heading, 1 being the largest size
`<P> </P>`	Start and end of paragraph
` `	Line break
`<HR>`	Horizontal line
`<PRE> </PRE>`	Opening and closing of preformatted text, all tabs, lines are preserved
`<B> </B>`	Bold characters
`<I> </I>`	Italic characters
`<OL> </OL>`	Ordered lists
`<A HREF=url>link</A>`	Hypertext or hot link to page or URL
`<FORM> </FORM>`	Enclose the form
`METHOD`	Post or get
`ACTION`	Address
`<INPUT...>`	Data entry
`NAME`	Name of variable
`SIZE`	Width of text box in characters
`TYPE`	Checkbox, radio, reset, submit
`<SELECT...>`	Drop down menu
`NAME`	Name of variable
`SIZE`	Number of items of the list to display
`<OPTION VALUE>`	Return selected option to NAME variable
`</SELECT>`	Close select list

If any of your scripts do not work, your first port of call should be the error logs as they are explicit in any errors that are generated. If you are using apache the logs are usually located in `/etc/httpd/logs` or `/usr/local/apache/logs`, depending on where you installed the Web server on your system. Scripts can also be tested by running them from the command line. Of course you will only get text output, but the output will help you in your debugging.

Let's create a cgi script. Type the following into a file, call it `test.cgi`, and save it in your `cgi-bin` directory. Do not forget to give it permissions of 755.

```
$ pg firstpage.cgi
#!/bin/sh
# firstpage.cgi
# display a page with text
```

```
echo "Content-type: text/html"
echo ""
echo "<HTML>"
echo "<H1><CENTER> THIS IS MY FIRST CGI PAGE</CENTER></H1>"
echo "<HR>"
echo "<H2><CENTER>STAND-BY TO STAND-TO!</CENTER></H2>"
echo "</HTML>"
```

The first line, as you probably know by now, is where the shell interpreter is located. The first echo line tells the server this is a MIME header; the second echo line is a new line. The output of cgi scripts will not work unless there is a new line after the MIME header.

Next, we echo out a start <HTML> tag, which informs the browser that the whole document now being displayed is in HTML format. Different character fonts can be displayed, graded from largest <H1> downwards to <Hn>. Usually <H6> is accepted as the smallest size to view with ease on the eyes. We centre the text on the page, so it appears pleasant to the eye. Next, we display a horizontal line. We will now use <H2> as the font size and use the <CENTER> tag to center the following text on the page, 'Stand-By To Stand-To'. The last line encloses the <HTML> tag.

If you forget to close off any tags, do not worry – you will soon spot them, because the tags will be displayed in your browser window when you try to load the document.

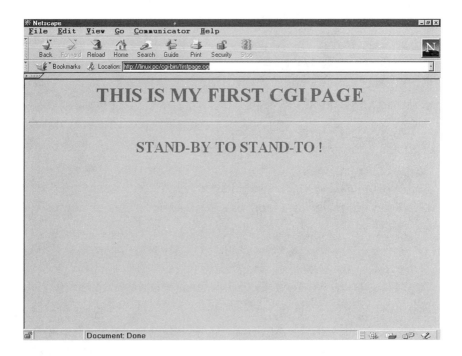

Figure 29.2 *Screenshot from the script* firstpage.cgi

Now to display the document, open up your URL window and type:

http://your_server/cgi-bin/firstpage.cgi

substituting `your_server` with your actual server name.

If you are networked and you get a 'DNS lookup failure' message, your browser is probably trying to look on the Internet for your page. Look at the connection tab on your browser; there should be an entry to bypass the proxy for local machines. Type in your server name and restart the browser.

Figure 29.2 shows how my page looks now.

29.4.2 Displaying the output of a shell command

Let's now put a shell command in the script so the output of the command is displayed in an HTML document.

We will see how many users are logged on. Using the `who` command we will filter it through the `wc` command to get the number of users. We will also print the date. Here's the script.

```
$ pg pagetwo.cgi
#!/bin/sh
# pagetwo.cgi
# display a page using the output from a unix command
MYDATE=`date +%A" "%d" "%B" "%Y`
USERS=`who |wc -l`
echo "Content-type: text/html"
echo ""
echo "<HTML>"
echo "<H1><CENTER> THIS IS MY SECOND CGI PAGE</CENTER></H1>"
echo "<HR>"
echo "<H2><CENTER>$MYDATE</CENTER></H2>"
echo " Total amount of users on to-day is :$USERS"
echo "<PRE>"
if [ "$USERS" -lt 10 ]; then
   echo  " It must be early or it is dinner time"
   echo  " because there ain't many users logged on"
fi
echo "</PRE>"
echo "</HTML>"
```

At the start of the script, we get the date and current connections. The date is echoed on to the centre of the page. The variable `USERS` is also displayed. A small if statement is used to determine if the number of users logged on is less than ten; if it is, type the message 'It must be early or it's dinner time'.

The tag <PRE> is used to preserve all formatting of white spaces and tabs. You should as a rule use <PRE> when you want to display the output of system

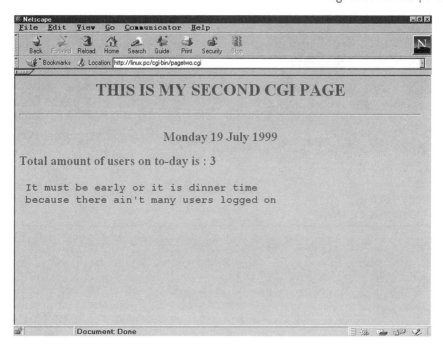

Figure 29.3 *Screenshot from the script* `pagetwo.cgi`

commands such as df or listings of files, or just several echo statements. I did not really need to use the <PRE> tag in this instance, but I thought I would introduce it at this early stage, in case you want to go off and do your own thing. To display the document, open up your URL window and type

    http://your_server/cgi-bin/pagetwo.cgi

substituting your_server with your actual server name.

    Figure 29.3 shows how my page looks now.

29.4.3 Using SSI

Using cgi scripts to open up a Web page to display a little information can sometimes be regarded as overdoing it a bit. For example, we displayed the date but we generated a cgi script to do that. Wouldn't it be great if we could embed a cgi script inside an HTML document so that the output of the script is displayed within a normal page? Well you can do this, and that's what we are going to do next.

    To embed cgi scripts into documents we have to enable Server Side Includes (SSI). When a document is displayed, it replaces the SSI command with the result of that command or script. Extra environment variables are also exported, containing additional information about your server and commands.

To enable SSI so that the server knows to look for SSI commands inside documents, you have to uncomment lines that have server-passed in the configuration files. In apache this is:

Addhandler server-passed.shtml
Addtype   text/htm   shtml

You will need to restart your server; use `kill -1` to make the server reread its config files. The documents that are going to have SSI in them need the file extension of `.shtml` instead of `.html`.

29.4.4 Access counter

Let's create a document that displays an access counter. You know the type: 'you are the nth vistor to this site'. We will also display the date when the page was last modified.

Don't forget to place this script in your cgi-bin directory; call it `hitcount.cgi`.

```
$ pg hitcount.cgi
#!/bin/sh
# hitcount.cgi
# hit page counter for html <cgi>
# counter file must be chmod 666
counter=../cgi-bin/counter
echo "Content-Type: text/html"
echo ""
read access < $counter
access=`expr $access + 1`
echo $access
echo $access >$counter
```

As you can see, the script reads the file `../cgi-bin/counter`, assigns the value that it reads to the variable access, adds one to it, then echos the result back into the file `/cgi-bin/counter`.

Let's now create a file called counter. All we need to do is put a start number in it; we will use 1. So create a file called counter and insert '1' (do not insert the quotes), then save and exit.

As everybody will need to use this file, the permissions need to be read and write for user, group and other.

```
$ chmod 666 counter
```

All that's left to do now is create the `.shml` file and place this file in your root Web directory, usually where all your other HTML documents are located, either in htdocs or html directory. Here's the file; do not forget to have an extension of `.shtml`:

```
$ pg main.shtml
<!- main.shtml>
<!- this is a comment line>
<HTML>
<H4> Last modified: <!--#echo var="LAST_MODIFIED" -->
</H4>
<HR>
<H1><CENTER> THE MAY DAY OPERATIONS CENTER </H1>
<H2>Stand-by to Stand-to
<HR>
This page has been visited <!--#exec cgi="/cgi-bin/hitcount.cgi"--> times
</CENTER>
</H2>
<HR>
</HTML>
```

The last modified variable as well as other variables are exported when using SSI. Check out the apache Web site (**www.apache.org**) for a full description of all the extra variables that are exported when you use SSI.

Looking at our SSI command:

This page has been visited < !--#exec cgi = "/cgi-bin/hitcount.cgi"-- > times

The general format is:

< !--# command argument = "value"-- >

In our case to run the cgi script hitcount:

The command is exec
The argument is cgi
The 'value' is the script name to be executed.

I've changed my configuration file so that this is the page that is displayed by default instead of index.html. You can still call the file by the full pathname though.

If you want to change your default page, edit the file srm.conf. There is an entry called:

DirectoryIndex

You will see that the filename index.html is located next to it. Change this filename to your new default page. Don't forget to close and re-start your Web server so that the changes can take effect.

To call the script, open your URL window and type:

http:// < server_name > /main.shtml

or

http:// < server_name >

if this is your default page.

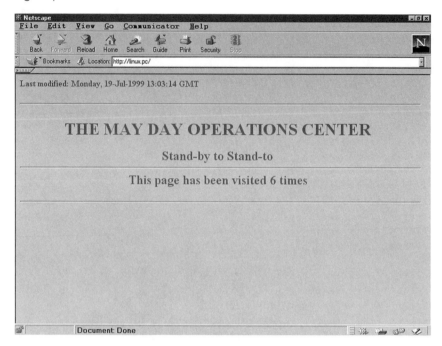

Figure 29.4 *HTML page with a simple page hit counter*

Figure 29.4 shows my page; just refresh the page to see the counter increase. Notice the LAST_MODIFIED variable is echoed.

You could of course reset the counter value each night by having a one-liner cron entry that echoes the number '1' to the file.

29.4.5 Printing out current Web environment settings using a link

When a cgi script is executed, a number of environment variables become available. You can use the env or set command to see most of the variables. Let's create a link from our main.shtml file to execute a script that displays these variables.

Here's the link entry we will use:

< A HREF = "/cgi-bin/printenv.cgi" > Environment < /A >

The A HREF marks the start of the link tag. The address or destination comes next surrounded by double quotes. The word 'Environment' is what will be displayed on the screen; this is what the user will 'click on' to send the form's contents. </A> marks the end of the link tag.

Here's how our `main.shtml` file looks now:

```
$ pg main.shtml

<HTML>
<! this is a comment line>
<! main.shtml>
<H4> Last modified: <!--#echo var="LAST_MODIFIED" -->
</H4>
<HR>
<CENTER>
<H1> THE MAY DAY OPERATIONS CENTER </H1>
<H2> Stand-by to Stand-to
<HR>
This page has been visited <!--#exec cgi="/cgi-bin/hitcount.cgi"--> times
<HR>
To see your environment settings just click
      <A HREF="/cgi-bin/printenv.cgi" >here</A>
</CENTER>
</H2>
<HR>
</HTML>
```

Here is the script called `printenv.cgi` that prints out the environment settings using the `env` command. We use the `<PRE>` tag to keep the tabs and white spaces intact.

```
$ pg printenv.cgi
#!/bin/sh
# printenv.cgi
# print out the Web server env using the command env settings,
echo "Content-type: text/html"
echo ""
echo "<HTML><PRE>"
env
echo "</PRE></HTML>"
```

Figure 29.5 shows how the page now looks with the link added.

When you click on the link, the environment settings appear (*see* Figure 29.6). Yours will be slightly different. As you run different scripts the settings will change to reflect the new environment.

29.4.6 Other common environment variables

Table 29.2 lists a collection of the most useful cgi environment variables. Some of these variables can be seen using the `env` or `set` commands.

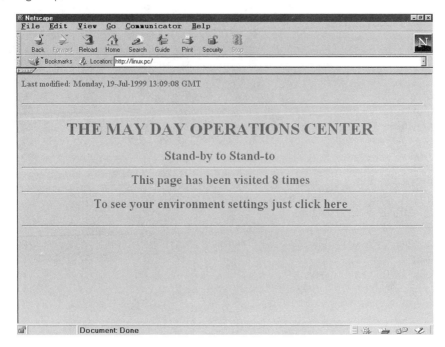

Figure 29.5 *A page with a link to see the environment variables*

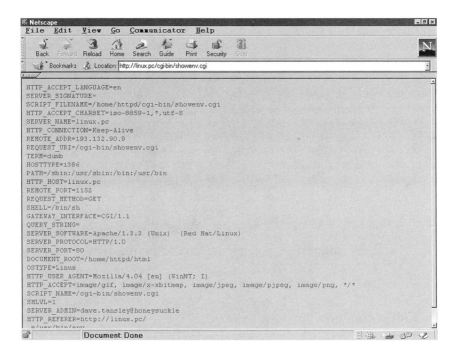

Figure 29.6 *A page displaying the current variables*

Table 29.2 *Common cgi Web server variables*

DOCUMENT ROOT	The main Web server directory, where the documents are loaded
GATEWAY_INTERFACE	The revision of cgi
HTTP_ACCEPT	The different MIME types accepted
HTTP_CONNECTION	The preferred HTTP connection
HTTP_HOST	The name of the local host machine
HTTP_USER_AGENT	The client browser
REMOTE_HOST	The remote host machine
REMOTE_ADDR*	The IP address of the remote host
REQUEST_METHOD	The method used to pass information
SCRIPT_FILENAME	The absolute pathname of the cgi script
SCRIPT_NAME	The relative pathname of the cgi script
SERVER_ADMIN	The email address of the Web administrator
SERVER_NAME	The server's hostname, DNS or IP address
SERVER_PROTOCOL	The protocol being used for the connection
SERVER_SOFTWARE	The Web server software name
QUERY_STRING	The passed data from the GET method
CONTENT_TYPE	The MIME type
CONTENT_LENGTH	The number of bytes passed using the post method

* Strictly speaking, this means the gateway address that you used to connect on to the Internet.

To display the variables you can put them in a little cgi script and call the script up as and when you need to check a variable value.

```
$ pg evncgi.cgi
#!/bin/sh
# envcgi.cgi
# print out the web server env
echo "Content-type: text/html"
echo ""
echo "<HTML><PRE>"
echo "CGI Test ENVIRONMENTS"
echo "SERVER_SOFTWARE = $SERVER_SOFTWARE"
echo "SERVER_NAME = $SERVER_NAME"
echo "GATEWAY_INTERFACE = $GATEWAY_INTERFACE"
echo "SERVER_PROTOCOL = $SERVER_PROTOCOL"
echo "SERVER_PORT = $SERVER_PORT"
echo "REQUEST_METHOD = $REQUEST_METHOD"
echo "HTTP_ACCEPT = $HTTP_ACCEPT"
```

```
echo "PATH_INFO = $PATH_INFO"
echo "PATH_TRANSLATED = $PATH_TRANSLATED"
echo "QUERY_STRING = $QUERY_STRING"
echo "SCRIPT_NAME = $SCRIPT_NAME"
echo "REMOTE_HOST = $REMOTE_HOST"
echo "REMOTE_ADDR = $REMOTE_ADDR"
echo "REMOTE_USER = $REMOTE_USER"
echo "AUTH_TYPE = $AUTH_TYPE"
echo "CONTENT_TYPE = $CONTENT_TYPE"
echo "CONTENT_LENGTH = $CONTENT_LENGTH"
echo "</PRE></HTML>"
```

29.5 Introducing the `get` and `post` methods

So far we have only displayed output to the screen. To be able to get information from the user we need to use forms, which is why cgi scripting has become so popular. You need the ability to process the user's input. With forms you can display text boxes, pull down menus and radio buttons.

Once the user has input or selected some information into the form, the user then clicks on `send` to send the information to a script, a cgi script in our case. How this information can be collected is where `get` and `post` come into play.

29.5.1 `get` method

The default action by any form is the `get` method. The `get` method is the one used to retrieve files from static HTML pages.

When a user clicks on `submit`, the information that was selected or chosen by the user is appended to the server's URL as an encoded string. The server's environment variable `QUERY_STRING` picks up this encoded string. The variable `REQUEST_METHOD` will also hold the form method used.

Creating a simple form

Let's create a simple form, creating a link from our `main.shtml` document to a script called `booka.cgi`.

Insert the following two lines after the last link entry we created in `main.shtml`:

```
<BR>
Basic form using GET method <A HREF="/cgi-bin/booka.cgi" >Form1</A>
```

Now type the following in and save it as `booka.cgi`; don't forget to put it in your `cgi-bin` directory.

```
$ pg booka.cgi
#!/bin/sh
# booka.cgi
echo "Content-type: text/html"
echo ""
echo "<HTML>"
echo "<BODY>"
# call booka_result.cgi, when user hits sent!
echo "<FORM action="/cgi-bin/booka_result.cgi" METHOD=GET>"


echo "<H4> CGI FORM</H4>"
# text box, input assigned to variable name 'contact'
echo "Your Name: <INPUT NAME=contact SIZE=30><BR><BR>"
# drop down menu selection assigned to variable name 'film'
echo "<SELECT NAME=film>"
echo "<OPTION>--  Pick a Film  --"
echo "<OPTION>A Few Good Men"
echo "<OPTION>Die Hard"
echo "<OPTION>Red October"
echo "<OPTION>The Sound Of Music"
echo "<OPTION>Boys In Company C"
echo "<OPTION>Star Wars"
echo "<OPTION>Star Trek"
echo "</SELECT>"
# drop down menu selection assigned to variable name 'actor'
echo "<SELECT NAME=actor>"
echo  "<OPTION>-- Pick Your Favourite Actor --"
echo "<OPTION>Bruce Willis"
echo "<OPTION>Basil Rathbone"
echo "<OPTION>Demi Moore"
echo "<OPTION>Lauren Bacall"
echo "<OPTION>Sean Connery"
echo "</SELECT>"
echo "<BR><BR>"
# check box variable names are 'view_cine' and 'view_vid'
echo "Do you watch films at the..<BR>"
echo "<INPUT TYPE="Checkbox" NAME=view_cine> Cinema"
echo "<INPUT TYPE="Checkbox" NAME=view_vid> On Video"
echo "<BR><BR>"
# input assigned to variable name 'textarea'
echo "Tell what is your best film, or just enter some comments<BR>"
echo "<TEXTAREA COLS="30" ROWS="4" NAME="textarea"></TEXTAREA>"


echo "<BR><INPUT TYPE=Submit VALUE="Send it">"
echo "<INPUT TYPE="reset" VALUE="Clear Form">"


echo "</FORM>"
echo "</BODY>"
echo "</HTML>"
```

The form action specifies that once the user hits 'Send it', the script `booka_result.cgi` is to be executed. We will use the `get` method.

The above form will display two text boxes, two pull down menus and a check box.

The text box for inputting your name is 30 characters long; the input will be assigned to the variable **contact**.

The first pull down menu lets you select your favourite film; the selected option is assigned to the variable **film**.

The second pull down menu lets you select your favourite actor; the selected option is assigned to the variable **actor**.

You select either or both of the check boxes by clicking on the required box. The ticked values are held in **view_cine** and **view_vid**. If the user ticks any of these check boxes, the variables will have the value 'on'.

The text box area lets you input more lines of text than a standard text box (30 columns with four rows of text, in our case), and all this information is assigned to variable **textarea**.

To send the data the word `submit` is used as an input type. To clear the form click on `clear`.

Type the following cgi script in and call it `booka_result.cgi` and save it in your `cgi-bin` directory.

```
$ pg booka_result.cgi
#!/bin/sh
# booka_result.cgi
# print out the web server env for a get
echo "Content-type: text/html"
echo ""
echo "<HTML><PRE>"
echo "<PRE>"
echo " Results from a GET form"
echo "REQUEST_METHOD : $REQUEST_METHOD"
echo "QUERY STRING   : $QUERY_STRING"
echo "</PRE></HTML>"
```

The above script displays a couple of cgi variables, the QUERY_STRING and REQUEST_METHOD. The QUERY_STRING will hold all data in an encoded string that was sent by the form that we just created with the script `booka.cgi`. The REQUEST_METHOD holds the type of method used, which will be `get`. Figure 29.7 shows how our form looks now, generated by the `booka.cgi` script.

Let's now enter some information and send it (*see* Figure 29.8). Clicking on 'Send it' displays the page shown in Figure 29.9. The contents of the QUERY_STRING can only be partly seen, due to the length of the string. Here's the full string below:

```
contact=David+Tansley&film=The+Sound+Of+Music&actor=Bruce+
Willis&view_cine=on&view_vid=on&textarea=%21%22%A3%A3%24%25
%24%25%5E*%5E%26*%28%29*%28%29%28*%0D%0A
How%27s+that+%21%21
```

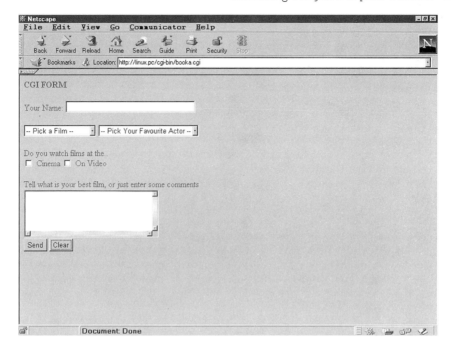

Figure 29.7 *A cgi form using the* get *method*

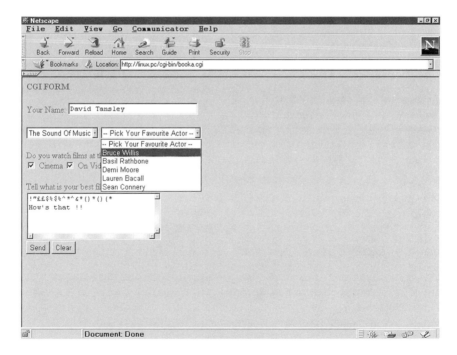

Figure 29.8 *Selecting and entering information into the form*

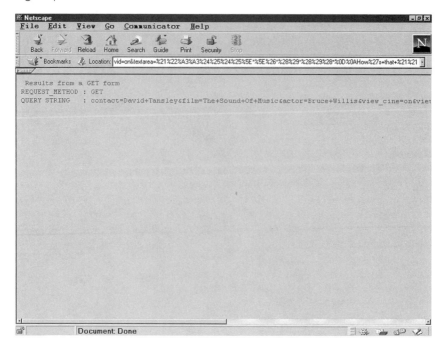

Figure 29.9 *The information sent by the form is now encoded*

From the information we sent we know we should have the following fields within the QUERY_STRING shown above:

Variable	Variable value
contact	David Tansley
film	The Sound Of Music
actor	Bruce Willis
view_cine	checked which means we have the value 'on'
view_vid	checked which means we have the value 'on'
textarea	!"££$%$%^*^&*()*()(*
	How's that !!

Decoding an encoded string

When the user clicks on 'submit' the information is assigned to the variable QUERY_STRING, and the string gets encoded in the following way:

All spaces are replaced by +

All value fields are separated by &

All values and their corresponding fields are separated by =

All symbols and some special characters are represented by %xy, where xy is the hexadecimal number of that character. Looking at our QUERY_STRING we have a lot of those in the textarea variable.

The cgi protocol states that any characters that are in the form of %xy (where xy is a hex number) should be converted to their ASCII character equivalent. These hex characters consist of the special characters &, %, +, =, (,) and all other symbols above the ASCII decimal range of 127. For instance the character (would be %29.

Hex characters are generated when the user enters these symbols or characters in free form text boxes. However, they can also be part of a menu text selection.

To break down the encoded string we now have to:

change all occurrences of & to line feeds
change all occurrences of + to spaces
change all occurrences of = to spaces
convert all %xy values to their ASCII character equivalents.

Once we have done all that, we need to be able to query or access each variable, so we can do something with the information sent. Decoding is only half the job, albeit the most task-intensive part. To be able to access the variables we can use the eval command.

The following script will carry out all the conversions needed and be able to access the variables. The script is heavily commented so you can understand what is happening.

```
$ pg conv.cgi
#!/bin/sh
# conv.cgi
# decode URL string
echo "Content-type: text/html"
echo ""
echo "<HTML><PRE>"
# display the method and the coded string
echo "Method       : $REQUEST_METHOD"
echo "Query String : $QUERY_STRING"
echo "<HR>"
# use sed to replace all & with tabs
LINE=`echo $QUERY_STRING | sed 's/&/      /g'`

for LOOP in $LINE
do
   # split the fields up into NAME and TYPE
   NAME=`echo $LOOP | sed 's/=/ /g' | awk '{print $1}'`
   # get the TYPE now replace all = with spaces and %hex_num with  \xhex_num
   # replace all + with spaces
```

```
    TYPE=`echo $LOOP | sed 's/=/ /g' | awk '{print $2}' | \
    sed -e 's/%\(\)/\\\x/g' | sed 's/+/ /g'`
    # use printf it does all the hex conv for you, display the variables
      printf "${NAME}=${TYPE}\n"
      # now assign the fields across to VAR ready to eval them, so
      # we can then address individual fields, double backslash needed
      # in case the fields have spaces in them
      VARS=`printf "${NAME}=\\${TYPE}\n"`
    eval `printf $VARS`
  done
  echo "<HR>"
  # keep using printf to preserve special chars...if any
  printf "Your name is                  : $contact\n"
  printf "Your choice of film is:       : $film\n"
  printf "Your choice of actor is       : $actor\n"
  printf "You watch films at the cinema : $view_cine\n"
  printf "You watch films on  video     : $view_vid\n"
  printf "And here are your comments     : $textarea\n"
  echo "</PRE>"
  echo "</HTML>"
```

You notice we are using printf to do the echoing – the reason for this is simple. Printf can do the same as the normal echo, but it can also do all the hex conversions for us. One note of caution here – when you use printf, it does not put a new line feed on for you; you have to do that so remember to use '\n' after every printf. The hex numbers held in the QUERY_STRING are in the form %hex_num; we simply convert them into the form \xhex_num using sed, and printf will then do all the conversion for us. Why make tasks harder for yourself when they can be solved in a simple way?

Save the above script as conv.cgi in your cgi-bin directory. Now all we need to do is to make a small amendment in the script booka.cgi so that the form calls conv.cgi instead of booka_result.cgi. Here's how the line should look now.

< FORM action = "/cgi-bin/conv.cgi" METHOD = GET >

If we now resubmit the form so that it executes conv.cgi (with the same information) we get the results shown in Figure 29.10.

Now we have the string in a more readable format, you can now do some processing with the information.

The get method is the default method to use with forms. Depending on your environment circumstances, there are two potential problems using the get method. The entire encoded string is appended to your URL when you send information, so information you send can be seen from your URL window. Though you might think this is not a big deal, it is if you are sending company or private information across the Web or network.

If you have a form with many input fields, the QUERY_STRING can become very long. Most people who use cgi use the post method for their forms. That's what we will look at next.

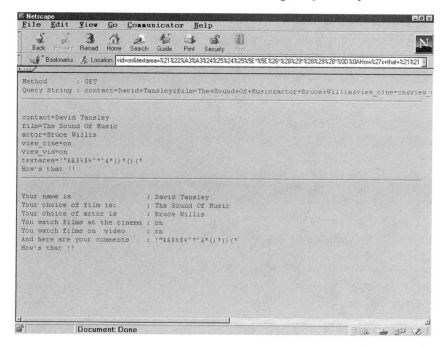

Figure 29.10 *The data in the form is fully decoded*

29.5.2 post method

The post method is the same as the get method with regards to how the string is encoded. The difference is how the post method gets the data; it reads it in from standard input. To send data using the post method, simply replace the get with post in the FORM action statement of your script.

> **< FORM action = "/cgi-bin/conv.cgi" METHOD = POST >**

The variable CONTENT_LENGTH will hold the total bytes sent when using the post method. We read in the string from standard input, and do the same conversion as we did with the get method. The read stops after the amount of bytes equal the amount contained in CONTENT_LENGTH.

All we need to do is to make a small change to the form action statement then we will have a generic form decoder. To read from standard input we can use the cat command. Here's the statement we need to add to our script conv.cgi, so it can handle both get and post methods.

> **if ["$REQUEST_METHOD" = "POST"]; then**
>   **QUERY_STRING = `cat -`**
> fi

Notice the hyphen in the cat command, this allows cat to read from standard input.

We simply test the QUERY_STRING – if it's a post method then we cat all the characters incoming on standard input into the variable QUERY_STRING. If the method is get then that's OK because we need to get that information from the QUERY_STRING anyway.

Amend the cgi script booka.cgi FORM action line from this:

< FORM action = "/cgi-bin/conv.cgi" METHOD = GET >

to this:

< FORM action = "/cgi-bin/conv.cgi" METHOD = POST >

We will also make some small amendments to the conv.cgi script, so we can test the values entered in the text and check boxes. Here is the newly amended script.

```
$ pg conv.cgi
#!/bin/sh
# conv.cgi
# decode URL string
echo "Content-type: text/html"
echo ""
echo "<HTML><PRE>"
# is it post ???
if [ "$REQUEST_METHOD" = "POST" ]; then
  QUERY_STRING=`cat -`
fi

# display the method and the coded string
echo "Method: $REQUEST_METHOD"
echo "Query String : $QUERY_STRING"
echo "<HR>"
# use sed to replace & with tab
LINE=`echo $QUERY_STRING | sed 's/&/    /g'`

for LOOP in $LINE
do
  NAME=`echo $LOOP | sed 's/=/ /g' | awk '{print $1}'`
  TYPE=`echo $LOOP | sed 's/=/ /g' | awk '{print $2}' | \
  sed -e 's/%\(\)/\\\x/g' | sed 's/+/ /g'`
  # use printf it does all the hex conv for you
    printf "${NAME}=${TYPE}\n"
    VARS=`printf "${NAME}=\\${TYPE}\n"`
  eval `printf $VARS`
done
echo "<HR>"
if [ "$contact" != "" ]; then
  printf "Hello $contact, it's great to meet you\n"
```

```
else
  printf "You did not give me your name ... no comment!\n"
fi

if [ "$film" != "-- Pick a Film --" ]; then
  printf "Hey I agree, $film is great film\n"
else
  printf "You didn't pick a film\n"
fi
if [ "$actor" != "-- Pick Your Favourite Actor --" ]; then
  printf "So you like the actor $actor, good call\n"
else
  printf "You didn't pick a actor from the menu\n"
fi
if [ "$view_cine" = "on" ]; then
  printf "Yes, I agree the cinema is still the best place to watch a
          film\n"
else
  printf "So you don't go to the cinema, do you know what you're missing\n"
fi

if [ "$view_vid" = "on" ]; then
  printf "I like watching videos at home as well\n"
else
  printf "No video!!, you're missing out on all the classics to rent or
          buy\n"
fi

if [ "$textarea" != "" ]; then
  printf " And here are your comments.....OK    $textarea\n"
else
  printf "No comments entered, so no comment !\n"
fi
echo "</PRE>"
echo "</HTML>"
```

Notice I have used `printf` throughout; I could have used some `echo` statements instead when I was not accessing the variables, but keeping `printf` makes the script clearer.

Load up the form and test it by sending some data across using the post method:

http:// < server_name > /cgi-bin/booka.cgi

Figure 29.11 shows the information I have entered on my Web page.

Now that some information has been entered, click on 'Send' – the results are shown in Figure 29.12.

The script now queries the different variables to see if information has been entered. You could then do further processing by making sure all fields have values,

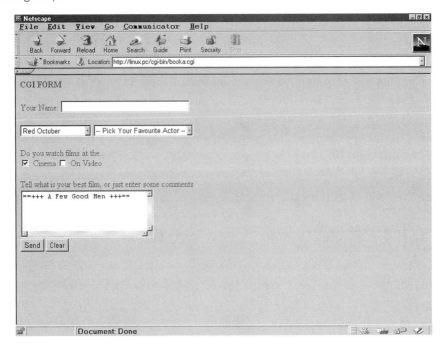

Figure 29.11 *A cgi form using the* post *method*

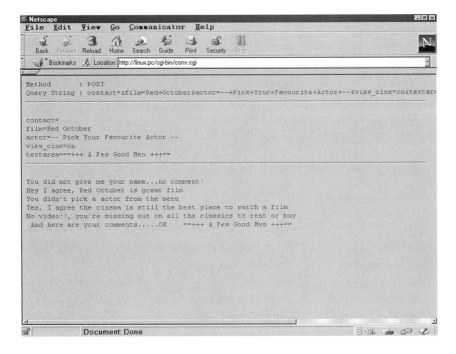

Figure 29.12 *The form's data is now fully decoded using the* post *method*

and if not then return the form to the user and ask the user to re-enter the information. Once you have a properly filled-in form, you could then append it to a file creating a mini-database.

A more useful cgi script

We will now create a script that actually does some useful processing (depending on your view). We will create a report for a fictitious company called Wonder Gifts.

An accounts file holds the number of items sold for each quarter of the year 1998. The file holds the items for the following departments: Stationery, Books and Gifts.

Our task is to generate a report based on the user's selection. The user can select by quarter, or by department. The processing required is to add together all the monthly items sold in that quarter. The output can go to the screen, printer or both.

Our form will have two drop-down menus, one for the quarter period and one for the department. A radio box will hold where the output is to go. Using radio boxes, the user can only select one button. Actually the report will only go to the screen; the radio buttons are for demonstration purposes only.

Here's the data file holding the quarter periods of items sold. The fields are as follows:

Department : Year : Quarter : Items sold in the months 1 to 3 for period1, and so on, for all four periods.

```
$ pg qtr_1998.txt
STAT        1998        1st        7998    4000    2344    2344
BOOKS       1998        1st        3590    1589    2435     989
GIFTS       1998        1st        2332    1489    2344     846
STAT        1998        2nd        8790    4399    4345     679
BOOKS       1998        2nd         889     430    2452     785
GIFTS       1998        2nd        9822    4822    3555     578
STAT        1998        3rd        8911    4589    2344    8690
BOOKS       1998        3rd         333    1489    6322     889
GIFTS       1998        3rd        2310    1483    3443     778
STAT        1998        4th        9883    5199    2344    6456
BOOKS       1998        4th        7333    3892    5223     887
GIFTS       1998        4th        8323    4193    2342     980
```

Here is the form script.

```
$ pg gifts.cgi
#!/bin/sh
# gifts.cgi .... using POST
echo "Content-type: text/html"
echo ""
echo "<HTML>"
echo "<BODY>"
# gifts_result.cgi is going to process the output from this form
echo "<FORM action="/cgi-bin/gifts_result.cgi" METHOD=POST>"
```

```
echo "<P>"
echo "<HR>"
echo "<H1><CENTER>GIFTS Inc <BR>"
echo "QUARTERLY REPORT</H1></CENTER>"
echo "</P><HR>"
echo "Department: <SELECT NAME=dept>"
echo "<OPTION>GIFTS"
echo "<OPTION>STATIONERY"
echo "<OPTION>BOOKS"
echo "</SELECT>"
echo "Quarter End:<SELECT NAME=qtr>"
echo "<OPTION>1st"
echo "<OPTION>2nd"
echo "<OPTION>3rd"
echo "<OPTION>4th"
echo "</SELECT>"
echo "<BR><BR>"
echo "Report To Go To:<BR>"
echo "<INPUT TYPE="radio" NAME= stdout VALUE=Printer >Printer"
echo "<INPUT TYPE="radio" NAME= stdout VALUE=Screen CHECKED>Screen"
echo "<INPUT TYPE="radio" NAME= stdout VALUE=Both >Both"
echo "<BR><BR><HR>"
echo "<INPUT TYPE=Submit VALUE="Send it">"
echo "<INPUT TYPE=Reset VALUE="Clear">"


echo "</FORM>"
echo "</BODY>"
echo "</HTML>"
```

The variable dept will hold the selected value for the department; the variable qtr will hold the value for the selected quarter. The variable stdout will hold 'printer', 'screen', or 'both'; the default is screen (this is specified using the word 'CHECKED'). Here's the script that will process the information received.

```
$ pg gifts_result.cgi
#!/bin/sh
# gifts_result.cgi
# decode URL string
echo "Content-type: text/html"
echo ""
echo "<HTML><PRE>"
# is it post ???
if [ "$REQUEST_METHOD" = "POST" ]; then
  QUERY_STRING=`cat -`
fi
# decode it
# use sed to replace & with tab
LINE=`echo $QUERY_STRING | sed 's/&/    /g'`
```

```
for LOOP in $LINE
do
  NAME=`echo $LOOP | sed 's/=/ /g' | awk '{print $1}'`
  TYPE=`echo $LOOP | sed 's/=/ /g' | awk '{print $2}' | \
  sed -e 's/%\(\)/\\\x/g' | sed 's/+/ /g'`
  # use printf it does all the hex conv for you
    VARS=`printf "${NAME}=\\${TYPE}\n"`
  eval `printf $VARS`
done
echo "<HR>"
echo "<H1><CENTER> GIFTS Inc</CENTER></H1>"
echo "<H2><CENTER> Quarter End Results </CENTER></H2>"
echo "<HR>"
# we need to change the fields name from STATIONERY to STAT to
# search properly
if [ "$dept" = "STATIONERY" ];then
  dept=STAT
fi


# Read in the file qtr_1995.txt
TOTAL=0
while read DEPT YEAR Q P1 P2 P3 P4
do
  if [ "$DEPT" = "$dept" -a "$Q" = "$qtr" ]; then
    TOTAL=`expr $P1 + $P2 + $P3 + $P4`
  fi
  continue
done </home/httpd/cgi-bin/qtr_1995.txt
echo "<H2>"
echo " TOTAL ITEMS SOLD IN THE $dept DEPARTMENT"
echo " IS $TOTAL IN THE $qtr QUARTER"
echo "</H2><HR>"
# where is the report going..
if [ "$stdout" = "Both" ]; then
  echo "This report is going to the printer and the screen"
else
  echo " This report is going to the $stdout"
fi
echo "</PRE>"
echo "</HTML>"
```

The first part of the script is really going to be much the same for any post form processing script. As we do not have any hex values to convert (because the input fields are all predefined menu options), we need not use printf, but there is nothing to stop you from using this command. The interesting part as far as this script is concerned is the reading in of the qtr_1995.txt file.

The while loop reads in and assigns all the fields to DEPT YEAR Q P1 P2 P3 P4 respectively. A test is then carried out against the $dept (value sent by the user) and the variable DEPT; this result is ANDed with the result of the other test. If the

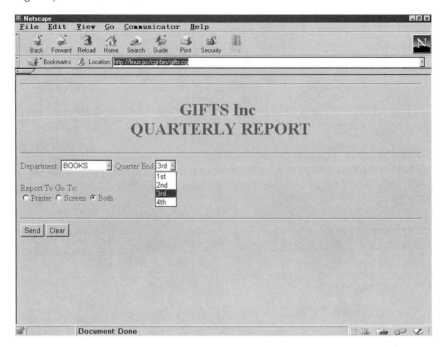

Figure 29.13 *Selecting quarter end information for further processing*

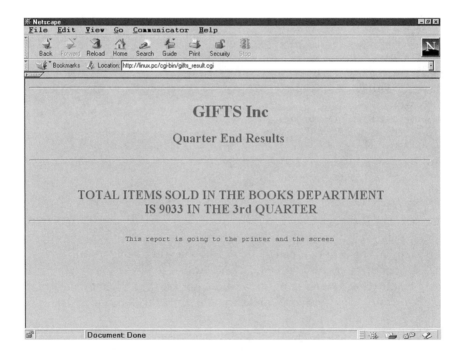

Figure 29.14 *Processing done, here's the output*

variable $qtr (value sent by user) is equal to the variable Q then we have a match. All numbers contained in this matched line are then added together.

Now that we have the form script and the script to process the information that the form sends, let's run it. Open up your URL window (or create another link in your main page) and type:

http:// < server_name > /cgi-bin/gifts.cgi

The results are shown in Figure 29.13.

The script processes the information that has been selected by the user producing the output shown in Figure 29.14.

29.5.3 Populating a list

For your HTML pages to be really dynamic, you will probably want to populate your lists or tables with current information from an existing file, instead of hard coding them in your cgi scripts.

In the following script, a pull down list is populated with information from a text file called list, which is situated in the temp directory, off the root wed server. A while loop is used to read in the contents (one line at a time) from the file to populate the list options. The code assignment to populate is:

echo " < OPTION > $LINE"

The selected option is assigned to the variable menu_selection.

Here's the script that will populate a menu, no form action is specified.

```
$ pg populat.cgi
#!/bin/sh
# populat.cgi
# populate a pull down list from a text file
echo "Content-type: text/html"
echo ""
echo "<HTML>"
echo "<BODY>"
echo "<H4> CGI FORM....populat.cgi..populate pull-down list from a text
    file</H4>"
echo "<SELECT NAME=menu_selection>"
echo "<OPTION>-- PICK AN OPTION --"
# read in the file into the list to populate the options
while read LINE
do
   echo "<OPTION>$LINE"
done < ../temp/list
echo "</SELECT>"
echo "</FORM>"
echo "</BODY>"
echo "</HTML>"
```

29.5.4 Automatically refreshing a Web page

When using cgi for monitoring or watchdog type tasks, it is sometimes more convenient to have your page continuously refreshed. To do this you call your own script or page. Here is a command that will refresh the script dfspace.cgi every 60 seconds.

> **< meta http-equiv = "Refresh" content = "60;URL = http:/linux.pc/cgi-bin/ dfspace.cgi" > "**

The keyword word here is Refresh. This lets the Web server know that this page is to be reloaded, and 'content = 60' is the number of seconds between each reload. To refresh your own script simply add your script name as part of the URL address.

I have quite a few monitoring scripts that poll all the major hosts on the network. I can tell at a glance if a host is up or down. To make it even prettier I use green and red balls, instead of displaying on and off in text.

Below is a script that uses part of the df output, and displays the file system and capacity fields in a table.

The following segment code is just a table header to put the table headings in. When using tables with raw output it really is a case of hit and miss until you get the desired table effect.

```
echo "<TABLE align="center" cellspacing="20" border=9 width="40%"
    cols="2">"
echo "<TH align="center">- Capacity % -</TH>"
echo "<TH align="center">- File System -</TH>"
```

Cellspacing sets the distance between the inner and outer borders of the table. Border holds a number that controls the thickness of the table border. Cols determines how many columns there are going to be in the table.

Here's the meat of the script.

```
df |sed 1d| awk '{print $5"\t"$6}' | while read percent mount
do
  echo "<TR><TD align="center"><B>$percent</B></TD><TD align="center">
      $mount</TH>
  </TR>"
done
```

Using df we pipe through sed to delete the heading, then pipe through to awk and read in the fifth and sixth columns, assigning the output to the variables percent and mount.

TR stands for table row and TD stands for table data. This is where the items of information go.

Here's the script. Admittedly 60 seconds is overdoing it a bit to monitor file systems, but if you are doing massive file migrations across file systems, it can keep you informed right up to the minute!

Here's the script.

```
$ pg dfspace.cgi
#!/bin/sh
# dfspace.cgi
echo "Content-type: text/html"
echo ""
# auto refresh every 60 secs
echo "<meta http-equiv="Refresh" content="60;URL=http:/linux.pc/cgi-bin/
dfspace.cgi">"
echo "<HTML>"
echo "<HR>"
echo "<A NAME="LINUX.PC Filesystems">LINUX.PC Filesystems</A>"

echo "<TABLE align="center" cellspacing="20" border=9 width="40%"
      cols="2">"
echo "<TH align="center">- Capacity % -</TH>"
echo "<TH align="center">- File System -</TH>"
# get the output from df, but first filter what we only need!
df |sed 1d| awk '{print $5"\t"$6}' | while read percent mount
```

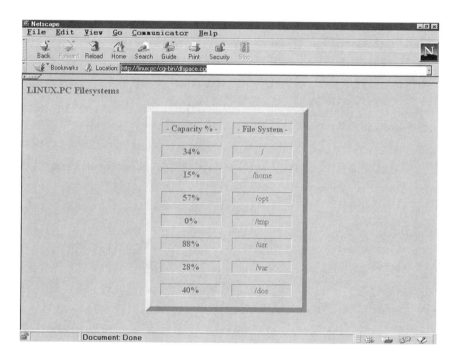

Figure 29.15 *Using output from the* df *command to generate tables*

```
do
    echo "<TR><TD align="center"><B>$percent</B></TD><TD align="center">
        $mount</TH>
    </TR>"
done
echo "</TABLE>"
echo "</HTML>"
```

Opening up the browser window gives me the output shown in Figure 29.15 – yours will most certainly be different.

http:// < server_name > /cgi-bin/dfspace.cgi

29.6 Conclusion

Creating cgi scripts enables you to create a much more interesting user interface. HTML pages could be the front end to all the common processing tasks that you run.

Scripts can be generated to carry out monitoring, front-ends, database queries, etc. HTML is now one of the standards for documentation that is shipped with application software.

APPENDIX A

ASCII chart

Character	Dec	Hex	Oct
Ctrl-@ (NUL)	0	00	000
Ctrl-A	1	01	001
Ctrl-B	2	02	002
Ctrl-C	3	03	003
Ctrl-D (EOT)	4	04	004
Ctrl-E	5	05	005
Crtl-F	6	06	006
Ctrl-G (BEL)	7	07	007
Ctrl-H (BS)	8	08	010
Ctrl-I (TAB)	9	09	011
Ctrl-J (NL)	10	0A	012
Ctrl-K	11	0B	013
Ctrl-L (FF)	12	0C	014
Ctrl-M (CR)	13	0D	015
Ctrl-N	14	0E	016
Ctrl-O	15	0F	017
Ctrl-P	16	10	020
Ctrl-Q	17	11	021
Ctrl-R	18	12	022
Ctrl-S	19	13	023
Ctrl-T	20	14	024
Ctrl-U	21	15	025
Ctrl-V	22	16	026
Ctrl-W	23	17	027
Ctrl-X	24	18	030
Ctrl-Y	25	19	031
Ctrl-Z	26	1A	032
Ctrl-[(ESC)	27	1B	033

Character	Dec	Hex	Oct
Ctrl-\	28	1C	034
Ctrl-]	29	1D	035
Ctrl-^	30	1E	036
Ctrl-_	31	1F	037
Space	32	20	040
!	33	21	041
"	34	22	042
#	35	23	043
$	36	24	044
%	37	25	045
&	38	26	046
'	39	27	047
(	40	28	050
)	41	29	051
*	42	2A	052
+	43	2B	053
,	44	2C	054
-	45	2D	055
.	46	2E	056
/	47	2F	057
0	48	30	060
1	49	31	061
2	50	32	062
3	51	33	063
4	52	34	064
5	53	35	065
6	54	36	066
7	55	37	067
8	56	38	070
9	57	39	071
:	58	3A	072
;	59	3B	073
<	60	3C	074
=	61	3D	075
>	62	3E	076
?	63	3F	077
@	64	40	100
A	65	41	101
B	66	42	102
C	67	43	103
D	68	44	104
E	69	45	105
F	70	46	106
G	71	47	107

Character	Dec	Hex	Oct
H	72	48	110
I	73	49	111
J	74	4A	112
K	75	4B	113
L	76	4C	114
M	77	4D	115
N	78	4E	116
O	79	4F	117
P	80	50	120
Q	81	51	121
R	82	52	122
S	83	53	123
T	84	54	124
U	85	55	125
V	86	56	126
W	87	57	127
X	88	58	130
Y	89	59	131
Z	90	5A	132
[	91	5B	133
\	92	5C	134
]	93	5D	135
^	94	5E	136
–	95	5F	137
`	96	60	140
a	97	61	141
b	98	62	142
c	99	63	143
d	100	64	144
e	101	65	145
f	102	66	146
g	103	67	147
h	104	68	150
i	105	69	151
j	106	6A	152
k	107	6B	153
l	108	6C	154
m	109	6D	155
n	110	6E	156
o	111	6F	157
p	112	70	160
q	113	71	161
r	114	72	162
s	115	73	163

Character	Dec	Hex	Oct
t	116	74	164
u	117	75	165
v	118	76	166
w	119	77	167
x	120	78	170
y	121	79	171
z	122	7A	172
{	123	7B	173
|	124	7C	174
}	125	7D	175
~	126	7E	176
Ctrl-?(DEL)	127	7F	177

APPENDIX B

Useful shell commands

This appendix lists and describes some useful shell commands. The options in the commands are not exhaustive, but should be enough for you to understand what the command does.

You may find further examples of these commands scattered throughout the book.

basename

Format:

basename path

Basename will strip the path from a supplied pathname and return just the filename. Commonly used in usage statements in scripts, in this case substitution is used when echoing out the filename.

```
$ basename /home/dave/myscript
myscript
```

echo "Usage: `basename $0` give me a file "
exit 1
...

If the above was part of a script called `myscript`, the output would be,

```
myscript: give me a file
```

The `$0` is a special variable that holds the current full pathname of the script.

`cat`

Format:

Cat options files

Option:

-v   to display control characters.

Cat is the most used file pager for text files.

```
$ cat myfile
```

Display the file myfile

```
$ cat myfile myfile2 >>hold_file
```

The above will combine two files (myfile and myfile2) into one file called hold_file.

```
cat dt1 | while read line
do
  echo $line
done
```

Cat is also used to read files in your scripts.

`compress`

Format:

Compress options files

Option:

-v   print results of compression

Compress is used to reduce the size of files. Once compressed the file is given the extension .Z. Use uncompress to restore them to their original state.

```
$ compress myfile
$ ls myfile*
myfile.Z
```

cp

Format:

```
cp options file1 file2
```

Options:

- -i   Prompt for confirmation for overwriting files
- -p   Preserve the permission modes and modification times
- -r   Recursively copy a directory

To copy the file `myfile` to `myfile1.bak`

```
$ cp myfile 1 myfile1.bak
```

To copy the file `get.prd` from `/usr/local/sybin` to `/usr/local/bin`

```
$ pwd
usr/local/sybin
$ cp get.prd../bin
```

To recursively copy all files and directories from `/logs` (downwards) to `/hold/logs`

```
$ cp -r /logs/ /hold/logs
```

diff

Format:

```
diff options file1 file2
```

Options:

- -c   Produce a different output from the standard format (*see below*)
- -I   Ignore character cases

Using the files file1 and file2 from our `comm` example, `diff` will output lines that are different between two files.

```
$ diff file1 file2
2,3c2,3
< The game
< Boys in company C
---
> The games
> The boys in company C
```

`Diff` has reported that lines 2 and 3 are different, with the second column in line 3 not matching.

dircmp

Format:

```
dircmp options directory1 directory2
```

Option:

-s   Do not display files that are different

Dircmp is very similar to diff – it will compare and then output the differences between two directories.

dirname

Format:

```
dirname pathname
```

The opposite of basename, dirname prints the pathname only:

```
$ dirname /home/dave/myfile
/home/dave
```

du

Format:

```
du options directory
```

Options:

-a   Display sizes for every file, not only directories
-s   Display the grand total only

Du prints the disk usage in 512 blocks. It is used mainly to print out the sizes of directories.

```
$ pwd
/var
$ du -s
14929    .
```

The size of the /var directory structure is 14929 (512) blocks.

file

Format:

file filename

This lets the shell determine the type of file.

```
$ file core
core: ELF 32-bit LSB core file of 'awk' (signal 6), Intel 80386,
version 1

$ file data.f
data.f: ASCII text

$ file month_end.sh
month_end.sh: Bourne shell script text
```

fuser

Format:

fuser options file

Options:

-k   kill all processes on file or file system
-u   show all processes on file or file system

The fuser command is used to show processes that are running on a file system or files that are being accessed. Some systems use -u and -m interchangeably. You can use the if command statement with the fuser command.

To list processes active on the device /dev/hda5:

```
$ fuser -m /dev/hda5
/dev/hda5: 1    1r     1c      1e     37     37r     37c     37e    144
    144r    144c    144e    158    158r    158c    158e    167r    167c
167e    178    17 8r    178c    178e    189    189r    189c
```

To kill all processes on the device /dev/hda5:

```
$ fuser -k /dev/hda5
```

To see if the file doc_part is open and what processes are running on it:

```
$ fuser -m /root/doc_part
/root/dt: 1  1r     1c      1e     37     37r     37c     37e    144
  144r    144c    144e    158    158r    158c    158e    167r    167c
167e    178    178r    178c    178e    189    189r    189c    189e    201
201r    201c    201e    212  212r    212c    212e    223    223r
```

Some `fuser` commands report the login IDs as part of the listing. If yours does not, use the numbers that have an 'e' on the end and `grep` this number through `ps xa` or `ps -ef`.

head

Format:

head -number files

`Head` is used to display the first ten lines of a file. To display less or more lines use the `-number` option. For example,

```
$ head -1 myfile
```

will display the first line of the file only, and

```
$ head -30 logfile |more
```

displays the first 30 lines of the file `logfile`.

logname

Format:

logname

This will display your current login name:

```
$ logname
dave
```

mkdir

Format:

mkdir options directory

Option:

    -m   set access when creating the directory

```
$ mkdir HOLD_AREA
$ ls -l HOLD*
-rw-rw-r--  1 dave   admin    3463 Dec 3 1998 HOLD_AREA
```

will create a directory called HOLD_AREA.

more
___

Format:

more options files

This command has the same functionality as page and pg, i.e. page the contents a screen at a time.

Options:

-c   Do not scroll text but page through instead
-d   Display a prompt message when paging a file
-n   Display n lines only instead of a full screen

```
$ more /etc/passwd
```

displays the passwd file.

```
$ cat logfile |more
```

displays the file logfile.

nl
___

Format:

nl options file

Options:

-I   Increment each line number by n; the default is 1
-p   Do not reset the numbering when a new page is met

nl is used to number a file, and is useful for printing out source code or log file listings.

```
$ nl myscript
```

will number the file myscript, and

```
$ nl myscript >hold_file
```

redirects the output of nl to the file hold_file, while

```
$ nl myscript |lpr
```

redirects the output of nl to the printer.

printf

Format:

printf format arguments

This command prints formatted text to the standard output, and is similar to awk's printf function.

Format:
Format can contain three different types of items; we will only look at formatting. The sequence to format is:

%[- +]m.nx

where the hyphen will left-justify a field. Generally speaking the m is used to represent the length of a field and n is the maximum length of the field.
The % sign is preceded with any of the following to format characters:

s	string
c	character
d	decimal
x	hexadecimal number
o	octal number

Printf by itself does not generate a new line; you have to use the escape sequence for that. Here is a list of the most common escape sequences.

\a	sound the bell
\b	backspace
\r	carriage return
\f	form feed
\n	new line
\t	tab

```
$ printf "Howzat!\n"
Howzat!
```

prints a string to standard output; use '\n' to force a new line, while

```
$ printf "\x2B\n"
+
```

converts the hex number 2B to its decimal ASCII character, which is a '+'.

```
$ printf "%-10sStand-by\n"
          Stand-by
```

prints a string left justified, starting 10 characters out from the left margin.

pwd

Format:

pwd

To display the current working directory, type:

```
$ pwd
/var/spool

$ WHERE_AM_I=`pwd`
$ echo $WHERE_AM_I
/var/spool
```

Substitution is used to grab the current working directory in a script.

rm

Format:

rm options files

Options:

-I   Prompt before each file is deleted (safe mode)
-r   Remove a directory if it exists

rm will delete files and/or directories.

```
$ rm myfile
$ rm -r /var/spool/tmp
```

will delete all files including directories from /var/spool/tmp and below.

rmdir

Format:

rmdir options directories

Option:

-p   Delete all empty directories that are found in the deletion process

```
$ rmdir /var/spool/tmp/lp_HP
```

will remove the directory lp_HP located in /var/spool/tmp.

script

Format:

script option file

Option:

-a   Append the output to a file

You can create a complete history of your session by using `script`. Simply invoke it at the command line. Script will terminate when you exit your session. Script copies what you type and appends it to a file.

`$ script mylogin`

will start the `script` session and log everything to the file `mylogin`.

shutdown

Format:

shutdown

This will shut down the system. Many vendors have their own specific command variation.

`$ shutdown now`

will shut down the system now, and

`$ shutdown -g60 -I6 -y`

will shut down the system in 60 seconds, then reboot the system.

sleep

Format:

sleep number

This command makes the system wait a specified number of seconds. For example,

`$ sleep 10`

means the system will do nothing for 10 seconds.

strings

Format:

strings filename

Strings can be used to view text contained in binary files.

touch

Format:

touch options filename

Option:

-t MMDDhhmm   Create a file with a month, day, hour, minute, date stamp

This creates a file with a current or new date stamp.

```
$ touch myfile
$ ls -l myfile
-rw-r--r--   1 dave      admin               0 Jun 30 09:59 myfile
```

The above creates a new empty file with today's date/time called myfile.

```
$ touch -t 06100930 myfile2
$ ls -l myfile2
-rw-r--r--   1 dave      admin               0 Jun 10 09:30 myfile2
```

The above creates a new empty file called myfile2 with the date stamp of June 10 at 09:30am.

tty

Format:

tty

Use tty to report what device or terminal you are connected to.

```
$ tty
/dev/tty08
```

Use **tty -s** to determine if your script is interactive. The return codes are:

0   for a terminal
1   for a non-terminal

`uname`

Format:

uname options

Options:

-a   Display all information
-s   System name
-v   Display the o/s version only or the date of o/s release

To display the current system name and other relevant information:

```
$ uname a
Linux bumper.honeysuckle.com 2.0.36 #1 Tue Oct...
```

`uncompress`

Format:

uncompress files

Use `uncompress` to restore any files that have been compressed.

```
$ uncompress myfile
```

The above uncompresses the file `myfile` that was previously compressed. Note that you do not have to specify the `.Z` extension of the file when uncompressing.

`wait`

Format:

wait process ID

This means wait until process ID has finished before carrying on, or wait until all background processes have finished before carrying on.

To wait until process ID has finished before carrying on with the script or task:

```
$ wait 1299
```

Wait until all background processes have finished:

```
$ wait
```

wc

Format:

wc options files

Options:

-c   Print character count
-l   Print line count
-w   Print word count

This counts the number of characters or words.

```
$ who|wc
      1       6      46
$ who|wc -l
      1
```

In the first example output the who command is piped through to wc, and the following columns are displayed:

number of lines, number of words, number of characters

In the second example, wc just prints the number of lines.

```
$ VAR="tapedrive"
echo $VAR | wc -c
10
```

The number of characters in the string VAR is output.

whereis

Format:

whereis command_name

Use the whereis command to locate the binary and manual page locations of a command.

```
$ whereis fuser
fuser: /usr/sbin/fuser /usr/man/man1/fuser.1

$ whereis sort
sort: /bin/sort /usr/man/man1/sort.1
```

Notice the binary is not displayed in the next two examples, because it is a shell built-in, but we have manual pages for the commands.

```
$ whereis times
times: /usr/man/man2/times.2

$ whereis set
set: /usr/man/mann/set.n
```

who

Format:

who options

Options:

-a   Display all output

-r   Report current run level (for LINUX use the command `runlevel`)

-s   List names and time fields

`whoami`   Display the name of the user running the command. This is not an option to the `who` command, and can be called by itself.

The `who` command reports who is logged on to to the system. To show users logged on:

```
$ who
root            console        Apr 22 13:27
pgd             pts/3          Jun 14 15:29
peter           pts/4          Jun 14 12:08
dave            pts/5          Jun 14 16:10
```

Who am I?

```
$ whoami
dave
```

Index